A History of the I. G. Farben Trial

Studies in German History

Published in Association with the German Historical Institute, Washington, DC

Recent Volumes:

Volume 31
A History of the I. G. Farben Trial: Armament, Exploitation, Auschwitz
Stephan H. Lindner

Volume 30
Encountering the Global in Early Modern Germany: Microhistories of Mobility, Materiality, and Belonging
Edited by Christina Brauner, Renate Dürr, Philip Hahn, Anne Sophie Overkamp, and Simon Siemianowski

Volume 29
Political Friendship: Liberal Notables, Networks, and the Pursuit of the German Nation State 1848–1866
Michael Weaver

Volume 28
Citizens into Dishonored Felons: Felony Disenfranchisement, Honor, and Rehabilitation in Germany, 1806–1933
Timon de Groot

Volume 27
Brewing Socialism: Coffee, East Germans, and Twentieth-Century Globalization
Andrew Kloiber

Volume 26
End Game: The 1989 Revolution in East Germany
Ilko-Sascha Kowalczuk

Volume 25
Germany on Their Minds: German Jewish Refugees in the United States and Their Relationships with Germany, 1938–1988
Anne C. Schenderlein

Volume 24
The World of Children: Foreign Cultures in Nineteenth-Century German Education and Entertainment
Edited by Simone Lässig and Andreas Weiß

Volume 23
Gustav Stresemann: The Crossover Artist
Karl Heinrich Pohl

Volume 22
Explorations and Entanglements: Germans in Pacific Worlds from the Early Modern Period to World War I
Edited by Hartmut Berghoff, Frank Biess, and Ulrike Strasser

For a full volume listing, please see the series page on our website: http://berghahnbooks.com/series/studies-in-german-history

A History of the I. G. Farben Trial

Armament, Exploitation, Auschwitz

Stephan H. Lindner

Translated by Sally Hudson Dill

berghahn
NEW YORK • OXFORD
www.berghahnbooks.com

Published in 2026 by
Berghahn Books
www.berghahnbooks.com

English-language edition, extended and revised

German-language edition

Originally published in German as
Aufrüstung—Ausbeutung—Auschwitz: Eine Geschichte des I.G.-Farben-Prozesses

Library of Congress Cataloging-in-Publication Data

Names: Lindner, Stephan H. author
Title: A history of the I.G. Farben trial : armament, exploitation, Auschwitz / Stephan H. Lindner.
Description: New York : Berghahn Books, 2025. | Series: Studies in German history; volume 31 | Includes bibliographical references and index.
Identifiers: LCCN 2025036687 (print) | LCCN 2025036688 (ebook) | ISBN 9781836952664 hardback | ISBN 9781836952671 epub | ISBN 9781836952688 adobe pdf
Subjects: LCSH: I.G. Farben Trial, Nuremberg, Germany, 1947-1948 | Nuremberg War Crime Trials, Nuremberg, Germany, 1946-1949 | War crime trials—Germany—Nuremberg | Farbenfabriken Bayer Aktiengesellschaft | World War, 1939-1945—Atrocities | Holocaust, Jewish (1939-1945)—Poland | Auschwitz (Concentration camp)
Classification: LCC KZ1179.I23 L565 2025 (print) | LCC KZ1179.I23 (ebook) | DDC 341.6/90268—dc23/eng/20250827
LC record available at https://lccn.loc.gov/2025036687
LC ebook record available at https://lccn.loc.gov/2025036688

British Library Cataloguing in Publication Data

A catalogue record for this book is available from the British Library

EU GPSR Authorized Representative

LOGOS EUROPE, 9 rue Nicolas Poussin, 17000, LA ROCHELLE, France
Email: Contact@logoseurope.eu

ISBN 978-1-83695-266-4 hardback
ISBN 978-1-83695-267-1 epub
ISBN 978-1-83695-268-8 web pdf

https://doi.org/10.3167/9781836952664

For Bettina

Contents

Figures and Tables

Figures

Tables

ACKNOWLEDGMENTS

It is a good and enjoyable custom to thank the people and institutions that helped and supported one on the long path to the finalization of a book. It would take pages upon pages to name all those who assisted me, generously provided valuable suggestions, discussed various aspects and problems of this book, and helped me to fix my errors. Therefore, I would like to limit myself to naming just a few—standing in for all these people—to whom I owe a particularly large debt of gratitude.

I almost always received exceptionally good support in my archival research. I am particularly grateful to Werner Renz of the Fritz-Bauer-Institut Frankfurt am Main, Annegret Neupert of the Bundesarchiv Koblenz, Gunther Friedrich of the Staatsarchiv Nürnberg, Anja Gillen of the Marchivum Mannheim, James A. Davis of the State Archives of North Dakota, Susan Becker of the Unternehmensarchiv BASF Ludwigshafen, and Michael Pohlenz and Hans-Hermann Pogarell of the Bayer-Archiv Leverkusen. I would also like to give a large thank you to Günther Nath, who generously gave me access to the private papers of his father.

I am grateful to Sally Falk Moore, a former member of the prosecution, for the important insights and suggestions that she provided and for giving me so much of her time when we met at her office at Harvard University. I am also grateful to Hans-Joachim Hecker and Ulf Hashagen for important suggestions.

I am very grateful to two great experts on the Nuremberg trials, Jonathan A. Bush and Kim Christian Priemel, as well as the foremost expert on the I. G. Farben company, Peter Hayes. I was able to discuss the subject matter of this book in detail with them. Kim Priemel and Peter Hayes also read the manuscript in great detail. At my department at Universität der Bundeswehr München, Donald Riznik, Roman Köster, and Christian A. Müller also gave the manuscript a thorough reading. All of them helped me to prevent mistakes and imprecisions, for which I am very grateful. I am also thankful for the many productive discussions I had with Donald Riznik, Daniel E. Khan, and the students who took part in our joint interdisciplinary seminars about the Nuremberg trials. My gratitude also goes out to the leadership of my university, which supported me on the project in many ways over the years, especially our chancellor, Siegfried Rapp.

I would also particularly like to thank Simone Lässig, the director of the German Historical Institute in Washington, DC, and Mark Stanton of Berghahn Books for including the book in this series. I am very grateful also to the four anonymous reviewers for their effort and their suggestions, which have been reflected in a series of edits and additions to the text. Thus, I added a section to provide more context about the company I. G. Farben to this English edition of the book.

For the translation I am very grateful to Sally Hudson Dill, who translated a difficult text with a great deal of patience and feel for the language and undertook the effort of finding the US quotes in the transcript. And I owe thanks to BASF—above all to Susan Becker—for financing the translation. Last but not least, I am very grateful to Patricia Casey Sutcliffe, from the German Historical Institute, Washington, for supervising the publishing process and editing the text.

Of course, I take sole responsibility for any errors or deficiencies that still remain in this book; without the support of those mentioned above, there would be more.

ABBREVIATIONS

AG	Aktiengesellschaft (stock corporation)
AllProz	Alliierte Prozesse (Allied War Crimes Trials)
CCL	Control Council Law
CDU	Christlich Demokratische Union (Christian Democratic Union of Germany)
DM	Deutsche Mark
FIAT	Field Information Agency, Technical
Gestapo	Geheime Staatspolizei (secret state police of Nazi Germany)
ICI	Imperial Chemical Industries
I. G. (Farben)	Interessen-Gemeinschaft (Community of Interests)
IHK	Industrie- und Handelskammer (Chamber of Industry and Commerce)
IMT	International Military Tribunal
JAG	US Army Judge Advocate General's Corps
JCS	Joint Chiefs of Staff (directive 1067)
KPD	Kommunistische Partei Deutschlands (Communist Party of Germany)
KZ	Konzentrationslager (concentration camp)
NARA	National Archives and Records Administration
NL	Nachlass (private papers)
NMT	Nürnberger Militärtribunale (subsequent Nuremberg trials)
NSDAP	Nationalsozialistische Deutsche Arbeiterpartei (National Socialist German Workers' Party)
OCCWC	Office of Chief of Counsel for War Crimes
OMGUS	Office of Military Government, United States
OPA	Office of Price Administration
OSS	Office of Strategic Services
RM	Reichsmark
RuSHA	Rasse- und Siedlungshauptamt der SS (SS Race and Settlement Main Office)
SA	Sturmabteilung (Storm Troopers)
SJ	Societas Jesu (Jesuits)
SPD	Sozialdemokratische Partei Deutschlands (Social Democratic Party of Germany)
SS	Schutzstaffel (Protection Squadron)

T4	Tiergartenstraße 4 (Berlin street address of coordinating center for "euthanasia" program)
UN	United Nations
USHMM	United States Holocaust Memorial Museum
VVN	Vereinigung der Verfolgten des Naziregimes (Association of Persecutees of the Nazi Regime)
W Agency	W standing for Wehrmacht (army liaison office of I. G. Farben)
WVHA	Wirtschaftsverwaltungshauptamt der SS (SS Main Economic and Administrative Office)

Introduction

Three grim dons, whose reputation
Rests on mass extermination
Stake their claim for chemistry:
Freedom and Democracy.

—Bertolt Brecht, *The Anachronistic Procession or Freedom and Democracy*

Shortly after the end of World War II, in August 1945, the Swiss historian Herbert Lüthy complained that German guilt—collective guilt, even—was discussed "so much and in such an undifferentiated manner." Perhaps this was the case, thought Lüthy, so that there would be no need for discussion of definable, differentiated, and gradated responsibility: "In the moral slurry that is being created, the specific responsibility of those who made Hitler's power possible is sinking into happy oblivion." In the best-case scenario, those who had gotten their hands dirty—"the ostensible protagonists of the Third Reich"—would be brought to justice. But the "beneficiaries and the clients" of the Nazi regime—"the bankers and *junkers*, the coal and steel lords, the chemical and electricity magnates"—would remain, according to Lüthy, "discreetly in the shadow of the tribunals against those fellow travelers who were caught."[1]

A prominent representative of private industry, Gustav Krupp, was set to be tried at the International Military Tribunal (IMT) in Nuremberg. Krupp was too sick and too afflicted by dementia, however, to represent himself before the court, and did not have to stand trial.[2] Plans were made for a second international military tribunal at which his son Alfried and a number of the managers at I. G. Farbenindustrie AG were to be put on trial. The trial did not take place, however. Instead, in twelve subsequent trials in Nuremberg, the Americans tried various representatives of the Third Reich's elite officials. Along with officials from various ministries, members of the judicial system, high officers of the Wehrmacht, doctors, and multiple different SS organizations, leading representatives of the German major industry sector were charged in three different trials: Alfried Krupp and Friedrich Flick as owners of their respective companies, some of their top managers, and twenty-four of the top managers at I. G. Farbenindustrie AG.[3]

I. G. Farbenindustrie AG was officially founded on December 9, 1925, with the signing of the merger agreement between the German chemical companies Bayer, BASF, Hoechst, Agfa, Griesheim-Elektron, Weiler-ter Meer, Cassella, and Kalle. On July 5, 1945, the management and control of the company and its assets were taken over by military officials in the US occupation zone. With the Allied Control Council Law No. 9 of November 30, 1945, I. G. Farben, or I. G., as it was referred to in abbreviated form, was confiscated, and the decision was taken to dissolve it. Though the history of the chemical company only spanned twenty years, I. G. Farben is still present in collective memory. The company was famous for its exceptional capacity for innovation and its wide range of products: dyes, pharmaceuticals, synthetic fibers, rubber, magnetic strips, fuels, and much more. I. G. Farben is best known to this day, however, for its disreputable connection with the policies of the Third Reich. In the twelve years of the Nazi regime, its management was not only "entangled" in the crimes of the Nazi regime; it was actively involved in them. I. G. Farben represented—and still represents—not just autarky and rearmament, but also exploitation and the horrors of Auschwitz.

This association exists despite the fact that the National Socialists had expressed disfavor toward the chemical company as "Jewish" or "international" as late as the early 1930s, not least for having quite a number of managers and supervisory board members who were Jewish or of Jewish heritage.[4] Starting in 1933, however, the company leadership quickly and willingly adapted to the conditions of the Nazi regime. Herbert Marcuse, one of the founders of the Frankfurt School, noted this in late November 1943 in a report for the American intelligence services: "The only large German trust which, at the end of the Weimar Republic, could still be considered as antagonistic to the Nazi regime, the I. G. Farbenindustrie, came into the Nazi camp shortly after 1933."[5]

For Telford Taylor, chief counsel of the American prosecution for the subsequent trials in Nuremberg, the trial against the managers of I. G. Farben was of particular importance. He described it as one of four key trials of the Nuremberg project, along with the Krupp trial, the Wilhelmstrassen trial, and the trial against the high command of the Wehrmacht.[6] The I. G. trial was clearly given a very important role at the time. As James Morris, one of the judges of the trial, wrote in mid-September 1947 to a US congressman, "This case is considered second in importance only to that of the International Trial of Goering and the other top Nazis."[7]

In May 1947, Taylor submitted an indictment against twenty-four high-level managers at I. G. Farben to the responsible military authority; the indictment was against the chairman of the supervisory board, all nineteen members of the board of directors, and four directors. The indictment contained five counts: Under count I, all managers were accused of having planned, prepared for, and carried out wars of aggression. Under count II, they were accused of war crimes and crimes against humanity for having participated in the plunder and spoliation of public and private property. Under count III, they were charged with having committed war crimes and crimes against humanity for having participated in the enslavement of the civilian population and concentration camp inmates, the use of prisoners of war in violation of international law, experiments on human beings, and the mistreatment and murder of human beings. Under count IV, three managers were accused of being members of a criminal organization, the SS. Under count V, all managers were charged with having taken part in a conspiracy to commit crimes against peace.

The trial *The United States of America v. Carl Krauch, et al.* began in late August 1947 before US Military Court VI against only twenty-three defendants, since one was seriously ill and his trial was separated from the others. The court consisted of three judges and one substitute judge: the presiding judge, Curtis Grover Shake (former judge of the Indiana Supreme Court), the aforementioned James Morris (judge of the North Dakota Supreme Court), Paul Macarius Hebert (dean of the law school of Louisiana State University), and Clarence F. Merrell, a lawyer from Indiana, as substitute judge.[8]

The taking of evidence was completed by mid-May 1948. The judgment was finalized in late July 1948. In it, all three judges acquitted all twenty-three managers of counts I and V, though Judge Hebert submitted separate reasoning for his consent in a concurring opinion. The three managers charged under count IV were also unanimously acquitted. Ten managers were acquitted of all counts by the majority of the judges. Thirteen managers were sentenced by the court to between eighteen months and eight years under counts II and III, though Judge Hebert submitted a dissenting opinion on count III. Those managers who were directly involved in the construction of the I. G. Farben factory in Auschwitz received the severest sentences.[9] Thus the trial against the twenty-three managers of I. G. Farben ended in the criminal conviction of thirteen defendants—among them all the top leaders of the company.

It is not particularly surprising that the court was criticized by the defendants and their counsel. They complained in particular of a supposed "victors' justice" on the part of the Americans. Heinrich Gattineau, one of the directors of I. G. Farben who were charged at the time, later wrote that the defense counsel had been "at a serious disadvantage." By his estimation, the judges had acquitted all the defendants of counts I, IV, and V, but under counts II and III, "a few problematic sentences" had been handed down. Because the concentration camp inmates in Auschwitz had, according to Gattineau, "benefited from the company's social services," one could not speak of it as "enslavement." He also claimed that I. G. Farben had not stolen or plundered; he claimed that the defendants had been sentenced "just because they were members of the supervisory board of a foreign company."[10] Other former managers at I. G. Farben, such as August von Knieriem and Wolfgang Heintzeler, largely shared Gattineau's assessments.[11]

However, due to the fact that the sentences were mild in comparison to those of most of the other Nuremberg trials, representatives of the prosecution also sharply criticized the judgment. After the judgment was issued, Telford Taylor remarked that the evidence against the managers at I. G. had been "the strongest of all the industrialist trials," but that it had "made little impression on two of the judges."[12] Josiah DuBois, the lead prosecutor in the I. G. trial, expressed his frustration about the judges and the judgment in especially strong tones in a book published in 1952: "The sentences were light enough to please a chicken thief, or a driver who had irresponsibly run down a pedestrian."[13]

With this appearance of a failed trial, it seems fitting that Judge Morris himself, who played a significant role in formulating the majority decision of the court, wrote to Judge Hebert after his return to North Dakota in mid-September 1948 that he was back at his desk at the supreme court "and should, therefore, not have too much time to let my mind dwell on the Nurnberg nightmare."[14]

Why, one asks, were the trial and the judgment clearly a negative experience, a "nightmare," even, for the majority of those involved? Why was it that the trial was seen negatively and continues to be seen negatively into the present day? What was it that went "wrong" at the time? Did the trial perhaps fall short owing to the biases of the majority of the "prairie judges," as they were disparagingly called?[15] Or did the prosecution perhaps botch the trial through lack of skill or through ideological zeal?[16]

In order to seek an answer to these questions, this book focuses on the I. G. Farben trial, including its prehistory, its progression, and the history of its reception. Particular attention is paid to the actors immediately involved in the trial. In addition to understanding their actions, the aim is to describe their goals and values to the extent possible. As Niklas Luhmann wrote in his book *Legitimation durch Verfahren* [Legitimation by Procedure], the fact that a court procedure has an uncertain outcome—rather than resembling the "ineluctable course of a ritual"—is one of its defining characteristics, and even serves as its "motor" and legitimating factor.[17] Consequently, the criminal proceeding against the managers of I. G. in this study will be understood as a trial that was open ended and whose outcome was uncertain—which requires that all the different phases of the trial be described in chronological order, without focusing exclusively on certain phases, arguments, or narratives.[18]

With that in mind, this study will unfold as follows: after the introduction, there will be a discussion of the prehistory of the trial and its legal foundations. This includes the debates that took place between 1942 and 1945, first in London, then in the United States, about how to address German war crimes, as well as the debates that led to the establishment of the IMT and the subsequent trials in the different military zones. Following this, the indictment and the establishment of the court will be addressed. The direct actors in the trial will be introduced—that is, the prosecution, the defendants with their counsels, and the judges. The subsequent chapter portrays the trial process, including the opening arguments and the explanation of the indictment, the reply of the defense, and, finally, the arguments of both sides. The judgment and its justification are then assessed in further detail, including both the majority opinion and the minority opinion. Next, the posthistory of the trial is addressed: the results of the judgment and how the prosecutors, the judges, the defendants, and the defense counsels all responded to the judgment. The final chapter analyzes and evaluates the trial and the judgment.

Except for the contextualizing overview of I. G. Farben added to this edition, the history of the I. G. Farben company itself is not addressed in great detail in this book since the focus of the description is not the company but the trial in Nuremberg.[19] Nor does the study focus in great detail on the charge of experiments on humans in the various concentration camps, since this charge did not play the role in the trial that one might have expected in light of the monstrosity of the crimes.[20] However, the victims, even if they were assigned only a secondary role in the trial, are omnipresent in the book as the trial was meant to bring justice to them.

The state of the academic literature related to the themes addressed by this study is excellent. In addition to a large number of descriptions of the IMT in Nuremberg, recent years have seen a thorough academic assessment of the subsequent trials, including the trials of the industrialists.[21] Three essential recent studies deserve particular mention: Kevin Jon Heller's work on the legal aspect of the subsequent trials, Hubert Seliger's dissertation on the defense counsels in Nuremberg, and finally Kim Priemel's overall presentation and interpretation of the Nuremberg trials in their entirety.[22] Recent anthologies about the Nuremburg trials published jointly by Alexa Stiller and Kim Priemel also deserve mention.[23]

The I. G. trial in specific is addressed by a number of journalistic, historical, and legal works of various levels of quality. In his aforementioned 1952 book, Josiah DuBois published his view of the I. G. trial from his point of view as former chief prosecutor. In the late 1970s, Joseph Borkin, a former employee of the Antitrust Division of the US Justice Department who had worked for the US prosecution in Nuremberg after the war, published a widely acclaimed book about the chemical company, which he described as his "Moby Dick." In it, like DuBois, he criticized the trial, the judgment, and the judges.[24] In 1981 the journalist Tom Bower picked up rumors published by the society reporter Drew Pearson alleging that Judge Shake had fraternized with the German defense counsels and that Judge Morris's wife had had close contact with the wives of I. G. managers standing trial.[25]

Josiah DuBois's and Joseph Borkin's negative assessments of the judges and of the judgment in the I. G. trial were taken up by the majority of historians, jurists, and journalists, in some cases even incorporating the rumors published by Tom Bower. In fact, DuBois and Borkin are often the primary authors they cite. In general, there is a tendency in the literature to yield to the temptation to continue the I. G. trial—most recently the work of Diarmuid Jeffreys, on the side of the prosecution, and Frank Gausmann, on the side of the defense.[26]

The archival sources on the trial are also very rich. It was possible to review the trial records and numerous documents connected to the trial, located in Frankfurt, at the Fritz-Bauer-Institut. It was also possible to study the Allies' records on the trials and the papers of defendant August von Knieriem in Germany, in the Federal Archive at Koblenz. The Nuremberg State Archive holds extensive and informative records on the war crimes trial, including records from the defense counsels. The company archives at Bayer, BASF, and Hoechst (now Sanofi) provided helpful information on the defendants and defense counsels. I also consulted the papers of defendants Eduard Wahl (Archive of the Konrad-Adenauer-Stiftung), Hermann Heimerich (City Archives Mannheim), Friedrich Wagner (City Archives Ludwigshafen), Friedrich Drischel (Baden-Württemberg Archives, Freiburg), and Herbert Nath (private papers, Munich/Grünwald).

For the prosecution, I consulted records in the National Archives, Washington, DC, as well as the papers of Telford Taylor (Columbia University), Drexel Sprecher (John F. Kennedy Presidential Library), Belle Mayer Zeck (Harvard University, also online), and Emanuel Minskoff and Benjamin Ferencz (United States Holocaust Memorial Museum). I also studied an interview with Josiah DuBois (Truman Presidential Library, online), and carried out a personal interview with Professor Sally Falk Moore (Harvard University), who was a member of the prosecution. With regard to the judges, I consulted the very informative papers of James Morris (North Dakota State Archives in Bismarck). The papers of Paul M. Hebert (Louisiana State University) are available online, but the documents are, in many cases, undated. With regard to Curtis G. Shake, I had access to transcripts of interviews with him (Indiana State Library) as well as a few copies sent to me from his papers (Vincennes University, Indiana).

Notes

1. Lüthy, "Die Verheerungen des Krieges," 76. The poet Bertolt Brecht was not the only one who agreed with Lüthy's assessment. His poem, quoted above, states further: "Next to celebrate the Night / Of the Long Knives, comes a tight / Knot of men who loudly call / For another free-for-all.—Then the faceless trust directors / Those men's patrons and protectors: / Pray, for our arms industry / Freedom and Democracy!" (Brecht, *Poems 1913–1945*, 410–11).

2. Neave, *Nuremberg*, on Alfried and Gustav Krupp see 32–33, also 54: "Gustav [Krupp] was discovered at his hunting lodge. Since the beginning of 1945, he had been unable to feed himself. He could say nothing but 'Donnerwetter!' Allied doctors declared him to be suffering from softening of the brain."
3. Priemel and Stiller, *NMT*; Ueberschär, *Der Nationalsozialismus vor Gericht*.
4. Hayes, *Industry and Ideology*, 65–66, 90–94.
5. Laudani, *Secret Reports on Nazi Germany*, 74–91; Marcuse, "German Social Stratification," quote from 81.
6. Priemel, *The Betrayal*, 274.
7. State Archives/State Historical Society of North Dakota, Bismarck, MSS 10154, James Morris Papers, Box 1, Folder 1: Morris to Charles R. Robertson, September 15, 1947 (hereinafter: James Morris Papers).
8. *The Judgement in the Farben Trial*, x–xii, 1–2, 9–17; *Trials of War Criminals*, vol. VII, 1–9.
9. *The Judgement in the Farben Trial*, xv, 2–3, 133–134; Taylor, *Final Report*, 195–201; Morris, "Major War Crimes Trials in Nurnberg," 97–109, here 100–102.
10. Gattineau, *Durch die Klippen des 20. Jahrhunderts*, 198, 202–203.
11. See von Knieriem, *Nürnberg. Rechtliche und menschliche Probleme*, who states, however, on 515 and 543, that the tribunal had been relatively fair to the defendants in the I. G. trial; Heintzeler, *Der rote Faden*, 81–108; Heintzeler, *Im Jahrhundert extremer Turbulenz*, 114–40.
12. Taylor, "Nuremberg Trials. War Crimes and International Law," 314–15.
13. DuBois, *The Devil's Chemists*, 338–47, quote from 339.
14. James Morris Papers, Box 1, Folder 2: Morris to Hebert, September 13, 1948.
15. Cf. Oberndörfer, "Recht und Richter: Verfahrensrechtliche Aspekte der Nürnberger Prozesse," 525–46, here 537–38; cf. Abelshauser, "Rüstungsschmiede der Nation? Der Kruppkonzern im Dritten Reich und in der Nachkriegszeit 1933–1951," 267–472, here 466: he speaks of "American provincial judges" who were "not living up to" their tasks.
16. Cf. Gausmann, *Deutsche Großunternehmer vor Gericht*, 239–49; see by contrast Bush, "New Dealer, Flüchtlinge und Radikale? Die Nürnberger Ankläger im Profil," 577–81.
17. See Luhmann, *Legitimation durch Verfahren*, 40, 114–16; cf. also Heinemann, "Rasse, Lebensraum, Genozid. Die nationalsozialistische Volkstumspolitik im Fokus von Fall 8 der Nürnberger Militärtribunale," 100–26, here 104–106, who, along with Luhmann, sees court proceedings as an "ambivalent communication process."
18. Brünger, *Geschichte und Gewinn*, 57–94: sees the I. G. trial, for instance, in the light of counteracting narratives.
19. On the history of I. G. Farben in the Third Reich, see, in particular, Hayes, *Industry and Ideology*. A problematic account (as it is in some cases apologetic) is Plumpe, *Die I. G. Farbenindustrie*; on individual I. G. factories, see Wagner, *IG Auschwitz*; Stokes, "From the IG Farben Fusion to the Establishment of BASF AG (1925–1952)," 206–361; Lindner, *Inside IG Farben*.
20. On this, in particular, see Weindling, *Nazi Medicine and the Nuremberg Trials*; Lindner, *Inside IG Farben*, 307–36.
21. Weindling, *Nazi Medicine and the Nuremberg Trials*; Earl, *The Nuremberg SS-Einsatzgruppen Trial*; Hébert, *Hitler's Generals on Trial*; Maguire, *Law and War*. Specifically on the Flick trial, see Jung, *Die Rechtsprobleme der Nürnberger Prozesse*; Drecoll, "Flick vor Gericht: Die Verhandlungen vor dem alliierten Militärtribunal 1947," 559–645; Frei et al., *Flick*, 401–41; Priemel, *Flick*, 616–49.
22. Heller, *The Nuremberg Military Tribunals*; Seliger, *Politische Anwälte?*; Priemel, *The Betrayal*.
23. Priemel and Stiller, *Reassessing the Nuremberg Military Tribunals*; Priemel and Stiller, *NMT*.
24. Borkin, *The Crime and Punishment of I. G. Farben*, ix—preface; on the judgment, see 149–56.
25. Bower, *Blind Eye to Murder*, 357–58.

26. Similar to DuBois, *Devil's Chemists*; and Borkin, *Crime and Punishment*: Boll, "Fall 6: Der IG-Farben-Prozeß," 133–43; Bush, "The Prehistory of Corporations and Conspiracy in International Criminal Law: What Nuremberg Really Said," 1094–1262, here 1213 (also footnote 445) and 1219; Greiner, *Die Morgenthau-Legende*, 384–91; Jeffreys, *Hell's Cartel*, 378–402; Heller, *The Nuremberg Military Tribunals*, 94–96. Critical of the prosecution: Hayes, "IG Farben und der IG Farben-Prozeß: Zur Verwicklung eines Großkonzerns in die nationalsozialistischen Verbrechen," 99–121; Spicka, "The Devil's Chemists on Trial: The American Prosecution of I. G. Farben at Nuremberg," 865–82; Stokes, *Divide and Prosper*, 54–55, 151–54; Lindner, "Das Urteil im I.G.-Farben-Prozess," 405–33. A more critical and even polemical interpretation with respect to the prosecution is the previously cited dissertation by Gausmann, *Deutsche Großunternehmer*, which speaks disparagingly of "Morgenthau Boys" and their supposed "naive political Messianism"—see inter alia 137–39, 283–84. At best a low level of understanding is shown by Hörner, *Profit oder Moral*. From a legal perspective, see Jeßberger, "Die I. G. Farben vor Gericht: Von den Ursprüngen eines 'Wirtschaftsvölkerstrafrechts'", 924–32. A very critical perspective on the I. G. trial from a point of view critical of capitalism is Baars, "Capitalism's Victor's Justice? The Hidden Stories Behind the Prosecution of Industrialists Post-WWII," 163–92.

Chapter 1

The Prehistory and Preparation of the Trial

The Lesson of Leipzig: The Allied Prosecution of German War Crimes

Since the start of World War II, multiple governments-in-exile of countries occupied by Nazi Germany and Italy, as well as Jewish organizations, had been calling for the punishment of war crimes committed by the Axis powers. These calls began to develop into practical action with the beginning of the racially motivated campaign against the Soviet Union and the systematic murder of the European Jews over the course of 1941. In the Declaration of St. James's Palace of January 1942, nine London-based governments-in-exile threatened the Germans and their allies who had committed war crimes with serious punishments. The United Nations War Crimes Commission was founded in the fall of 1942, and by the end of 1943, it had created a list of known war criminals.[1] At the same time, intensive Allied discussions began to take place in London about how to deal with the war crimes of the Axis powers, especially the Germans, after a victorious end to the war. All agreed that this time, in contrast to what had occurred at the end of World War I, the Allies would take the punishment into their own hands. There should not be another "farce"—which is how many of the Allies had perceived the trials against war criminals at the Leipzig Imperial Court of Justice.[2]

Starting in the first half of 1942, an unofficial consultative body under the framework of the United Nations—the London International Assembly—started a series of debates on the question of the punishment of the war crimes of the Axis powers, which culminated in a joint resolution in late June 1943.[3] Professor Marcel de Baer, president of the Court Militaire de Belgique and a "significant figure in the microcosm of the governments-in-exile," led the group.[4] Other prominent participants included Frederic Herbert Maugham, Viscount Maugham, the former lord chancellor of Great Britain and older brother of the author W. Somerset Maugham; René Cassin, a jurist of Free France and a later

Nobel Peace Prize recipient; and American criminologist Sheldon Glueck, who would later serve as an advisor to Robert H. Jackson, the chief prosecutor at the IMT.[5]

Maugham took a juridically conservative stance in the debates and rejected retroactive laws on general principle. He also wanted to limit international war crime trials to crimes that were so grave "as to cause a feeling of horror in all civilised countries"—in other words murder, torture, rape, or the forced prostitution of women or girls. He did not think that crimes such as theft or plunder should fall under the jurisdiction of such courts. In general, he was of the opinion that establishing international tribunals should lead to "simple" and "fair" solutions and that the plan for them ought not be "too ambitious."[6] Over the course of the discussions, Maugham decisively rejected the idea of having military tribunals pass judgment on war criminals, especially if they did so under martial law.[7] German war crimes, however, ought to be prosecuted by the Allies, the family of "civilised states": "In Lord Maugham's opinion Germany had, for the present at least, ceased to be a member of that family and in their recent conceptions of law her people could not be distinguished from savages so that they could not legitimately complain if the allied powers took steps to punish horrible crimes against their own nationals."[8]

René Cassin, who had served as a French delegate to the League of Nations for fourteen years prior to the war, was much less conservative than Maugham; in fact, he saw a necessity to take political action. According to Cassin, it was important to prevent those who were guilty from getting off as they had done after World War I. He did not think that the Germans themselves should be responsible for the trials or that the war criminals and their accomplices should be able to find cover in neutral territory abroad. In 1914 a war would still have been considered a tool of international politics; in 1939, however, after the signing of the Kellogg-Briand Pact, a war of aggression was a crime. He also saw the consequences of the war as "illegal." The rules of the Hague Convention certainly applied, and violations of them should be punished. However, certain crimes committed by the Germans were of a "collective nature," he argued—not just because they related to entire categories of the population of a country, but also because they were carried out by an "anonymous mass of soldiers and civilians": "Whether it be legal or not, all the oppressed nations demand that those who have participated in these great collective crimes, of which the mass deportation of civilian populations is the most striking example, should be punished." Cassin was aware of the fact that punishments such as these were not easy to carry out, since they went against established legal traditions. People were used to the idea of individuals and their accomplices being tried, not groups of people: "One cannot, however, deliberately refuse to study a legal problem because it happens to be a new one. The Germans have invented crimes, and they will only have themselves to blame if laws and sanctions are specially instituted to deal with them." Cassin also wondered whether German war criminals should be tried in front of regular courts or military courts, the latter having the advantage of an easier process and a shorter duration. And he opposed accepting the argument of superior orders as a defense, in full recognition of the dilemma of either infringing on the principle of superior orders as a valid legal principle or allowing guilty parties to evade justice. If the latter were to occur, the Germans, in Cassin's view, would feel justified in their track record of violence. The purpose of criminal justice was to deter people who might feel inclined toward criminality—and the Germans had shown ample evidence of deep-rooted criminal tendencies, in his opinion. International criminal law would be failing in its most important purpose if it emboldened these instincts by recognizing the argument of superior orders. In addition, all civilized people, and especially the Germans' victims, would perceive it to be a great injustice if those who committed such atrocities got away without punishment: "There is no better means of destroying the confidence of the nations in the law than to sacrifice justice for the sake of a legal principle."[9]

Sheldon Glueck, in turn, expressed the opinion in a letter to Marcel de Baer that the vast majority of the war criminals should be tried in national courts. He thought that an international court should also be established, if only to prevent leaders of states, who had previously benefited from immunity, from violating the laws and customs of war. Founding a new court of this type would not present the problem of retroactivity: "No civilized nation believes in ex post facto legislation. But we must look at substance rather than form." The court would not have to use ex post facto legislation because there was plenty of public international law, codified international law, national law, and forms of punishment. One merely had to apply them properly and appropriately and carry out a fair trial. That being the case, it would be irrelevant whether the defendant were facing a new court: "it is the shell of the matter, so far as his rights are concerned, not the kernel."[10] In a later article, Glueck further elaborated the idea of punishing German war criminals in front of a new international court—and saw no problem with it.[11]

Marcel de Baer summarized the debates over the punishment of war criminals and the associated legal questions in late September 1942 as follows: This war called for "retribution," he argued, which could be carried out in two ways: "indiscriminate reprisals" or "just punishment." Reprisals are carried out during a war, he argued, whereas punishment is carried out after the war under ordinary jurisdiction. The principle of punishment had been established thanks to the Declaration of St. James's Palace and various speeches by Franklin Delano Roosevelt and Winston Churchill. But if one wanted to carry out punishment, he argued, one had to be sure of how one intended to do it: "The punishment of the war criminals is one of the complicated and difficult problems of international law. It has not been satisfactorily solved and I suggest that this is due to the absence of positive law on the matter." German war criminals should have been tried after World War I, but the corresponding paragraphs in the Versailles Peace Treaty had been insufficiently developed. This had resulted in the "fiasco" of the punitive measures: "We are often told that we must not look back and that this is no time for inquests on past events. But what is the value of experience if it is always to be ignored?" In addition, it had been a mistake, in his opinion, that the punishment process had been so drawn out—in some cases taking as much as five years. The public no longer had an interest in the punishment at that point and had wanted to let what was in the past stay in the past. If one wanted to carry out punishment this time, one had to proceed quickly; thus, the United Nations should address these legal questions without delay. It was important, first, to determine what the term "war crime" meant and on what legal basis such crimes would be tried. Then, a decision had to be made about the corresponding "machinery," with a large majority of the participating commission members, according to de Baer, considering the creation of an international court necessary.[12]

The minutes, memoranda, and letters on these debates about the punishment of German war criminals clearly show the difficulty of the legal questions that the representatives of the United Nations had to deal with: the challenges of punishing individuals in the framework of international law, the validity of the superior orders principle, and the type of court. A simple perusal of the views of a few prominent participants in the discussion, briefly summarized here, suffices to show how much they diverged on how to proceed. The one thing that clearly united all sides was the view that war criminals should not be allowed to get away this time—this was the lesson of Leipzig.[13]

The Moscow Declaration of November 1, 1943, was the most decisive step from legal debates to a concrete Allied prosecution of German war crimes. At this time, US President Franklin D. Roosevelt, British Prime Minister Winston Churchill, and Soviet leader Josef Stalin came to the agreement that German war criminals, the "Hitlerite Huns," were to be tried at the place of their crimes after the occupied territories had been freed. Major criminals whose atrocities were not linked to a certain geographic location were to be tried and judged jointly by the Allied governments.[14]

What the declaration did not specify, however, was how the German war criminals would be punished. There were contentious debates over this question even within the US government. Some in the US government wanted to pursue harsh reprisals against war criminals. Others were of the opinion, as were the majority of the London International Assembly, that one had to search for solutions that were legally tenable, even if they were innovative, as long as they ensured some form of punishment for German war criminals.[15]

The first group was represented by US Secretary of the Treasury Henry Morgenthau, a friend of President Roosevelt's. He wanted to smother Germany's simmering aggression in Europe for good and was thus in search of what amounted to a Carthaginian peace settlement.[16] On September 5, 1944, he presented his plan to the president to have "the arch-criminals" swiftly executed by firing squads drawn from UN soldiers as soon as they were identified by "an officer of the General rank." In addition, he suggested that all members of the SS and the Gestapo, high officials in the police and the SA, all high government and Nazi Party functionaries, and all leading public officials who were closely associated with the Nazi regime be arrested until a determination could be made as to their individual guilt. He also wanted Nazi Party members, *Junkers*, army and navy officers, and "Nazi sympathizers who by their words or deeds materially aided or abetted the Nazi program" to lose the right to vote and to be limited in their choice of careers.[17]

The second group was represented by Secretary of War Henry L. Stimson, a Republican who had been an enthusiastic supporter of an international court since his time as secretary of state under President Herbert Hoover.[18] The same day that Morgenthau submitted his plan, Stimson called General Myron C. Cramer, the judge advocate general of the US Army, to investigate the possibility of establishing Allied military courts in Germany with American civilians in order to pursue war crimes. In the phone conversation, Stimson expressed rather pragmatic ideas about how such a trial process for war criminals should look: "They must have some sort of charge against them—they must have some sort of an opportunity to reply to that charge. I'm not even sure of counsel but of course counsel can be given to them by the court but it must be slender enough but substantial—it must give them—well we must not put ourselves in the position where it can be said we convicted these people without a trial. But it must be free from all the delays that would go with the technicalities of courts-martial or the United States jurisprudence procedure should go in, absolutely [*sic*]."[19]

That same day General Cramer sent Secretary Stimson an article written by his colleague Major Willard B. Cowles on the subject. The influence of this text on further developments is hard to definitively demonstrate. In any case, in this document Cowles described the possibility of having military tribunals prosecute and judge war crimes. Military tribunals had jurisdiction as long as a state of war technically persisted, he argued—this included a ceasefire or a military occupation. The tribunals could be mixed Allied courts. He also argued that there was no legal reason why a civilian could not be a member of such a tribunal. However, the prosecutor—generally, but not necessarily—should be an army officer. A defendant had the usual rights, including the right to counsel, the right to challenge the members of the commission, the right to be confronted with the witnesses against him—and the defendant's guilt had to be proven "beyond a reasonable doubt." According to Cowles, it was a common misperception that international law did not allow for prosecution; on the contrary, he argued, it was thoroughly capable of this. Finally, Cowles suggested, as had Marcel de Baer, that these trials be carried out as quickly as possible, because they would otherwise lose their effectiveness.[20]

In addition, Colonel Murray C. Bernays introduced the legal concept of conspiracy, which was common in the United States, to the War Department as a means of judging the many German war criminals while maintaining constitutional practices.[21] The idea was that members of the Nazi government, the Nationalsozialistische Deutsche Arbeiterpartei (National Socialist German Workers' Party; NSDAP), and public institutions should be tried by an international court for conspiracy to commit murder, terrorism, and the destruction of peaceful populations in contravention of the rules of war. The prosecuting states would then be able to sue individuals whom they selected as representative of the organization in question: "Proof of membership, without more, would establish guilt of participation in the mentioned conspiracy, and the individual would be punished in the discretion of the court."[22] This concept appealed not just to Stimson, but also to Secretary of State Cordell Hull and Secretary of the Navy James V. Forrestal. In drafting a joint memorandum, they pointed out that providing evidence in the individual prosecution of so many war criminals would be so difficult that it would be nearly impossible to try them. They also argued that the Nazis' crimes were not just a few scattered atrocities, which might occur in any context, but rather the result of a preplanned policy to achieve world supremacy: "To such a state of facts the well recognized principles of the law of criminal conspiracy are plainly applicable, and may be employed. An indictment upon a charge of conspiracy will properly include the leaders of State, the governmental and party agencies such as the SS and Gestapo, and other individuals and groups who during the time in question have been in control of formulating and executing Nazi policy."[23]

Over the course of further discussions, the Treasury Department, in a memorandum spearheaded by Morgenthau and apparently drafted by his associate Josiah DuBois, suggested a simplified court procedure, with close to no rights for the defendants.[24] In the end, however, Stimson and Hull, along with Attorney General Francis Biddle, prevailed over Morgenthau. In late January 1945, they called for a regulated legal procedure and pushed back against executions without criminal proceedings or hearings—because these stood contrary to the most important legal principles that all members of the United Nations shared. They therefore suggested creating an international military commission or military court, consisting "of civilian or military personnel, or both" for the main war criminals. Subsequent trials should be held in front of tribunals of the occupying forces, national courts, or national or international military tribunals. Furthermore, they suggested that in order to prepare for the criminal procedure, the United Nations War Crimes Commission should be dissolved and replaced by an "executive group" with representatives from the military and qualified staff of the four Allied powers: the British Commonwealth, the United States, the Soviet Union, and France.[25]

For Harry S. Truman, a former judge and Roosevelt's successor as president after his death in April 1945, an orderly legal procedure was especially appealing, and he used the January 1945 memo "as a guideline for official American policy." In late April, Truman selected US Supreme Court Justice Robert H. Jackson as representative of the United States and "Chief of Counsel for the Prosecution of Axis Criminality." Jackson was officially appointed on May 2, 1945.[26]

The controversial nature of proper trials of German war criminals, however, can be seen in a letter from Ernest Gruening, the governor of the Alaska Territory, to Francis Shea, a leading member of Jackson's team. Fully aware that his views might stand counter to the Anglo-American legal tradition, in late May 1945, Gruening called for a punishment of the perpetrators that would reflect the monstrosity of their crimes. Any attempt to try individuals and use American rules of procedure would end disastrously, he argued. Instead, he called for summary executions: "It will never be possible to provide adequate punishment. For the many millions of people slaughtered and deliberately tortured to death, the only adequate justice is the killing of those who were responsible for those deaths, those in high places who established the policies, those in middle places who were part of the machinery of executing the policies, and those lesser people on the ground who carried them out."[27]

Instead, the group around Secretary of War Stimson wanted to hold fast to constitutional methods and legal customs and rejected summary executions. Looking back at the IMT in Nuremberg, Stimson wrote in 1947 that the defendants, whom he saw as the perpetrators of the worst crimes in history, had not ended up on the dock through "trickery," but through the "massed angered forces of common humanity." The Allies could have dealt with the imprisoned Nazi leaders in three ways: "release, summary punishment, or trial." Release had been unthinkable, since it would have appeared to be an admission that there had been no crimes. Summary punishment had been frequently recommended; it would have been emotionally satisfying in the short term and corresponded to the Nazi legal understanding. But this was the very reason why this solution ought to be avoided: "Our anger, as righteous anger, must be subject to the law. We therefore took the third course and tried the captive criminals by a judicial proceeding. We gave to the Nazis what they had denied their own opponents—the protection of the Law. The Nuremberg Tribunal was thus in no sense an instrument of vengeance but the reverse."[28]

I. G. Farben Managers in the Dock

A consideration of the discussions that took place over the course of the war reveals that the war criminals who were to be sought out for prosecution were mostly individuals and high officials who had carried out "heinous criminal offences," in the words of Viscount Maugham, on the front and in the occupied countries.[29] Representatives of industry were of less interest as potential defendants. Only a few of those involved in the discussions—Sheldon Glueck or the Labour politician Clement Attlee, for instance—considered the possibility at the time of trying representatives of private industry as war criminals.[30]

But over the course of the pursuit of the "four Ds"—"denazification, demilitarization, democratization, and decartelization"—soldiers and leading representatives of private industry, in addition to high-level Nazis, came into the crosshairs of the investigation.[31] Apparently taking up essential aspects of Franz Neumann's study of the Third Reich, some of the Americans did, in fact, emphasize the high level of responsibility that traditional German elites bore for the policies and the crimes of the Nazi regime. This became clear when representatives of the traditional elites, in addition to representatives of the political leadership of the Nazi regime, were put in the dock at the IMT. It became even clearer in the subsequent trials at Nuremberg, which were carried out by the Americans alone, where doctors, soldiers, government officials, and representatives of large companies were tried alongside SS officials.[32]

The German Chemical Firm I. G. Farbenindustrie AG

I. G. Farbenindustrie was founded in early December 1925, with its headquarters in Frankfurt am Main, with the signing of the merger agreement between the chemical companies Bayer, BASF, Hoechst, Agfa, Griesheim-Elektron, Weiler-ter Meer, Cassella, and Kalle. The company was not only by far the largest chemical company in Germany between 1925 and 1945; it was, along with the Vereinigte Stahlwerke, one of the two largest private companies in the entire German economy. I. G. Farben was also one of the largest private companies in the world. It was a leader in the global chemical industry—the largest company in the sector in terms of sales and number of employees, edging out Imperial Chemical Industries (ICI) in Great Britain and DuPont, Union Carbide and Carbon Corporation, and Allied Chemical and Dye Corporation in the United States.[33]

Efforts to unite the chemical industry in Germany dated back to 1904. Despite the German chemical companies' already strong position, Carl Duisberg, a member of Bayer's board of directors, wanted to merge the most important companies so that they could avoid ruinous competition with each other abroad, obtain better sale and purchase prices, achieve greater economies of scale, and secure a good rate of return for years to come. Though Duisberg's project failed, the same year saw the merger of the companies Hoechst and Cassella; this alliance was expanded into an "association of three" with the addition of Kalle in 1907. This stood opposite the "triple alliance" of Bayer, BASF, and Agfa, which had also been founded in 1904.[34]

In 1915, at an early stage of World War I, Duisberg presented a revised version of his 1904 memorandum for discussion, basing it on the possible consequences of the war for the German chemical industry. At the time, factories located in enemy countries were already under sequestration or military supervision; it was unclear what would become of them and the assets still in enemy territory as well as any outstanding debts after the war, he argued, but one must count on losses. Domestically, too, the war was having negative consequences because of limits or prohibitions on the use of certain raw materials. There would also be problems with exporting. While the war and its consequences might hit different companies differently, in his view consolidation would mean that the negative consequences of the war could be distributed more evenly. In August 1916 the community of interests contract (*Interessengemeinschafts-Vertrag*) between Agfa, BASF, Bayer, Cassella, Hoechst, Kalle, the Griesheim-Elektron chemical factory, and the chemical factories that had previously been Weiler-ter Meer was signed. The companies in the syndicate remained largely independent despite having to make a series of decisions jointly—and the association, although it was set to last fifty years, could be dissolved at any time.[35]

The German chemical industry was particularly affected by the provision of the Versailles peace settlement that allowed the states of the Entente to confiscate German patents and German assets abroad. The fact that the dye factories were able to utilize only around 40 percent of their production capacity during the postwar years made the leading chemical companies more willing to form a closer alliance. Once again, it was Duisberg who submitted a proposal, this one in fall 1924. At the time, however, he sought not a merger of the companies, but a shared holding company. However, the majority of the companies in the community of interests rejected this solution and pursued an immediate and direct merger. The leading figures at the time—Carl Duisberg at Bayer and Carl Bosch at BASF—finally reached a gentleman's agreement about the form of association despite their differences in opinion in what was called the "founders' compromise." Both had sought a "combination of centralist and decentralist elements in the structure of the new large company," as Wolfram Fischer explained it.[36]

In his study of I. G. Farben, Gottfried Plumpe wrote that its organizational development could be divided into three phases: in the first phase, the time of the "founders' compromise," with its so-called "decentral centralization," the individual factories were given significant autonomy. In the second phase, a divisional structure was formed in order to handle the problems that arose from the early compromises and the global economic crisis. The third phase, according to Plumpe, was a time of "polycentrism" because of the period of exceptional expansion in the 1930s.[37]

As chairman of the board of directors of I. G. Farben in the mid-1920s, Carl Bosch explained to a Reichstag committee the development away from the early "decentral centralization" toward a greater level of cooperation among the individual factories and clear consultation processes, agreements, and rationalization measures. He pointed out that as a result of World War I, the loss of patents through the Versailles Peace Treaty, and a widespread protectionist tariff policy, sales had decreased by half. With no prospect of an improvement to the situation, the decision had been made to merge. After this had been done, the task had been to draw the necessary conclusions. First, a series of products had to be consolidated. Then, they had begun to trim down the dye program. The sales division had then finally been consolidated. Bosch also explained that, organizationally, the original decision to bring all the members of the boards of directors of the member companies into I. G. Farben's board of directors had led to the formation of a Working Committee of twenty-six members that met every three to four weeks in Frankfurt under his chairmanship and that was a driving force in the company. The supervisory board had also taken on all the members from the individual companies. However, only ten directors from the former companies who had switched to the supervisory board were called to the Supervisory Council—and it was only the latter that served important functions such as supervising the board of directors, naming directors, and approving contracts. In addition to the Working Committee, there was a series of expert committees—for example on dyes, pharmaceuticals, or technical matters—which, according to Bosch, carried out the actual work.[38]

Over the course of the global economic crisis, the leadership of I. G. Farben increased rationalization measures, Bosch related. While until then the old companies of Bayer, BASF, and Hoechst had essentially continued to exist as regional Works Groups, a commission had been set up in 1929 on the initiative of Duisberg to determine how to cut costs. I. G. Farben's various areas of activity were divided into three major divisions, and Bosch placed three managers whom he especially valued in charge of investment decisions for these divisions. Carl Krauch was put in charge of Division I, referred to as Sparte I, which covered the fields of nitrogen and mineral oil synthesis; Fritz ter Meer led Division II, or Sparte II, which included dyes, inorganic substances, intermediate products, solvents, pharmaceuticals, and pesticides; and Fritz Gajewski was put in charge of Division III, or Sparte III, covering the fields of photo and synthetic fibers. The leadership at I. G. Farben soon realized that the divisional structure was well suited to managing the company from a technical standpoint. It significantly reduced, however, the former autonomy of the regional works groups.[39]

In 1930, under the leadership of Bosch, I. G. Farben's Central Committee was founded to succeed the Working Committee as a leading organ in essential matters. It handled important staff matters and "confidential matters."[40] Until well into the 1930s, the Central Committee was in many ways the pinnacle of the company, the nexus where the important strategic decisions were made.[41] During the Third Reich, the following members of the board of directors of I. G. Farben also served as members of the Central Committee: Carl

Bosch (chairman until 1935, then chairman of the supervisory board) Hermann Schmitz (chairman starting in 1935), Wilhelm Gaus (until 1937), Erwin Selck (until 1937), Carl Krauch (until 1940, then chairman of the supervisory board), Georg von Schnitzler, Fritz Gajewski, Heinrich Hörlein, Fritz ter Meer, August von Knieriem, and Christian Schneider.[42] Eight of these individuals were tried in 1947 in Nuremberg.

When Bosch transferred to the supervisory board in 1935 after Duisberg's death, the Central Committee lost influence. This was also related to the fact that because of changes in stock corporation law in 1938, the Working Committee was dissolved, and in its place, the board as a whole became the top decision-making organ of the company. It consisted at the time of twenty-seven members. Over the course of the war, the number stabilized at around twenty-one—therefore, I. G. Farben's whole board was approximately as large as the original Working Committee.[43]

After the war, Fritz ter Meer described meetings of the board of directors as "discussions among good friends"; there had been differences of opinion, but "never fights." This was because each board member, in light of the considerable level of independence and the division of work, was aware of needing to be "the most knowledgeable one in his field of expertise" and to act accordingly.[44] I. G. Farben's substantial growth in the 1930s was what drove, as Peter Hayes put it, the "centrifugal forces in the company"—starting in 1938, the members of the board of directors only had access to the minutes and statistical data that related to their work.[45]

In the interwar years, the company stood on the two pillars of traditional economic liberalism: "free trade abroad and free enterprise at home."[46] It made an effort, however, to achieve greater market share and higher profits through consultation and cooperation with national and international competitors. At the same time, the company sought to be innovative—above all, technically innovative—and to develop new markets, business lines, and products.[47] In this process, decisions were made more from technical than from commercial points of view. This technical approach shines through Carl Bosch's statement that I. G. Farben did not exist to bring in high dividends: "Our pride and our duty is to work for those who come after us, to establish the processes on which they will work."[48]

Hitler's seizure of power in 1933 changed the environment for the company. Nazi economic steering, efforts to achieve autarky, and promotion of the armaments industry created their own market rules and market structures in the years that followed, ones that were hard to compare to the economic situation prior to the Nazi takeover. I. G. Farben quickly adapted to the new circumstances, however; it sought to profit from them and knew how to do so.

Not long after the Nazi seizure of power, I. G. Farben contacted the new government. Since the onset of the global economic crisis and the massive drop in oil prices, the field of synthetic fuels—an important one for the company and one that it had bet on with the factory in Leuna—had become highly unprofitable.[49] That same year, in December 1933, I. G. Farben and the German government signed the "*Benzin-Vertrag*," or "gasoline agreement," after complicated negotiations. The Leuna factory agreed to increase its production of synthetic fuels in support of the Nazi autarky policies, and the government in turn agreed to purchase these at a guaranteed price, though the potential profit was capped. Raymond Stokes summarized this arrangement as follows: "This agreement effectively halted the hemorrhaging of IG funds into the Leuna plant, and ensured that the trust's substantial investment would be recouped in the long term. The government, on the other hand, attained its goal of increasing domestic German fuel supplies at very little cost."[50]—or, in the words of Peter Hayes, "Testifying to the length and intensity of the negotiations that produced it, the *Benzin-Vertrag* astutely balanced the interests of the contracting parties."[51]

In May 1934, Wilhelm Gaus, a member of the board of directors, developed some basic thoughts about the future development of the company. He expected that the industrialization of formerly commodity-producing countries and the reduction in exports would continue gradually but inexorably. This would surely lead to massive losses with regard to export and production volumes. Until that point, the company had been able to compensate for losses through contracts or rationalization measures, but this would no longer be possible if there were a further retreat in production and export volumes: "In this context, the problem of autarky appears in a different light. We are convinced of the fact that autarky is inexpedient and that exporting as much as possible is of critical importance for Germany. But I. G. Farben should not fail to recognize the facts of the major upheavals in the life of the nation and for this reason should focus on the problem of how Germany will feed itself and employ itself in the coming decades. It is worth considering whether the company should already commence research activity to prepare for later manufacturing for the domestic market, which would then build I. G. Farben's shrunken production volumes back up." For many imported goods, he argued, "the possibility of replacement through chemical products [could] be assumed"—for example, for textile fibers, rubber, tanning agents, or resins: "I. G. Farben should not hold back from engaging in research in this field because of its current lack of profitability."[52]

The Benzin-Vertrag of 1933 was therefore only the beginning of close cooperation between the chemical company and the Nazi regime. I. G. Farben was prepared to carry out research and production that was not profitable over the short or medium terms but could be lucrative over the longer term in the context of economic autarky and the armaments economy. I. G. Farben started to go into mobilization planning rather early and established the "W Agency" (W standing for Wehrmacht), an army liaison office, already under Carl Krauch's leadership in September 1935—a year before the official Second Four-Year Plan of 1936, through which Hitler wanted to ensure that war preparations would be finished within four years. From 1936 to 1938, Krauch worked directly for the Four-Year Plan under Hermann Göring as the head of the research and development department of the Amt für deutsche Roh-und Werkstoffe (Office for German Raw Materials).[53] The leader of organic research at the Hoechst factory, Georg Kränzlein, proudly announced in 1943, "When in 1936 the *Führer* handed the Four-Year Plan to Reich Minister Hermann Göring, I. G. Farben had already pre-prepared a good 80 percent of the plan's demands through its forward-looking research and development work, for instance in the fields of new high-performance explosive, newly developed types of Buna, plastics, textile auxiliary agents, detergents, tanning agents, camouflage material, pharmaceutical products such as serums, vitamins, hormones, disease and pest control products, and the same time addressed many other new problems."[54] This description might be exaggerated, but in light of the company's voluntary cooperation with the Nazi regime, one would certainly not be wrong to speak of self-mobilization on the part of I. G. Farben. However, it would also be too simplistic to assume that I. G. Farben was fully oriented toward autarky and the arms economy. I. G. Farben's board of directors, especially the leadership of Division II under Fritz ter Meer, also pursued a strategy of diversification and modernization throughout the Third Reich.[55]

During World War II, the company grew, as did its importance for the regime. By 1938 Carl Krauch had become an important associate of Hermann Göring as plenipotentiary for special issues in chemical production under the Four-Year Plan. In 1940 I. G. Farben took part in Nazi planning for an economic New Order in Europe, which Peter Hayes described as "a real turning point in IG Farben's relationship to the Third Reich."[56] The company was now no longer focused on international free trade, but increasingly on the Nazi ideology of a *Grossraum* economy under German leadership. The aim was to profit from this policy in the occupied countries.[57] Even during the challenging wartime workforce situation, the company did not struggle much. There was no particular enthusiasm at I. G. Farben about the idea of using forced labor, but the company knew how to use it: "Despite the influx of putatively inferior foreign workers, Farben's sales income per worker in the core corporation was 580 marks higher in 1941 and 806 marks higher in 1943 than in 1939; expenditures for wages, insurance, and social services had fallen by 407 and 194 marks per head respectively." Toward the end of the war, of the approximately 333,000 employees of the company, half were foreign or forced laborers or concentration camp inmates. Summing this up, Peter Hayes came to the conclusion: "For all its defects, the Nazi labor system paid, both for Farben and for the Third Reich in general."[58]

In general, in Nazi Germany, I. G. Farben, according to Peter Hayes, was "the apparent main winner" from the Nazi policy "of autarky, armament, aggression, exploitation, and destruction."[59] The economic development of the company during the Third Reich was striking: In 1943 total sales added up to more than three billion reichsmarks, and net profits were 300 million reichsmarks. Total sales thereby amounted to two and a half times the company's best results prior to the Great Depression. And profits between 1933 and 1943 increased no less than fivefold. In 1943, the company had 334 factories and shares in around 400 companies in Germany as well as 600 around the world—this included many that had been added through "Aryanization" or "Germanification" in the territories annexed and occupied by Nazi Germany. Without I. G. Farben's products, the Nazi regime could hardly have carried out the war—in 1943, I. G. Farben provided no less than 8 percent of the Wehrmacht's demand for aluminum, 25 percent of its demand for synthetic fibers, 33 percent of its demand for gasoline, around 50 percent of its demand for ammunition and chemicals, and 100 percent of its demand for synthetic rubber.[60]

I. G. Farben had already begun producing synthetic rubber in the 1920s under the name of "Buna" (butadiene sodium, or Butadien-Natrium, in German). The development process had mostly been halted owing to the global economic crisis and the sharp fall in the price of natural rubber, however.[61] In the Third Reich, the effort was taken up again, especially since the Reichswehr took a great interest in the product in its efforts to achieve autarky. In 1937, during the course of the Four-Year Plan, the decision was made to build a first production facility for Buna in Schkopau, near Leuna. In 1938 the decision was made to build another factory in Marl, which became the chemical factory Hüls. The government quickly demanded an expansion of Buna production, especially from 1940 onward, as the expected victory over Great Britain failed to materialize. Plans were thus made for the construction of a factory near Ludwigshafen/Oppau and for a fourth factory in the East.[62]

After assessing multiple sites and at first favoring Rattwitz, near Breslau, I. G. Farben's leadership finally selected Auschwitz. At the turn of 1940/1941, according to Peter Hayes, "in Auschwitz the interests and the racist dreams of Heinrich Himmler's SS, the logics of the Nazi regime's work policy and the industrial strategy of I. G. Farbenindustrie became interwoven."[63] Auschwitz was advantageous, above all, because it was close to water and coal and had close transportation connections. Whether the nearby concentration camp, which was still relatively small at the time, was an essential factor in the choice of location remains controversial.[64] I. G. Farben's responsibility for the use of slave labor and for the Holocaust would not be reduced in either case, though, Hayes maintains: I. G. Farben, with its choice of location, accepted as a matter of course that in the case of workforce scarcity, forced labor would need to be used and that nearby concentration camp inmates would be used for this purpose. I. G. Farben's decision also had the effect of increasing Himmler's already high level of interest in the camp. Göring's instruction to Reichsführer-SS Himmler to make workers from the Auschwitz concentration camp available for the construction of the factory, on the initiative of Krauch, opened up to Himmler and the SS promising economic opportunities such as the lease of concentration camp inmates and cooperation with private industry.[65]

Since the productivity of concentration camp inmates during the construction of the I. G. Farben factory was very low, delaying the timeline, the company's leadership called for the establishment of a separate concentration camp immediately next to the factory grounds. In late October 1942, this camp was opened, close to the former town of Monowitz, near Auschwitz.[66] In order to proceed more quickly with the construction of the new I. G. Farben factory, the concentration camp inmates were more brutally exploited and those who had been weakened were "selected" and returned to Auschwitz to be killed: "Thus began the rolling of a grisly human conveyor belt between the SS's rail sidings and Monowitz. Able-bodied Jews were brought from Auschwitz, billeted three to a bed in stifling and verminous barracks, provided minimal food and clothing supplements to the standard camp issue, subjected to lengthy predawn roll calls in all sorts of weather, and put to work on eleven-hour shifts hauling or carrying heavy loads at a trot. Within three to four months of their arrival, such treatment literally consumed the inmates, reducing them to walking skeletons. Those who did not drop dead were sooner or later reclaimed by the SS and gassed."[67] In total, 23,000 to 25,000 concentration camp inmates died during the construction of the I. G. Farben factory. To these were added multiple thousands of dead inmates who had had to work in the direst conditions in I. G. Farben's coal mines and had an even higher rate of mortality. Overall, at least 27,000 concentration camp inmates died either while working for I. G. Farben or after being sent back to Auschwitz, where they were killed with Zyklon B, the product of a subsidiary of I. G. Farben and Degussa.[68]

When the name I. G. Farben is mentioned, it is therefore not the variety of its products or the successes of its innovations that come to mind, but rather its manager's share in the responsibility for the crimes at Auschwitz. As Peter Hayes wrote, "Nothing contributed more to making I. G. Farben into the model of a 'Nazi corporation.'"[69]

I. G. Farbenindustrie AG Under Attack

During the Weimar Republic, I. G. Farben had already been viewed with great mistrust because of its preeminent position in the German economy. The journalist Helmut Wickel, for instance, published a book about the company in 1932, the year prior to Hitler's accession to power, with the telling title *I.-G. Deutschland. Ein Staat im Staate* [I. G. Germany. A State within the State] in which he argued that Duisberg had already foreseen that "a state within the state would emerge" when he had first "developed the plan for a trust that could comprise the entire German chemical industry" in 1904. At the time, chemistry was not even yet what it would become: "The trust, which became reality after the war, permeates and influences the entire German economy." The trust was a constantly changing organic configuration, the roots of which were in "the researcher's laboratory." From there, it extended "into the other branches of the economy and conquer[ed] them, both technically and also with regard to capital."[70] In late 1931 I. G. Farben was "so much the recognized economic powerhouse of Germany" that a journalist could "coin the term 'I. G.-Germany.'"[71] I. G. Farben's managers, above all Duisberg, had been able to ensure their influence over Heinrich Brüning's government despite all setbacks and the failure of various plans: "Very much in keeping with Duisberg's wishes, things are no longer decided today in the Reichstag, but rather in unaccountable committees of representatives of industry, so-called government advisors." The most important among them was Hermann Schmitz, the financial director of I. G. Farben, who, according to Wickel, could even have become the "dictator of the economy."[72]

Helmut Wickel was convinced that I. G. Farben had become "a politically decisive force, a true state within the state." In the event of possible further development of European cooperation, "the correspondingly expanded chemical trust [would] maintain the same importance." The chemical industry was now, in his view, "the most active group in capitalism," and its importance for the economy would only increase. Not only domestically, but also in foreign policy—in the efforts to achieve stronger European cooperation—I. G. Farben was a leader: "Leverkusen, Oppau and Leuna came together and became I.-G.-Germany, and they are growing and expanding and want to become I.-G.-Europe."[73]

Because of its important position in the Nazi economy, especially during the war, and its close connections with the Nazi state, I. G. Farben stood, in the words of Kim Priemel, "for everything that was wrong with the German economy." The company was seen as a "fifth column" supporting the Axis powers and seeking to damage the Allies.[74] I. G. Farben was accordingly viewed with even greater mistrust than during the years of the Weimar Republic and became the target of journalistic attacks in the Allied countries, especially the United States.

Shortly after the entry of the United States into the war, in early 1942, John Boylan published a work with the sensational title *Sequel to the Apocalypse. The Uncensored Story: How Your Dimes and Quarters Helped Pay for Hitler's War.*[75] The foreword was by Rex Stout, who at the time, according to Andreas Marquet, was regarded as an "enemy" by German immigrants since he "propagated his hatred for all Germans and spread the thesis of collective guilt."[76] As one of the most prominent American representatives of Vansittartism—the idea that National Socialism was "no coincidence," but rather was "anchored deep in the German mind"—Stout called for Americans to learn to hate the Germans.[77]

Boylan's book portrayed multiple representatives of I. G. Farben alongside Gustav Krupp, Fritz Thyssen, and Hjalmar Schacht as conspirators against democracy and peace, aiming at global dominance: Carl Duisberg, his secretary Heinrich Gattineau, Hermann Schmitz (the chairman of the board of directors since 1935), and his nephew and fellow board member Max Ilgner.[78] In 1925, through the merging of the most important German chemical companies, Duisberg and Bosch had founded the massive I. G. Farben trust, which the author described as "the octopus": "It was ready for world conquest!"[79] According to the book, Adolf Hitler was merely a puppet of big industry, which sought to use him to achieve global supremacy. Ilgner's Berlin office NW 7, which primarily produced studies about global financial and economic trends,[80] was depicted as a center of espionage which financed "fifth columns" abroad. According to the book, Schmitz and Ilgner had built up their centers of influence in North and South America and sought to profit from them with the start of the war: "The history of I. G. Farben's plundering in Europe continued to parallel the ravages of Hitler's war machine." The result was impressive: "From a monster corporation in the chemical world, I. G. Farben had accompanied Adolf Hitler through a holocaust of blood and tears until it had become the largest corporation anywhere in the world. Farben now dominated oil, coal, electric power and other fields in addition to its pre-war European monopoly of chemicals and synthetics."[81] In this description, I. G. Farben was one of the horsemen of the apocalypse, whose terrible role the Americans had been unaware of when they had purchased its products and thereby fed the "beast of the apocalypse." Because of the "supreme crime of total war against civilization," he argued, Schmitz, Ilgner, and Gattineau, among others, but also Duisberg and Bosch, who had died by that time, should be tried.[82] Boylan ended his book with a reference to I. G. Farben's connection to American companies such as Ford and Standard Oil: "Is there no sure, fool-proof way to uproot these hidden tentacles of the German I. G. Farben Octopus? Will countless other millions of American money paid in the purchase of household chemicals, family medicines and camera supplies be drained away through secret channels to feed and propel Hitler's juggernaut in its assault upon civilization?"[83]

It is hard to determine how influential or how widely read the book was. The prosecution, in any case, not only read it but also cited it—for example in an important memorandum by Leo Drachsler on the industry trials.[84] The image of I. G. Farben as an octopus also reappeared in a series of other written materials. And Belle Mayer, a lawyer at the Department of Treasury who later worked for the prosecution, seems to have been connected with the Society for the Prevention of World War III, an organization founded in late 1943 that gave institutional expression to Vansittartism in the United States and had Rex Stout as a leading member.[85]

In 1943, while the war was still going on, the American Joseph Borkin, an employee of the Antitrust Division of the Department of Justice, and Charles Welsh, an employee of the Office of Price Administration, published a book about the German "master plan" for war and conquest: "The sweep of German aims in German history has had one all-embracing theme: world conquest."[86] According to Borkin and Welsh, the cartels in particular, which had always represented German national interests, were aimed at military conquest and subjugation. This could best be understood by looking at I. G. Farben: "The record of I. G. in the twentieth century is a recital of Germany's attempt to use scientific achievements to control the world. I. G.'s commercial peacetime monopolies have been the support for its services to German militarism."[87] Monopolies and democracy did not go hand in hand, however, since monopolies such as that of I. G. Farben meant rigid control of economic life: "The political integrity of the individual, and the right to engage in enterprise, are the freedoms for which we fight. Democracy and an I. G. could not dwell together in Germany, nor could they do so here."[88] Capitalism was based on free enterprise, whereas cartels were based on rigidity, stabilization measures, and private economic planning. Germany and I. G. Farben had planned for a "total war" in advance. And thanks to their ingenuity and ruthlessness, they had been repeatedly able to push through an "industrial Munich"—in other words, appeasement agreements like that of 1938.[89]

According to Borkin and Welsh, therefore, Hitler and the National Socialists should not be declared the primary enemy. It would be dangerous to misjudge the form for the substance: "For Hitler is only one incarnation of the ruthless Teutonic vanity that finds release in war." In their argument, the National Socialists had been selected by the generals and the industry barons once the framework of the war economy was ready; and the Junkers had brought Hitler to power when his star was already beginning to fade. In so doing, though, they had made a misstep: "Along with his canting theories went his intuition, which they could not control. Hitler became the State, enforcing his nightmare orders with the sadism of the Gestapo. Neither wealth nor station could protect the man who dared to question the Fuehrer's wisdom." Hitler did not have the "icy logic" of those who had made the "master plan," and had slid into war: "He is the sorcerer's apprentice, wielding the warlock's powers he cannot fathom."[90] At that time the master plan was failing, because Germany's Blitzkrieg had not brought victory by the end of 1942 and the war was dragging on. But an Allied victory did not mean that the cartels had experienced defeat. Germany had lost World War I, but I. G. Farben had, Borkin and Welsh argued, won the peace. The Versailles Treaty had robbed Germany of its colonies, but since then, the cartels had acquired more "colonies" than the German empire had ever controlled.[91] Therefore, it was important in a new peace planning process not to let the cartels thrive again. Terrible wars would result from mistakes made during the peace process: "We want no private planners nor do we need a paternal democracy. The weakness of democracy lies not in its lack of planning but in its tolerance of industrial oligarchy, the economic twin of Fascism."[92]

Thurman Arnold, Borkin's superior as the head of the Antitrust Division and a well-known trust buster of the Roosevelt administration, wrote an enthusiastic foreword for the book—after all, the fight against large companies and cartels was central to the New Deal.[93] The German exile and lawyer Heinrich Kronstein, another colleague of Borkin's, was also expected to support the book but refused to do so, since, as he later wrote, he did not see the Nazis' plans of global conquest as inherent in the German psyche. He seems to have been put under increasing pressure at his agency as a result.[94] But according to Kronstein, in 1943, no one at the agency thought "even remotely about destroying German industry" or any "similar ideas": "Quite the opposite: There was an interest in doing everything to build up an open market, including Germany, as soon as possible after the end of the war."[95]

However, the opponents of the power of the German cartels were gaining influence in Washington, DC. Under the leadership of Senator Harley M. Kilgore of West Virginia, hearings were initiated in the Senate about the question of cartels and national security. Over the course of these hearings, the Subcommittee on War Mobilization came to the conclusion that the Allies, in order to prevent the risk of another war, must not only remove Germany's political and military leaders; "They must destroy Germany's industrial leadership as well." The democratic states must not repeat the error of thinking that German industry was politically "neutral" or that German aggression was only the domain of political fanatics. In order to destroy German imperialism for good and pave the way for a peaceful and democratic Germany, the power structures of German industry had to be changed such that they could no longer serve the waging of war. To this end, the monopolies and cartels had to be broken up. Furthermore: "Punishment of 10,000 of the leading imperialist-minded German industrialists will be more effective than punishment of 1,000,000 Nazi underlings who carried out orders of the conspirators."[96] In this report, not least to support their own recommendations, the drafters quoted from a letter from Roosevelt to Secretary of State Cordell Hull in which he explicitly referenced the danger represented by I. G. Farben: "The history of the use of the I. G. Farben trust by the Nazis reads like a detective story. Defeat of the Nazi armies will have to be followed by the eradication of these weapons of economic warfare."[97]

Then, in 1945, Roosevelt's treasury secretary, Henry Morgenthau, published a book entitled *Germany Is Our Problem*, in which he argued for the deindustrialization of Germany. In the writing process, he was assisted by, among others, Josiah DuBois, Belle Mayer, and Emanuel Minskoff, all of whom were later on the prosecution in the I. G. Farben trial.[98] I. G. Farben played a prominent role in Morgenthau's portrayal of aggressive trusts and cartels, and like Boylan, Morgenthau depicted the company as an octopus: "The Farben Octopus."[99]

In the fall of 1945, shortly after the end of the war, the "Bernstein Report" was submitted to General Lucius D. Clay, the deputy military governor of Germany at the time. Under the leadership of Colonel Bernard Bernstein, who had been appointed by the Treasury Department as a financial advisor to General Dwight Eisenhower in 1942, a team studied I. G. Farben and prepared a report on its military importance and its foreign investments. According to the report, I. G. Farben had provided massive support to the Nazis. The company, it argued, was of major importance for the German war economy, and its foreign subsidiaries had been transformed into centers of German intelligence and espionage. During the war I. G. Farben had profited significantly through a series of acquisitions in the occupied territories, and during the summer of 1940, it had even started postwar planning aimed at reordering the global chemical industry according to its wishes. The report's foreword stated that it would illustrate "the methods by means of which I. G. Farben advanced into foreign countries in order to achieve global supremacy over the chemical industry, and the camouflage techniques that it used to hide its foreign investments and holdings." According to the authors, the report described how I. G. Farben "expanded after military conquest through plundering of foreign industrial companies and foreign assets." In addition, evidence had been newly discovered that "relate[d] to how the activities of I. G. Farben and its branches were embedded in the military requirements of the Third Reich in preparing a war of aggression."[100]

The report seems to have been received favorably by, among others, General Eisenhower. It did not have the effect desired by the authors, however, with regard to the treatment of I. G. Farben. Bernstein was also kept at arm's length by General Clay at the time. He returned to Washington, DC, where he revised the report with Belle Mayer and submitted it to the Kilgore subcommittee in late November.[101] At the same time, Belle Mayer was working on a publication about I. G. Farben with Richard Sasuly, who had worked on Bernstein's staff.[102]

In early July 1945, before the Bernstein Report had been submitted, I. G. Farben and its assets in the US occupation zone were placed under the leadership and control of the sitting American military commander on the basis of General Order No. 2 of July 5, 1945, based on Military Government Law No. 52.[103] The Americans' position on how to deal with companies like I. G. Farben was not clear, however. Emanuel Minskoff, who was in Germany with Colonel Bernstein on behalf of the Treasury Department, wrote on July 7, 1945, only shortly after the seizure of the I. G. Farben factories in the US occupation zone, that the company was being treated far too well. The group in the US occupation forces that was then responsible for the factories was powerful and oriented only toward production: "The clear purpose and intention of the General order is the destruction of I. G.—not merely a change of its name or ownership but actually to deprive Germany of the war potential it represents." Officers were now being sent to seize I. G. Farben's factories. But the orders stated that the most important goal was to have the factories that were still functioning continue to run and, insofar as possible, to bring those at a standstill back into operation: "Instead of destroying I. G. such a program would be the only thing that could save it." Minskoff presumed that General Clay had signed the order with the best intentions of destroying I. G. Farben, but that the responsible officers were executing it such that the company would be saved: "From where I stand, it seems clear that the only thing that will close I. G. is a lack of coal."[104]

With the Allied Control Council Law No. 9 of November 30, 1945 (CCL No. 9), I. G. Farben was seized in all four occupation zones, and the decision was made to dissolve it. Behind this move by the victorious Allied powers were two driving forces: the accusation that I. G. Farben had been an accomplice to Nazi crimes and the importance of the company for the German war economy. Correspondingly, the Control Council Law, which focused solely on I. G. Farben, was introduced as follows: "In order to insure that Germany will never again threaten her neighbours or the peace of the world, and taking into consideration that I. G. Farbenindustrie knowingly and prominently engaged in building up and maintaining the German war potential, the Control Council enacts as follows."[105] This Allied administrative act already, to some extent, declared the company and its managers co-conspirators in planning and carrying out the war and accessories to crimes against peace.

The lawyer Hermann Heimerich, a prominent member of the SPD who had served as the mayor of Mannheim during the Weimar Republic until his removal by the Nazis in spring 1933, protested against an "agitation" he considered "unfair" against I. G. Farben that was taking place through the Control Council Law, in the press, and on the radio.[106] In a letter he wrote to a friend in mid-December 1945, Heimerich described his client Carl Krauch as "one of the most important chemists in Germany" and as "a man of stature in every respect, who naturally thinks along the lines of a planned economy, and surely never was a convinced Nazi." Serving as Krauch's legal representative had allowed Heimerich to get to know the "whole I. G. Farben complex" in more detail: "I am deeply shocked by the agitation that is being carried out, which in style reminds me of the methods that were used in the German Propaganda Ministry, which we believed could never be repeated again anywhere." This propaganda also fell on fertile soil in Germany, in his view, since the company was seen by many Germans as "big business," as a "state within a state." He doubted whether all that was being said at the time was true. The "hateful agitation" preempted, according to Heimerich, a "clear determination of the facts" and denied those who were accused the chance to defend themselves. It was therefore important to give them a chance to speak for themselves—and not "condemn [them] too quickly."[107]

In fact, at the time German newspapers were reporting on I. G. Farben's role on the basis of Colonel Bernstein's statements to the Kilgore Senate subcommittee. According to these, the company had "produced the deadliest poison gas in the world" in Wuppertal and used human beings as "guinea pigs" for experiments. This was known, according to these sources, despite the fact that when the victory of the Allies seemed assured, the Germans had tried to destroy "all of I. G. Farben's important documents" that might implicate them. According to Bernstein, German industry had "started a war to enslave the world twice within one generation." And the center of industrial might "around which Germany was organizing the wars of aggression," he claimed, was I. G. Farben.[108]

Preparation of the Indictment

According to Kim Priemel, the "economic dimension" played an important role in the prosecution's efforts to understand the structures and dynamics of the Third Reich by means of the Nuremberg trials. It even stood at the center of the debates about National Socialism—not least because of the imperative to rescue the reputation of capitalism, which had suffered owing to the complicity of German companies with the Nazi regime and its crimes. This attempt was carried out by differentiating the "good" American version of capitalism from a German version beset by flaws—even crimes: "By putting corporations in the dock in all but name, Nuremberg became a forum in which two variants of capitalism clashed and where the path of reform was laid out just as retribution was exacted."[109]

However, in June 1945, there were no leading representatives of private industry on the list of Nuremberg defendants. The economy was represented at that point only by Reich Ministers Hjalmar Schacht, Walther Funk, and Albert Speer.[110] On July 12, 1945, American Chief Prosecutor Jackson asked his associate Francis Shea to address the "economic aspects" of the trial, which the latter did with a memorandum that he submitted later that month. In it, Shea presented as potential defendants Schacht, Funk, Speer, General Plenipotentiary for Labor Deployment Fritz Sauckel, and, in addition to a few others, Alfried Krupp and Hermann Schmitz. According to Shea, the businessmen's guilt consisted in providing Hitler and the Nazi regime with the material foundations for rearmament and the means of war—with full knowledge that Hitler sought to use these to wage war, making them accomplices. While the former was easy to prove, the latter, according to Shea, could prove difficult. If relevant documents could not be found, one would have to use speeches by Hitler or Göring to demonstrate that their plans were so well known that industrialists or financiers who supported the Nazi regime had to be aware of them. On this basis, according to Shea, one could conclude that they aimed at wars of aggression to achieve world supremacy. "We would try to build up something of this case in any event, but it is much much [!] more dependent on inference."[111]

Two other high-ranking staff members of the prosecution, Robert Storey and John Harlan Amen, clearly felt skeptical about a trial against private businessmen. Amen supposedly said in reaction to Shea's draft that their task "was to convict the major war criminals and then go home," but not to "reform European economics." Shea's plans would "overload things" and turn a war crime trial into an "anti-trust case." And Storey is said to have argued that the trial against businessmen was a "balloon that [would] burst" and "make us all look silly."[112] Heinrich Kronstein, a member of the American occupation forces at the time, also expressed doubts. In late August 1945, he wrote the following in his journal: "I am quite worried about the dangerous possibilities that this war crime trial holds in certain cases. I bet that Schacht, Schmitz, and other economic 'criminals' will behave as follows: They will say that they were in agreement with companies like Standard Oil, Dupont, ICI, Shell, and others about the necessity of a war against Russia." Kronstein closed with the frustrated remark: "Only the deplorable disorganization of the War Crimes Commission, where there is much infighting due to personal jealousies, explains why no clear policy has been developed by which the investigations might demonstrate a smoking gun."[113]

The British also had reservations about trying representatives of private industry. A staff member of the British Foreign Office argued in this vein against trying Hjalmar Schacht and Gustav Krupp. He wrote as follows about Schacht: "He is, I believe, in many ways an unpleasant and unreliable character. But, in my considered view, he is not a war criminal in the sense of the prosecution. His defense would be so strong that, if it did not secure an acquittal, the authority of the Tribunal would be seriously reduced."[114] And with regard to Gustav Krupp, Alfried's father, he said that to his knowledge there was "no evidence" to suggest that Krupp "ever had any part in the political decisions on foreign policy of the Nazi or any other German Government."[115] In addition, one could not charge him with "any direct responsibility for war crimes in the narrower sense."[116]

According to Telford Taylor, US Chief Prosecutor Jackson "regarded the charges against German industrialists as a vital part of the case."[117] Jackson therefore planned, together with Soviet and French prosecutors, to try some businessmen and managers—that Krupp would be included was a given.[118] In this case, however, the charge proved to be a complete failure. Shea had wanted to try Gustav's son Alfried, who had had sole responsibility for the firm from 1943 onward; other members of the criminal prosecution agency thought, however, that Gustav Krupp, who had been head of the company until 1943, should be charged. Because of the choice of the elder Krupp, who was seriously ill and in the end incapable of standing trial, the private sector was missing on the dock. The majority of the tribunal rejected Jackson's attempt to quickly replace Gustav with Alfried in the indictment, with the British judge playing a not insignificant role.[119] However, because the French side clearly wanted industrialists to be charged as well, the British and French chief prosecutors agreed on a statement that an indictment of Alfried Krupp and other leading German industrialists would be assessed in case another trial were to take place. According to Taylor, this was the "first official indication" that there would be further war crimes trials.[120]

In late 1945, Jackson had been able to convince President Truman to let him select his own successor as chief prosecutor for possible subsequent trials. He suggested his associate, Colonel Telford Taylor, for the position. Taylor was officially appointed through General Memorandum No. 15 on March 29, 1946, as deputy chief of counsel, with responsibility for leading the Subsequent Proceedings Division.[121]

Prior to his official appointment, Taylor had already created lists of possible defendants. According to a memo from his staff member Drexel Sprecher on January 21, 1946, Taylor was especially interested in a list of "potential criminals in the industrialist field." This included leading managers of banks and major companies such as Krupp, Vereinigte Stahlwerke, and I. G. Farben and the leaders of the industrial associations.[122] Taylor wrote a memo to Jackson on January 30, 1946, stating that he was planning another international trial "at which the list of defendants will include a heavy concentration of industrialists and financiers."[123] A draft by Taylor for his staff in early February 1946 made this clear: "Plans are being made for the trial of those big German industrialists who a) supported the Nazis in their rise to power; b) participated with the Nazis in preparing Germany for aggressive war; c) assisted the Nazis substantially in waging aggressive war; d) participated in the economic spoliation of occupied countries and in the slave labor program." Corresponding documents or payments were to be sought and collected as evidence of participation in all points mentioned.[124]

In mid-April 1946, Taylor received a list of twenty-nine industrialists, financiers, and members of the Nazi regime for future criminal proceedings from Jackson's staff member Walter Rapp. Figures from I. G. Farben on the list included the board members Hermann Schmitz, Georg von Schnitzler, and Heinrich Bütefisch.[125]

At the start of 1946, Jackson seemed still to support the plan to establish a further international court in which primarily businessmen would be tried.[126] But in mid-May 1946, he officially informed President Truman that he was not in favor of a second IMT. He saw the possible acquittal of Schacht as a precedent that would be nearly "fatal." The body of evidence against industrialists in a second international court proceeding would be worse, not better, than the one against Schacht, one of the weakest cases at the IMT. The plans at the time were to try industrialists and financiers in a second IMT, but that would create the impression, according to Jackson, that they were only being tried because they were industrialists—even more so since they would be tried by the Americans together with the Soviet communists and the French leftists. The main reason for the trial was that the industrialists would otherwise escape any form of criminal proceeding. Here, though, the American balance was good, since in the IMT, according to Jackson, there was the desire to try many of them, but it had been too hard to get the other three Allies on board. Demonstrating how tense the relationship with the Soviet Union was already at the time, he rhetorically asked whether one could try German businessmen who had produced panzers for Germany's campaign against Poland without also trying Russian commissars who had produced tanks to invade Poland. Jackson also saw it as a problem that a Frenchman or a Russian could be elected as presiding judge of the tribunal even though neither would be particularly familiar with the common law system or could guarantee a fair procedure. The industrialists could nonetheless, according to Jackson, easily be brought to justice for their crimes without a second IMT: "Practically every industrialist in Germany can be convicted of using slave labor, and many can be proven guilty of illegal use of prisoner-of-war labor. These are specific crimes easily established."[127]

Taylor, however, disagreed with Jackson's argumentation and conclusions. Because of the "Krupp episode"—that is, the suit against Gustav Krupp, who was unable to stand trial—and Jackson's unrealized desire to replace him with other industrialists, not a single industrialist had been tried at the IMT. Therefore, a second IMT should be focused on German industrialists and finance magnates. All four Allied delegations wanted, if it came to it, a short, approximately three-month trial with just a few defendants. They had even agreed upon Alfried Krupp, a few I. G. Farben managers in whom the United States was particularly interested, the banker Kurt von Schröder (on the recommendation of the British), and the industrialist Hermann Röchling (on the recommendation of the French). The Soviets could nominate a few defendants, but the total number of defendants was not supposed to comprise more than six people—eight at the most.[128]

Taylor was supported in his efforts by the French and the Soviets, but the British side too seems to have seen itself obligated to support a second IMT because of the joint declaration with the French mentioned above.[129] Thus, in early June 1946, Drexel Sprecher provided a preliminary draft for a possible lawsuit against eight leading figures from business and politics in Nazi Germany, which, as the author told Taylor himself, was "hastily drawn" and "almost slavishly" followed the IMT indictment. He also claimed the draft was too complex, redundant, and wordy and that "the technique of alleging responsibility for 'institutional' activities" was "primitive." In the draft, Sprecher saw the concept of an undifferentiated conspiracy as central to the charges against industrialists—a first charge was to include conspiracy for aggression and conspiracy to commit war crimes and crimes against humanity.[130]

At the same time, Taylor sent around a circular requesting the cooperation of numerous American agencies and announcing the investigation of twenty-six leading industrialists and financiers. The possible defendants now included additional I. G. Farben managers: Schmitz and von Schnitzler were now joined by Ilgner; Carl Krauch, the chairman of the supervisory board; and Fritz ter Meer, a member of the board of directors.[131] In late June 1946, Taylor made a push to ensure that preparations had been made to try the potential defendants in a possible second IMT. His staff member Jim Heath's group was supposed to prioritize work on von Schnitzler, Schmitz, and Alfried Krupp, while Drexel Sprecher's group was to focus on Schröder, Röchling, and Flick.[132]

Finally, in late July 1946, Taylor finished a memorandum for the US secretary of war in which he once again voiced his support for a second IMT against representatives of the German private sector. The Soviet and the French governments wanted a second IMT along these lines, while the British government was "lukewarm" about the opportunity but would support it in the end, according to their head prosecutor at the IMT, Sir Hartley Shawcross. Seen from a diplomatic perspective, it would now be problematic, he argued, if the Americans were to draw back. All powers involved were in agreement, according to Taylor, that it should be a short procedure with just a few defendants. All also agreed, he stated, on the trial of Alfried Krupp, Hermann Röchling, Kurt von Schröder, and I. G. Farben managers Hermann Schmitz and Georg von Schnitzler. The Americans were responsible for the trial against the two I. G. Farben managers; the Americans and British were jointly responsible for Krupp, while the British were responsible for von Schröder and the French for Röchling. The Soviets reserved the right to later nominate one or two industrialists or bankers. The second IMT would be solely focused on industrialists and bankers, since they had not been represented in the IMT that was already underway. Focusing on a single group would strongly abbreviate the procedure. It was to be carried out in parallel with zone-based court proceedings against SS leaders, soldiers, state functionaries, and possibly other defendants. Because the potential defendants had been involved in bringing Hitler to power, waging wars of aggression, plundering occupied countries, and deporting civilians as slave labor, it ought to be possible to try them on the basis of the Hague Convention and the crimes defined in Article 6 of the IMT statute. And they could not claim that they had changed their views: "None of the listed defendants is in any position to use the defense of 'change of heart' which Schacht has capitalized on in the present proceeding." Finally, a fair trial could be ensured through an informal agreement with the British, which would ensure that the tribunal was led by a Briton or an American. The trial also should take place in Nuremberg again, not least to avoid further delays and the high costs of a move to Berlin—the Soviet preference.[133]

A few days later, the prosecution prepared a list of possible defendants, which included more than twenty leading business figures. Those from

I. G. Farben included supervisory board chairman Carl Krauch and board members Hermann Schmitz, Georg von Schnitzler, Fritz ter Meer, Max Ilgner, and Otto Ambros.[134] What was entirely unclear at this point (and would remain so until fall 1946) was whether the tribunal would be organized by zone or whether it would once again be an international military tribunal; it was also unclear which of the individuals listed would ultimately be tried. Leading managers of I. G. Farben, however, would certainly be included among the potential defendants.[135]

In mid-August 1946, Sally Falk Zeck, a young lawyer on Taylor's team, wrote the following in an internal memorandum: "It is contemplated that in about a month and a half or slightly more there will be a trial of about eight of the most prominent German industrialists, probably before an international tribunal." She explained further that it was the role of the American delegation to lead the case against managers Hermann Schmitz, Max Ilgner, and Georg von Schnitzler of I. G. Farben and against Alfried Krupp of the Krupp company. Besides the briefs against these four individuals, " 'economic' briefs" were prepared "against Farben and Krupp as corporations." Like the IMT, where both individuals and organizations such as the SS had been tried, the new trial would pursue both an individual and an institutional approach. According to Zeck, it was possible to find material that would incriminate the company, but this was more difficult for the four listed individuals: "It cannot be too much emphasized that as desirable as documents might be signed by the four defendants showing them clearly guilty of black crimes, such documents will be found rarely, if ever, since these men were in positions of such importance that they rarely carried their plans into the realm of action themselves."[136]

In light of this problem, it was important to think over how to proceed against representatives of the private sector. The prosecutor's office saw the potential of the legal construct of conspiracy and of an institutional indictment. Looking back, Taylor wrote in the early 1990s that the "Bernays additions," as he called them, "did more harm than good," but that this could not be foreseen at the time.[137]

The central analysis regarding the charge of conspiracy for the industrial trials was drafted by Leo Drachsler, a staff member of the prosecution who had immigrated from Slovakia with his parents as a child and had studied in New York City at City College and Columbia University's law school. After his studies, he had worked as a lawyer at the Department of Justice's Antitrust Division in New York. He spoke fluent German and seems to have been personally recommended for Nuremberg by Assistant Attorney General Tom Clark.[138]

On September 28, 1946, he submitted a memo entitled "Indictment of the Industrialists."[139] The "basic charge" for Drachsler was to be conspiracy. And there were four different approaches for the charge: First, a Nazi conspiracy; second, a conspiracy organized by individual industrialists; third, two or more independent conspiracies of the Nazis and the industrialists, who had combined forces after 1933 with the consolidation of the Nazi regime, carried out rearmament, and planned a war of aggression; and fourth and finally, the "'[i]nstitutional' approach," which Drachsler considered the most promising, whereby companies such as I. G. Farben and Krupp themselves were the conspirators, making them "criminal organizations."

The first approach, according to Drachsler, was impractical, because a lack of resistance did not represent participation in a Nazi conspiracy. The second approach was also problematic, because if the industrial conspiracy was the only true conspiracy, the IMT itself would be rendered less important. It was doubtful whether one should pursue the theory that the Nazis had been a mere vehicle for a conspiracy of industrialists, even if some historians supported it. The German industrialists would not be tried as monopolists, however, but as adherents of the criminal Nazi regime, with which they had joined forces in order to achieve global supremacy. It would be easy to produce evidence that German industry had been fully integrated into the war machine and that the industrialists had been "free partners" of the regime. The third approach, despite being historically accurate, was not airtight and could allow for the defense of "personal innocence." Thus, the institutional approach, for Drachsler, was "the soundest, because it embraced the advantages of the other three, testimony-wise, yet avoids the pitfalls and opportunities for specious defenses they present." This could be used to clearly show the criminal and conspiratorial character of the I. G. Farben, Krupp, and Flick companies. And it had its advantages: "By first establishing corporate or organizational guilt, the problem of personal guilt of the responsible executives (joined as defendants in their individual as well as official capacity) is simplified. There are left for determination only questions of degrees of guilt raised by personal defenses." Drachsler even saw, as in the third approach, two conspiracies among industrialists and the National Socialists that had been established prior to 1933 with the goal of achieving global domination. They had come together in 1933 in order to make their shared goal a reality through a war of aggression: "In the face of corporate guilt so overwhelmingly established, pleas of personal innocence on the part of corporate executives become difficult, if not impossible, to sustain."

The legal theory for the charge was to be the common law concept of conspiracy. In trials such as these, according to Drachsler, concrete evidence was not necessary: "It is elementary that circumstantial evidence is sufficient to establish a conspiracy. … We need only show that the industrialists, at opportune moments in the development of Nazi Germany enthusiastically adopted Nazi objectives, and efficiently implemented means used to attain a common criminal end." This is because those engaged in conspiracy act in secret and attempt to hide their tracks. "Search for detailed documentary proof of every last act or activity is unnecessary." Even so, the German obsession with orderly paperwork would certainly aid the prosecution in gathering the evidence. Equally helpful, though, were the facts that the IMT's statute allowed circumstantial evidence to the greatest degree possible and that the court was not bound by "technical rules of evidence."

In the second part of the memorandum, Drachsler dealt with the "Symbolic Treatment of Individual and Institutional Guilt. Possibilities of a Combined Presentation."[140] In order to properly pursue an institutional approach, according to Drachsler, it was desirable to have "one big trial" in which prosecutors could lay out the whole picture with its corresponding historical background. Then, the evidence against the individual industrialists could be presented. However, Drachsler conceded that the prosecutor's office, with its limited resources, could not take on such a project. Nor was the court chamber the appropriate location for a long seminar on German economic history. The only alternative was a series of individual trials against a certain number of German companies and their leadership. The disadvantage of this option was that it would make it hard to convey the full historical picture—that German industry had been a unified instrument and an important spearhead of Nazi aggression in the effort to achieve global supremacy. A series of disconnected trials would provide only an "atomized picture," he argued.

The German industrial and financial sector was, according to Drachsler, the "third column" of the Nazi regime, alongside the NSDAP and the Wehrmacht. This raised the question, he argued, of how best to symbolically show that not only the leadership of Krupp and I. G. Farben but all high-level German industrial managers were part of the Nazi conspiracy and how to prove how individual industrialists maintained their control over German industry "as a Nazi institution" through voluntary and public economic organizations. One could not ignore the dual role of German industrialists as powerful people in their economic sector and powerful people in the institutional life of the German economy. If one could show that the industrialists were the third major column of the conspiracy, then one could better pursue the goal of disarmament. This was not a Vansittartist-aligned program, he argued, nor was it an effort to fully suppress German economic activity. But the special relationship between government and industry in Germany needed to be ended, and trusts, cartels, and other similar institutions had to be prohibited. Chief Prosecutor Jackson had called for the conviction of the organizations tried in the IMT and had reminded the court that the acquittal of these organizations would be worse than acquittal of individual defendants: "This applies with equal force against German cartelism and its institutions, and how much greater a catastrophe would it be not to indict and try them at all!" This is because these German economic institutions, both in their goals and in their methods, were criminal and just as culpable as the six Nazi organizations that, according to Drachsler, were soon to be convicted by the IMT.

Taylor immediately commented on Drachsler's memorandum—though not until after the IMT had pronounced its verdict, in which the Reich cabinet, the general staff, and the high command of the Wehrmacht were not declared to be criminal organizations. He agreed with Drachsler that "one big trial" was infeasible and shared his view that a series of individual trials would not properly communicate the significance and scope of the issue unless they could somehow be portrayed as a whole. However, he did not agree with Drachsler's idea of having companies declared criminal organizations—the reasons for this had been made clear in the IMT. It also seemed unnecessary to Taylor: "There is no reason why we cannot adopt an 'institutional approach' if we select our defendants intelligently and utilize the legal concept of conspiracy fully." Taylor was in full agreement, however, that there should be an effort, in the presentation of the cases, to emphasize that the industrialists on the dock "appear[ed] as individuals, as corporate officers, and as quasi-governmental representatives of the German associations which they led." Taylor also came to the conclusion that witnesses should play an important role in the trials of the industrialists: "I doubt that we will ever have documentary evidence on the 'industrial conspiracy' which will compete with the documentary evidence in Case No. 1 [the IMT]. I am hopeful that we can 'jazz up' the program and emphasize the 'unified conspiracy' element by using a carefully selected panel of eminent witnesses such as Thyssen, Schroeder, von Papen and others."[141] With this, Taylor also seems to have abandoned the second IMT that he had long promoted, even if the plans for it were not clearly set aside until early 1947.[142]

In late February 1947, Taylor finally wrote a memorandum for his office stating that a "semi-final decision" about the list of defendants had to be agreed upon by early March on orders of General Clay.[143] During this phase, Raphael Lemkin suggested that the prosecution consider raising the charge of genocide—a criminal concept of which he was the originator—in the trials of the industrialists.[144] Clearly, a number of matters related to the indictment were still unclear. This was also true with regard to the precise charges to be raised in relation to the preparation, planning, and waging of a war of aggression. In "rough notes" dictated by Taylor and circulating at the prosecutor's office in March 1947, he addressed the corresponding judgments in the IMT and concluded that it would be best not to rely too heavily on the legal concept of conspiracy in raising the charge of waging a war of aggression: "The Court adopted a very narrow view of the conspiracy theory, and I think its usefulness is now largely exhausted." The judgments of Sauckel and Speer, thought Taylor, should raise more concerns than should the acquittal of Schacht: "In general, in the industrialists [*sic*] cases, I think it will be wise to develop, as fully as possible in the indictments, all circumstances showing fore-knowledge, to use their acts during the early years of the Nazi regime to show intent, and to center our criminal charges on acts committed in 1937 and thereafter."[145] Even with an advantageous legal framework, however, finding incriminatory evidence was no mean feat for the staff of the prosecution.

Debates on the Legal Framework

In a 1949 legal assessment of the trials of the industrialists in Nuremberg commissioned by the Ruhr industrialist Theo Goldschmidt, legal scholar Hans Ficker wrote that the "legal source" of the twelve subsequent trials had, above all, been Control Council Law No. 10 of December 20, 1945 (CCL No. 10). The procedural law for the trials had, however, been "separated from the material law and submitted to Order No. 7 of the military government about the constitution and responsibility of certain military courts."[146] Thus, it is essential to fully understand these two legal bases of the subsequent trials in Nuremberg.[147]

Control Council Law No. 10, on the "punishment of persons guilty of war crimes, crimes against peace and against humanity," was issued by the Allied Control Council, which consisted of representatives of the four Allied victorious powers and went into effect on December 20, 1945.[148] The law was therefore published while the IMT was still carrying out its proceedings. Its "actual purpose," as the legal expert Herbert Kraus argued in a commentary at the time, was to "create a substantive legal basis for all the war crimes trials."[149] A major author of the law was apparently Charles Fahy, then the director of the legal department of the American occupation authority (Office of Military Government, United States, or OMGUS) and a close advisor of General Lucius D. Clay.[150]

The text of the law began by stating its aims. It was promulgated, it stated, in order to "give effect" to the determinations of the Moscow Declaration of October 30, 1943, and the London Agreement of August 8, 1945, as well as the subsequent IMT statute "and to establish a uniform legal basis in Germany for the prosecution of war criminals and other similar offenders."

Drawing on the IMT statute, the first section of Article II defined four categories of crimes:

1) Crimes against peace—planning for, preparing for, or waging a war of aggression or a war in violation of international laws and treaties;
2) War crimes—crimes against body, life, or property in violation of the laws of war, in particular the Hague Land War Order, and the customs of war;
3) Crimes against humanity—murder, extermination, enslavement, or deportation of civilian populations as well as "persecutions on political, racial, or religious grounds whether or not in violation of the domestic laws of the country where perpetrated;" and
4) A new punishable offense consisting of "membership in categories of a criminal group or organization declared criminal by the International Military Tribunal."

Crimes against peace also now included terms such as "invasions" and "wars," which made it possible to include the annexations of Austria, Bohemia, and Moravia in the charges. The concept of crimes against humanity was likewise expanded to apply to acts that were not connected with a war as the IMT had defined it.[151]

The second section of Article II stated that an individual, without any regard to nationality, could be found guilty of such crimes as a principal or accessory, for having abetted them, for having "[taken] a consenting part therein," for having been "connected with plans or enterprises involving its commission," for having been "a member of any organization or group connected with the commission of any such crime," or—under point 2(f)—for having held a "high political, civil, or military (including General Staff) position … or held high position in the financial, industrial, or economic life" of Germany or one of its allies. The "very broad definitions of involvement," according to Herbert Kraus, went beyond the IMT statute; and they were "detailed, but not systematically ordered." Kraus also pointed out that incitement was not mentioned as a basic form of implication.[152]

The third section addressed punishments ranging from loss of civil rights to forced labor and death. The fourth section ruled against the immunity of sitting heads of state, who until that time had been widely accepted to have immunity in international law, stating that "[t]he official position of any person, whether as Head of State or as a responsible official in a Government Department, does not free him from responsibility for a crime or entitle him to mitigation of punishment." The defense of "superior orders" was also strongly limited. The text stated that acting on the order of the government or of a superior did not free a person from responsibility for a crime but could reduce the sentence. Finally, the fifth section stated that there was no statute of limitations for crimes committed in the time period of January 30, 1933, to July 1, 1945; nor would any immunity, pardon, or amnesty granted by the Nazi regime prevent trial or punishment.

The determination under 2(f) was particularly important for the trials of the industrialists, because the formulation "high position," translated into German as 'gehobene Stellung,' gave the prosecution significant discretion. Herbert Kraus considered this stipulation "the least understandably written stipulation of Law No. 10." He found no clearly defined limits between "persons in a high position" and those "who do not fall under this concept." He also saw a translation issue in the German version. Considering the use of the phrase "high position" in the English version and "*haute situation*" in the French, Kraus stated, "This phrase would be better translated *hohe Stellung* instead of *gehobene Stellung*."[153]

No less problematic for businessmen and managers was the fourth section, which severely limited the widely recognized defense of superior orders, whether concrete or presumed.[154]

The other stipulations of CCL No. 10 on the authorizations and tasks of the occupation authorities, the modalities for the arrest of those suspected to be war criminals, and the forms of punishment do not require further explanation here. What is important is that its scope was significantly broader than the London Statute, since it was not limited to crimes without a specific location and since it did not require the linking of crimes against humanity with crimes of a war of aggression.[155]

The concrete legal processes were set up in the form of military tribunals by the American military government through Ordinance No. 7 of October 18, 1946, as modified by Ordinance No. 11 of February 17, 1947.[156] Ordinance No. 7 was apparently substantially co-drafted by William Zeck, a staff member of the prosecution, which could be seen as problematic since he was not neutral but a party to the case.[157]

The aim of Ordinance No. 7 was "to provide for the establishment of military tribunals which shall have power to try and punish persons charged with offenses recognized as crimes in Article II of Control Council Law No. 10, including conspiracies to commit any such crimes." Each tribunal consisted of three or more members determined by the military governor. An alternate member could also be named if the military governor considered this advisable. Members and alternate members of the tribunals had to be lawyers who had spent at least five years at one of the highest US state courts or at the US Supreme Court. The military governor also determined the presiding judge of the tribunal. The tribunals and their members could not be challenged by the prosecutors or the defendants or their counsels, which represented a major breach of the trial rights that were otherwise customary. If a member of the court were to get sick or be unable to participate for another reason, they could be replaced by an alternate. If there were no alternate, the remaining judges were to bring the trial to a conclusion. Decisions and judgments were to be determined by majority vote, and in the case of a tie the trial was to be ceased.

The charges against individuals who were to be tried based on this ordinance were to be submitted by the Office of Chief of Counsel for War Crimes, in other words the office of the main American prosecutor for war crimes. In order to protect their rights, defendants had to receive the indictment and related documents in a language they could speak and within a specific timeframe. The indictment was also supposed to "state the charges plainly, concisely and with sufficient particulars to inform defendant of the offenses charged." The main proceedings were also to be carried out in, or translated into, a language that the defendant understood. The defendant had the right to select a defense counsel as well; if the individual rejected one, then the court would choose one. Through their defense counsels, defendants could bring evidence to their defense and cross-examine the prosecution's witnesses. Defendants could also request that the court bring in certain witnesses or documents.

The tribunal had the right to summon witnesses and place them under oath, to interrogate defendants, to "require the production of documents and other evidentiary material," to appoint officers for certain tasks, and to set the rules of procedure. It also had the right to discuss these and other matters and make decisions on them in plenary sessions of the military tribunals. The courts were to ensure the trial was confined "to an expeditious hearing of the issues raised by the charges" and to "take strict measures to prevent any action which will cause unreasonable delay, and rule out irrelevant issues and statements of any kind whatsoever."

Article VII, which threatened to majorly limit the established rules of evidence in common law courts, stood to be of major significance for the proceedings: "The tribunals shall not be bound by technical rules of evidence. They shall adopt and apply to the greatest possible extent expeditious and nontechnical procedure, and shall admit any evidence which they deem to have probative value." This determination could be very useful for the prosecution if a court decided in its favor. According to William Zeck, the judges were even obligated to apply this rule as broadly as possible; they were, it was stated, "required by Ordinance No. 7 to admit virtually all captured documentary evidence."[158]

It was also important for the courts to know that the IMT's rulings that "invasions, aggressive acts, aggressive wars, crimes, atrocities or inhumane acts [that] were planned or occurred" were not to be called into question and constituted factual evidence, "in the absence of substantial new evidence to the contrary."

Ordinance No. 7 also determined the trial procedure and the role of the Central Secretariat. It finally stated that the tribunals' judgments were "final and not subject to review." There was, therefore, no possibility of appealing the sentence to a higher court, as is typical in a normal legal process. Only the punishment itself could be reviewed, but by the military governor, not by judicial authorities. The military governor, who was responsible for the implementation and carrying out of the punishments determined by the courts, could "mitigate, reduce or otherwise alter" them, but not make them more severe.

With regard to the proceedings, matters of objections and similar instances were governed by the "uniform rules of procedure" established by the committee of presiding judges. At first the regulations of April 1, 1947 (which had already been revised) applied. One section was revised in December, which made things easier for the German lawyers with regard to the "Motions and Applications" section—they hurriedly translated it and submitted it to the defense parties. In early January 1948, there was a new version of the uniform rules of procedure. The changes to the original April 1947 draft related in particular to the sections on "Motions and Applications" and "Interviewing of Witnesses."[159] In the daily procedural work of the tribunals, the "elaborately formulated rules of play" served "a very important role" for all those involved in the trials—the judges, the prosecution, and the defense.[160]

The American occupation forces also presented briefings to the Germans about the legal bases of the trial and the responsibilities of the various parties. For instance, Robert Kempner, a leading staff member of the prosecution, delivered a talk at the University of Heidelberg about the material legal bases for the trials, the differences between civil and common law, and the concept of conspiracy.[161]

In the fall of 1946, an American general presented detailed information to German lawyers about the defense counsels' responsibilities in the Nuremberg trials. In so doing, he emphasized that the trial procedure had been unknown to German lawyers until that point, but that "much greater support from the lawyers [had been] hoped for" than had been seen "from the majority of the lawyers." It was, he argued, "of great importance for the courts in their efforts to find the truth that everything on behalf of the parties was presented and explained reasonably and conscientiously." It was expected that the defense counsels would take on the case "in detail," and as "the most important responsibility," that they would exactingly assess the evidence proffered by the prosecution—in particular through the cross-examination of the prosecution's witnesses. This method of hearing evidence corresponded to the one used in common law courts, he explained. Through the examination and assessment of the evidence, the hope was to do justice to the witnesses and to the defendants. This process had the sole goal of "determining the true facts with the greatest possible degree of precision." The trial procedure was such that a witness would first be questioned by the party who brought him or her in—this was the direct examination. Then, the witness would be questioned by the counter-party or -parties—this was the cross-examination. Then the first party could ask questions again, but only with regard to topics from the cross-examination. The direct examination had to be carried out "properly and based on the rules of the taking of evidence." The witnesses could "only be asked questions about matters of importance for the trial." And the court had to ensure that the witnesses were not asked leading questions or questions that could incriminate the witness himself or herself. Leading questions in the direct examination were "one of the most frequent mistakes of German lawyers." They were allowed, however, in the cross-examination, and there was even the right to question statements from the direct examination in a way "that served no other purpose than to discomfit a witness" if they were suspected of making false statements. The cross-examination, therefore, differed substantially from the direct examination and the one following cross-examination. The general also pointed out that it was solely the responsibility of the prosecution to "prove the guilt of the defendant"—and only once this had been "sufficiently proven" was the defense to begin. Those on the defense could also ask the court to "declare the accusation insufficient." If the court decided that there was enough evidence for the charges, then it would be the defense counsel's turn. The lawyers had to give the judges "at all times their greatest respect and not forget that they were fitted with the power and authority of the court." This did not limit the agency of the defense. A member of the defense, however, should "never present things as true fact to the court if he was not sure that they were true." If this were to happen by accident, the defense counsel should "clarify this mistake as soon as possible." A member of the defense should never furnish evidence "that he knows is erroneous." He should believe the statements of his charge; the decision about the truth or untruth of the evidence was incumbent solely on the court. Similarly, the court alone would decide whether someone was guilty or innocent—not the lawyer. Therefore, a lawyer was to defend their client "with all their strength," even if they considered the latter guilty.[162]

Seen as a whole, the military tribunals used a mixture of civil and common law, though the latter dominated: The trial was a "duel" between the public prosecution and the defense with the goal of winning the judges over to one side or the other. The prosecution was only required to present incriminatory material, not exculpatory material. However, the prosecution had the sole responsibility for proving guilt. The defense, in turn, only had the responsibility of exonerating the defendant. The judges were to hold back during the trial and be as open as possible to the evidence and argumentation presented to them. In general, they were also only infrequently to ask follow-up questions. In the end, though, the judges made their judgment in Nuremberg without a jury and without any possibility of objection: "The Nuremberg judges act as court and jury; they find fact, and express law."[163]

Former Secretary of War Henry Stimson, in a 1947 article, described the mixture of civil and common law (or Continental and Anglo-American law) that had been used in the IMT as particularly accommodating and fair for the defendants: "Each defendant was allowed to testify for himself, a right denied by Continental law. At the conclusion of the trial, each defendant was allowed to address the Tribunal, at great length, a right denied by Anglo-American law. The difference between Continental and Anglo-American law was thus adjusted by allowing to the defendant his rights under both."[164]

Francis Biddle, the former US attorney general and a judge in the IMT, wrote in the same year about the charge of planning, preparing, and waging a war of aggression based on the London Statute: "Those who framed it, I believe, had in mind the punishment of the politicians, military leaders, and industrialists who were responsible for unleashing war against a world at peace. They did not propose to authorize the indictment of every soldier or civilian who had taken part in the war. Such a construction would have been absurd, and would have led to a gravely unjust result."[165] The court was also hesitant about the legal concept of conspiracy, according to Biddle, not least because it was not equally recognized in civil law. Therefore, the successful prosecution of conspiracy would require the clear demonstration of a criminal aim, and the conspiracy could not be too far separated from the decision to act—and the act itself.[166]

In the article, Biddle also addressed the question of criminal organizations. Just one month after the start of the proceedings of the IMT, the Control Council had issued CCL No. 10, according to which membership in an organization declared criminal by the IMT could be punished with penalties ranging from the loss of civil rights to execution. This had raised concerns at the IMT, since the application of the law could lead to major injustices. Biddle knew of no other law by which one could be convicted merely for membership in an organization without involvement in its crimes. The law, according to Biddle, was by no means supposed to permit arbitrariness: "In net result therefore it will be necessary to establish individual guilt in subsequent proceedings."[167] Thus, Schacht's acquittal had been based on the fact that he could not be proven guilty of the charges against him beyond a reasonable doubt: "It is interesting to note that the Tribunal used the 'reasonable doubt' formula in weighing the evidence of guilt."[168]

The authors of another 1947 article on the IMT verdict—all members of the prosecution—pointed out that the IMT verdict would not make things uniformly easier for subsequent trials. The IMT had, they argued, made very narrow judgments; Biddle had emphasized the same. This article in the *Harvard Law Review* is particularly interesting, not least because Judge Hebert studied it carefully in connection with the I. G. Farben trial.[169]

The authors began by pointing out that in the IMT, the US part of the indictment was the first charge—that of a "joint plan or conspiracy." From the beginning, conspiracy to commit terrible crimes had been understood as "the core of the case."[170] The prosecution had had access to a large number of documents—and the official documents in particular had been evidence of the highest quality. For crimes against peace, where knowledge of the aggression to come had only been limited, only a few witnesses would have been able to make statements. In general, the testimony of the prosecution's witnesses, who had been Nazis or Nazi sympathizers, had been seen as problematic.[171] The court had been somewhat critical of the prosecution for the way it proceeded and for its evidentiary strategies. It had acknowledged the defense's right to cross-examination to a great degree, the article argued, always striving to ensure a "fair trial," despite the fact that the statute made a simpler procedure possible.[172] The evidence provided for the first charge had been excellent. Sufficient material had been provided to show that the Nazi state had aimed from the beginning to make Hitler's aggressive goals reality. A whole series of documented discussions between Hitler and small groups of high-ranking military and government representatives had proven this.[173] Despite the fact that the charge affected all the defendants, it had led to the least number of convictions: Only eight of the defendants were convicted, comprising four members of the military, two foreign ministers, and two high-ranking Nazi officials. The authors of the article saw these convictions as "the most significant achievement of the Nuernberg verdict," since, in keeping with the charter, they underscored the fact that a war of aggression was a crime and that all those involved in this conspiracy could be brought before a court. However, conspiracy—the joint plan—was limited by the tribunal to crimes against peace. This may have resulted from an ambiguous formulation in the statute, but might also reflect a lack of sympathy for the concept of conspiracy.[174]

The rejection of a broad theory of conspiracy as promoted by the prosecution had multiple explanations, according to the authors. First, the judges wanted conspiracy with the goal of carrying out a war of aggression to be clearly demonstrated, as a precisely planned criminal endeavor: "To have accepted the prosecution's theory in toto would have required a holding, in substance, that the Nazi government from 1933 on was an open conspiracy." American courts, according to the authors, tended to be cautious when ruling on the crime of conspiracy. It was also clear that the IMT wanted to avoid being too innovative and inviting accusations of ex post facto judgments. The objections of the defense against the concept of conspiracy may also have had an effect.[175] The defense had succeeded in raising doubts about the evidence in the case of defendants who were not part of the military. There had also been substantial gaps in the evidence in these cases. The inconsistent Nazi propaganda, sometimes bellicose, sometimes peaceful, claiming only to want to rearm in the case of a war of defense, had also aided the defense. This came through most clearly in the case of Hjalmar Schacht. None of the defendants had done more for Germany's rearmament potential than Schacht in his roles as president of the Reichsbank, economics minister, and general plenipotentiary for the war economy. But "armament," according to the court, was not a crime within the meaning of the IMT statute, unless the prosecution could prove that Schacht was engaging in armament for a planned war of aggression. For the authors of the article, it was hard to understand that such a central figure of the German rearmament program could not have known about its eventual goals. They also considered his decision to step back as economics minister to be the result mainly of a disagreement with Göring, since he remained Hitler's "personal advisor." In 1938 he had warned about inflation caused by high public expenditures and had lost his last post, but he had remained a minister without portfolio until 1943. However, the court had considered the evidence that Schacht had personally planned the war with Hitler to be insufficient. In the end, only eight defendants fulfilled this criterion, a fact the authors rued: "Personal participation in the planning of the small group around Hitler seems to have been made the practical measure of guilt under Count One. Such a test appears excessively narrow."[176] The authors argued that perhaps this narrow interpretation of conspiracy and joint planning was due to the fact that with a lack of concrete evidence, especially in the case of Schacht, only those for whom the evidence was clear were convicted. It could also be due to the fact that the court wanted to avoid controversial charges, such as the planning of a war of aggression. And it could finally have been due to a "dislike of the conspiracy theory in general."[177]

The prosecution of crimes against humanity also suffered, according to the authors, from the narrow definition of a conspiracy or joint plan. Crimes that had been carried out starting in 1937 could have been prosecuted, they argued. However, the IMT had decided only to prosecute crimes against humanity, such as war crimes, starting with the outbreak of the war in September 1939.[178]

The prosecution of criminal organizations proved to be another problem. Since individual trials were highly impractical and difficult to carry out, the

IMT statute provided for determining individual punishable guilt on the basis of membership in organizations that had been defined as criminal. According to the authors, this approach would have solved enormous procedural difficulties and problems of evidence for "hundreds of thousands" of people. It would also have supported the Allies' aim of preventing the revival of National Socialism.[179] However, this approach had not been to the taste of the tribunal, which had described this procedure as one that was expansive and new and that, absent sufficient monitoring, could lead to major injustices. Therefore, membership in an organization declared to be criminal, such as the SS or the Gestapo, was not sufficient for a conviction. The tribunal decided to utilize further criteria: the individual could not have been forced to be a member of the organization, and that individual had to have known personally about the crimes committed or to have personally taken part in them. Articles 9 and 10 of the IMT statute were thus undermined to a certain degree—and the prosecution had to provide evidence of guilt: "The effectiveness of the organization trials at Nuernberg, then, appears questionable."[180]

The authors summarized their argument by concluding that the IMT judgment exhibited real limits as a precedent. Despite the fact that some of the defendants were convicted on all counts of the indictment, a careful reading of the judgment showed that the most relevant charges were long-recognized war crimes. The authors were critical of this limitation: "In future trials for Crimes against Peace the prosecution would be handicapped if it were confined to the limits set in the opinion. If industrialists were among the defendants, the prosecution would be faced with the ruling that 'production' is no part of the crime of 'waging' aggressive war. It would be faced with the need of proof, a fatal omission in the Schacht case, that rearmament was carried out with actual knowledge of aggressive war plans." In the corresponding footnote, the authors also directly addressed the question of whether this would set a precedent for the I. G. Farben trial: "The extent to which the Nuernberg verdict will be followed as precedent may be shown by the pending case against I. G. Farben officials."[181]

In a 1948 article, prosecution staff member William Zeck explicitly demanded that the judges of the subsequent trials fulfill the tasks that the IMT had not taken on. The IMT had only been one step in the development of international law. At the time, only the war criminals at the highest levels of government had been convicted. Now, he argued, it was equally important, perhaps even more important, to try industrialists, field marshals, jurists, members of "goons and gun squadrons," or doctors who had supported the regime and incriminated themselves. The judges, Zeck argued, had to act with knowledge, courage, and imagination. They had to make judgments that answered society's demand for an international authority and that would rein in the evil impulses of people and nations—and in so doing, they should set aside national interests and political or economic prejudices. Unfortunately, he argued, very few had used this "monumental opportunity."[182] Zeck cited the judgment in the Flick trial as a negative example. It read like "a lengthy apology for the Nazi industrialists who built and fed Hitler's war machine before and during the war, used vast quantities of foreign slave labor and prisoners of war in their war plants, and coerced Jewish owners of private businesses into making forced sales of their enterprises so that the Flick Organization could achieve a position of industrial domination in Germany and throughout Europe." In addition, it was the shortest of all the judgments, at only fifty-one pages: "The Flick Judgment contains the scantiest review of the proof submitted by the prosecution despite the fact that, except for the Justice opinion, its statement of the law purports to be the most comprehensive."[183] Zeck saw the judgment as "completely unsound" because of its generous treatment of superior orders with reference to the count of "slave labor." He regarded the court's interpretation of the ostensible threat represented by the Nazi police state as "excessively charitable" to the defendants. This being the case, he argued, the judges had to fulfill their duty in the remaining trials—such as the I. G. Farben trial—and use the opportunities at their disposal.[184]

Hans Ficker saw things very differently from Zeck in the assessment he wrote for Theo Goldschmidt—which, it should be said, he did not want published under his own name. He was clearly of the opinion that "the assessment would lose a good amount of its impact if the Kempner-Hagannah clique exposed and discredited the author [Ficker] from the outset as a former advisor to the Reich cabinet."[185] Ficker, who had been at the International Institute for the Unification of Private Law in Rome until 1935, had, in fact, quickly become attached to National Socialism and had even managed to attain membership in the NSDAP in early 1934 even though the party had been closed to new members toward the end of 1933. Dieter Rebentisch described his work for the Nazi regime—at the Reich Justice Ministry from 1935 until the outbreak of the war and then in the Reich Chancellery as a close associate of Heinrich Lammers until the end of the war—as "a bit more than unavoidable adaption."[186] Ficker's Nazi past and his antisemitic comments about Robert Kempner, a former ministerial advisor in the Prussian Ministry of the Interior, and other Jewish members of the prosecution should not prevent a consideration of and engagement with his perspective as a subject matter expert—precisely in the spirit of *audiatur et altera pars*.

Ficker viewed the legal framework in Nuremberg as a "quite complicated legal situation seen purely in formal terms." The acts being prosecuted were, he argued, "far too broad and not expressed simply enough," which is what led to the abundance of material in the trials: "An experienced judge will find himself facing the difficult question of whether there was overreach from a procedural standpoint, and legal experts and attorneys general will not be able to shake their worry about whether this incredible excess of material is not based on the fact that in reality there are no clearly delineated punishable offences or crimes of individuals being submitted to the judges for review, but rather an entire historical period and a great country in the form of its clearest representatives are being put on the dock."[187] For Ficker, the Nuremberg trials were the result of the common law idea of an enemy, because according to traditional international legal thinking, it was "impossible to accuse simple citizens of an enemy country of 'violating international law.'" Nuremberg therefore represented "a major incursion of Anglo-Saxon international law into Continental international law." The legal consequences were significant, and the "victim" was, in his view, "the individual citizen, who is facing an immediate international liability that he cannot accede to without coming into conflict with the state to which he belongs."[188]

According to Ficker, the Nuremberg trials had subjected the defendants to a "legal system of an entirely different structure" from the one under which they had functioned and worked. This violated the basic legal prohibition of ex post facto treatment in criminal law. All the Nuremberg courts had ruled that the legal sources of the trials—the Moscow Declaration, the London Agreement, and CCL No. 10—were "a codification of international law that was unwritten at the time of the incriminating acts," and had, according to Ficker, "associated themselves with retroactive laws in a way that evokes the adherence to the letter of the law of German judges."[189] In stark contrast to the existing international law, CCL No. 10 was making "the net of threatened punishments more stringent and casting it wider than any national criminal law has ever done." Ficker continued, "Is there a single international jurist—to say nothing of criminal lawyers—who truly believes that all of these criminal acts and threatened punishments, if only *in nuce*, truly exist in international law, even if only in Anglo-Saxon international law? To ask the question is to answer in the negative." The London Statute as well as CCL No. 10 were "an ex post facto law-making" that were "subsequently tailored to the acts to be condemned." In addition, the legal norms were seen as binding only on Germans and Italians, not the citizens of the Allied nations, leading "to the most serious doubts" about whether these laws were part of international law. The war criminals, he argued, should have been convicted through national criminal law, whether Nazi criminal law or Weimar Republic law.[190]

However, the tribunals had made an effort, as Ficker noted with approval, to lay out CCL No. 10 so as "to narrow it down and to get rid of the worst injustices that would have resulted from a literal application of its expansive subject matter." Nonetheless, there were plenty of cases remaining that would be unsatisfactory from the Continental legal perspective: "If the foundations of the material law on which these historically unique trials rested were unbalanced and controversial, the difficulties from a procedural viewpoint were no less so." International criminal law had been "always a step-child" of international law; the entire mindset of international law had refused "even to think about the possibility of international criminal proceedings against individuals." This even raised the question, he argued, of whether the courts in Nuremberg were international courts or American courts—the courts had certainly answered this question in different ways. The courts that considered themselves international did so on the basis that they were applying international law: "It is true that they believed they were doing this." But a "conclusion drawn from the legal nature of the law being applied as to the character of the court applying it" was "not allowed." The courts had also argued for their international character by pointing out that the Nuremberg courts could not be American courts because they were not provided for under the US Constitution. This was an incorrect conclusion, however, because they were "special American courts established [by a] special act." They were therefore American courts, he argued, "that were not provided for in the US Constitution, but were subject to US laws."[191]

The lack of clarity about the status of the court had the natural result of a "lack of clarity about the procedural law to be applied": "It is an old and well-proven principle that a court, even if it is applying foreign material law, carries out proceedings based on its own procedural law, its *lex fori*. In moments where the courts saw themselves as international, they were acting, so to speak, in a void. Because there was no rule of procedure for international criminal law." The actual rules of procedure therefore lay "fully in the court's discretion." Ordinance No. 7 did include a regulation for the Nuremberg courts: "But when one considers the fact that this ordinance comprises in its entirety 23 articles, and notes by contrast that a modern criminal procedure ordinance, such as the Italian one, contains 653 paragraphs, then one can conceive how many matters remained unregulated." Ficker added that the ordinance not only established rules but also dispensed from them. The common-law rules of evidence were lifted to some degree by Article 7 of the ordinance. Testimony from hearsay, self-incrimination, and the mutual incrimination of the defendants were possible, as this had also been formulated in the Flick judgment: "Because of the elimination of these rules of evidence of common law, which were based on centuries of old legal conviction and development, the defendants were in a worse position than they would have been in front of an American court in America." Thus, the procedural law had mostly remained "in the shadows"; procedural guarantees were not given to the court but instead were "left to the determination of the judge." The judges had mostly solved the procedural problems on the basis of their own procedural law. But the solution had not been foreseeable: "Every court decided as it wished to. Therefore, no lawyer could draw on his procedural experiences in front of one court before another."[192]

This discussion of the legal framework of the subsequent trials in Nuremberg clearly illustrates the courts' significant room for interpretative discretion. The actors involved were also clearly fully aware of this—and what one side saw as an advantage, the other perceived as a disadvantage. If Ficker, for instance, complained about the lifting of the common-law rules of evidence in Article 7 of Military Ordinance No. 7, which was in fact problematic, Zeck saw in this very article a duty for the judges. When the courts did not apply these procedural possibilities in practice, Zeck complained—while Ficker praised them.

In May 1948, toward the end of the I. G. Farben trial, similar procedural questions were raised at a German-American Youth Club event about whether the Nuremberg trials were fair and just. On behalf of the prosecution, Benjamin Ferencz emphasized how fair the Americans were to the defendants, all of whom received a counsel of their choice, even if they had been National Socialists. Karl Hoffmann, on the side of the defense, also saw the trials as mostly fair. However, he presented the view that the prosecution had a stronger hand than the defense. This had always been the case in Germany, however, he claimed—the state was simply stronger than one person representing an individual. In addition, according to Hoffmann, the courts had made an effort to even out the differences. Drexel Sprecher, who was also part of the discussion, regretted on behalf of the prosecution that international law was now enforced, but by four victorious states. The most important evidence for the trials had been documents, which still existed in great number despite attempts to shred them because the Germans had made "too many copies." The trial had not been too technical, but had allowed many things that would not have been possible in front of American courts, he claimed. The trial process had also been very easy after the IMT, with its hesitant judges. The only truly new thing in Nuremberg had been the offense of a war of aggression. Wolfgang Heintzeler, as a representative of the defense, pointed out, however, the defense's disadvantages with respect to the prosecution. He also criticized the fact that the prosecution would only present incriminatory material, whereas under civil law it would have been required also to present exonerating material. In the "duel" between prosecution and defense, equality of arms was important. This equality was not assured in a completely destroyed country, however, even if everyone tried to ensure it. Equality was also hampered by the fact that the prosecution was part of the military government, had its support, and could move entirely freely—whereas the defense, for instance, could not leave the country. Ferencz again argued against the accusation that the judgment had been a victors' justice, though he admitted that the trial in principle was not unproblematic. However, Ferencz stated, one should take into account that, metaphorically speaking, no one had been arbitrarily shot as a criminal. There was, rather, an open procedure: "However where a policeman with a gun goes out and catches a criminal and takes his gun away from him, and then takes him to court, and the courtroom is opened, and the criminal's friends are invited to attend, and they have a careful trial, where every word is written down, where the law is clear, where everyone can criticize, and then they shoot the criminal—I say it's been perfectly fair proceeding—even if the man with the gun is the one who conducted the trial."[193]

Ferencz's metaphor, no doubt formulated with his audience at the youth club in mind, demonstrates a relatively pragmatic view from at least part of the prosecution. But this did not make the Nuremberg trials "political trials" of the victors over the vanquished. The debates during the war in London and

Washington, DC, in which the participants thoroughly discussed legal questions and problems and sought a constitutional way of proceeding—even if with the help of problematic legal constructions or constructions unfamiliar to continental Europeans, such as "criminal conspiracy"—show that there was an effort to administer justice. The effort to achieve constitutionality found its limits, however, in the simultaneous desire to punish "heinous crimes." This desire to punish was so great that people were willing to limit legal principles that had been widely accepted until then, such as the recognition of superior orders. At the same time, the trials of German war criminals were supposed to stay within the legal framework—revenge should not be enacted. Belle Mayer's personal papers contain a memorandum on the punishment of war criminals in which this issue becomes clear. It states, "I do not mean to suggest or imply that German war criminals should not be given a fair trial by military tribunals. But I do feel strongly that such trials must be simple, expeditious, and unencumbered by the technical delays and defenses which even under our own system frequently impede the execution of essential justice."[194]

Early in the I. G. Farben trial, Judge Morris himself had remarked, "The practice here is not as technical as that governing trials at home, nevertheless, there are certain basic rules governing fair trials which must be observed."[195] Overall, on the basis of the applicable legal foundation (so in particular Allied Control Council Law No. 10 and US Military Ordinance No. 7), the courts in Nuremberg ensured that the defendants received a fair trial and were judged not in an undifferentiated manner, but according to their level of responsibility, with verdicts ranging all the way from acquittal to detainment to execution. It was the fine balance between the firm desire for a fair and just trial and the firm desire to punish horrific crimes—as well as the shortcomings of the legal framework—that led to discussions and disputes in the everyday practice at Nuremberg but generally resulted in well-reasoned judgments. Thus Judge Morris defended the work and results of the Nuremberg courts in a 1953 letter to the lawyer Heinrich Kronstein: "I am inclined to agree with you that the Nurnberg trials, taken as a whole, lack uniformity, both in procedure and in the concept and application of substantive law. That is a natural result of a dearth of statutory law and a lack of precedent." Morris added: "But it does not mean that the Nurnberg trials should never have been held, or that the result was, in general, not an approximation of justice."[196]

Notes

1. Taylor, *Anatomy*, 23–26; Smith, *Reaching Judgment at Nuremberg*, 21.
2. On the Leipzig trials: Willis, *Prologue to Nuremberg*; Hankel, *Die Leipziger Prozesse*; Matthäus, "The Lessons of Leipzig: Punishing German War Criminals after the First World War," 3–23.

3. Boot, *Genocide, Crimes Against Humanity, War Crimes*, 180–82.
4. This is according to Priemel, *The Betrayal*, 62; cf. Bush, "'The Supreme … Crime' and Its Origins: The Lost Legislative History of the Crime of Aggressive War," 2342–43.
5. Cf. on this von Lingen, "Setting the Path for the UNWCC: The Representation of European Exile Governments on the London International Assembly and the Commission for Penal Reconstruction and Development, 1941–1944," 45–76; Priemel, "'A Story of Betrayal': Conceptualizing Variants of Capitalism in the Nuremberg War Crimes Trials," 69–108; Bush, "Supreme … Crime," 2343–47.
6. London International Assembly, *Reports*, 39–41: Confidential Memorandum on the Trial of War Crimes (Viscount Maugham), July 1942. I am grateful to Dr. Donald Riznik for suggesting this book.
7. London International Assembly, *Reports*, 119: Proceedings of a Special Meeting of the London International Assembly, October 12, 1942.
8. London International Assembly, *Reports*, 132: Proceedings of the Twelfth Meeting of the London International Assembly, September 28, 1942.
9. London International Assembly, *Reports*, 43, 53: Prof. René Cassin, Note of violations of the laws and customs of war, no date. On Cassin, cf. Winter and Prost, *René Cassin and Human Rights*; on superior orders, see Dinstein, *The Defence of 'Obedience to Superior Orders'*; Lippman, "Conundrums of Armed Conflict," 1–111; van Sliedregt, *The Criminal Responsibility of Individuals*, especially chapter 7, 316–41; van Sliedregt, *Individual Criminal Responsibility*, 287–306.
10. London International Assembly, *Reports*, 106–108: Sheldon Glueck to M. de Baer, September 9, 1942.
11. Glueck, "By What Tribunal Shall War Offenders Be Tried?," 1083.
12. London International Assembly, *Reports*, 122–39, with de Baer's arguments on 124–31, quotes from 124 and 125.
13. See also Weinberg, "The Setting and the Significance of the Nuremberg Trials," 35–36.
14. Taylor, *Anatomy*, 26–28; Smith, *Reaching Judgment at Nuremberg*, 21; Smith, *The American Road to Nuremberg*, 13–14: Document 1; see also Bush, "Supreme … Crime," 2347–49.
15. This debate has already been portrayed in great detail in the relevant literature, especially by Smith in the following two books: *Reaching Judgment in Nuremberg*, 20–45; *The Road to Nuremberg*. See also Kochavi, *Prelude to Nuremberg*.
16. Cf. Blum, *From the Morgenthau Diaries*; in German, see Blum, *Deutschland ein Ackerland?*; Mausbach, *Zwischen Morgenthau und Marshall*; Greiner, *Die Morgenthau-Legende*.
17. Smith, *American Road*, 27–29: Document 12.
18. Pomerance, *The United States and the World Court*, 112–16.
19. Smith, *American Road*, 24–27: Document 10. Also as a copy in the John F. Kennedy Presidential Library, Boston: Drexel Sprecher Papers, Box 50, Procedures/Press File, Folder 1, Law and Legal Problems (hereinafter: Drexel Sprecher Papers).
20. Drexel Sprecher Papers, Box 50, Procedures/Press File, Folder 1, Law and Legal Problems: Copy of the article by Major Cowles "Trial of War Criminals by Military Tribunals." Drexel Sprecher was one of General Taylor's closest associates. The article is located in his papers along with the transcript of the telephone call. According to Kraus, *Kontrollratsgesetz Nr. 10*, 65, Cowles was employed at the agency of the judge advocate general.
21. Bush, *Prehistory*, 1100: after which the judge Learned Hand in 1925 names conspiracy "that darling of the modern prosecutor's nursery." On the legal concept of conspiracy, see Safferling, "Die Strafbarkeit wegen 'Conspiracy' in Nürnberg und ihre Bedeutung für die Gegenwart," 65–82. On Bernays, see Mouralis, "Outsiders du droit international: Trajectoires professionnelles et innovation juridique à Londres, Washington et Nuremberg, 1943–1945," 122–23.
22. Smith, *American Road*, 33–37, Document 16, quote from 36.

23. Smith, *American Road*, 41–44, Document 19, quote from 42.
24. Blum, *Deutschland ein Ackerland?*, 259; Smith, *The Road to Nuremberg*, 148–49; cf. also Gausmann, *Deutsche Großunternehmer*, 60–61.
25. Smith, *American Road*, 117–22: Document 35; see on this Taylor, *Anatomy*, 38–39; Kochavi, *Prelude to Nuremberg*, 205–13.
26. Smith, *Reaching Judgment*, 37–38; Taylor, *Anatomy*, 39–40.
27. Harvard University, Harvard Law School Library, Belle Mayer Zeck Papers, Nuremberg Related Material, Correspondence, Box 3, Folder 18: Ernest Gruening, governor of Alaska, to Francis M. Shea, May 25, 1945 (copy) (hereinafter: Belle Mayer Papers).
28. Stimson, "The Nuremberg Trial: Landmark in Law," 179–80.
29. London International Assembly, *Reports*, 132.
30. Priemel, "A Story of Betrayal," 87; Priemel, *The Betrayal*, 80.
31. Cf. Priemel, "A Story of Betrayal," 90.
32. Cf. Herbert, *Geschichte Deutschlands*, 566–69.
33. Plumpe, *Die I.G.*, 175, 182–83.
34. Lindner, *Inside IG Farben*, 13–15.
35. Lindner, *Inside IG Farben*, 15–18; Plumpe, *Die I.G.*, 96–99.
36. Fischer, "Dezentralisation oder Zentralisation – kollegiale oder autoritäre Führung? Die Auseinandersetzung um die Leitungsstruktur bei der Entstehung des I.G.-Farben-Konzerns," 483; Plumpe, *Die I.G.*, 136–44; Lindner, *Inside IG Farben*, 15–26.
37. Plumpe, *Die I.G.*, 163.
38. Bosch on I. G. Farben, in Ausschuss zur Untersuchung der Erzeugungs- und Absatzbedingungen der deutschen Wirtschaft, Verhandlungen und Berichte des Unterausschusses für allgemeine Wirtschaftsstruktur (I. Unterausschuß), 3. Arbeitsgruppe: Wandlungen in den wirtschaftlichen Organisationsformen. Erster Teil: Wandlungen in den Rechtsformen der Einzelunternehmungen und Konzerne, 437–43. See also Lindner, *Inside IG Farben*, 27–30.
39. Hayes, *Industry and Ideology*, 19–21; Plumpe, *Die I.G.*, 147–49; Fritz ter Meer, *Die I. G. Farbenindustrie Aktiengesellschaft*, 30–32.
40. Ter Meer, *Die I.G.*, 56–57.
41. Hayes, *Industry and Ideology*, 23; Plumpe, *Die I.G.*, 149–52.
42. Heine, *Verstand und Schicksal*, 34.
43. Hayes, *Industry and Ideology*, 23–24; Plumpe, *Die I.G.*, 156–58.
44. Ter Meer, *Die I.G.*, 54–55; Lindner, *Inside IG Farben*, 36–37.
45. Hayes, *Industry and Ideology*, 24; cf. Plumpe, *Die I.G.*, 158.
46. Hayes, *Industry and Ideology*, 44.
47. Plumpe, *Die I.G.*, 200–203.
48. Hayes, *Industry and Ideology*, 3: Bosch's words quoted from Hayes.
49. Hayes, *Industry and Ideology*, 37–42.
50. Stokes, "From the IG Farben Fusion to BASF AG," 256.
51. Hayes, *Industry and Ideology*, 118.
52. BASF Unternehmensarchiv, IG Archiv C 121/11: Report on the 44th meeting of the technical leadership on May 4, 1934.
53. Hayes, *Industry and Ideology*, 142–43, 155–58; Lindner, *Inside IG Farben*, 266–67.
54. Hoechst Archiv, Personalakten Kränzlein: Manuskript Kränzlein, Kunststoffe für den Flugzeugbau, April 19, 1943 (translation also in Lindner, *Inside IG Farben*, 266–67).
55. Lindner, *Inside IG Farben*, 267.
56. Hayes, *Industry and Ideology*, 268.
57. Hayes, *Industry and Ideology*, 268–71; on France, see 278–90; on Norway, see 290–97. Hayes sees I. G. Farben more as reactive than as proactive; see 316–17.
58. Hayes, *Industry and Ideology*, 343–45, quotes from 344; Hayes, "IG Farben und der IG Farben-Prozeß," 99–100.

59. Hayes, "IG Farben und der IG Farben-Prozeß," 99–100.
60. Hayes, "IG Farben und der IG Farben-Prozeß," 99–100.
61. Plumpe, *Die I.G.*, 349–53.
62. Cf. on this Plumpe, *Die I.G.*, 356–80; Stokes, "From the IG Farben Fusion to BASF AG," 280–82, 299–301.
63. Hayes, "Die IG Farben und die Zwangsarbeit von KZ-Häftlingen im Werk Auschwitz," 129–48, quote from 130.
64. Hayes, "Die IG Farben und die Zwangsarbeit von KZ-Häftlingen im Werk Auschwitz," especially 134–36; cf. Stokes, "From the IG Farben Fusion to BASF AG," 299–306. For a detailed assessment, see Wagner, *IG Auschwitz*.
65. Hayes, "Die IG Farben und die Zwangsarbeit von KZ-Häftlingen im Werk Auschwitz," 137–39; Plumpe, *Die I.G.*, 380–83, however, does not mention Krauch's level of initiative. See also Wagner, *IG Auschwitz*, 49–55.
66. Wagner, *IG Auschwitz*, 94–102.
67. Hayes, *Industry and Ideology*, 359.
68. Hayes, *Industry and Ideology*, 359–60; Hayes, "Die IG Farben und die Zwangsarbeit von KZ-Häftlingen im Werk Auschwitz," 129, 144; Wagner, *IG Auschwitz*, 288.
69. Hayes, "Die IG Farben und die Zwangsarbeit von KZ-Häftlingen im Werk Auschwitz," 129–30.
70. Wickel, *I.-G. Deutschland*, 185–86.
71. Wickel, *I.-G. Deutschland*, 200.
72. Wickel, *I.-G. Deutschland*, 207–208.
73. Wickel, *I.-G. Deutschland*, 213.
74. Priemel, *The Betrayal*, 197–98.
75. Boylan, *Sequel to the Apocalypse*. A copy is located at the Bayer Archive, 207/007–001.
76. Marquet, *Friedrich Wilhelm Wagner*, 294.
77. Reuther, *Die ambivalente Normalisierung*, 146–49, also quotes Stout's article entitled "We Shall Hate, or We Shall Fail" from 1943. On Lord Vansittart and on Vansittartism, see Später, *Vansittart*.
78. Boylan, *Sequel to the Apocalypse*, 5–6.
79. Boylan, *Sequel to the Apocalypse*, 17.
80. Stokes, "From the IG Farben Fusion to BASF AG," 247–48.
81. Boylan, *Sequel to the Apocalypse*, 51–52.
82. Boylan, *Sequel to the Apocalypse*, 60–61.
83. Boylan, *Sequel to the Apocalypse*, 62–64.
84. National Archives and Record Administration (hereinafter: NARA), RG 238, Entry 165, Box 1, Folder 11: Memorandum from Leo Drachsler, September 28, 1946: Indictment of the industrialists. II. Symbolic treatment of individual and institutional guilt: possibilities of a combined presentation—here footnote on 18. Also in Drexel Sprecher Papers, Box 50 Procedures/Press File, Folder 4, Law and Legal Problems: Intra-office memorandum of Drachsler for Heath, September 28, 1946, Indictment of the industrialists. Symbolic treatment of individual and institutional guilt: possibilities of a combined presentation—here footnote on 7.
85. Reuther, *Ambivalente Normalisierung*, 149–50; Gausmann, *Deutsche Großunternehmer*, 246, 356–57.
86. Borkin and Welsh, *Germany's Master Plan*, 13.
87. Borkin and Welsh, *Germany's Master Plan*, 16–17.
88. Borkin and Welsh, *Germany's Master Plan*, 49.
89. Borkin and Welsh, *Germany's Master Plan*, 76–77.
90. Borkin and Welsh, *Germany's Master Plan*, 142.
91. Borkin and Welsh, *Germany's Master Plan*, 143–45.

92. Borkin and Welsh, *Germany's Master Plan*, 146.
93. Borkin and Welsh, *Germany's Master Plan*, 7–9. On the New Deal and antitrust, see Freyer, *Antitrust and Global Capitalism*; Phillips-Fein, *Invisible Hands*.
94. Kronstein, *Briefe an einen jungen Deutschen*, 218–20.
95. Kronstein, *Briefe an einen jungen Deutschen*, 214.
96. Cartels and National Security, 8.
97. Cartels and National Security, 3. This quote from September 8, 1944, is also in OMGUS, *Ermittlungen*, xii.
98. Priemel, *The Betrayal*, 67–68; see also footnote 37.
99. Morgenthau, *Germany Is Our Problem*. On the image of an octopus, see also Priemel, *The Betrayal*, 198–99.
100. OMGUS, *Ermittlungen*, 13–14.
101. OMGUS, *Ermittlungen*, xxxviii (introduction by Karl Heinz Roth).
102. Sasuly, *IG Farben*. On the role of Belle Mayer, see Acknowledgments, v.
103. *The Judgement in the Farben Trial*, 162–64. On the Hoechst I. G. Farben factory, cf. Lindner, *Inside IG Farben*, 341–42.
104. United States Holocaust Memorial Museum Archives (USHMM Archives), Emanuel E. and Dorothy Minskoff Collection, RG 10.154*01, Correspondence, Folder 1: report/letter Minskoff, July 7, 1945 (hereinafter: Emanuel Minskoff Papers).
105. Printed in *The Judgement in the Farben Trial*, 158–59.
106. Marchivum. Stadtarchiv Mannheim, Nachlass Hermann Heimerich 24/1972a–449: Note Heimerich from December 21, 1945, with regard to Prof. Dr. Krauch (hereinafter: NL Heimerich). On Heimerich, cf. Heimerich, *Lebenserinnerungen*, 66–68, about the years 1934–44; biography of Heimerich in Parzer, *Mannheim*, 20–55.
107. NL Heimerich, 24/1972a–449: Heimerich to Helmut Cron, Dec. 19, 1945. On Cron, see Parzer, *Mannheim*, 34, footnote 122. It is interesting that here the concept of a planned economy is given a positive connotation.
108. NL Heimerich, 24.1972a–449: Excerpt from *Frankfurter Rundschau* from December 28, 1945: "Die Rolle der IG-Farben."
109. Priemel, "A Story of Betrayal," 70–71; see also the detailed assessment in chapter 6 of Priemel, *The Betrayal*, 196–240.
110. Smith, *Reaching Judgment at Nuremberg*, 63–64.
111. Cf. Taylor, *Anatomy*, 80–81; for the memo from Shea on July 23, 1945, Bähr et al., *Der Flick-Konzern*, 880–84, Document 30, quote from 881.
112. This is according to Taylor, *Anatomy*, 81–82; cf. also Gausmann, *Deutsche Großunternehmer*, 146; Priemel, *The Betrayal*, 85.
113. Kronstein, *Briefe an einen jungen Deutschen*, 24–25: Journal entry, August 22, 1945.
114. Memorandum from E. J. Passant on August 15, 1945, quoted in Taylor, *Anatomy*, 87–88.
115. Memorandum from E. J. Passant, quoted in Taylor, *Anatomy*, 92.
116. Memorandum from E. J. Passant, quoted in Taylor, *Anatomy*, 92.
117. Taylor, *Anatomy*, 93. Contrary to this, cf. Gausmann, *Deutsche Großunternehmer*, 155, also footnote 425.
118. Cf. Bower, *Blind Eye*, 334–35.
119. See Taylor, *Anatomy*, 91–94, 151–61; Priemel, "A Story of Betrayal," 95; Bush, *Prehistory*, 1111–12; cf. also Bower, *Blind Eye*, 334–35.
120. Taylor, *Anatomy*, 161.
121. Columbia University, Rare Book and Manuscript Library, MS 1684, Telford Taylor Papers, Box 299, Nuremberg War Crime Trials, Office of Chief Counsel for War Crimes: Robert Jackson, General Memorandum No. 15, March 29, 1946 (hereinafter: Telford Taylor Papers).
122. NARA, RG 238, Entry 159, Box 3, Folder 2: Drexel Sprecher memorandum, January 21, 1946: List of potential criminals for Nazi industrialist cases.

123. Taylor, *Anatomy*, 286.
124. NARA, RG 238, Entry 159, Box 3, Folder 2: Taylor, draft, February 4, 1946: research for evidence involving Nazi industrialists in war crimes.
125. Drexel Sprecher Papers, Box 57, History File, Administrative Matters: Robert Jackson/Walter Rapp, April 18, 1946, memorandum for Colonel Taylor.
126. Bush, *Prehistory*, 1115–17.
127. Telford Taylor Papers, Box 299, Nuremberg War Crime Trials, Office of Chief Counsel for War Crimes: Robert Jackson, May 13, 1946: memorandum for the President on American participation in further international trials of Nazi war criminals. Printed in Taylor, *Final Report*, Appendix J, 276–79, quote from 279; cf. also Bush, *Prehistory*, 1123–27.
128. Telford Taylor Papers, Box 299, Nuremberg War Crime Trials, Office of Chief Counsel for War Crimes: Taylor memorandum for Benjamin Cohen on American participation in further international trials of Nazi war criminals, June 18, 1946. Printed in Taylor, *Final Report*, Appendix J, 279–82.
129. Taylor, *Anatomy*, 286–88.
130. Drexel Sprecher Papers, Box 50, Procedures/Press File, Folder 4, Law and Legal Problems: Sprecher to Taylor, June 6, 1946. On the draft, cf. Bush, *Prehistory*, 1135–40, in particular 1140.
131. Drexel Sprecher Papers, Box 51, Procedures/Press File, Trial Preparation: Taylor, OCCWC, to agencies listed, June 6, 1946, on "Investigations of war crimes in the industrial and financial field."
132. Drexel Sprecher Papers, Box 57, History File, Administrative Matters: Sprecher inter-office memorandum for Colonel Tomlinson, June 27, 1946.
133. Telford Taylor Papers, Box 299, Nuremberg War Crime Trials, OCCWC: Taylor memorandum for the Secretary of War on American participation in a second international trial of Nazi war criminals, July 29, 1946. On the British position, see Hartley Shawcross to Jackson, July 25, 1946, printed in Taylor, *Final Report*, 283–84.
134. NARA, RG 238, Entry 159, Box 1, Folder 5: OCCWC, August 1, 1946, Leading industrialists, financiers and economic figures in Nazi Germany who may be subject to prosecution under CCL No. 10. Also in Drexel Sprecher Papers, Box 51, Procedures/Press file, Trial Preparation.
135. For detailed information on a second IMT, see Bloxham, "'The Trial That Never Was,'" 41–60.
136. NARA, RG 238, Entry 203, Box 1, Folder 3: Sally F. Zeck, August 13, 1946: Memorandum to all research analysts. The Farben and Krupp cases.
137. Taylor, *Anatomy*, 637–38.
138. Bush, *Prehistory*, 1157; Telford Taylor Papers, Box 188, TTP-14-4-3-48: Taylor to Paul F. Hannah, Raytheon Manufacturing Company, January 16, 1951. Here Taylor seemed not particularly convinced about Drachsler's legal skills, which he described merely as "good": "He showed an unusual ability both to master a large amount of factual detail, and to devise reasonable and workable methods of procedure."
139. NARA, RG 238, Entry 165, Box 1, Folder 11: "Indictment of the industrialists," September 28, 1946, parts I and II; part II also in Folder 25. Cf. on the memorandum, Priemel, *The Betrayal*, 164–65; Bush, *Prehistory*, 1157–60; Gausmann, *Deutsche Großunternehmer*, 225–30.
140. Gausmann, *Deutsche Großunternehmer*, 230, calls these "symbolic trials."
141. Drexel Sprecher Papers, Box 50, Procedures/Press File, Folder 4, Law and Legal Problems: T[elford] T[aylor] memorandum for Mr. Pomerantz, October 4, 1946: Mr. Drachsler's memorandum of Sept. 28. Cf. on this Bush, *Prehistory*, 1160–63.
142. Cf. on this Priemel, *The Betrayal*, 156–57; Bush, *Prehistory*, 1129, writes that the idea of a second IMT "just withered away."
143. Drexel Sprecher Papers, Box 57, History File, Administrative Matters: Taylor to prosecution team, February 20, 1947: Semi-final decision as to what defendants we will prosecute.

144. See Bush, *Prehistory*, 1178–81; Priemel, "A Story of Betrayal," 87–88.
145. Drexel Sprecher Papers, Box 51, Procedures/Press File, Trial Preparation: T[elford] T[aylor] memorandum, March 19, 1947, Rough notes on aggressive war.
146. Bundesarchiv, AllProz 3/281, Manuskript Dr. Hans Ficker, Die Nürnberger Industrieprozesse (1949), 2.
147. For a detailed assessment of the legal framework, see Heller, *The Nuremberg Military Tribunals*, in particular chapter 5: Jurisdiction and Legal Character of the Tribunals, 107–38, and chapter 7: Procedure, 159–78.
148. Printed in *The Judgement in the Farben Trial*, 146–50; Jung, *Rechtsprobleme*, 226–31. On the Allied Control Council, see Kraus, *Ministerien für das ganze Deutschland?*; Mai, *Der Alliierte Kontrollrat*.
149. Kraus, *Kontrollratsgesetz Nr. 10*, 20.
150. Priemel, *The Betrayal*, 155.
151. Printed in *The Judgement in the Farben Trial*, 146–50, here 146–47.
152. Kraus, *Kontrollratsgesetz Nr. 10*, 28, 94–95.
153. Kraus, *Kontrollratsgesetz Nr. 10*, 101–102.
154. Cf. Kraus, *Kontrollratsgesetz Nr. 10*, 114–26 and 136–37 on acting under orders in the Flick judgment.
155. Bishai, "Leaving Nuremberg: America's Love/Hate Relationship with International law," 437; Heller, *The Nuremberg Military Tribunals*, 138.
156. Printed in *The Judgement in the Farben Trial*, 151–57; also printed in von Knieriem, *Nürnberg*, 555–61.
157. According to Bush, *Prehistory*, 1166, it was drafted by William Zeck together with Bessie Margolin.
158. Zeck, "Nuremberg: Proceedings Subsequent to Goering et al," 379. See also Control Council Law No. 10 and Ordinance No. 7.
159. See on this Drexel Sprecher Papers, Box 50, Procedures/Press File, Folder 1, Law and legal problems: Uniform rules of procedure, military tribunals, rev. to April 1, 1947; Secretary General, December 11, 1947, Subject: Uniform rules of procedure, military tribunals; Uniform rules of procedure, military tribunals, rev. to January 8, 1948.
160. Oberndörfer, "Recht und Richter," 530–36, quote from 535.
161. NL Heimerich, 24/1972a–449: Sketches, apparently by Heimerich himself, from the presentation by the English [*sic*] representative of the prosecution Kampner [*sic*] about the legal bases for the Nuremberg trials on January 19, 1946, in the old auditorium of the University of Heidelberg.
162. NL Heimerich, 24/1972a–449: Excerpt from a speech by Brigadier General Ingles on the occasion of the meeting of the presidents of the bar associations in Bad Pyrmont on September 25, 1946.
163. Zeck, *Nuremberg*, 379.
164. Stimson, "The Nuremberg Trial," 186.
165. Biddle, "The Nurnberg Trial," 689.
166. Biddle, "The Nurnberg Trial," 690–91.
167. Biddle, "The Nurnberg Trial," 691–93.
168. Biddle, "The Nurnberg Trial," 695.
169. Leventhal, Harris, Woolsey, Jr., and Farr, "The Nuernberg Verdict," 857–907. On Hebert, see Paul Macarius Hebert Papers, Louisiana State University, Law Center, Digital Commons, Hebert Nuremberg Collection: https://digitalcommons.law.lsu.edu/nuremberg_docs/37 (last retrieved on April 29, 2019): detailed Harvard Law Review Memo (hereinafter: Paul Hebert Papers). Cf. also Zuppi, "Slave Labor in Nuremberg's IG Farben Case: The Lonely Voice of Paul M. Hebert," 513, esp. footnote 73.

170. Leventhal et al., "The Nuernberg Verdict," 859.
171. Leventhal et al., "The Nuernberg Verdict," 860.
172. Leventhal et al., "The Nuernberg Verdict," 862.
173. Leventhal et al., "The Nuernberg Verdict," 865–66.
174. Leventhal et al., "The Nuernberg Verdict," 867–69.
175. Leventhal et al., "The Nuernberg Verdict," 871.
176. Leventhal et al., "The Nuernberg Verdict," 874–79, quote from 879.
177. Leventhal et al., "The Nuernberg Verdict," 881.
178. Leventhal et al., "The Nuernberg Verdict," 885–86.
179. Leventhal et al., "The Nuernberg Verdict," 887–89.
180. Leventhal et al., "The Nuernberg Verdict," 893–902, quote from 901.
181. Leventhal et al., "The Nuernberg Verdict," 902–903, and footnote on 203.
182. Zeck, "Nuremberg," 377–78.
183. Zeck, "Nuremberg," 379–80.
184. Zeck, "Nuremberg," 388–89.
185. Bundesarchiv, AllProz 3/281: Note by Nagel, November 30, 1949, on the discussion of Ficker, Nagel and Knittel on November 25, 1949.
186. Rebentisch, *Führerstaat und Verwaltung im Zweiten Weltkrieg*, 66.
187. Bundesarchiv, AllProz 3/281, Manuskript Dr. Hans Ficker, Die Nürnberger Industrieprozesse (1949), 2.
188. Bundesarchiv, AllProz 3/281, Manuskript Dr. Hans Ficker, 4.
189. Bundesarchiv, AllProz 3/281, Manuskript Dr. Hans Ficker, 5–6.
190. Bundesarchiv, AllProz 3/281, Manuskript Dr. Hans Ficker, 7–8.
191. Bundesarchiv, AllProz 3/281, Manuskript Dr. Hans Ficker, 9–11.
192. Bundesarchiv, AllProz 3/281, Manuskript Dr. Hans Ficker, 11–13.
193. Telford Taylor Papers, Box 32: TTP-5-1-7-111, German-American Youth Club, Nurnberg, Hans Lamm Chairman, Forum Discussion: Are the Nurnberg trials just and fair?, Main court room, Palace of Justice Nurnberg, May 19, 1948, quote from 42.
194. Belle Mayer Papers, Post Nuremberg Material, Personal, Box 10, Folder 9: Writings on the punishment of war criminals, undated.
195. James Morris Papers, Box 1, Folder 2: Morris to Mr. and Mrs. Vernon Cooper, August 29, 1947.
196. James Morris Papers, Box 1, Folder 5: Letter from Morris to Kronstein (copy), March 25, 1953, with excerpts from the I.G. Farben judgment; Folder 4: Kronstein's reply on March 29, 1953. With regard to the debate at the time about the Nuremberg trials between Kronstein and Telford Taylor, see Priemel, *The Betrayal*, 361.

Chapter 2

The Indictment and the Composition of the Court in Case VI

Nuremberg 1947/1948: Working and Living Conditions

Since Thucydides, every event has been assigned a place and a date—*illic et tunc*.[1] The place of the events to be described here was Nuremberg, where the prosecution, the General Secretariat, and the courts were located. The city was largely in ruins after the war; around 80 percent of the buildings in the city center were damaged or completely destroyed. In September 1945, someone who would later become a member of the prosecution described his impressions from a visit to Nuremberg, which he called "the hot-bed of racial doctrines and practices and the inspiration for racial persecutions." Nuremberg was one of the oldest cities in Germany, he continued, "But you ought to see it now. The air raids have literally crushed it." Kilometer after kilometer, one saw only the remains of structures, parts of walls, the inside of buildings with no exterior walls, similar to the landscape depicted in Figure 2.1: "In places, rubble is piled stories high, and in some districts the odor of decay still lingers on. Thousands of bodies are probably still buried in the debris."[2] Yet Nuremberg still had very good rail connections and a courthouse with an attached prison that were largely preserved. According to Telford Taylor, it was the US Army that had suggested Nuremberg as the location for the IMT and also made it possible for both this and the subsequent trials to take place there.[3] Apparently the fact that Nuremberg was Julius Streicher's city, as well as where the Nazi Party rallies had taken place, did not play a significant role in the choice of location. But the choice of Nuremberg also made it clear that this was a tribunal of the victors over National Socialism, as Taylor later wrote, "Symbolically the city was quite appropriate for a trial of the Nazi leaders, as it was here that the Nazi Party had staged its annual mass demonstrations and where the anti-Semitic 'Nuremberg Laws' had been decreed in 1935."[4]

On October 18, 1945, the IMT, in which twenty-four leading proponents of the Nazi regime were originally supposed to be indicted, was officially opened in the plenary hall of the Berlin Chamber Court (Kammergericht) building, only to then immediately adjourn. On November 20, the trial against twenty-one defendants began in Courtroom 600 in the Nuremberg Palace of Justice (see Figure 2.2). These defendants included Reich Marshal Hermann Göring; Deputy Führer Rudolf Hess; the Reich Ministers Alfred Rosenberg, Wilhelm Frick, Albert Speer, and Hjalmar Schacht; the high-ranking SS official Ernst Kaltenbrunner; as well as the leading military officers Wilhelm Keitel, Alfred Jodl, and Karl Dönitz, the last of whom was also Hitler's successor as Reich president. The three absent defendants were Gustav Krupp von Bohlen und Halbach, who was not fit to stand trial, Martin Bormann, who was indicted in absentia, and Robert Ley, who had committed suicide. The trial entailed the presentation of over 5,000 documents over a total of 218 days, interviews with 240 witnesses, and the screening of documentaries on Nazi crimes. In the verdict handed down on September 30 and October 1, 1946, three defendants were acquitted, including Schacht, twelve defendants were sentenced to death, and the other defendants were sentenced to prison.[5]

Instead of holding a second international tribunal against leading figures in business, as originally planned, the American zone trials began in Nuremberg after the IMT verdict was issued.[6]

From early December 1946, the first trial, the "Doctors' Trial," addressed, for one thing, the criminal experiments SS doctors had conducted on prisoners in concentration camps in Auschwitz, Buchenwald, and Dachau. These included therapy experiments with substances provided by I. G. Farben, which company leaders had known about at the time. For another, the trial was about the "euthanasia campaign," that is, the murder of thousands of mentally and physically disabled people under the code name "Aktion T4" (named after the Berlin address of the perpetrators, Tiergartenstrasse 4).

In the second trial, the inspector general of the German Air Force, Erhard Milch, stood accused. The third, the "Lawyers' Trial," brought leading figures from the Nazi legal system, especially from the Reich Ministry of Justice, to trial. In the fourth, employees from the SS Main Economic and Administrative Office (Wirtschaftsverwaltungshauptamt or WVHA) were tried, above all, its head, Oswald Pohl, who was also responsible for the exploitation of concentration camp prisoners in Auschwitz. Finally, the fifth case dealt with the responsibility of industrialist Friedrich Flick and some of his senior managers. This launched the industrial trials, with the I. G. Farben trial, the sixth case, immediately following; later, the trial against Alfried Krupp and some of his managers was added as the tenth case.

The trial of the managers of the I. G. Farben conglomerate, which is addressed in detail here, lasted from spring 1947 to summer 1948—this is, thus, the "date" of this historical event. On May 3, 1947, the indictment "against Carl Krauch and others" was filed in Nuremberg. The trial began in mid-August 1947 with the arraignment, when the accused appeared in court to receive the charges, and lasted until the verdicts were announced on July 29 and 30, 1948.

The year 1947, when the trial began, was not only a turning point for Western Europe; as historian Tony Judt put it, it was the year in which the fate of the entire European continent was decided.[7] At that time, there was little confidence in Europe; chaos and poverty reigned everywhere. In particular, food supply issues had not been resolved at all.[8] One of the defendants recalled years later: "The winter of 1946/47 was worse than any other period of the evil years between capitulation and currency reform. First of all, because it was bitterly cold for an unusually long time, but, above all, because there was an almost complete breakdown in provisioning."[9] In Germany the daily food intake in the British occupied zone fell from 1,500 calories in mid-1946 to just 1,050 calories in early 1947.[10] The coldest winter since 1880 was followed by one of the hottest and driest summers. One of the judges reported in the fall of 1947 that Germany—indeed, all of Western Europe—was suffering from a drought so bad that the harvest for potatoes, one of the most important foods, was only half its normal size.[11]

Figure 2.1. Nuremberg 1945/46. Source: Stadtarchiv Nürnberg, A65_I_RA_411; reproduced with permission.

Shortly before the beginning of the I. G. Farben trial, in the spring of 1947, well-informed Americans regarded Europe as already on the brink of the abyss and on the verge of a communist takeover. In this situation, disappointed by what was perceived as a non-constructive stance of the Soviet Union on the German question and disturbed by the poor economic and mental state of Western Europeans, US Secretary of State George C. Marshall announced a European reconstruction program at Harvard University on June 5, 1947. Although this European Recovery Program was intended primarily to benefit Great Britain and France, in principle, it was open to all European countries. Not only was it set up to be long term, but it also gave the receiving countries great freedom in how they used the money because it was seen as helping people help themselves.[12]

Yet, Stalin and his foreign minister, Molotov, were hostile to the Marshall Plan, not least because it was incompatible with the Soviet economic system, so they banned the communist governments of Poland and Hungary from participating in it. Czechoslovakia, which was then ruled by a coalition government under communist leadership but was not yet part of the Soviet sphere of power, also bowed to pressure from Moscow and refrained from participating although it had originally aimed to do so. In late February 1948, the communists, led by Klement Gottwald, initiated "a cold coup," completely taking over the government of Czechoslovakia, whereupon it joined the Soviet bloc.[13]

In the shadow of these events, the Brussels Pact established a Western defense alliance consisting of Great Britain, France, and the Benelux countries. During this time, West Germans were seen less and less as enemies and more as possible future partners of the free West. Accordingly, the Marshall Plan was also to be extended to the three West German occupation zones. Planning also began for a West German state. The Soviet representative in the Allied Control Council protested these developments, ultimately leaving the council in late March 1948. This Soviet step ended the joint administration of Germany by the four Allied powers.

The situation between East and West worsened even more when the Soviet Union completely blockaded West Berlin in response to the currency reform in the three West German occupation zones enacted on June 20, 1948. Berlin thus went from being the capital of the criminal Nazi regime to a symbol of freedom from Soviet oppression. The Cold War had begun.[14]

It was during this short but eventful and even decisive phase in European postwar history in 1947/48 that the I. G. Farben trial took place in Nuremberg.

At that time, the US Army provided, supported, and financed all the personnel necessary for the Nuremberg trials, including judges, prosecutors, defense lawyers, interpreters, and assistants. It established and took care of all the necessary infrastructure because the American military authorities had to take care of more than the Palace of Justice and the prison owing to the city's massive destruction; they also had to ensure that the staff for the prosecution, the judges, the defense lawyers, the members of the press, and international delegations found accommodation and office space. The US Army also provided food, supplies for heating, and vehicles and drivers.[15]

For example, after arriving in Nuremberg, Judge Morris and his wife stayed in a hotel for a few days before moving into a house on the outskirts of the city: "We have a cook, a maid, and a part-time man who takes care of the furnace and yard. For transportation I have a staff car and a driver. That sounds better than it actually is for the cars over here have seen hard usage and are unreliable while the drivers are inexperienced and frequently get lost."[16] Morris was dissatisfied with his access to legal literature in Nuremberg, especially since Berlin had a good law library: "It is strictly in keeping with the tradition of War Department and army inefficiency that the court should be located in Nurnberg without a library, and that the library should be kept in Berlin where there is little use for it."[17] Nevertheless, Morris was able to convince the War Department to allow his personal secretary to join him in Nuremberg: "Thus I have competent assistance in the office, which means a great deal in this world of inefficiency."[18]

Against Morris's criticism of a lack of efficiency in Nuremberg, one must consider the conditions—the abovementioned destruction, logistical problems, and supply deficiencies—the Americans faced in organizing the subsequent trials in

Figure 2.2. The Palace of Justice in Nuremberg 1945/46. Source: Stadtarchiv Nürnberg, A65_I_RA_424; reproduced with permission.

Nuremberg. Seen from this perspective, the achievements of the US Army and occupation authorities were quite remarkable.

Alongside the courts with judges appointed by the military governor, Nuremberg had the General Secretariat, which served as a central administrative and support site for the judges and the defense lawyers.[19] The office for the prosecution, the "Office, Chief of Counsel for War Crimes" (OCCWC), founded in late October 1946 for the subsequent trials carried out by zone, was subordinate to the military governor. Accordingly, as defense lawyer Wolfgang Heintzeler quipped in May 1948, it was an agency of the US occupation. As the circumstances in Nuremberg were constantly changing, the organization of the office remained flexible, as its director Telford Taylor noted.[20] In addition to various teams that prepared the indictments, there was an Evidence Division that located and interrogated witnesses and defendants, a Document Control Branch that was responsible for registering and securing documents and preparing books of documents, and a Public Information Office. Moreover, there was the indispensable Language Division, whose employees worked on the translation of countless documents or as simultaneous interpreters at the court.[21] Taylor mentioned the Translation Branch of the Language Division as an example of the work done in Nuremberg in his "Final Report": Between September 1, 1947, and September 1, 1948, this branch translated and reproduced 133,262 pages for the courts. This number included 45,387 pages for the prosecution and 87,875 for the defense. Considering the number of working days in this period, the average daily output was no less than 520 pages.[22]

In the beginning, in October 1946, the OCCWC had over 400 Americans and Allies on staff, with this figure rising to 1,000, including some Germans, by the end of the year. Staff size peaked between May 1947 and January 1948, with around 1,700 employees in August 1947, 1,500 at the beginning of 1948, and only around 900 that September. The "language problem," that is, the need to communicate across languages and via translations in the trials, accounted for the office's many employees, its "overhead," according to Taylor.[23]

These many employees of the US military government, whether US military personnel or American civilians, whether Allies or Germans, performed countless services for the courts, the prosecutors, and the defense lawyers, so that all involved in the trials could perform their functions as well as possible. Overall, despite various problems, the US Army's organizational and logistical achievements in Nuremberg were exceptional.

The German defenders benefited from this as well. They were well or very well equipped right from the start, even though there were some problems in the day-to-day in Nuremberg. This related in particular to the search for accommodation. In late November 1946, one of the lawyers was informed that "several hundred rooms had been seized by the military government" to make them available to the defense lawyers working in Nuremberg.[24] Housing was apparently often allocated from the seized holdings of the military court's housing office. For this to occur, an application for the relocation of an employee to Nuremberg had to be submitted to the General Secretariat. The lawyers were apparently also able to apply for rooms through the local housing office. In order to hire someone who did not live in Nuremberg, one had to obtain a work permit and approval of the move from the employment office. A permit for the relocation also depended on the refugee commissioner's approval, as the municipal housing office would not otherwise allocate any rooms.[25]

The lawyers who did not live in the greater Nuremberg area also had to worry about their residences back in their usual hometowns, as well as transportation. For example, the lawyer Rudolf Dix wrote to a colleague that problems cropped up that he had not thought possible when he had agreed to defend Friedrich Flick "already in mid-1945." In early 1947, he was not able to travel from Berlin to Nuremberg because he would have had to face the risk of "completely disgraceful accommodation" and perhaps even homelessness since people were required to make their old spaces available when they moved. And without a "travel order," he was not able to leave Berlin at all.[26]

The Americans provided for their employees through the PX, a local store run by the US occupying army, and a cafeteria in the courthouse, where the German lawyers were also allowed to eat three times a day for fifty pfennigs per meal. This was a great privilege, given material conditions in Germany at the time. They were remunerated at a rate of 3,500 Reichsmark (RM) per month for the first defendant, an additional 1,750 RM for a second, and the same for a third defendant in the same case, or an additional 3,500 RM for a second defendant in a different case from the first; the total compensation was not to exceed 7,000 RM per month. The fees were not paid by the US military government but by the Bavarian Ministry of Justice. Moreover, there were other important benefits. According to Benjamin Ferencz, the pay and care the US military government provided the defenders in Nuremberg were better than that of public defenders in the United States: As "hard workers," they received the largest food ration: 3,900 calories a day—more than American soldiers and almost three times as much as Germans on average. In addition, Ferencz wrote, the defenders received "a very highly-prized carton of American cigarettes" every week; no other employees of the military government received this, regardless of nationality or rank. They also had access to office space, equipment, and the impressive pay already mentioned: "Their salaries of 3500 marks per defendant are paid by the local government and may be as high as 7000 marks per month as contrasted with the 200 marks received monthly by the averaged skilled worker." What's more, the defenders were also allowed to use American airlines, railroads, and automobiles, and if they used their own vehicles for business purposes, they received gasoline for them.[27] A letter from a member of the prosecution to a friend in the United States shows what the entire remuneration in cash and kind was worth at the time: "The mark economy makes every American a king in his own right. For one carton of cigarettes one can obtain approximately 800 Reichsmarks. A well-paid German earns approximately 50 Reichsmarks a week. A pound of American coffee sells for about 300 to 350 Reichsmarks."[28] The ID (Figure 2.3) and mess card (Figure 2.4) of the lawyer Herbert Nath give a glimpse of some of the benefits

Figure 2.3. Office of Chief of Counsel of War Crimes: ID card of the lawyer Herbert Nath. Source: NL Nath; reproduced with permission.

Figure 2.4. Mess card of the lawyer Herbert Nath. Source: NL Nath; reproduced with permission.

the lawyers enjoyed. Thus, it was not very surprising that the Bavarian authorities who paid the money believed that the defense lawyers earned more than enough, if not too much, and tried to reduce their fees accordingly.[29]

So the circumstances for the judges, prosecutors, and defense lawyers involved in the trials were significantly better than for most people living in Germany's occupied zones. This also allowed them to make the evenings entertaining and festive at times. One should not think that the prosecutors and defense attorneys did nothing but work day in and day out in the courthouse and their offices. Perhaps because they had to deal with horrific aspects of the Nazi regime during the day, they tried to enjoy life in the evening—albeit strictly separated. While the Allies celebrated in the Grand Hotel or in their clubs, the defense lawyers and their employees enjoyed life in restaurants or their own rooms. Professor Herbert Kraus, who had worked with the lawyer Walter Siemers at the IMT, wrote to him after his return to the University of Göttingen that the atmosphere there was "a mixture of mustiness, depression and decay": "We miss the hustle and bustle of nefarious Nuremberg; and, above all, we miss you, your nightly visits, waiting for you, your turban, etc."[30]

After all, many men and women in Nuremberg were away from their partners, and it seems to have been somewhat common—after the war, given the separation from their partners it had caused, as well as the widespread partying mood—for people there to enter into extramarital relationships. Even people present together as a couple could experience the breakdown of their relationship, as happened with the marriage of William and Sally Falk Zeck, who briefly worked together preparing the industrialists' trials for the prosecution in 1946.[31]

Last but not least, those imprisoned in Nuremberg, whether as defendants or witnesses, also had relatively good living and prison conditions. One of the defendants later wrote, "Because of the physical strain of the procedure of the trial, the defendant was entitled to better food than the witness or pretrial prisoner. As early as May 6 [1947], we learned that the rations would be immediately set to 2,900 calories. That wasn't far from three times the German ration at the time."[32] According to an internal American report on the treatment of prisoners in Nuremberg, they received decent food, with the authorities taking particular care to remove cutlery after meals because of the risk of suicide. Medical care was provided around the clock by three civilian German doctors and a dentist. When they were initially incarcerated, the prisoners were examined for all possible weapons, and all their personal belongings were confiscated, inventoried, and stored. Afterward they were given blankets, a cup and a spoon, and items for washing up, but no razors. Instead, they were shaved every day and were allowed to shower and get a haircut once a week. The prisoners were also able to go for a walk or do sports in one of the four prison yards every day. Conversations with one's lawyer and interrogations had to be registered, and the prisoners were escorted to these and picked up again. Prisoners could obtain books and journals from the prison library. In the winter, the cells were heated, and on Sundays the prisoners could attend Catholic or Protestant worship services. All inmates were grouped together by case, but the cases were separated from each other to prevent cross-contact. There was a dressing room where defendants changed into and out of the clothes they wore in court, and they left them there overnight to pick up on the next day of the trial. At least once a month, the clothes were cleaned and, if necessary, mended. For lunch, the prisoners usually returned to the prison to eat—"except the I. G. Farben group, which had their noon meal served in the Court house (ante room) the reason being nearly all of the group were rather old, and it would take to [*sic*] much time, traveling back and forth."[33]

Nevertheless, there was significant differentiation among the inmates' own views of their circumstances—not only, as the internal report said, because mail and packages were censored, examined, and, if necessary, kept from their intended recipients. When the accused I. G. Farben managers were told they needed to be placed two to a cell in the summer of 1947 "to prevent suicide attempts from happening again," their lawyers protested. The lawyers argued that the defendants, half of whom were over sixty and a third of whom were almost seventy, were "mostly already in their third year in prisons, camps and penitentiaries" and suffered severe physical and mental strain owing to a whole series of measures. Yet, as none of the defendants was considering suicide, there was no need to crowd them together. This even posed a threat to their health, the lawyers maintained, because it was stressful physically as well as psychologically since the cells were too narrow, with too little air for two people, and were too dark, making it difficult for all to work and prepare for the trial.[34] Toward the end of the trial, the physical and psychological strain on the defendants was apparent, not least because sessions grew longer and also took place on the weekends.[35]

Summarizing the working and living conditions in Nuremberg in 1947/48, one has to speak of an unusual situation for occupied Germany. The living and working conditions there were special, on the one hand, because the food and pay were particularly good, but, on the other hand, particularly stressful, as one was confronted with the atrocities and crimes of the Third Reich in the courtroom every day. As prosecutor Robert M. W. Kempner wrote in retrospect, Nuremberg was "extraterritorial in every way." According to Kempner, living and working in Nuremberg at the time "did not mean a return to Germany" because the city "was under military orders, had military quarters; neither food nor anything else was German."[36] Not only was Nuremberg "fairly independent," but in Kempner's words, those working there also felt as though they were in "a legal ivory tower within the political system."[37]

The Prosecution in the I. G. Farben Trial

The Prosecution Team

In March 1946, at the suggestion of Robert Jackson, Telford Taylor (see Figure 2.5) was officially appointed by President Harry S. Truman as deputy chief counsel for the subsequent trials. In his new role, Taylor quickly became "the heart and soul of the 'Subsequent Proceedings' at Nuremberg,"[38] as a staff member of the prosecution wrote.

Taylor, who came from a well-off New England family, had been born in 1908 in Schenectady, New York, where his father had worked for General Electric. He had attended the prestigious Williams College in Massachusetts, where he had earned a Bachelor of Arts in 1928. He had then moved to Harvard Law School, where he had been particularly fostered by professors James Landis and Felix Frankfurter, who would later serve as a US Supreme Court justice; he would continue to work with them even after finishing his studies. He had found his first job at the US Department of the Interior. After that, he had moved to the Agricultural Adjustment Administration, where he had had direct experience with the massive conflicts between conservatives and progressives associated with the New Deal. Subsequently, he had held numerous positions in various institutions of the Roosevelt administration, including the Department of Justice, where he had met Robert Jackson and Francis Biddle. Taylor's brilliant career had not been interrupted by the war. During World War II, he had served predominantly and apparently very successfully as a liaison officer with the British intelligence service in Bletchley Park, ultimately with the rank of colonel. At the end of the war, he had wanted to return to civilian life in the United States, not least to save his marriage, as he wrote in his memoirs. Even so, he had then followed Jackson's call to Nuremberg, where he represented the prosecution in the case against the Wehrmacht High Command as a criminal organization in the IMT. From 1946, Taylor, as deputy chief counsel, prepared the subsequent trials.[39]

The biggest problem Taylor faced at the time was the personnel situation. In late January 1946, he determined that it would be "quite impossible" to carry out the planned subsequent trials "with the present legal staff of the Office Chief of Counsel." Most of its staff were not interested in further proceedings and wanted to go home. In addition, there were already so few employees with legal training in the prosecution team that it would be impossible to dispense with anyone in the planned new trials. Ultimately, according to Taylor, only six to eight of the lawyers working for the prosecution at the time might remain in Nuremberg.[40]

In order to recruit both young and experienced lawyers who were ambitious and self-sacrificing, and thereby solve his personnel problem, Taylor traveled to Washington, DC, in early 1946. He also hoped for a military rank suitable to his new task. With the active support of Colonel David "Mickey" Marcus,

Figure 2.5. Telford Taylor, chief counsel in the Nuremberg subsequent trials. Source: NARA 238-OMT-VI-P-1; NL Nath; public domain.

the very committed officer in charge at the Pentagon, he managed to recruit numerous qualified staff. And he was promoted to brigadier general. Moreover, Taylor was promised that his wife could accompany him to Nuremberg and that other employees in his agency could also take their spouses with them. For many recruits, this was a prerequisite for even going to Nuremberg.[41]

After returning to Nuremberg in May 1946, Taylor organized his agency's legal and research staff into six groups. One group was tasked with compiling a list of leading German figures. Two groups were expected to prepare the charges against German industrialists and financiers. The first of these two groups, under the leadership of James Heath, was to take over the trials against Krupp and leading I. G. Farben managers. This group included, among others, Leo Drachsler, Benjamin Ferencz, Russell Thayer, William Zeck, and his wife, Sally Falk Zeck. The second group was led by Drexel Sprecher and was expected to deal with the general structure of the German economy, as well as with different industrialists and financiers from those the first group was handling. The library, likewise, was under the charge of Sprecher, who would also serve as an advisor to the other five groups. Three other groups were tasked with collecting and analyzing material in preparation for trials against other possible war criminals. The first of these groups was to deal with the "cases of organizations" and the collection of evidence against military war criminals, the second with the leaders of the SS and the German health system, and the third with the leading officials of the German Foreign Office. What Taylor found important at this point was that his agency be as flexible as possible and that the various groups cooperate closely.[42]

In late June 1947, Taylor explained his program to representatives of the Soviet press: concentration camp guards or similar individuals were not to be charged in Nuremberg because they would be tried in Dachau or other places. Those who had given the orders to the concentration camp guards or had developed the rules in force at the time would be charged in Nuremberg: "Therefore, the defendants in these trials are, in general, the principal Nazis in each of the major fields of German activity under the Nazi regime." At that time Taylor wanted to bring sixteen cases, which fell into four categories, with about 225 defendants, to trial: The first category for him was the SS as the most important criminal Nazi organization; these trials were held against the leaders of the SS Main Economic and Administrative Office, the SS Race and Settlement Main Office, and the SS Einsatzgruppen. The second group included the leading German military officers, such as Field Marshal Milch. The third group of defendants involved representatives from politics, the state, and the administration, such as in the trial against jurists that was ongoing at the time. Finally, the fourth group comprised the leading men in industry and finance—the trial against Flick was underway, and twenty-four leading managers of I. G. Farben had been charged. According to Taylor, the crimes the defendants were charged with in the industrial trials were usually deportation and mistreatment of slave laborers, financial support of Himmler and the SS, and plunder and spoliation in the occupied territories. When asked about any delays, Taylor replied that the trials were taking longer than originally planned but should not be sped up, for one thing, to ensure the best possible conditions for the defense and, for another, so that as much as possible could be learned about the Third Reich and its functioning—historical facts that could then be made available to the public.[43]

After all, Taylor was also pursuing didactic goals with the trials, as he noted in a lecture to the German-American Youth Club in the summer of 1947: "I want to say very emphatically that the object of these trials is not revenge and that only part of the object is the punishment of such of the accused as may be found guilty. A very much more important object is to bring about a clear understanding, both in Germany and abroad, concerning exactly what was going on in Germany during the years of the Hitler regime, under the government which became known as the Third Reich."[44] Taylor wanted to use the trials, as Mark Spicka and Kim Priemel have already shown, to inform the German people especially about the crimes of the Third Reich, as well as the reasons and preconditions for them, and reform German society in the process.[45]

Of what turned out to be twelve subsequent trials in Nuremberg, Taylor once described four as most important to him; one of these was the I. G. Farben trial.[46] A trial against managers of I. G. Farben had been planned from the start, although it was originally intended to be part of a second international tribunal.[47] The extent to which the industrialists' trials were part of Taylor's personal agenda became clear in his opening speech at Flick's trial, where he also explained his understanding of the Nazi state: "The Third Reich dictatorship was based on this unholy trinity of Nazism, militarism, and economic imperialism."[48] This core statement of the "unholy trinity" was obviously based largely on the concept of the four pillars that supported the Nazi regime, which Franz Neumann, who was working for the prosecution at the time, had developed during the war in his book *Behemoth*: The four pillars of the Third Reich were the NSDAP, the ministries, the military, and—relevantly in this context—the economy.[49] In the Flick trial Taylor also described his attitude towards the accused industrialists: "We are not dealing in this case with murderous fanatics to whom one may pay the single compliment of sincerity. We are dealing with men so bent on the attainment of power and wealth that all else took second place."[50]

Taylor apparently had intended for the New York lawyer Abraham L. Pomerantz, who had made a name for himself as a lawyer for small shareholders, to be the chief prosecutor in the originally planned second IMT. However, it is likely that many in the prosecution thought he played fast and loose with the rules and did not share his support of a "crude condottiere interpretation of how German big business had controlled the Nazi regime." Frustrated by the developments in Nuremberg, Pomerantz returned to the United States after just a few months.[51]

His successor, Drexel Sprecher, was one of the few who had been there since the IMT. Like Pomerantz, Sprecher was not universally admired in the prosecution team—and apparently many called his analytical skills, especially, into question.[52] Sprecher had come from a wealthy Midwestern family, had studied at the London

School of Economics, and then, like Taylor, had completed his law studies at Harvard University. After that, he had worked for several years as a lawyer at the National Labor Relations Board, a prominent New Deal agency, where he had led numerous labor litigation cases. During the war, he had served in the American secret service, the Office of Strategic Services (OSS). At the end of the war, he had been sent to the IMT with several other OSS employees, where, among other things, he had worked with Franz Neumann on the Baldur von Schirach case. Taylor recruited him early for the subsequent trials. By February 1946 he had already become the head of the Economics Division in the Subsequent Proceedings Division and then of the group that prepared the I. G. Farben trial.[53]

However, rather than Sprecher, Taylor appointed Josiah DuBois as the chief prosecutor of the I. G. Farben trial (see Figure 2.6). DuBois, born in Camden, New Jersey, in 1912, had studied law at the University of Pennsylvania, graduating at just eighteen years of age. He had then worked in the Foreign Funds Control Division of the Department of the Treasury. According to Rebecca Erbelding, he was one of the youngest members of Morgenthau's executive staff and had a reputation as a "hothead," being passionate, articulate, and fearless.[54] In 1940, he began working as an investigator at the Treasury Department,

Figure 2.6. Josiah DuBois, chief prosecutor in the I. G. Farben trial. Source: NARA 238-OMT-VI-P-2; NL Nath; public domain.

confiscating foreign assets, then moved to Bernard Bernstein's staff under General Eisenhower. In 1943 he became aware that the State Department was dragging its feet on the Jewish refugee problem. He helped draft a report for Treasury Secretary Morgenthau, "on the Acquiescence of This Government in the Murder of the Jews," so that Morgenthau could intervene with Roosevelt.[55] In order to quickly advance the course correction he was calling for, DuBois also secretly informed the society journalist Drew Pearson about the US government policies he was critical of. Accordingly, one can regard the War Refugee Board, which was finally set up to save European Jews in 1944 and headed by John Pehle, with DuBois as general counsel, as one of his achievements. That same year, DuBois, who, as one of the treasury secretary's closest employees, also worked on the Morgenthau Plan and Morgenthau's book *Germany Is Our Problem*, became an assistant secretary. Like the treasury secretary, DuBois initially opposed trials for German war criminals. In 1945, under President Truman, he took part in conferences in Moscow and Berlin as an advisor on reparations issues. In early 1946 he stopped working for the government and returned to the United States. Then, in December of that year, Taylor asked him to come to Nuremberg and serve as the chief prosecutor in the I. G. Farben trial.[56]

According to Mark Spicka, DuBois was the "perfect lawyer" to lead the lawsuit against the I. G. Farben conglomerate, especially on the charges of waging a war of aggression and conspiring against peace. He adhered to Morgenthau's line that the Third Reich was a monolithic, totalitarian regime that was entirely in keeping with German authoritarian and militaristic traditions. During the trial, DuBois thus pursued the ideas of the Morgenthau Plan, which, as described above, called for a Carthaginian peace, that is, extremely harsh punitive actions against Germany, and for Germany to undergo deindustrialization. While the New Deal trustbusters likewise mistrusted the cartels and big corporations, they had different goals from those of DuBois. Whereas the former, like Taylor, wanted to reform the power structures of the German economy, DuBois wanted to remove the totalitarian elements—and the roots thereof—endemic to German society and destroy them.[57]

In her analysis of the Nuremberg trials, Elizabeth Borgwardt came to the following conclusion: "The Nuremberg criminal trial might best be understood as an alternative to competing schemes such as the Morgenthau Plan, which emphasized the reparatory justice approach of disassembling industrial plants and the exporting of German labor to rebuild war-torn Allied countries."[58] Seen in this light, it was by no means unproblematic that members of the defeated Morgenthau group like Josiah DuBois could be found in prominent positions among the prosecutors in Nuremberg. But, according to Kim Priemel, Taylor did not seem to be aware of the "irony" of DuBois's appointment as deputy chief prosecutor in the I. G. Farben trial: just two years earlier, as an employee of Morgenthau, DuBois had still disputed the need for trials.[59]

The Preparation of the I. G. Farben Trial

According to Mark Spicka, DuBois led the prosecution against the I. G. Farben managers under the assumption that the Third Reich reflected the aggressive and militaristic characteristics inherent in German culture and the German people. German companies, DuBois felt, also had these characteristics, so they needed to be punished to no longer pose a threat in the future. Spicka thus concluded that " … Dubois's desire to obtain retribution lent itself to the construction of a trial plan concentrating on the count of crimes against peace instead of the easier to prove charges of slave labor and plunder and spoliation."[60] But the prosecution's focus on conspiracy against peace could by no means be attributed solely to DuBois. None other than Taylor himself regarded Count V, that is, the conspiracy against peace, as particularly important. It was partly for this reason, Taylor argued, that the preparations for the I. G. Farben trial took a relatively long time: "Out of strong personal conviction no less than because it was my official duty to enforce the provisions of Law No. 10—including its proscription of war-making—I directed that the staff of OCCWC should concentrate a large share of its time and energy on the analysis of evidence and the preparation of charges relating to 'crimes against peace.' The proof necessary to support these charges is, as a rule, more extensive and complicated than in the case of war crimes and atrocities."[61]

Nevertheless, the search for reliable evidence, especially on the particularly important counts of war of aggression and conspiracy against peace, proved to have difficulties beyond their complexity and extensiveness for the prosecution staff, as Taylor had said. It also suffered from the problem, as Francis Shea and Sally Falk Zeck mentioned in their memoranda, that it was difficult, if not impossible, to find personally incriminating material against the defendants on these charges.

Along the same lines, a June 1946 letter from Hyman B. Ritchin, an employee of the Justice Department, was not very encouraging. Ritchin had collected evidence against industry early on with Sam Harris, a friend of Taylor's: "We had tentatively agreed at that time that it would be best to convict the corporation and hang on to the corporationarly [*sic*] individuals we wanted. We thought it would be a grave mistake to attack the individuals per se." This was because it would hardly have been possible to convict the two I. G. Farben managers they were thinking of prosecuting at the time, von Schnitzler and Schmitz. It would have been difficult to point to one person and say that person was primarily responsible for the company's activities: "Von Schnitzler, unfortunately for him, had wide notoriety, but in fact, he was nothing more than a super salesman. Personally, I think Krauch, chairman of the supervisory board, is the one individual in the company who is more guilty [*sic*] than the others."[62]

In addition to the problem of finding reliable evidence against specific individuals, the case also struggled from the prosecutors' being left largely alone to do their work. Celia Goetz, who worked as a lawyer for the prosecution on the trials against Flick and Krupp, noticed immediately upon arriving in Nuremberg that there was a lack of systematic organization. She was assigned to the Flick team and told to collect evidence for the trial without any help or introduction. After she complained about the vagueness of the task, she was transferred to the Krupp team. Summing up her experience, Goetz noted, "There was good reason for some level of disorganization in all the cases. As I came to appreciate, the entire staff, lawyers and support personnel, and even judges, had been put together from scratch. The members had little or no experience working with one another, and few had any experience working on the issues before us. Like myself, most of the prosecutors knew no German, and every legal act broke new ground."[63]

Moreover, the American military authorities were often uncooperative toward American prosecutors. Taylor himself wrote in retrospect, "At the higher levels of command, especially among the regular officers, there were few who applauded and some who openly questioned the wisdom of the Nuremberg undertaking." And their doubts grew ever stronger, especially after Winston Churchill's speech about the "Iron Curtain" between Eastern and Western Europe.[64]

A young lawyer on Taylor's team noted this lack of support from segments of the army and the occupying authorities.[65] Sally Falk Zeck, who had studied law at Columbia University, described in her memoirs the frustrating experience of searching for evidence: In 1946, she and William Zeck, her husband at the time, had applied to work for Taylor in Washington, DC, and both had been hired. When Taylor asked her what interested her especially, she mentioned the industrial trials, whereupon he assigned her to the I. G. Farben case. In Germany, she then drove to Frankfurt with several German-speaking assistants to search for evidence at I. G. Farben's headquarters. To her surprise, she learned that it was not an American who was responsible for the "tremendous warehouses full of documents" but rather a German who supposedly knew nothing about those documents. She then complained to the American officer in charge, but he did not want to provide her any support. On the contrary, "[H]e criticized the Nuremberg trials for persecuting Germans who were doing nothing wrong, and suggested that a bunch of Jews were doing this." Subsequently, she sought the help of an American chemist who was doing research there for the US government: "I asked him if he would be of any help; absolutely not as he had one objective himself and he was not going to help the Nuremberg people; it was clear to me that certain of these military people were anti the Nuremberg trials." After only six months, a very unhappy time, she recalled in 2014, she felt too young and unimportant to be capable of achieving anything in Germany. She left Nuremberg at the end of 1946, got divorced, and also rejected an offer from Taylor to work for his agency in Washington.[66]

Mary Kaufman had similarly frustrating experiences when American officials apparently refused to provide her with documents and witnesses.[67] Benjamin Ferencz also described problems with the US military in a letter: "Major Hanson, the gentleman in charge of all these bon mots is a very fine gentleman, but he would sooner part with his right leg than a slip of paper from these buildings [I. G. Farben's]." Ferencz therefore decided to enlist the help of three I. G. Farben managers: Hans Kugler, who was later indicted; Ernst Struss from the TEA office, I. G. Farben's centralized administrative office on technical questions, who became an important witness for the prosecution; and Paul Dencker: "I carefully explained to these gentlemen that I was from Noooremburg [*sic*], letting it rolll [*sic*] significantly off my tongue, and was interested in certain operations of their little company. I suggested that we were concerned with the details as they pertained to 2 or 3 of the top men, for there was talk of re-organizing Farben with a new directorate, and we would have to know which of the top 2 or 3 would be affected by our denazification policy. Meanwhile my good cigarettes are going round the table. Somehow the idea became prevalent that if they played ball in the right way they might possibly be the new top men in their beloved industrie [*sic*]. (So help me I made no promises!) The effect was most amazing. Before I could say 'Heil Hitler' these 3 characters start bringing me the most amazing reports." Thus, he concluded that a former I. G. Farben manager working on the files for them was worth thirty qualified Washington employees.[68]

As Kim Priemel noted, this letter was symptomatic of Ferencz's failure to recognize the difference between corporate responsibility and evidence of individual guilt.[69] Indeed, it was easier to determine a company's responsibility—that is, to pursue an institutional approach—as Hyman Ritchin and Sally Falk Zeck had already discovered. In late March 1947, shortly before the indictment was submitted, the lawyer Randolph Newman wrote a memorandum on the question of whether it would be possible to indict a company under CCL No. 10, the Moscow Declaration, or the London Agreement. He concluded, "A careful reading of those three statutes leads to the conclusion: Corporations cannot be made defendants under Control Council Law No. 10." Even if one were to interpret CCL No. 10 very broadly and declare companies to be "persons," the question would remain as to whether it would really be wise. Newman's answer was a resounding no: "Why should we create a new problem, which, no doubt, will lead to an extensive discussion and which, if passed upon against the prosecution, would do more harm to our cause ('I. G. Farben acquitted!') than it could ever help us if decided in our favor." Drexel Sprecher forwarded the memorandum to Taylor with the comment "I assume the issue of a corporate defendant is 'dead'. If not I believe you might find further 'worries' in the attached study."[70]

Nevertheless, in the trials of the industrialists, the companies were often named before the accused persons. According to Kim Priemel, this was typical of the blurred distinction between legal and natural persons; this got around the question of clarifying the relationship between an individual and a company, which were rhetorically mixed together—and often resulted in only the responsibility of the company's being proven. This gave the defense counsels an open flank they could assail in the prosecution, which was a real stroke of luck for them.[71]

The prosecution, for quite some time, had little more evidence than the Bernstein Report and the Kilgore Report. But Ritchin had already made the following comment on the Bernstein Report: "It is badly written and I would recommend that you do not rely on it."[72] In addition, an undated document with no named author, apparently from mid- to late 1946, also stated that the copies of the two reports were in many cases illegible and not properly authenticated. It also noted that the interviews were signed, but the interviewees had not been under oath, and, although they contained valuable information for the prosecution, they lacked precise data and source citations on important points. As a result, the document's author argued, many of the interrogations needed to be carried out again. Moreover, many of the reports' statistics were incomplete and did not contain the necessary information.[73] Even Bernd Greiner, who was very positive about the prosecution, wrote, "One would not be able to do much with Bernstein's black book from the autumn of 1945: no court would accept unsworn witness statements or documents without a date; no judge would be satisfied with general statements about the company's policies."[74]

Thus, it made a lot of sense to ask the Allies for assistance in obtaining evidence, which Taylor's deputy counsel, Pomerantz, did, asking the French in late October 1946.[75] And it was sensible to make an effort, as William Zeck did in 1946, to gather evidence against I. G. Farben and its managers in Washington, DC, as well. At that time, Zeck turned to Belle Mayer, who, in the course of her work in the Treasury Department, including for Bernstein, had compiled extensive material about I. G. Farben. He managed to convince Mayer not only to make the material available to the prosecution but also to join the team in Nuremberg. In fall 1946 Mayer joined the prosecution.[76] Soon after her arrival in Nuremberg, however, she discovered that the team still had little more than the Bernstein Report for the trial.[77]

This was likely due, not least, to the fact that the prosecution suffered from considerable turnover, fueled by personal animosities, members jockeying for position, and differences of opinion regarding the strategy to be pursued. Some staff came and went for largely personal reasons, as was the case with Sally Falk Zeck, who, when she left Nuremberg, also left her marriage to William Zeck behind. But some turnovers had to do with frustration with the work, as was the case with Abraham L. Pomerantz.[78] Leo Drachsler, who had played a key role in setting the strategy for the industrial trials, also moved to a different American agency in frustration.[79] And Jan Charmatz, who had taught law at Charles University in Prague before the German occupation of Bohemia and Moravia in March 1939 and who, as a Czech, was a member of the prosecution, reported in a letter to Belle Mayer in early May 1947 on tremendous conflicts within the prosecution team. At that time he himself moved into a different office because he had fallen out completely with Drexel Sprecher. Some on the team, he wrote, would no longer exchange a word with him or even greet him.[80]

William Zeck also left Nuremberg frustrated because he did not get along with his new superior Josiah DuBois, who had probably come to Nuremberg, along with Morris Amchan, at the suggestion of Belle Mayer.[81] As Zeck explained in an interview years later, the prosecution had initially wished to indict only members of I. G. Farben's board of directors until DuBois arrived. Zeck noted that a lot of time had been spent collecting conclusive evidence of board members' personal guilt with the help of I. G. Farben employee Paul Dencker.[82] But then, despite Zeck's protesting, DuBois had decided to indict I. G. Farben director Erich von der Heyde: "[H]e had seen a picture of an ugly SOB [son of a bitch] in an SS uniform, who somehow worked for I. G. Farben in some capacity, named von der Hyde [*sic*] and he said, 'I've got to have this man in the dock,' and I said, 'The man doesn't belong in our dock because of the careful selection we've made with respect to background.'"[83] Apparently, von der Heyde was indicted instead of Ulrich Haberland, who was not a member of I. G. Farben's board but had headed the Upper Rhine Works Group since 1943:[84] "I didn't know what DuBois's background was, but that didn't matter if all he could see himself doing, fresh off a plane, on the basis of a photograph he saw, was make an arbitrary decision to replace a vulnerable defendant with a guy in an SS uniform, I figured I'd had enough, you know. Belle was there, there was a new team, another one arrived while I was busy interrogating in Frankfurt, in the coldest winter they'd seen in a hundred years, a man came in off a plane named Morris Amchen [*sic*], and he looked around and he saw what I was doing, and he said have I examined their income tax returns? So I figured this was another one who was going to brighten my life as I try to proceed with this prosecution. I decided to go home." Although Taylor had tried to change his mind, Zeck left the team and returned to the United States.[85]

Thus, it was hardly surprising that another suggestion from Mayer, namely, to hire the author Howard Armbruster as a staff member for the prosecution, was met with skepticism. In a letter to the OCCWC, Armbruster was described as "a very determined man" who would probably be difficult to lead, adding, "I mention this because I know that you have a great many 'personality problems.'"[86] And, indeed, the trial team was caught up in tussles over authority and arguments about members' respective status, but also about the strategy and the assessment of the evidence, for months.[87]

As a result, the overall working conditions for the prosecutors were not particularly good, as Charles LaFollette, a former congressman employed at that time by the prosecution, noted: There was no real cooperation among the team members, and both the translation and copying departments were bad; a lot of things did not work, he felt, but a lot was expected from the trial teams. The existing problems had to be solved if several courts were to work simultaneously: "You can't even operate three [tribunals] now without killing the lawyers who are trying the cases or without making their experience so unpleasant that compared with stateside practice it is incomprehensible that any lawyer would want to impose such conditions upon any other lawyer."[88] After all, the prosecution teams in the various trials were relatively small, including the prosecution team against the I. G. Farben managers—the prosecution seriously suffered from a lack of qualified personnel.[89]

Eventually, Taylor and DuBois's explicit goal of proving the charges of waging a war of aggression and conspiring against peace against the I. G. Farben managers took an extraordinary amount of time and effort, but the other charges also required a lot of work.

Just a few weeks before the trial began, in early May 1947, Charmatz wrote with resignation that, although he was working twelve to fourteen hours a day, working with the document books had shown him how little progress had actually been made in preparing for the trial: "I realise now after I am pretty well advanced in the preparation of the document books how sketchy our evidence still is; how much additional research in the various document centers and plants has still to be done; and that at least for my part I have not even started yet to think of rounding up witnesses for our count."[90] Emanuel Minskoff, who came to Nuremberg in April 1947 at the request of DuBois, with whom he had worked at the Treasury Department, described similar experiences. In a letter dated February 1948, Minskoff, working on Count III, "Slavery and Mass Murder," complained: "Since joining Belle Mayer and Joe DuBois in April of last year I have been literally enslaved by the prosecution of the I. G. Farben case. It is with true nostalgic reflection that I recall the easy days in the Treasury when 60 or 70 hours were considered a hard week's work."[91]

On account of these working conditions and probably also the conflicts within the prosecution, the staff members Thomas Ervin and Jan Charmatz suffered breakdowns; both then had serious health issues for some time.[92]

On the team prosecuting I. G. Farben, Belle Mayer took the lead on the charges of war of aggression and conspiracy against peace. The German entrepreneurs and managers, Mayer wrote in her draft indictment, were not ordinary capitalists, even if they had attempted this "masquerade." They had committed all the monstrous crimes they stood accused of: "[I]t must be exposed to the world once and for all if the honest businessmen and industrialists of the world are to be relieved of the unjustified stigma and suspicion which has attached to them as a result of the monstrous crimes of these pseudo-businessmen." She averred that this masquerade had to be stopped: "If they are businessmen, their business is war and their market the world. If they are scientists, theirs is the science of organized murder."[93]

According to Kim Priemel, the prosecution wanted to show that I. G. Farben's managers were not "normal" businessmen or managers as understood in the United States.[94] To do this, the team had to explain precisely the crimes against peace and not just the war crimes and crimes against humanity because, according to DuBois, the latter were an integral part of crimes against peace. The prosecuting attorneys did not want the accused managers to be perceived as "simple criminals": "From their perspective the men in the dock—and those they represented—had not only plundered and coerced, murdered and supplied the instruments of murder, they had been planning to do this all along or, at the very least, had known of and consented to the Nazi plans."[95] For the indictment, Belle Mayer extensively argued with traditions from German history, such as enduring feudalism, aggressive militarism, and the absence of antitrust regulations. Kim Priemel viewed Mayer's historical approach and her strategy of portraying German entrepreneurs and managers as "pseudo-businessmen" as effective: "Despite the colourfulness of her narrative and a sincerity that verged on naïveté, the rationale behind Mayer's emphasis on history was highly astute. If the prosecution was to win guilty verdicts the judges needed to be convinced that the men in the dock were nothing like the entrepreneurs they knew at home."[96]

Frank Gausmann, whose portrayal of the prosecution is even more negative than the above-quoted one of Mark Spicka, on the other hand, saw them as ideologically obstinate "Morgenthau boys" who wanted to destroy the German economy. In Gausmann's view, after their efforts to restructure the German economy in 1945 were defeated, these "Morgenthau boys" obviously began to focus more and more on the "initially rather secondary indictment of major businessmen in Nuremberg." Seeking to reform the German economy "via the detour of the war crimes trials" and trade out its leading figures, they did not indict the most criminally liable entrepreneurs but instead the "most prominent or best-known representatives" of Germany's major industries "in a blanket manner and with as much publicity as possible" in order to discredit these industries.[97] Gausmann saw his view confirmed by the example of the I. G. Farben prosecutors. In the industrial trials, he noted, in addition to "the many idealistic young lawyers" who sought to prove the conspiracy charge "out of more or less naive enthusiasm," the prosecution also included "several proven American anti-trusters as well as stubborn Vansittartists" in important positions. From the beginning, people like Drexel Sprecher and Leo Drachsler had been hired from the Justice Department's Antitrust Division, which would have been particularly hostile to big business. However, in late 1946, "some important, albeit particularly questionable, personnel decisions" had been made concerning the I. G. Farben trial.

Gausmann holds that with Josiah DuBois's appointment on the recommendation of Belle Mayer, whom he regards as radical, the I. G. Farben trial grew even more ideological. According to Gausmann, Mayer, DuBois, and Minskoff were "proven supporters of the radical variant of Morgenthau's world of ideas" that Taylor recruited "from left-wing government circles" because of their views and reputation.[98]

Karl Heinz Roth regarded the trial in a manner similar to Gausmann but assessed it positively. According to Roth, it could be assumed that DuBois's group, which largely came from the Treasury Department, saw in the trial against the I. G. Farben managers "a real opportunity to effectively slow down the restoration process that had begun [in the West German occupation zones] after their long-lost political power struggle."[99]

In fact, the prosecution (see Figure 2.7) for the I. G. managers' trial did include some of Morgenthau's close associates from the Treasury Department, such as Belle Mayer, Josiah DuBois, and Emanuel Minskoff. There were also some Jews of American or European descent such as Belle Mayer, Mary Kaufman, Benjamin Ferencz, William Zeck, Morris Amchan, Emanuel Minskoff, and

Figure 2.7. The prosecution team led by Josiah DuBois (seated third from left), here with Drexel Sprecher (seated second from left) and Emanuel Minskoff (standing on the far right). Source: NARA 238-OMT-VI-P-14; NL Nath; public domain.

Randolph Newman, who was born Rudolf Heinrich Neumann in Germany and had practiced law there.[100] Even so, Jews and remigrants did not hold any leading positions in the I. G. Farben prosecution. Nevertheless, Josiah DuBois reported about grumblings that many, indeed too many, Jews were working for the prosecution.[101] Even Bishop Aloysius Muench, the apostolic nuncio in the American occupied zone, regarded the prosecution as being under the influence of Jews and "39ers," i.e., German emigrants who had received American citizenship before the war. He also insinuated that they were seeking retribution.[102] Such claims can also be found in Frank Gausmann's work.[103]

To be sure, Jews and re-migrants were not necessarily friendly toward Germans. Emanuel Minskoff wrote to a colleague in the Treasury Department in early 1948 that Germans worked only as much as necessary; the rest of the time they were busy with black market transactions. But their "favorite activity" was feeling sorry for themselves. Pointing to their destroyed cities and factories and the meager food rations, they constantly complained about the hard blow fate had dealt them: "There is no feeling of guilt or sorrow for the war itself or for the mass destruction of human beings, both apart from, as well as in conjunction with, the waging of war." The fact that the British, French, Italians, Greeks, and many others who were worse off during the war than the Germans were still suffering from lack of food and clothing was irrelevant to them. They complained about unfair distribution, and if the Americans did not give them as much as Hitler did, they claimed they would have been better off under Hitler.[104]

The publicist Tom Bower characterized the prosecution as "certainly" having "Jews amongst the American staff at Nuremberg," as well as a probable "sprinkling of left-wingers," yet, overall, as being in the hands of a "Harvard Law School mafia": "Young, inexperienced, wholly ignorant about Germany and faced with immense obstacles, they diligently tried to convert a group of undistinguished and conservative American judges to a radical theory: that educated, respected and otherwise normal businessman could be guilty of murder."[105] Among the I. G. Farben prosecutors, only Telford Taylor and Drexel Sprecher were Harvard graduates. And the inexperience of the prosecutors was already noted by Judge Morris in early 1948: "The prosecution is being conducted by a group of inexperienced refugees from Washington bureaucracy."[106]

In sum, one can agree with Bower and Morris that most of the prosecutors in the I. G. Farben trial in Nuremberg had little courtroom experience. There were also a number of Jewish staff members, but none of them held a leading position on the trial team. Nor was there a "Harvard Mafia." Perhaps the trial team did not have the best lawyers, as Belle Mayer said in retrospect: "I think that what we were lacking was top-notch trial counsel." According to Mayer, the prosecution needed some lawyers with real experience in criminal homicide cases, and if such lawyers had been present, the team may have been more successful.[107] In fact, DuBois repeatedly brought Mayer back in, even though she had also returned to Washington in frustration, because he was not satisfied with the team. At his request, she collaborated on the important brief on the war of aggression at the end of 1947 because at that time, DuBois did not have enough faith in Morris Amchan.[108] And Mayer was even involved in writing the closing statement in the spring of 1948.[109]

Yet even better and more experienced lawyers would likely have struggled in Nuremberg due to Taylor's and DuBois's chosen approach. DuBois's decision to abandon the responsibility criteria that William Zeck had helped to develop and to charge not only board members but also mid-level managers, in other words the four directors, with the crime of waging a war of aggression and crimes against peace rendered the prosecution vulnerable. The IMT's acquittals for Hjalmar Schacht and Albert Speer on charges of crimes against peace already presented a major problem for the prosecution in its trial against industrialists—and the problem was not made any smaller if mid-level managers were also indicted instead of top managers. Some members of the prosecution were well aware of this.

The IMT verdict made the prosecution's work more difficult because CCL No. 10 emphasized its special status as a precedent, even though Taylor later said that, although it was an important precedent, it was "not binding on the subsequently-constituted Nuernberg tribunals."[110] At that time, however, a memorandum recorded that the IMT ruling of September 30, 1946, was "not favorable to a conspiracy count." It would not be enough to prove that I. G. Farben had produced armaments and supplied them to the Nazi regime for its wars of aggression because then almost all German industrialists would have to be convicted. Rather, it would be important to work out I. G. Farben's special role. Since the I. G. Farben trial was the first case to charge industrialists for a war of aggression, it needed to clearly demonstrate industrialists' willingness to cooperate with the Nazi regime. The case against the industrialists could not be compared to that against Schacht and Speer since the industrialists had been involved in planning the wars of aggression from the beginning and had fully supported Hitler long before 1939. In order to plausibly demonstrate that I. G. Farben had played a major or minor role in crimes against peace, it was, therefore, necessary "to show the general economic and military importance of I. G. Farben in order to distinguish it from the average German soldier or civilian." For that, it might be necessary to show a complete picture of the entire German system of war preparations: "This lengthy method, however, should be chosen only if it will not be possible to prove a good case of crimes against peace on our theory that I. G. Farben planned, prepared and actually waged wars of aggression by producing before and during the war in full knowledge of Hitler's plans to wage wars of aggression."[111]

Yet this was exactly what would become one of the biggest problems of the I. G. Farben trial: the prosecution would present a mass of material—often lacking in concrete evidentiary value—in order to then build up chains of evidence and draw conclusions. The indictment material against I. G. Farben's managers was not much better than in the other proceedings, and the prosecution was not, as Karl Heinz Roth claimed, so "excellently prepared," even though its key members consisted of "top-class lawyers from the Treasury Department."[112] The indictment and the trial strategy were the very elements that would prove to be problematic over the course of the trial, and Telford Taylor and Josiah DuBois shared responsibility for them.

The Indictment

When the indictment was officially filed, the prosecution made it clear how guilty it believed the accused I. G. Farben managers were. The excerpt from the indictment used for the press release is worth quoting in detail: "The indictment against these 24 top officials of FARBEN charges these persons with committing as grave, if not graver, crimes against civilization than were charged in the indictment filed before the IMT against Göring and other leaders of Germany. On the doorstep of the defendants is laid the murder, torture, starvation, enslavement, and robbery of millions of people; the laying in ruin of millions of homes; the destruction of tremendous industrial capacity necessary to maintain the standard of living of peoples all over the world; the laying in waste of agricultural land capable of feeding millions of people; and the leaving of a large part of the world in economic and political chaos." According to Taylor, the I. G. Farben trial would get to the heart of Germany's guilt for the unspeakable crimes against civilization in the last war: "In a very literal and real sense these defendants and others like them—not Hitler and his half-mad street-fighting colleagues—are the principal war criminals. And what is more important, these defendants and others like them will, if their guilt is unexposed and unpunished, be an immeasurably greater threat to the future peace of the world than would Hitler if he were alive today." Up until that point, the indictment continued, the focus had been on the strange and frightening groups of opportunistic madmen in senior positions in the German government, whose guilt was undeniable. But now, Taylor argued, it was important to turn to the madmen's "principals," that is, the clients and the main liable parties who had burdened themselves with an even greater guilt—and without whom the National Socialists would have remained just "a band of common fellons [*sic*]."[113]

In this way I. G. Farben's managers were declared to be the main perpetrators whose actions were even worse than those of the National Socialists. It made clear what the defendants had to prepare themselves for. This was stated, among other places, in an article in the *Frankfurter Rundschau* in late March 1947 that emphasized the connection between I. G. Farben and the Auschwitz concentration camp: "In a few weeks, twenty I.G.-Farben employees will be brought before a court as war criminals and the death penalty will be requested for them."[114]

In the end, the indictment of May 3, 1947, charged twenty-four managers of I. G. Farben:

- Carl Krauch, chairman of the supervisory board of I. G. Farben and plenipotentiary of special issues in chemical production in the Four-Year Plan
- Hermann Schmitz, chairman of I. G. Farben's board of directors
- Georg von Schnitzler, board member and chairman of the Commercial Committee
- Fritz Gajewski, board member and head of Division III
- Heinrich Hörlein, board member
- August von Knieriem, board member and chief legal officer
- Fritz ter Meer, board member, head of Division II, and chairman of the Technical Committee
- Christian Schneider, board member, head of Division I, chief operating officer, and member of the SS
- Otto Ambros, board member
- Max Brüggemann, board member
- Ernst Bürgin, board member
- Heinrich Bütefisch, board member, member of the Freundeskreis Himmler and the SS
- Paul Häfliger, board member
- Max Ilgner, board member, head of Berlin NW 7, and nephew of Hermann Schmitz
- Friedrich Jähne, board member
- Hans Kühne, board member, head of the Leverkusen Works Group
- Carl Lautenschläger, board member, head of the Maingau Works Group, Frankfurt-Hoechst
- Wilhelm Mann, board member
- Heinrich Oster, board member
- Carl Wurster, board member, head of the Ludwigshafen Works Group
- Walter Dürrfeld, director of I. G. Farben's Auschwitz factory
- Heinrich Gattineau, head of the Economic Policy Department of Berlin NW 7
- Erich von der Heyde, Berlin NW 7, member of the SS
- Hans Kugler, member of the Commercial Committee.[115]

Of the twenty-four defendants, the first eight defendants listed were members of the former Central Committee of I. G. Farben. Carl Krauch (see Figure 2.8) had not been on the board of directors since 1940 but had become the chairman of the supervisory board after Bosch's death. The other seven were leading members

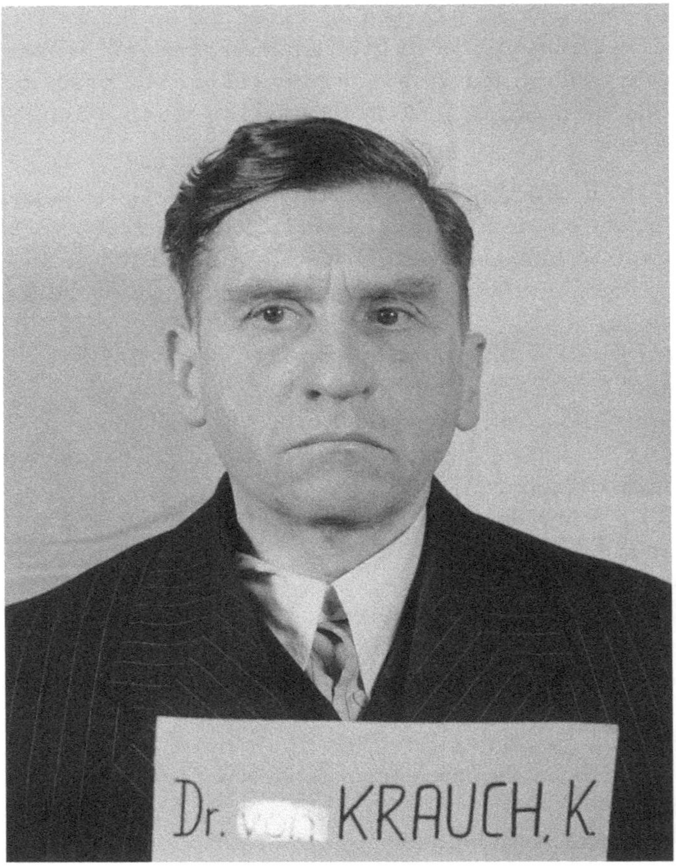

Figure 2.8. One of the top leaders of I. G. Farben—Carl Krauch. Source: NARA 238-OMT-VI-D-1; NL Nath; public domain.

of the board of directors of I. G. Farben. Hermann Schmitz (Figure 2.9), Fritz ter Mer (Figure 2.10), and Georg von Schnitzler (Figure 2.11) occupied special positions among them, Schmitz as its chairman, ter Meer as the most important technical director, and von Schnitzler as the most important commercial director. Those named alphabetically after these eight defendants—from Otto Ambros to Carl Wurster—were also members of I. G. Farben's board of directors, a number of them only since 1938. At the end of the list came Walter Dürrfeld, Heinrich Gattineau, Hans Kugler, and Erich von der Heyde, four I. G. Farben managers who were not board members.

William Zeck had wanted to bring only members of the board of directors to trial as defendants. In an interview years later, he pointed out that being a board

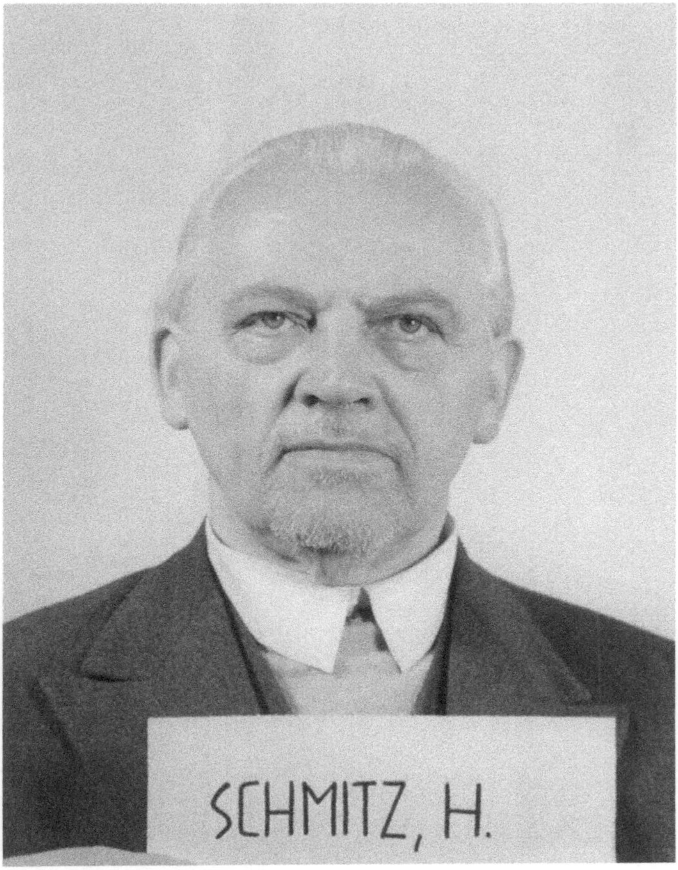

Figure 2.9. One of the top leaders of I. G. Farben—Hermann Schmitz. Source: NARA 238-OMT-VI-D-2; NL Nath; public domain.

member alone was not enough to prompt a charge. For an indictment to be brought, the individual responsibility of a board member had to be established. Defendants had to have an important function in the company and in cooperation with leading National Socialists like Göring in the Four-Year Plan: "You couldn't just use a broad brush and decide because a man was on the Vorstand, we'll put him in the dock." Rather, incriminating evidence and background information had to be collected, using documents and interrogations for each individual member of the board of directors to be indicted. In particular, the interrogations of Paul Dencker, whose name Zeck had found in Belle Mayer's documents, were very helpful as Dencker was extremely well-informed about

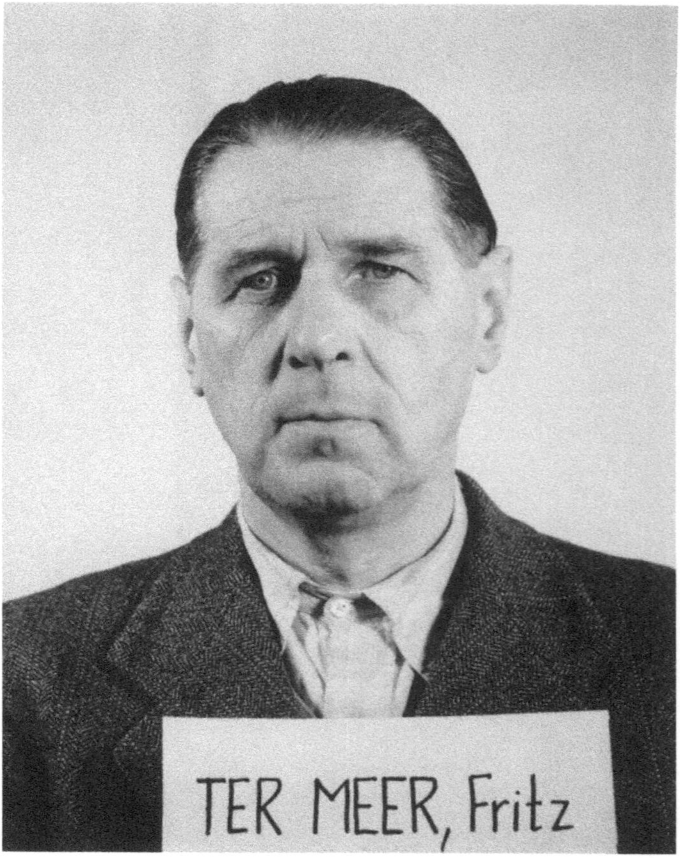

Figure 2.10. One of the top leaders of I. G. Farben—Fritz ter Meer. Source: NARA 238-OMT-VI-D-7; NL Nath; public domain.

the firm.[116] Accordingly, Zeck was particularly frustrated when DuBois decided, in a way Zeck felt was completely arbitrary, to abandon the principle that had applied up until then and to select defendants as he saw fit, like the "ugly SOB in an SS uniform" Erich von der Heyde.[117] William Zeck's suggestion that only members of the board of directors be prosecuted for whom special responsibility could be proven was ignored in the indictment; this led him to resign in frustration and return home before the trial began. Nevertheless, he was listed in the indictment among the members of the prosecution as responsible for "corporate organization" and the individual responsibility of the defendants.[118]

In contrast to the trials of Krupp and Flick, in which the owners and some of the leading managers stood accused, the defendants in the I. G. Farben trial were

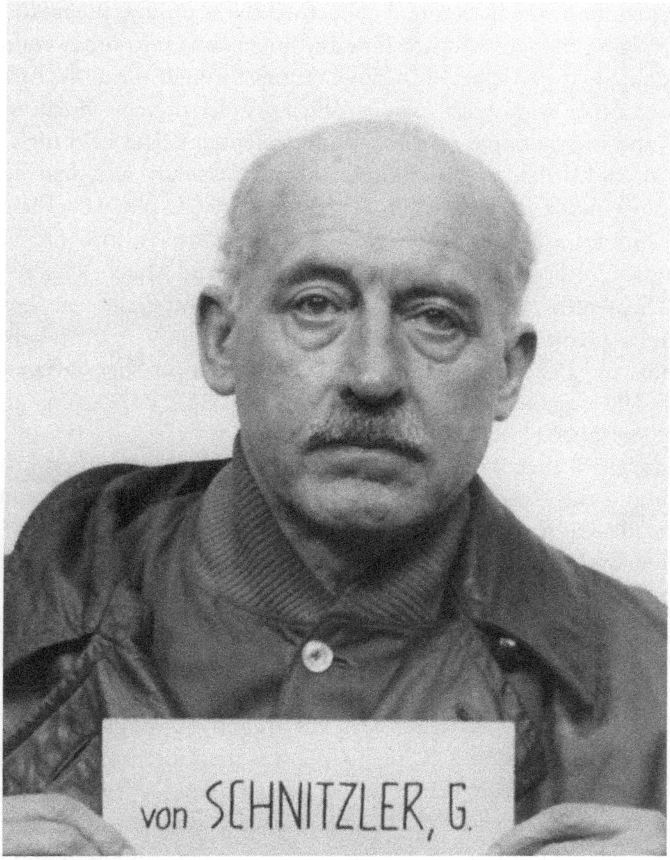

Figure 2.11. One of the top leaders of I. G. Farben—Georg von Schnitzler. Source: NARA 238-OMT-VI-D-3; NL Nath; public domain.

exclusively employed managers. Hans Kugler later wrote in his memoirs that people were amused when a security guard in the dining room asked, "which of the twenty-three guests was 'Mr. IG-Farben.'" The security guard had "gotten to know Mr. Krupp and Mr. Flick, who gave the name to the other two industrial trials and now wanted to take a closer look at the 'boss' among us."[119] Among the I. G. Farben managers, however, no "Mr. I. G. Farben" stood accused—but rather merely employees.

It should also be noted here that no Nobel Prize winner counted among the twenty-three or twenty-four accused I. G. Farben managers, as has been noted in the literature again and again since Josiah DuBois wrote this in his book about the defendant Heinrich Hörlein.[120]

The first count in the indictment concerned the planning, preparation, initiation, and waging of wars of aggression and incursions into other countries: All the defendants had participated in these crimes through the I. G. Farben company and in other ways with various other people, thereby violating international law and international treaties. All the defendants had held high positions in financial, industrial, and economic life in Germany and had committed crimes against peace, as defined in Article II of CCL No. 10. The following invasions and wars of aggression were listed: against Austria on March 12, 1938; against Czechoslovakia on October 1, 1938, and March 15, 1939; against Poland on September 1, 1939; against Great Britain and France on September 3, 1939; against Denmark and Norway on April 9, 1940; against Belgium, the Netherlands, and Luxembourg on May 10, 1940; against Yugoslavia and Greece on April 6, 1941; against the Soviet Union on June 22, 1941; against the United States on December 11, 1941.

The indictment then went into detail about an alliance between I. G. Farben and Hitler and the Nazi Party. While most of the points here pertained to the company's alliance with the Nazi movement, three defendants were also mentioned by name. This affected Bütefisch and Gattineau, who were the I. G. Farben representatives who had visited Hitler in 1932, and von Schnitzler, who was present at the meeting of industrialists and financiers with Hitler and Göring on February 20, 1933, and had made the largest single donation to the Nazi Party on behalf of I. G. Farben. Prosecutors also detailed the synchronization of I. G. Farben activities with the military through the "W Agency," mentioning Krauch by name. Krauch's role was then discussed in detail in connection with the Four-Year Plan and war preparations. A few other defendants were named in this, especially in connection with their positions in industrial associations and committees: Schmitz, von Schnitzler, Bütefisch, Wurster, and Jähne. According to the indictment, I. G. Farben also had contributed to weakening Germany's potential enemies through cartel agreements. I. G. Farben had maintained a spy network for Nazi Germany and contributed to German espionage and propaganda activities, especially via Berlin NW 7. When the war had begun, I. G. Farben had increased these activities. The accused managers had not left the country like Fritz Thyssen had done, nor had they given up offices like Hjalmar Schacht had done. Pursuing the goals of the greater German-controlled economic area, using Nazi terminology, the indictment stated that I. G. Farben had always followed directly after the military into the occupied territories with precise plans for exploiting them for the war economy and for the company's profit.[121]

The second count concerned plunder and spoliation. Again, all twenty-four managers were charged with looting private and public property, exploitation, spoliation, and other crimes against property in countries occupied by German troops. The Germans' methods had differed from country to country; there had also allegedly been sham negotiations with owners as Germans had tried to give the impression that they were paying for confiscated goods or raw materials. I. G. Farben had marched with the Wehrmacht and had played a significant role in the German program of exploitation and appropriation through conquest. The crimes of spoliation and looting also included cases in Austria and Czechoslovakia. The defendants Schmitz, von Schnitzler, ter Meer, Kühne, Ilgner, Häfliger, Wurster, and Kugler were all named in this context. Von Schnitzler was the name most associated with I. G. Farben's crimes in Poland, Norway, and France. Krauch, Oster, and Ambros were named in connection with I. G. Farben's looting and spoliation in the Soviet Union.[122]

Under the third count, all twenty-four defendants were accused of having participated in the enslavement and deportation of civilian population groups in occupied countries, in the enslavement of foreign and German concentration camp prisoners, in the use of prisoners of war for producing armaments, and in the mistreatment, terrorization, torture, and murder of enslaved people. All the defendants were accused of perpetrating or contributing to war crimes as defined by the Hague Land War Code and to crimes against humanity as defined in CCL No. 10 in that the defendants had allegedly ordered, aided, or abetted these crimes. The indictment went into detail about I. G. Farben's role in the slave labor program, emphasizing the roles specific individuals had played in it: Krauch, as the plenipotentiary of special issues in chemical production in the Four-Year Plan, ter Meer and the other members of the Technical Committee, Schneider as chief operating manager, and the site group leaders. All in all, the prosecution felt that I. G. Farben's board of directors bore overall responsibility for the concern's role in the crimes.[123]

Although the indictment devoted only a few lines to the use of poison gas and experiments on humans under this count, it presented I. G. Farben's role in Auschwitz and the construction of the Buna plant in Monowitz in more detail, describing the crimes in Auschwitz and the process of murder in the gas chambers. The three defendants Krauch, Ambros, and Bütefisch were named under this point as partners of Göring and the SS; strangely, however, Dürrfeld, as head of the I. G. Farben plant in Auschwitz, was not mentioned.[124]

The three SS members among the defendants—Schneider, Bütefisch, and von der Heyde—were accused under the fourth count of membership in the SS, which the IMT verdict had categorized as a criminal organization.[125]

Under the fifth count, that of a common plan or conspiracy, all twenty-four defendants were once again regarded as guilty of having participated as leaders, organizers, instigators, or accomplices in formulating and executing a common plan or conspiracy to commit crimes against peace or to commission such crimes. At the same time, all the defendants were held individually responsible for their actions, as well as for all acts committed by each person involved in the execution of such a common plan or conspiracy.[126]

Because of the indictment, which, with the exception of count IV, always accused the entire group of twenty-four I. G. Farben managers together, the defendants found it extremely difficult, if not impossible, to pursue their own interests. Although Randolph Newman had made it very clear that a company could not be indicted under the London Statute and CCL No. 10, the indictment against the twenty-four I. G. Farben managers read largely like an indictment against an institution. It followed almost exactly the suggestions of Leo Drachsler in his memoranda of September 1946, in which he expressed his desire to see the guilt of the individual managers proven by proof of the institution's guilt. On this point, Kim Priemel wrote, "That more often than not companies were named first and individuals later mirrored the hazy distinction between judicial and natural persons that was typical of Nuremberg's 'economic' trials."[127]

The defense also registered the quasi-institutional approach in the indictment, which named the defendants in the introduction but mostly referred to "I.G." in the charges themselves and then, finally, listed all the defendants with their offices in Appendix A in order to present the connection between business and the Nazi regime. Carl Krauch's lawyer, Hermann Heimerich, who had been a Social Democratic mayor of Mannheim until the National Socialists had dismissed him in 1933, had already seen the need for some "chief defense counsels" to share a larger office space together before the indictment was published. Without such a special office, he felt it would be "hardly possible" to process "the entire I.G. conglomerate."[128]

But after the publication of the indictment, Heimerich found himself faced with "a completely changed and unexpected situation" that had "given him strong reservations about finally taking over the defense of Professor Krauch"—because charges against individuals "just appear here and there in the reasoning of the indictment" and other people could be added as defendants at will: "The indictment is primarily and in all its key points directed against the institution and the overall activities of IG. This is clear from the table of contents preceding the indictment, in which, significantly, not a single person's name is mentioned, but rather it states again and again 'IG took part,' 'IG operated,' 'IG in Austria, in Poland, in Norway,' 'The role of IG in the slave labor program,' 'IG in Auschwitz,' etc. When reading the indictment, one waits, in a way, to come across the allegation at the end that IG was a criminal organization, as was the case in the first war crimes trial, for example, regarding the General Staff. Instead, at the end there is the extremely brief justification for the charge of conspiracy, although the possible widening of scope of this conspiracy charge is pointed out." Thus, the prosecution, Heimerich concluded, "apparently assumes collective guilt" and concentrates it on the previously accused individuals.[129]

Emanuel Minskoff, an employee of the prosecution, was not very happy with the indictment, either. In a letter of February 1948, he wrote that he only found out much later "that, included in the vague and general language of the 100-page

Indictment," there was but "one sentence which, if carefully read, charged Farben's participation in criminal medical experiments and also charged Farben's participation in manufacturing and providing the poison gas which killed millions of concentration camp inmates." At the beginning of the trial, Minskoff averred, the defense strongly opposed this part of the charge as it was not supported by evidence. At least one member of the prosecution saw it the same way, but Minskoff wanted to find out what the evidence for this charge was: "Of course the real answer was that in typical DuBois fashion, enough extra phrases were thrown in to cover evidence that we suspected existed but which we had not quite reduced to possession."[130]

Thus, it has to be concluded that the prosecution was not "excellently prepared." Nor did the indictment bring the two defendants the prosecution had long sought to charge, Hermann Schmitz and Georg von Schnitzler, to trial "along with a well-selected group of I.G. [Farben]'s top managers."[131] Members of the prosecution, such as William Zeck and Emanuel Minskoff, already contradicted this. The problems of the trial also became clear in an interview with William Zeck and Belle Mayer Zeck, the latter having largely formulated the part of the indictment on the war of aggression.[132] Belle Mayer wanted to convince the judges at the time that the defendants should not be viewed as friendly businessmen, because they were murderers, even though they looked and talked like businessmen.[133] For her, as the indictment also notes, individual evidence and a clear assignment of responsibility to individuals were not so important; she considered their guilt already proven: "Many of us felt as the British felt in London—that the crimes that these people had committed had been repeated so often and were of such common knowledge that the courts should take res adjudicata of some of these events and acts that had been publicized on a worldwide basis. Take judicial notice of the fact that they were committed, without the necessity of these very labored proofs."[134]

The Defense

Arrests, Interrogations, and the Kransberg Memorandum: The Defendants on the Search for a Defense Strategy

A number of I. G. Farben managers, including multiple members of the board, were immediately detained or interned by the Americans after they occupied Frankfurt on the basis of occupation directive JCS 1067. A few remained in jail in Frankfurt-Preungesheim until late 1945 or early 1946, including Georg von Schnitzler, a member of the board of directors of I. G. Farben and head of the Commercial Committee. According to the description of an American official who was trying to interrogate him, von Schnitzler first adopted an aristocratic, arrogant manner and acted relieved that the "unpleasantness"—the Third Reich and the war—were over. He had apparently had nothing to do with the Nazis and their crimes: "One would never have guessed that von Schnitzler was a criminal, one of the financial mainstays of the Nazi regime, and a mastermind of the I. G. Farben foreign organization." In the interrogations, von Schnitzler had lied through his teeth—but was not surprised when he was then arrested for making false statements to officials.[135]

Hermann Schmitz, the former chairman of the board of directors, had also been detained at the end of the war. The intention from the beginning had been to prosecute both men, Schmitz and von Schnitzler, in a war crimes trial—either a second IMT or a trial by the Americans in their occupation zone on the basis of CCL No. 10.

While some of the defendants had been interned or detained since the end of the war, in some cases with interruptions, and had to count on being tried, a number of the defendants did not know for some time whether they had been detained to serve as witnesses or to face trial themselves. For some, such as Carl Krauch, the detainment primarily consisted of house arrest, though Krauch spend a good portion of that time being treated at a hospital.[136] Carl Ludwig Lautenschläger, the former head of the Hoechst factory who had in the meantime moved to the laboratory in Elberfeld, did not know for some time after he was arrested whether he was to be a witness or a defendant.[137] Director Hans Kugler, who cooperated with Benjamin Ferencz, among others, was still hoping for a leading position at Hoechst in 1946–47.[138] In prison Kugler met Ulrich Haberland, the head of the Leverkusen factory, who was apparently one of William Zeck's candidates for the dock but as it turned out, as Kugler later wrote, "had only been 'borrowed' by the English for interrogations and was soon released."[139] Instead of Haberland—according to Zeck—Erich von der Heyde was put on the dock.[140] Hans Kühne, who had been Haberland's predecessor in Leverkusen and therefore had been largely out of his position already during the war, was first arrested by the French in March 1947 in Lindau and brought by car to Nuremberg on May 1, where he found himself serving as a defendant: "The food was sufficient and in some cases even good. The oppressive thing was just always being in a locked cell from which one could only see part of the sky, and the strict surveillance if one had to leave one's cell."[141]

According to a May 1948 list (Table 2.1) compiled by the prosecution, the defendants had been under arrest at the following locations for varying periods of time. The judges requested this list in order to determine how long the individual defendants had already been under arrest or interned.[142]

As is clear from Table 2.1, some of the I. G. Farben managers had been under arrest since the end of the war, though apparently with some interruptions. This put a strain on those affected, in particular Hermann Schmitz and Georg von Schnitzler, both of whom became more and more talkative with the members of

Table 2.1. Period and place of detention/internment of the I. G. Farben managers tried in Case VI (May 10, 1948). Source: Drexel Sprecher Papers, Box 47, Case Files, Case VI—Tribunal Orders: Period and Place (or Nature) of Detention of the Defendants in Case No. VI (Farben) since the Allied Occupation of Germany, Nuremberg May 10, 1948: for prosecution, Sprecher and Taylor, for defense, Dix; "approved and ordered filed": Judge Shake, May 13, 1948. Table created by Stephan H. Lindner.

Name	Period of detention or internment	Location of detention or internment
Ambros, Otto	Jan. 17, 1946–May 1, 1946	Ludwigshafen
	Since Dec. 13, 1946	Ludwigshafen, Baden-Baden, Nuremberg
Bürgin, Ernst	Since June 23, 1947	Chateau Arnoux, Strasbourg, Nuremberg
Bütefisch, Heinrich	Since May 11, 1945	Leuna, Versailles, Kransberg, Wimbledon, Nuremberg
Dürrfeld, Walter	June 9, 1945–June 17, 1945	Merseburg
	Since Nov. 5, 1945	Ziegenhain, Ludwigsburg, Nuremberg
Gajewski, Fritz	Since Oct. 5, 1945	Munich, Kransberg, Nuremberg
Gattineau, Heinrich	Oct. 11, 1945–Aug. 6, 1946	Garmisch I.C.
	Since Oct. 11, 1946	Altötting, Nuremberg
Häfliger, Paul	May 11, 1945–Sept. 30, 1945	Frankfurt am Main
	Since May 3, 1947	Nuremberg
von der Heyde, Erich	Since Apr. 28, 1947	Hamburg, Nuremberg
Hörlein, Heinrich	Since Aug. 16, 1945	Kransberg, Nuremberg
Ilgner, Max	Since Apr. 7, 1945	Würzburg, Versailles, Kransberg, Nuremberg
Jähne, Friedrich	Since Apr. 16, 1947	Grevenbroich (Brit. zone), Nuremberg
von Knieriem, August	Since Apr. 7, 1945	Würzburg, Versailles, New York, Nuremberg
Krauch, Carl	Since Sept. 3, 1946	Heidelberg, Nuremberg
Kühne, Hans	Since Apr. 29, 1947	Lindau, Nuremberg
Kugler, Hans	July 11, 1945–Oct. 6, 1945	Frankfurt am Main
	Since Apr. 18, 1947	Frankfurt am Main, Nuremberg
Lautenschläger, Carl L.	Since Dec. 11, 1946	Düsseldorf, Nuremberg

(*Continued*)

Table 2.1. (*Continued*)

Name	Period of detention or internment	Location of detention or internment
Mann, Rudolf Wilhelm	Sept. 19, 1945–Oct. 16, 1945	Sonthofen
	Since Apr. 26, 1947	Tiefenbach, Nuremberg
Oster, Heinrich	Since Dec. 31, 1946	Schlüchtern (US zone), Nuremberg
Schmitz, Hermann	Since Apr. 7, 1945	Würzburg, Kransberg, Nuremberg
Schneider, Christian	Since Feb. 6, 1947	Rosental (US zone), Nuremberg
von Schnitzler, Georg	Since May 7, 1945	Frankfurt am Main, Kransberg, Nuremberg
ter Meer, Fritz	Since June 7, 1945	Versailles, Kransberg, Nuremberg
Wurster, Karl	Since Apr. 25, 1947	Ludwigshafen, Nuremberg

the prosecution interrogating them, eventually leading to major rifts among the I. G. Farben managers.

Apparently in response to a question that arose during the I. G. Farben trial as to whether von Schnitzler had been put under too much pressure, Abe Weisbrodt, who had interrogated him in the summer of 1945 in Frankfurt, referred to three phases of interrogation. During the first phase, von Schnitzler had not been cooperative. The interrogators had then studied the available documents, enabling them to point out inconsistencies between his statements and what was recorded therein. Thus, they had regularly pointed out that it contravened the laws of the military occupation to lie during interrogations. During the second phase, von Schnitzler had endeavored to answer in such a way as not to contradict documents that he believed the interrogators had in hand. When he noticed that they also had documents that he had believed to have been destroyed, he became very cooperative—the third phase. He spoke about friends and family and told anecdotes about I. G. Farben managers: "During such periods, we found that von Schnitzler was a source of valuable information." During this phase, von Schnitzler increasingly provided his statements in written form—and was allowed to state as much as he wanted. Finally, he was also brought into the interrogations of other I. G. Farben managers: "At such times, von Schnitzler would often contradict the statements of these other Farben officials, pointing out to us any inaccuracies contained in them."[143]

However, von Schnitzler was not the only one to undergo numerous interrogations and prepare a series of affidavits. Schmitz also put statements on the record, which the prosecution wanted to use in the trial. Under pressure from Fritz ter Meer, however, Schmitz changed his statements in early 1946. In late March 1946, ter Meer wrote to the Field Information Agency, Technical (FIAT) that during an interrogation on September 17, 1945, in which von Schnitzler had also taken part, Schmitz had signed a statement drafted by Weisbrodt that contained "substantial misstatements with regard to important points, namely in the matter of technical questions." Ter Meer explained that as the former head of the Technical Committee, he was enclosing a written document with his letter and asked that he henceforth be interrogated in cases of doubt. This, he stated, had been agreed to by the other members of the board of directors who were interned at the camp, who also assented to his statements, he stated.[144]

A draft of the "Comprehensive Correction" of Schmitz's statement of September 17, 1945, disagreed, for example, with the statement that I. G. Farben's new investments were connected with the rearmament program. Armaments, strictly defined, had been a very small share of the company's business, it stated. It was a commonplace truth that the chemical industry served as "a supplier industry for all other industries," in wartime for the armaments industry as well as for agriculture. Ter Meer also corrected the statement about the W Agency (W standing for Wehrmacht) in this draft, stating that it had not been responsible for the relationship between the various I. G. Farben factories and the Wehrmacht, but had only been established in order to avoid economic treason when exchanging technical knowledge with foreign countries.[145]

Schmitz finally prepared a new statement to replace that of September 17, 1945. He explained that Weisbrodt had interrogated him in von Schnitzler's presence shortly before leaving for the United States and, in order to save time, had then dictated a comprehensive statement and provided it for them to sign. Despite having a few problems with the text, he, Schmitz, had signed it, "in order to avoid the impression that I was not willing to help shed light on the business dealings of I. G. Farben." He and von Schnitzler had pointed out multiple times that "substantial parts of the subject of the interrogation" had not been their responsibility and that technical questions should be directed to ter Meer. The subject matter was now correctly presented in Fritz ter Meer's memorandum of March 30, 1946, he argued, which had been drafted "in coordination with the members of the board of directors present here." Schmitz's statement of September 17, 1945, which he now formally rescinded, was therefore "objectively obsolete."[146]

This new and supposedly correct presentation of the facts was a detailed thirty-seven-page document known as the "Kransberg memorandum."[147] In the memorandum's introduction, Fritz ter Meer described its origins. In April 1945, he had been arrested by the Americans in Italy, where he had spent most of his time since September 1943, and in June 1945 had been brought to Kransberg, where he had remained until fall 1946. In spring 1946, von Schnitzler and Ilgner had also been brought to Kransberg. Since being arrested, he and the other managers at I. G. Farben had been repeatedly interrogated; he therefore wanted to provide the examiners with "the full truth according to the best of my knowledge and conscience." In Kransberg they had also discovered that a trial of the leading I. G. Farben managers was planned. After this, they had been allowed to discuss their defense. In March 1946 Schmitz had informed the others about his statement of September 17, 1945, which caused "great dismay among the entire group of leading men" of I. G. Farben, "since it was assumed that the report contained mistakes and false conclusions." Since Schmitz was not a technical expert, but most of his statements had addressed questions of this nature, the I. G. Farben managers had decided to prepare a "comprehensive report" in which they sought to provide "the correct depiction of the matter." The majority of the memorandum had been written by him—ter Meer—but with the help of von Schnitzler, Ilgner, and von Knieriem.[148]

Karl Heinz Roth tells this story differently. He writes that there had been "serious criticism on the part of the 'specialists' with regard to the talkative 'salesmen' " in Kransberg. After it became known that a trial was impending, ter Meer had written "a detailed counter-memo on the history and organizational structure of I. G. Farben" on March 30, 1946: "Then, the 'salesmen' were put under pressure. After 'detailed meetings multiple times a week,' Schmitz put forward a 'correction.'" Von Schnitzler also revised his statements, but not as significantly as the other I. G. Farben managers clearly wished he would do.[149] Sebastian Brünger also emphasizes the pressure put on the commercial division managers, in particular by ter Meer. They then corrected or rescinded their statements after having previously spoken "frankly" with the Allied interrogators.[150]

This matter was also discussed during the trial. During Sprecher's cross-examination, ter Meer conceded that during the second half of 1945 he and von Schnitzler had shared a room and that von Schnitzler had requested to be moved from the cell because ter Meer had criticized him "for certain things": "Yes, we had a violent argument."[151] Von Schnitzler had said that "he had been put under a great deal of pressure by his former colleagues" on the board of directors, especially by ter Meer. Ter Meer and his defense team did not want to leave this uncontested. According to ter Meer, von Schnitzler had arrived at Kransberg at Christmas 1945, where ter Meer himself had been since June 1945. They had shared a room, and their relationship had been normal, but von Schnitzler had been "in a physical and mental state of depression." In March 1946, ter Meer and a few colleagues had discussed Schmitz's statement in the shared room in the presence of von Schnitzler. The discussion resulted in ter Meer's "memorandum," which he sent to FIAT in Frankfurt on March 30, 1946. According to ter Meer, von Schnitzler had not been put under any pressure with reference to it. The statement by Schmitz, who had not wanted to support the "memorandum" at first, had led to the conclusion, however, that it needed to be corrected due to its misstatements. The conflict with von Schnitzler had resulted from the fact that the two men were "persons of very varying natures," and the "small personal friction" came out, ter Meer went on, "for some minor reason, something became too much for me." Since ter Meer saw von Schnitzler as the "spiritual father of the incriminating statements" of Schmitz, he had told him this "in a very unmistakable manner" in June 1946. He and his colleagues had known that von Schnitzler had been interrogated, and they asked him "very urgently about the situation," since they feared that he had perhaps made "some erroneous or wrong statements or other statements which might incriminate our firm erroneously." But von Schnitzler did "not want to make any detailed statements about those things at the time."[152]

What becomes clear from the conflict is that the prisoners were not originally acting in concert. Schmitz and von Schnitzler, the only ones who were expecting to be indicted from the beginning, clearly hoped to improve their situation through cooperative behavior. Von Schnitzler in particular was very forthcoming after his arrest. His wife Lilly considered her husband to have been initially quite naive and unprepared for the situation he was in. In late November 1946, she wrote to a friend, the jurist Carl Schmitt, that Georg had by that point been apart from her for a year and a half and had gone through personal growth during that time. Beforehand, he had "remained truly a child who had only known lovesickness." Lilly von Schnitzler, who had converted to Catholicism in the interim, wrote that God had given him a "guardian angel and the grace of faith," which he also needed, as the "most difficult phase" lay ahead of them.[153] Von Schnitzler was in fact not very popular among his fellow prisoners because of the statements he had made. In December 1947, his lawyer, Siemers, wrote to the defense counsels of the other defendants as follows: "As you know, many of the defense counsels were very upset about v. Schnitzler's affidavits and declared that the affidavits had to be corrected no matter what. Despite these frequent declarations, however, I never received information about which points had to be corrected." Providing a list of all of von Schnitzler's statements, he asked for precise information about the wishes of the other defense counsels.[154]

Returning to the Kransberg memorandum, ter Meer argued in the document that the merger of the most important German chemical companies to form I. G. Farben was intended to further advance the "great scientific and technical successes of the past": "The guiding principle of the new company was to open new territories in the world of chemistry." Nor had this development been a specifically German or an isolated phenomenon: "The decade after the end of the First World War was a remarkable era of large-scale industrial development for the entire global economy"—in the oil and automotive industries, too, for instance. The development of the chemical industry was also "not specific to Germany" but rather had led to major developments and advances in research and technology around the globe. It had been "simply a logical conclusion of all these developments" that I. G. Farben "had received its own share of these fruits," not least because of an intensive exchange of know-how among I. G. Farben's individual factories, which enabled a "thorough modernization process" on all levels.[155]

He first addressed the period after 1933. Those outside Germany now incorrectly assumed that all governmental measures during that period had served to enable a future war of aggression: "For I. G. Farben as for the German economy as a whole, the picture is very different—it was about work and bread for the German people!" The government had used a number of measures to battle high unemployment. Since it increasingly lacked the foreign exchange necessary to import critical raw materials as well as food items and luxury foods, the country had taken the "path of autarky ... based on the Russian and Italian model." It was, however, according to ter Meer, "entirely erroneous to assume" that I. G. Farben had allowed itself to be governed "primarily, or exclusively, by autarky planning" starting in 1933; it "rather restarted its expansion and development from exactly the point where they had ground to a halt during the crisis." The memorandum thus emphasized continuity in the company's strategy during this phase. I. G. Farben's large-scale investment had also been made "based on purely private economic assessments, free of governmental planning"—continuing to pursue the goal of "implementing the latest achievements of science and technology in all its fields of work." This became ever harder to achieve, however, since the chemical industry found itself compelled to play an important role in the autarky efforts. Nonetheless, I. G. Farben had made an effort, he argued, to limit political influence as much as possible, to maintain its financial framework, and to limit itself to fields which it saw as important for its industrial development: "It is in keeping with I. G. Farben's tradition that it carried out the establishment and construction of these autarky plants based on strict economic measures and with a healthy expansion policy focused on the long term."[156]

The memorandum also provided a plausible explanation for I. G. Farben's role in rearmament. For one, "I. G. Farben's comprehensive involvement" in the chemicals field made it "natural" that the Nazi regime sought the company's "collaboration" in rearmament. But the chemicals industry did not produce much in the way of armaments in the narrower sense, according to ter Meer. Thus, until 1939 I. G. Farben had "only a relatively modest share" of armaments production, which could not be precisely determined, however, due to a lack of documentation.[157]

By the mid-1930s, the planned economy, fed by "Social-Democratic thinking," had taken a more solid shape, leading, among other consequences, to production secrets' having to be disclosed. With the Four-Year Plan, free economic activity had become difficult: "The initiative for all economic output moved increasingly into the hands of central state agencies; the economy itself had to accept the dark side of this planned economy and take up the battle against bureaucracy, the constant encroachment of unsuitable and inexperienced officials, and mountains of paperwork."[158]

Ter Meer also went into delicate points in his memorandum: the W Agency, Krauch's role in the Four-Year Plan, and I. G. Farben's international contracts.

According to his account, the W Agency had been established only in order to avoid committing "economic treason" when the company was exchanging technical information with foreign countries. Only during the war had it increasingly taken on additional responsibilities, he argued. Krauch had been made available for the Four-Year Plan only so that "an energetic and above all knowledgeable person" was involved instead of one who was political and "unsatisfactory in terms of technical knowledge." Here ter Meer also stated that having a key figure from I. G. Farben play a public role was "the natural consequence of a given situation." In the case of international and purely privately motivated contracts, I. G. Farben had made a general effort at contractual fidelity but also had to dispel any suspicion of economic treason. This had often been achieved in the contracts, not least in the contracts with Standard Oil.[159]

Ter Meer emphasized that the pressures and limitations on the economy were even greater during wartime—and sought to downplay I. G. Farben's role. During the war, the conglomerate's activities had been increasingly "dictated" by the "necessities of war." Management had not prepared a mobilization plan for itself or for the entire German chemical industry, as Schmitz's statements seemed to imply. With the intensification of the aerial war over Germany, a series of western factories had been moved to more central, eastern, or southern territories. Due to the loss of important natural rubber imports, the company's Buna capacity had been greatly expanded. Finally, I. G. Farben had not been able to maintain its negative attitude toward chemical weapons and had begun to work on them—in response to Allied preparations. Nonetheless, I. G. Farben had "steadfastly held its position to fight the use of gas weapons with all the means at its disposal."[160]

In its conclusion, the memorandum again explicitly states that its goal was "the correction of certain information" in Schmitz's statement of September 17, 1945. The wording of this statement, as a summary of a number of interrogations, could, according to ter Meer, "create an entirely false impression about I. G. Farben's activities from 1933 onward." It had been necessary to clarify that I. G. Farben, since its founding in 1925, had only "followed the course of the industrial development of the world in general and of the chemical industry in particular." These developments had had a larger influence, he argued, "than government policy and rearmament." I. G. Farben's contracts abroad had also been "without exception" motivated purely by business reasons.[161]

Ter Meer's remarks, which, as previously mentioned, were prepared in the spring of 1946, were then followed, in an affidavit of April 15, 1947, by statements by Schmitz and von Schnitzler, a brief economic history of the development of I. G. Farben, and a few pages about the division of labor and of responsibility among members of the company's board of directors and its top managers.[162] Sebastian Brünger summarizes the memorandum as follows: "Even before the start of the trial, the document made clear the central theme of the defense and its favored portrayal of Nazi history: It was the victim narrative of the patriotic businessman or scientist whose peace-loving capacities were forced willy-nilly into a wartime economy … Fritz ter Meer successfully pushed for this exculpatory narrative with his colleagues and laid the foundation for a unified defense. No pattern of interpretation would be worked over by the participants in the trial and over the years that followed with more intensity than this attempt to clearly delineate roles."[163]

Even if one does not entirely agree with Brünger's interpretation of the Kransberg memorandum, it was in any case a response, a counternarrative to how I. G. Farben was being depicted in the American publications previously mentioned—and by Belle Mayer. However, one can also view the memorandum more simply as an attempt by company managers, detained and facing a trial that they found unpredictable, to develop a coherent defense. The defendants were rightly worried that they stood the chance of facing harsh verdicts.

In the winter of 1946, after the apparent discussions during the imprisonment in Kransberg, the trial seemed to be getting closer. Hans Kugler wrote in his memoirs that in November 1946 "initial contacts with leading lawyers and legal experts of the I. G. Farben circle" took place in Frankfurt.[164] According to Kugler, a delegation from the prosecution had been based since October 1946 in the Hotel Carlton, which had been taken over by the military occupation, and was beginning to question witnesses and potential defendants. Many topics related to I. G. Farben, specifically the "holdings in Germany and abroad acquired by I. G. Farben after 1937," were discussed once more. And "detailed biographies" were requested for "nearly one hundred members of the board of directors and former top managers at I. G. Farben." Kugler himself was expecting only to have to live in the Nuremberg witness quarters for two months as a witness for the prosecution, not least so that he would be barred from being a witness for the defense: "When German newspapers were then announcing that twenty death sentences would be meted out in the coming I. G. Farben trial, this understandably did not much lift my mood."[165]

On April 18, 1947, Kugler was finally fired as an employee at Hoechst by the American military authorities and immediately arrested. He was taken from Frankfurt to Nuremberg—not, as he had hoped, to the witnesses' quarters, but to the prison. Only in early May 1947 did it become fully clear to him that he would be standing trial.[166]

The Defense Counsels and the Role of the Former I. G. Farben Factories

In reference to the IMT, Telford Taylor wrote, looking back, that without defense lawyers there never would have been "either court or case": "A plainly incompetent group of defense lawyers would have made a farce of the case; a rowdy contingent could have shattered the court's dignity." The selection of the defense counsels, for which in the case of the IMT British officer Airey Neave was responsible, had been largely satisfactory. The well-known criminal defense lawyers Rudolf Dix and Otto Kranzbühler, moreover, were "not the only first-rate lawyers among the defense counsel."[167] In fact, a proper defense was of exceptional importance to the judges of the IMT as the foundation of a fair trial—and they were accordingly "very intent on the protection of the lawyers."[168]

The defense counsels at Nuremberg had a mixed reputation in Germany at first, and in some cases even faced hostility.[169] For instance, three of the lawyers working in Nuremberg—Rudolf Dix, Walter Siemers, and Martin Horn—had issues with their bar associations in Cologne, Hamburg, and Munich. They were to be assessed politically for their supposedly "Nazi-leaning" defense of high-level Nazi figures in Nuremberg and possibly expelled from the bar. Rudolf Dix, the defense counsel for Hjalmar Schacht, who had been acquitted by the IMT, not only made efforts with the American General Secretariat to deal with the Cologne bar association. In an extensive correspondence he also vehemently defended himself against the accusations and urged Horn to keep his spirits up: "By the way, do not let yourself get gray hairs over this matter. We acted in a justified and appropriate manner at the time. Should poor decisions be made by bar councils in the future, we can fall back on our good consciences. We know at least as much about the propriety of lawyers as these gentlemen and truly survived the trial by fire of lawyerly tact in Nuremberg more than the men who are now lining up to reprimand us based on information from one-sided interests and [they] prove by these very actions that they most likely would have slipped on the parquet floors of Nuremberg."[170] Dix also expressed himself strongly against the council of the Hamburg bar association in response to the accusations and even submitted a formal complaint against its president, Professor Walther Fischer. Dix explained that he had embarked on this process in response to an official press release that disparaged him as a lawyer. He knew that Fischer liked to accuse him of jumping the gun. Fischer had done the same before the Nazis had seized power, Dix wrote: When Dix was protecting Jewish colleagues, Fischer had harshly attacked him for it.[171] The degree to which the accusation rankled Dix became clear again in 1949 when he declined an invitation to speak at the Conference of German Lawyers. He did not consider it "tactful" to discuss an important question there "after the joint bar associations, around two years ago, found it appropriate" to initiate disciplinary proceedings against him and Siemers at their respective bars in Hamburg and Berlin, accusing them, "as it suited the joint bar associations to express it, that we 'had seriously damaged the reputation of German lawyers at home and abroad.'"[172]

Even if the defense counsels clearly faced mistrust or even rejection from their German colleagues, they had a genuinely privileged position thanks to the support of the Americans—with generally good working conditions and very good compensation in the form of money and noncash benefits. The defense counsels' work in Nuremberg was not merely lucrative, however; it could also have positive implications for future business. Thus, the Munich lawyer Horn wrote to a colleague that, thanks to his work in Nuremberg defending Joachim von Ribbentrop at the IMT, he could "now select only interesting clients."[173] Telford Taylor noted in retrospect that by contrast to the "great exodus of prosecutors" the "vast majority of the German defense lawyers" stayed in Nuremberg in order to participate in the subsequent trials. Only ten of the defense lawyers left, whereas twenty-three of them wanted to continue in Nuremberg.[174]

According to the records of the prosecution, a total of 373 Germans and two Americans served as defense counsels in the twelve subsequent trials—as compared to 131 lawyers of the prosecution. In Case VI, according to this list, there were fifty-four defense counsels, not all of whom were lawyers. The list of chief defense counsels also included their Nazi past, which was investigated by the US authorities. In Case VI, according to this list (Table 2.2), of the nineteen chief defense counsels at the end of the trial, ten had been members of the NSDAP—just over half.[175]

This list of defense counsels was not complete, however, since it did not include those who assisted on the defense, nor did it include the chief defense counsels who had given up or lost their clients since the start of the trial. Nor did it include Professor Eduard Wahl, who served as general counsel for the entire defense team. Overall, based on a list by Hubert Seliger, approximately 61 percent of the defense counsels at Nuremberg had been members or candidates for membership in the NSDAP. This percentage was far above the average for the German population as a whole, which, with 8.5 million NSDAP members, stood at around 10 percent.[176]

In his memories of the IMT, the lawyer Herbert Nath wrote, "It is certain that some of the defense counsels are still caught up in Nazi thinking. How could it be otherwise." With the trials occurring so shortly after the end of the Nazi regime and in light of the fact that the defendants were free to select their own defense, including former Nazis or collaborators, this was not particularly surprising. However, according to Nath, the majority of the defense counsels attempted to distance themselves from the Nazis and only wanted to serve the law.[177] The fact that the American prosecution checked the defense counsels makes it clear, however, that they were mistrustful of the German lawyers.

Looking back in late 1948, Taylor wrote of the German defense counsels, "These well-educated professional men, by no means homogeneous from a political standpoint (many of them were Nazi party members and a number were active Nazis) were thrown into close contact with the documentation which revealed the inner workings of the Third Reich, with the responsibility of doing the best that they could for their clients." At first the defense counsels had acted cautiously, but then they realized that they could take a "bold and intransigent

Table 2.2. List of the defendants and their counsels based on a list prepared by the prosecution on January 27, 1949. Source: Drexel Sprecher Papers, Box 62, Publication Project File, Publications—Staff in all cases: Public Information Office OCCWC, January 27, 1949: List of Defense Counsels. Table created by Stephan H. Lindner.

Defendant	Counsel
Ambros, Otto	Dr. Hoffmann, Karl, Nuremberg, NSDAP
Brüggemann, Max	Dr. Klefisch, Theodor, Cologne, NSDAP
Bürgin, Ernst	Dr. Schubert, Werner, Augsburg, NSDAP
Bütefisch, Heinrich	Dr. Flächsner, Hans, Berlin
Dürrfeld, Walter	Dr. Seidl, Alfred, Munich, NSDAP
Gattineau, Heinrich	Dr. Aschenauer, Rudolf, Munich, NSDAP
Gajewski, Fritz	Dr. von Metzler, Wolfram, Hamburg
Häfliger, Paul	Dr. von Metzler, Wolfram, Hamburg
von der Heyde, Erich	Dr. Hoffmann, Karl, Nuremberg, NSDAP
Hörlein, Heinrich	Dr. Nelte, Otto, Heide bei Siegburg, NSDAP
Ilgner, Max	Dr. Nath, Herbert, Prien
Jähne, Friedrich	Dr. Pribilla, Hans, Coburg, NSDAP
von Knieriem, August	Pelckmann, Horst, Wiesbaden
Krauch, Carl	Dr. Böttcher, Conrad, Stuttgart, NSDAP
Kühne, Hans	Dr. Nath, Herbert, Prien
Kugler, Hans	Dr. Henze, Helmut, Frankfurt a. M.
Lautenschläger, Carl	Dr. Pribilla, Hans, Coburg, NSDAP
Mann, Wilhelm	Dr. Berndt, Erich, Frankfurt a. M.
ter Meer, Fritz	Bornemann, Karl, Frankfurt a. M., NSDAP
Oster, Heinrich	Dr. Henze, Helmut, Frankfurt a. M.
Schmitz, Hermann	Dr. Dix, Rudolf, Berlin
Schneider, Christian	Dr. Dix, Hellmuth, Fischen/Allgäu, NSDAP
von Schnitzler, Georg	Dr. Siemers, Walter, Hamburg
Wurster, Carl	Dr. Wagner, Friedrich, Ludwigshafen

attitude" without having to fear "any unpleasant consequences." After this, a number of the lawyers had taken "what appear to be very extreme positions" in the defense of their clients.[178]

Theodor Klefisch, who had been practicing law since 1905 in Cologne and who was considered "the senior among all the defense counsels at the Nuremberg trials," was considered a staunch National Socialist. He could, according to Hubert Seliger, "look back to a long career as a well-known criminal defense lawyer, in particular in commercial criminal law." During the IMT, Klefisch had been able to have Gustav Krupp pulled out of the trial due to illness—and was then able to do the same with the defendant Max Brüggemann.[179] Alfred Seidl, who practiced law in Munich as a young lawyer, had also been a staunch Nazi who had excelled as a "good soldier of the movement" in the Third Reich. Hubert Seliger described him as "the most provocative and also most influential figure of the Nuremberg trials."[180] Whether or not one agrees with this assessment, Seidl was in any case very prominent. Herbert Nath described Seidl, who, at the IMT, had introduced the secret agreement between Hitler and Stalin, as "the pyrotechnician," because "his main role seems to consist in setting off 'political bombs.'"[181] And Nath noted that Göring and other defendants referred derisively to Schacht's defense lawyer, Rudolf Dix, as a "swine of a lawyer"—Seidl by contrast received from them the "dubious honor of being titled a 'German lawyer.'"[182]

In addition to the lawyers who were or had been staunch Nazis, there were also those who to varying degrees had accommodated themselves to the Nazi regime. The most prominent among them was the aforementioned Rudolf Dix (Figure 2.12), who was also the spokesman for the defense team in the I. G. Farben trial starting in late 1947. Hailing from a left-liberal home, his first position after completing his law studies had been in the German colonial administration. After World War I he had worked at the Reich Ministry for Economic Demobilization before opening a law office in Berlin in 1920, at which he would be joined by his brother Hellmuth. Rudolf Dix was considered an excellent lawyer whose conciliatory nature could diffuse conflicts during trials. Starting in the mid-1920s, he had begun moving politically to the right and seems to have become a proponent of elitist young conservative views. In contrast to his brother Hellmuth, Rudolf Dix, who had served at the end of the Weimar Republic as chairman of the lawyers' association, did not get involved in the NSDAP after 1933.[183] Hubert Seliger counted Rudolf Dix among the "patriotic pragmatists."[184] After the war, in 1946, he was threatened with a professional tribunal and in 1948 was even first denied permission to practice law in Berlin by the Soviet occupation authorities owing to supposed "Nazi propaganda."[185] Telford Taylor saw Dix as a very capable criminal defense lawyer and as the "dean of the defense counsel," who, making a "dignified and reasonable appearance," represented it as its spokesman.[186]

Figure 2.12. The lawyer Rudolf Dix. Source: Stadtarchiv Nürnberg, A65_IV_RA_039; reproduced with permission.

The lawyer Walter Siemers, by contrast, was not so positively assessed by Taylor. He was "pain-staking and intelligent," but had problems with the common law trial procedure. In his defense of Admiral Erich Raeder, he had "not played his cards well."[187] Siemers, a Hamburg corporate lawyer of high repute, had not joined the NSDAP, like Dix, and seems to have also represented German Jews during the Nazi era on matters relating to their financial assets. As the company lawyer of the armaments company Electroacustic in Kiel, he had close connections to the navy.[188] He reflected on his work in Nuremberg and his position with respect to the Nazi regime in a letter to his mother in early 1946. The coming decade, Siemers wrote, would hopefully be "under a better sign" than the last, "which had been overshadowed by the Nazis until its end." "I am just happy that this terrible nightmare is over, which we had always had the same opinion about from the beginning; it just seems somewhat strange to me that I of all people must now still be so intensively and exclusively focused on this era of the past."[189]

Nor was the lawyer Herbert Nath an NSDAP man, but, like Siemers, he had sought out his niche in the Third Reich. The stepson of a colonial officer who had served in South West Africa, he had joined the cadet school in Lichterfelde in 1914, but had had little relish for it. Starting in 1924, he had studied law in

Berlin, but had had to interrupt his studies for multiple years because of a tuberculosis infection. In late 1932 he had finally completed his state examination. In 1936 he had finished his studies and had been appointed an associate judge. The following year, 1937, he had married the lawyer Agnes Schreiber and had opened a law office in Berlin with her, something quite unusual for the time. In terms of politics, he claimed to have already been a supporter of the SPD at this time. Since he had not been drafted into the military because of his illness, he had worked throughout the entire Nazi era as a criminal defense lawyer. At the end of the war, he and his family had moved to Prien am Chiemsee, where he and his wife worked as lawyers. Through Rudolf Dix, who knew his wife's family well, Nath had received an appointment at the IMT. Later, his wife also worked at Nuremberg.[190]

There were also those who did not adapt to the Nazi regime or who even suffered under it. Erich Berndt, the defense counsel for Fritz ter Meer and Wilhelm Mann, had been forced from his position as a judge at the regional appeal court in Frankfurt and sent to the filing department at the Frankfurt municipal court because he had a Jewish wife.[191] Hermann Heimerich, Carl Krauch's lawyer and a prominent member of the SPD, had been removed from his office as mayor of Mannheim by the Nazis in spring 1933. He had survived the Third Reich in Berlin as a business consultant, having been refused admission to the bar. After the war, he had been briefly politically active on behalf of the American occupation force as the interim president of the supervisory authority of the Saarland-Palatinate-South Hesse province. Afterwards, he had settled down in Heidelberg as a lawyer. In Mannheim, the SPD had declined to select him as the candidate for mayor in 1945 because the party leadership considered him "too bourgeois" in light of his role as a corporate lawyer and his lifestyle.[192]

Friedrich Wilhelm Wagner, who represented Carl Wurster, was considered by Hubert Seliger to be a "special case."[193] Wagner, born in 1894 to a worker in Ludwigshafen, had studied law and become a lawyer after finishing his studies. He had joined the SPD early on and had held an important position in the Reichsbanner Schwarz-Rot-Gold association. From 1930 to 1933, he had served a direct mandate as a representative in the Reichstag for Ludwigshafen. He had also been involved in the Free Religious Community and in a masonic lodge. He had been arrested in early March 1933 because of his support of the Weimar Republic against the National Socialists but had been able to flee. First exiled in France, he had fled after the German occupation of the country to the United States, where he had remained until late 1946. In early 1947, he had returned to Ludwigshafen, where he had opened a law office. For a returned emigrant seeking to rebuild his life, taking on Wurster's defense seems to have been a smart decision. For Wurster, a defense counsel with such a high reputation and of such eloquence was a stroke of good luck. Wagner showed a strong presence at Nuremberg despite his many political commitments. His assistant,

Wolfgang Heintzeler, who had switched from the Reich Justice Ministry to I. G. Farben, later liked to exaggerate his role at Nuremberg, writing that he had carried the main burden of Wurster's defense—an account that Hubert Seliger believes.[194] Reading the trial records conveys a very different image, however. The prosecutor Robert M. W. Kempner wrote later that Rudolf Dix and Herbert Kraus, as Schacht's defense lawyers, served as something like "oath helpers," as they existed "previously in old German trials": "If two good men stand up on behalf of the defendant, then there must be something to it."[195] The effect must have been even more significant with an "oath helper" such as Friedrich Wilhelm Wagner.

The defense, to which we turn now, began organizing early on. Ilse Bethge, Krauch's secretary and close confidante; Professor Eduard Wahl; Professor Carl Bilfinger; and Weiß, a director about whom there is no further information, met in December 1945 at Hermann Heimerich's. The meeting was held in response to an announcement on the radio that thirty leading I. G. Farben managers would be tried at a Nuremberg court, possibly by January 1946. The notes on the meeting read as follows: "As much as the men present were convinced of the absurdity and horror of such a trial, there was general agreement about the fact that in any case preparations for such an eventuality had to be made as quickly as possible." Bilfinger saw the criminal war of aggression as the "centerpiece of the indictment" in the IMT, one which would likely form the basis for the trials of the industrialists. In light of this, Bilfinger wanted to draft a memorandum, "giving particular attention to the interests of Prof. Krauch." Heimerich, however, developed an organizational plan for the entire defense. This seemed to him to require cooperation among the defense lawyers. First, contact had to be made with Hermann Schmitz, who was detained at Kransberg, and with Georg von Schnitzler and Fritz ter Meer, who had apparently been released by that time, "in order to find out their plans with respect to a defense." In addition, apparently on Heimerich's initiative, an archive was to be created, in which reports on the trials would be collected and filed, including those published in foreign newspapers. Finally, Heimerich wanted to get in contact with other lawyers. Director Weiß was to acquire a series of I. G. Farben documents for the defense, in particular on the transition from a peacetime to a wartime economy; collect information about the results of the interrogations of other I. G. Farben managers; and search for materials "on the question of the destruction of I. G. Farben as a cartel or conglomerate." The defense was anticipating costs of around 100,000 RM, of which "the absolutely necessary cost layout (excluding the fees) of the entire defense establishment" alone was estimated to be around 50,000 RM. Heimerich also wanted to get in contact with German press representatives and representatives of the churches in order to create an atmosphere well disposed toward I. G. Farben. For Nuremberg, Heimerich wanted to bring in Bilfinger and possibly Wahl as "advisors."[196]

After this meeting, however, nothing seems to have happened for some time. Not until October 1946—after the verdicts at the IMT had been announced—did Heimerich hear from the lawyer Philipp Möhring that he had not learned anything new "about your client or mine." Only in November would it become clear, Möhring stated, how things would proceed. Presumably, instead of the international court, "an English-American one [would] preside." According to Rudolf Dix, Möhring explained, there would first have to be a coming to terms with Schacht's verdict before other indictments could be considered. New trials would be unlikely to occur before 1947.[197] This was also the view of Hans Kugler, who wrote that in the winter of 1946, the trial seemed to be getting closer: "In November 1946 the first contacts with leading lawyers and jurists in the I. G. Farben circle took place in Frankfurt. I took part in them, though I was not among those whose prior positions meant they could expect an indictment more or less automatically."[198]

Some lawyers clearly were of the view that Speer's IMT verdict and its justification "created a precedent that would make a trial of the industrialists much more difficult, if not impossible." In any case, a leading position in the armaments industry alone would not be "decisive or sufficient for a guilty verdict."[199] As late as January 1947, Heimerich told the lawyer Horst Pelckmann that despite pronouncements to the contrary, a trial against German industrialists was not likely to occur in the near future. Nothing had given him the impression "that the trial against German industrialists is prepared to such an extent that it could be expected to proceed anytime soon."[200] In his response, Pelckmann endorsed this insofar as he concluded "with certainty that the I. G. Farben conglomerate will be the last of the industrialist trials to be held." That said, the investigations of I. G. Farben were continuing "unswervingly" and the prosecution was attempting, during the ongoing preliminary investigations for the other trials, to "find material against I. G. Farben."[201]

In late February 1947, however, it became clear that a trial of the I. G. Farben managers would start soon. The lawyer Helmut Henze, who had worked as a jurist at I. G. Farben's central financial department, was apparently to serve as the coordinator of the defense in the trial on behalf of the former company. Since the trial was to start in May or June, Henze wanted to talk things over with Heimerich and Pelckmann. Thus, under Henze's direction, a meeting occurred before the indictments had even taken place among the lawyers who would be involved in the trial as defense counsels.[202] Their first agreement was that above all, the various defense teams would coordinate closely, not least, it was claimed, in order to avoid the duplication of work. This would require mutual consultation about affidavits to be collected, subpoenas, reports, and trips. In addition, they would found an office to serve as a depository for certificates, reports, and "written documents of general interest" for the defense. Last, Henze informed the lawyers present which reports and assessments had already been requested.[203]

It seems that by winter 1946–1947, Siemers had established a document archive in Nuremberg (referred to as the "industry office") that was intended to provide material for the defense counsels involved in the upcoming industrialists' trials. Heinz Nagel, a lawyer and former officer in the Army High Command, took over the leadership; he seems to have gotten the job primarily because he was the brother-in-law of Professor Herbert Kraus, a well-known expert in international law and Schacht's defense lawyer.[204] According to the lawyer Friedrich Silcher, the office was, however, only useful for the defense "before and at the very beginning of the I. G. Farben trial … before the special I. G. Farben defense office, with Dr. Rolf Müller as its de facto head, was established and took up its work." It should be added that Müller had, at least originally, worked for Siemers.[205]

Siemers, the lawyer who represented von Schnitzler in the I. G. Farben trial, seems on the whole to have earned good money from the trials in Nuremberg. The lawyers did have to use their income to finance the costs of an office and an assistant. These were not insubstantial, but they clearly generally did not exceed their income. This can be seen in the example of Siemers: His costs for the IMT from April to early October 1946—approximately six months—amounted to 4,379.19 RM. With an income of 3,500 RM per month, or 21,000 RM over six months, based on the records of the Bavarian authorities, this made for a respectable profit margin. But some of Siemers' line items remain cloudy—for instance, in 1946 his expenses included an account at the reinsurance company Munich Re involving multiple thousands of reichsmarks for the lawyers Günther von Rohrscheidt and Egon Kubuschok.[206] In addition to his official remuneration, Siemers clearly received, or was promised, considerable sums from various "clients." Thus, Siemers wrote to Horn in March 1947 that it was possible that a trial "against our mutual client" would start before the Flick trial was over: "It remains the case that our clients place value on your and my collaboration. Unfortunately, I cannot give you a specific timeframe, because it is not clear when a trial will begin against I. G. Farben, the iron-producing industry, including Krupp, and possibly Dresdner Bank."[207] But Horn, who had a flourishing law office in Munich, found this unsatisfying; he would only return to Nuremberg, he stated, if there were "firm obligations of an immediately pressing nature," not for "discussions held in such elastic form."[208]

It is clear that money was exchanging hands beyond the official payments. This is also mentioned in a letter from Krauch's original defense lawyer, Hermann Heimerich, to Eduard Wahl: "In the meetings that I conducted in Nuremberg, it emerged that only certain general costs of the defense, related to the overall defense, are covered by a special fund, the provenance of which is unknown to me; all the further costs of the defense fall on the family or friends of the defendants involved, insofar as they are not covered by the fees that are paid by the military court."[209] It is also clear that the Ruhr industry financially supported the defense in Nuremberg, as Jonathan Wiesen has determined.[210] Otto Ambros, for instance, expressed his thanks for the support that he had received from the Essen industrialist Theo Goldschmidt.[211] Colleagues from the former I. G. Farben factories in Ludwigshafen, Leverkusen, and apparently Hoechst also supported the defendants with personnel, money, and various other services.[212]

In late April 1947 Henze finally wrote to the lawyers Rudolf Dix, Walter Siemers, Hans Flächsner, and Horst Pelckmann that the indictment should be expected in a few days, but that while the "number of defendants is not yet set, on the other hand more than 30 gentlemen from this company are under arrest here." He asked the four lawyers to be accommodating if the I. G. Farben defendants turned to them: "Some time ago, in order to prevent these gentlemen from feeling uncertain in the selection of their defense counsel upon receipt of their indictments and in order to ensure that the defense is adequately composed, I, serving as the representative of a number of them, advised their relations to recommend to them that they appoint one of you as their lawyers upon receipt of the indictment." However, according to Henze, there was "clarity on both sides that in some cases this was not to be seen as a final arrangement."[213]

With the presentation of the indictment in the I. G. Farben trial in early May 1947, which signaled the impending start of the trial, it became necessary for each defendant to choose a defense counsel. A defense staff was also to be formed, which apparently was less than simple, as a defendant later remembered: "Differences of opinion among the defendants about who ought to take on whose defense, tensions and certain rivalries in the circle of lawyers seeking nominations—this all meant that the defense front was slow to form."[214] Another defendant wrote that the indictment was accompanied by a list of lawyers who "were permitted by the court and from which we were to select our defense lawyers." There were two opportunities per day to meet with them in the "so-called gymnasium," where "around 60 confessional-style cells" had been erected in which the defendants, "monitored by guards, separated by grating," sat opposite their defense counsels.[215]

On May 3, Henze, coming from Nuremberg, met with Heimerich (Figure 2.13), Krauch's lawyer, to discuss the defense once again. In the discussion, Heimerich suggested that "around four main defense lawyers—maybe Dix, Siemers, Zutt, and I" jointly secure larger quarters "in which the I. G. Farben complex as a whole can be dealt with." The office ought to be led, Heimerich thought, by Henze, who would simultaneously serve as his assistant. Henze seemed to accept this idea, but at the same time wanted to "defend a less important defendant, Mr. Kugler for instance, in order to thereby obtain a spot among the defense counsels." But Heimerich wanted to "define the specific task" that Henze would have to take on. He was not sure, however, whether Henze had "certain commitments" with Dix, Siemers, or Pelckmann. In any case, Heimerich

Figure 2.13. Hermann Heimerich, as Carl Krauch's lawyer, had a substantial role in the preparation of the defense. Source: Marchivum, City Archives of Mannheim, Bildsammlung, KF013123; reproduced with permission.

wanted a special office, because he considered "handling the I. G. Farben complex as a whole" to be "hardly possible" otherwise.[216]

However, after the indictment was published, Heimerich got cold feet. He wrote to Henze that the "completely changed and unexpected situation" caused him "great doubts about definitely taking on the defense of Professor Krauch": "In reading the indictment one expects to some degree to eventually run into the claim that I. G. Farben was a criminal organization." Heimerich continued: "It is simply very clear that collective guilt is assumed and is being concentrated on the individuals who in the meantime have been indicted." And his client Carl Krauch stood at the fore among the individual defendants precisely "because of the alleged connection between his work for the Third Reich with his position and work at I. G. Farben." Therefore, Heimerich concluded, "It will, in my opinion, necessarily result during the trial that Krauch's defense lawyer will first of all also have to study the entire I. G. Farben conglomerate, with all its complexities, and understand it thoroughly. Prof. Krauch's lawyer will be forced into the responsibility of guiding and leading the defense as a whole to a certain degree." This could be discerned from the structure and design of the indictment: "I had never imagined a task of this scope and level of responsibility when I stated that I was on principle prepared to look after Prof. Krauch's interests. Nor would I be up to the task." By way of justification, he cited his advanced age, his excess of work, his lack of vigor, and the prosecution's advantages over the defense. He also claimed that his knowledge of the American trial procedure was too limited and that he lacked "any feel for the Nuremberg milieu." Heimerich finally added: "It should be taken into account that my political and professional past by themselves make me too ideologically distant from I. G. Farben and mean that I have dealt too little with this company." All of these were decisive reasons, as Heimerich argued to Henze, to place the defense of Krauch, "the central person in this giant trial against an economic institution," in other hands. He stated, however, that he was willing to continue to contribute, just not in the leading role.[217]

Under these new circumstances, Henze scheduled a meeting of the defense on May 15, 1947, in which Heimerich also took part. The meeting addressed the strategy for the overall defense—which clearly did not appeal to all.[218] On the following day, it was not just Heimerich who officially informed his client Krauch that he would not be representing him.[219] The lawyer Fritz Sauter informed his clients Heinrich Hörlein, Carl Ludwig Lautenschläger, and Friedrich Jähne about his exasperation with the discussion and withdrew from the defense that same day because he saw and wanted to avoid "the danger of regular and serious differences of opinion with the other defense lawyers," which could damage the interests of his clients: "I am gaining a stronger and stronger impression that there are efforts underway to tightly organize the defense of the I. G. Farben people under a united leadership, disregarding the special interests of the individual defendants and the special circumstances of their cases." This was counter to his professional ethos: he did not take instructions from anyone other than his client, whether from a co-defense counsel, a codefendant, or someone outside of the trial. To this was added, for Sauter, the fact that there was clearly an attempt "to influence the distribution of the clients and even to remove defense lawyers who have already been appointed in favor of others" who were expected to have a more "willing attitude" with regard to a "centralized defense." Finally, he found it onerous for his clients that the trial was to be coupled with the Flick trial.[220]

Other lawyers seem to have been able to work with the intended strategy, or at least deal with it better than Sauter, who beside Rudolf Dix had been considered the second "dean" of the defense in the IMT, but was also perceived to be very problematic, as someone who during the Nazi regime "had oscillated between informer and defender putting his life at stake on behalf of his clients."[221] For Telford Taylor, Sauter was "a tall, rather excitable man who prefaced his questions with explanatory remarks calculated to give witnesses more than a hint of the answers he expected."[222] In any case, Sauter and Heimerich did not simply abandon their clients, but helped line up new defense counsels for them. The lawyer Otto Nelte replaced Sauter in the defense of Hörlein, and the lawyer Hans Pribilla took over the defense of Lautenschläger and Jähne.[223] Heimerich planned at first to have Krauch be represented by the renowned economic lawyer Professor Karl Geiler, who had been the prime minister of Greater Hesse after the war, leading a coalition government. The second candidate was Conrad Böttcher, a well-respected economic lawyer who was then serving as an advisor to the Ministry for Political Liberation in Stuttgart. Eduard Wahl, a professor of civil law, civil procedural law, and foreign and international private law at the University of Heidelberg, whom Heimerich had already called in for advice on multiple occasions, was to serve as the second defense counsel. The intention at the time was also to send the lawyer Ernst Achenbach to the United States in order to recruit an American lawyer for the overall defense of Krauch, Schmitz, and von Schnitzler.[224] In late May it became clear that Krauch's defense would be taken on by Conrad Böttcher as chief counsel and Eduard Wahl as secondary counsel. Heimerich wanted to function as a third defense counsel as needed.[225]

While Sauter dropped out entirely, Heimerich continued to be involved in organizing an overall defense and an individual defense for Krauch—apparently with the support of Henze. In a June 17 meeting, Henze, Heimerich, Siemers, and Hellmuth Dix discussed the question of who would be dean of the defense. They came to an agreement, as Heimerich had anticipated, on Conrad Böttcher, Krauch's lawyer. They also discussed the request of the lawyers Wahl and Gierlichs to postpone the trial and—relatedly—the possible hiring of an American defense counsel, which was supported in particular by Siemers. Heimerich reported that there were Americans based in Germany at the time who were interested in working on the defense. He also spoke about his efforts to create positive press for I. G. Farben and the indicted managers. At the end, Henze expressed his willingness to finance the costs of the "Fehsenbecker office" from a "general I. G. Farben fund" if its work was "of importance for the defense as a whole."[226]

Wolfgang Heintzeler spoke in a letter to Heimerich in late June 1947 against the possibility of bringing in American lawyers or consultants, considering it "dangerous" to "bring any members into the defense who have not been recommended wholeheartedly based on long-standing personal acquaintanceship or other grounds."[227] But Heimerich was pleased with himself and his work, as he reported to Krauch's wife.[228] However, he was now being ousted by Böttcher.[229] In late October 1947, Böttcher made it clear to Heimerich that he did not want him to continue his work, nor did he value it. He regretted that Heimerich had not been able to make the decision to "take part in frontline service in Nuremberg, which is what this all relates to." The development of the trial justified his view "that everything depends on this work at the front." Expert opinion did not make much of a difference, and the press, whose attention Heimerich wanted to draw toward the trial, proved "entirely uninterested" except for a connection that the lawyer Achenbach had made.[230] Heimerich drew the necessary conclusion and pulled out entirely—though not without pointing out that his petition for "improving and clearing up the overall atmosphere" unfortunately had not been recognized or supported.[231] He did not prove to be vindictive toward Böttcher, however.[232] When Böttcher was replaced by Rudolf Dix as dean and speaker of the defense at the end of the year, he seemed to become aware that he had not always been respectful of others, in particular of Heimerich.[233]

A peculiarity of the I. G. Farben defense, which, as Hubert Seliger writes, was organized "with almost military precision," consisted in the position of "Special Counsel" for the overall defense.[234] This position personified in certain ways the joint and mutually agreed-upon defense of all defendants that had been called for by the former chairman of the board Hermann Schmitz at the start of the trial. Schmitz had written to his codefendants urging them to come together to form a "mutually supportive and collegial defense front worthy of the impressive history and tradition of I. G. Farben."[235]

Professor Eduard Wahl, who held this position in the trial, was also Krauch's secondary counsel, a position in which he was particularly involved in the preparation for the trial but also active later. On September 3, 1947, shortly after the start of the trial, he was admitted by the court as "Special Counsel for all defendants."[236] Wahl, born to a school principal in 1903, had completed his law studies and passed his state exam in 1923. In 1927, after his second state exam, he had switched to the Kaiser-Wilhelm-Institute for Comparative Law and International Private Law, where he had worked with Ernst Rabel, assisting him in various trials. In 1932 he had completed his postdoctoral studies at the University of Berlin on the subject of third-party contractual rights in French law and had become an adjunct lecturer (*Privatdozent*). In 1935 he had been appointed to a professorship in Göttingen, and in 1940, now a member of the SA and the NSDAP, he had moved to Heidelberg, where he had run into problems, however, because of his so-called "pro-Jewish views." He had apparently been arrested in 1944 and then sent as a medical orderly to the front. After the war he had been hired again by the University of Heidelberg, and in 1947, he had been "exonerated" in his denazification proceeding. He had also been one of the founders of the Heidelberg Christlich Demokratische Union (Christian Democratic Union of Germany; CDU).[237] Wahl was so successful in the I. G. Farben trial that the lawyer Otto Kranzbühler, who had the leading role in the defense in the Krupp trial, wanted to win him over for this trial as well, which Wahl declined, however.[238]

On the whole, the majority of the chief defense counsels were in fact, as Hubert Seliger writes, a "who's who" of the economic lawyers working in Nuremberg. In addition to the Dix brothers, Siemers, Pelckmann, Nath, and Böttcher, this also included the politically uncontaminated Wolfram von Metzler.[239] A number of the above were not just veterans of the IMT but also had earned themselves a reputation in the Flick trial—this was true of Rudolf Dix, Siemers, Pelckmann, Flächsner, and Nath.

In addition to these personal defense counsels, chosen by the defendants or their families, there were Henze, the coordinator of the defense, and a whole series of I. G. Farben workers who assisted the lawyers. As Hubert Seliger writes, "Practically every defense lawyer had the 'structural support' of an I. G. Farben employee or company lawyer."[240] Henze himself, in addition to coordinating the defense, took on the defense of two clients, Heinrich Oster and Hans Kugler. Even if, like Sauter, one saw this coordination as more of a disadvantage, the support provided by the former I. G. Farben and its staff harbored enormous advantages for the defense of each client and of the defendants overall. The role of the I. G. Farben employees was very important, not least because the defense was clearly fully or partially financially supported by the factories in Leverkusen and Ludwigshafen—and had additional resources available. It was therefore logical that Wolfram von Metzler wrote, full of gratitude, to Wolfgang Heintzeler just a few weeks after the trial took place, "I think that what was achieved could certainly not have been achieved without the help of the I. G. Farben lawyers, and I must tell you that I always found the exceptionally comradely collaboration with the I. G. Farben lawyers, irrespective of the subject matter, to be particularly pleasant and enjoyable."[241]

One of the defendants, Hans Kugler, praised the court for permitting "lawyers also from the former I. G. Farben circle on the defense": "The mixture on the defense of routine criminal defense lawyers and expert jurists who knew both the internal workings of I. G. Farben and the defendants themselves personally was an advantage. It counteracted to some small degree the lack of evidence from which the defense suffered for a variety of reasons—from the two-year head start of the prosecution to the impediments to looking at company documents and the restrictions on communications and travel."[242] The factories of Leverkusen and Ludwigshafen and the old Frankfurt headquarters, in particular, sent top employees to provide support. This included not just lawyers but also engineers. The most important ones were in-house counsel staff members Wolfgang Heintzeler, from Ludwigshafen, who worked as assistant to Wurster and Oster's defense counsels, and Friedrich Silcher, from Leverkusen, who worked as assistant lawyer for von Knieriem and delivered an important concluding plea.[243]

The defendants themselves and their lawyers often bewailed the fact that the defendants and their counsels were at a serious disadvantage to the prosecution's team with regard to staff numbers, resources, and the prosecution's years of preparation.[244] This may have been true in a few trials, but certainly not for the trials of the industrialists. As a matter of fact, in his study of the Nuremberg lawyers, Hubert Seliger states that "with regard to the defense counsels of big industry at latest" this thesis must be considered "disproved." Already in the case of Gustav Krupp, there had been an effort to assemble a team of well-respected lawyers from the Weimar Republic era, a company lawyer, an international law specialist, and a British lawyer to carry out a task that then proved unnecessary because of his health: "This mixture of the remnants of the legal establishment of the Weimar Republic, company lawyers as assistants, foreign lawyers, and lawyers specializing in international law would prove typical for the composition of the defense of the industrialists in the subsequent trials."[245]

In the case of I. G. Farben, the effort to bring on an American lawyer as part of the defense did not succeed; the candidates who had been considered ultimately did not work out.[246] However, as Judge Morris stated, "The defendants are being represented by a large number (I do not as yet know how many) German lawyers and one Swiss [the lawyer Walter Vinassa]. Defense Counsel includes many of the best lawyers in Germany."[247] In this regard, at least, the judges and the prosecutors were in agreement. As William Zeck wrote in the first half of 1948, prior to the announcement of the verdict in the I. G. Farben trial, "The Nuremberg accused have been represented by the very best legal talent in Germany. In point of experience and ability, German counsel have frequently been considerably more impressive than the American lawyers on the Chief of Counsel's Staff."[248]

The lawyers, for their part, despite complaints about the working conditions in Nuremberg that ranged from the occasional to the frequent, were clear about the fact that they were fulfilling an exceptionally important role. Eduard Wahl reported in a letter that Rudolf Dix had said to him that "his work in Nuremberg was the apex in his rich legal career."[249]

The Court

From the beginning, General Clay and Chief Counsel Taylor had struggled to find enough qualified judges for the trials. In early September 1946, Clay requested, after consultation with Taylor, about twenty-four judges for the subsequent trials, who were to begin as soon as possible after the verdict in the IMT and ought to conclude by December 1947. Taylor could begin with the indictment as soon as the needed judges were available. They wanted judges with as much experience as possible and whose judgments would be respected in the US legal field—army officers were to be avoided as far as possible. Clay and Taylor had the idea that leading law schools could provide legal experts as judges and that the federal government and individual states could provide a series of judges from the various judicial systems.[250]

However, in early November 1946, Fred Vinson, the chief justice of the US Supreme Court, made the decision not to send federal judges to Nuremberg, since resulting labor shortages would lead to even more delays in the federal courts. This meant that the War Department had to draw on judges from the individual states and prominent members of the bar associations. In the end, most of the thirty-two judges who served as judges or substitute judges in Nuremberg were from the supreme courts of the individual states. They were and continue to be derided as "prairie judges," but their experience in jurisprudence mostly compensated for their inexperience in matters of international law and German history and politics.[251]

The judges in Nuremberg were invited on the recommendation of politicians, other judges, or representatives of different agencies. If they agreed to serve, they traveled via Washington, DC, to New York, where they boarded a ship to Bremerhaven. From there, they continued, for instance, by train to Frankfurt, then by car to Nuremberg. At this point, they would quickly be assigned to a court. The formal appointment of a tribunal was in the hands of General Clay, the military governor in the American zone.[252] Clay appointed not just the judges of the various courts but also the presiding judges. Fulfilling his task Clay was apparently acting on the advice of both Charles Fahy and Herman Phleger.[253]

In the case of Tribunal No. VI, the "Farben Case," the judges were appointed by General Order No. 87 of August 9, 1947. Curtis Grover Shake was appointed as presiding judge, James Morris and Paul Macarius Hebert as judges, and Clarence F. Merrell as substitute judge.[254]

Curtis Grover Shake, born in 1887 in Knox County, Indiana, had grown up in a family of limited means. His maternal grandfather had been a German immigrant.[255] He had first studied to be a teacher at Vincennes Junior College in Indiana. After following this career path for two years at a small rural school, he had decided to pursue law. Starting in 1907, without a formal high school diploma and financed by a local patron, he had studied law at Indiana University in Bloomington, graduating in 1910. It was there that he had met his wife, who had been pursuing the same course of study.[256] At the beginning of his career, he had primarily litigated against coal and railroad companies, which had then, in turn, began to hire him. Shake, a member of the Democratic Party, had also pursued a political career between 1910 and 1937: He had served as city attorney; Knox County attorney; US commissioner for the Southern District of Indiana; and, from 1926 to 1928, as member of the Indiana Senate. In 1928, he had run for state attorney general. In the election, he had strongly attacked the Republicans and their connections with the Ku Klux Klan, which had been powerful in Indiana at the time. Shortly before the vote he had been accused of himself having been a member of the Ku Klux Klan since 1924—which is not inconceivable. In any case, Shake had lost the vote and returned to his law office.[257]

In 1937, Shake had been appointed by the Democratic governor, on an interim basis, as a judge on the Supreme Court of Indiana, and then properly elected to the position in 1938 for a six-year term. During this time, he had served as chief justice three times. In 1944 he had not stood for re-election to the supreme court, since he had assumed that the Republicans would win and had wanted to avoid the "stigma" of having lost. He had returned to his work as a lawyer from 1945 to 1947. During this period, in 1946, his wife had died. He was most likely invited to Nuremberg on the recommendation of Frank Richman, who was serving as a judge in the Flick trial. He accepted the offer and traveled to Germany alone. In addition to his work on the Supreme Court of Indiana, he had apparently also made a name for himself as a mediator of numerous labor conflicts, some large and problematic.[258]

Shake arrived in Nuremberg relatively early and participated in the joint session of all the tribunals that took place on July 9, 1947. In November 1947 he was elected by his peers to the important role of chairman of the Supervisory Committee of Presiding Judges. He held this position until the end of the I. G. Farben trial in late July 1948.[259] Shake was thus an experienced lawyer and a judge with a high reputation. When the I. G. Farben trial began, the prosecution welcomed the news of his appointment. The lawyer Mary Kaufman referred to Shake, for instance, as an "intelligent person … completely fair, honest, and objective."[260]

James Morris was also assigned to Case VI. Born in 1893 in Bordulac, North Dakota, he had also grown up in very simple circumstances—as a homesteader in a sod house on the North Dakota plains. After the early death of his father, he had increasingly had to take on his role on the family's small farm. At the age of sixteen, he had decided to pursue higher education and had moved in with relatives of his mother's in Cincinnati, Ohio, where, after high school, he had attended the University of Cincinnati Law School, graduating in 1916. That same year, he had been admitted to the bar in Ohio, and the following year to the bar in North Dakota. He had served in the US Army during World War I, after which he had become a lawyer in North Dakota. Like Shake, Morris had also been very involved in politics. As a member of the Republican Party, he had taken on multiple public roles at the local and regional levels. His highest political office in North Dakota had been that of attorney general during the 1929–1932 term. Starting in 1935, he had served as an elected judge of the Supreme Court of North Dakota, serving multiple times as chief justice.[261]

In his first election for the supreme court in 1934, Morris had campaigned along with Judges William Nuessle and A. G. Burr as independents; they had also advertised in local German-language newspapers such as the *Dakota Freie Presse* and *Der Staatsanzeiger*.[262] They had won against the political machine of William and Lydia Langer, who had been seeking at the time to control the supreme court and had been strongly opposed to their candidacy.[263] William Langer had been elected governor of North Dakota in 1932 as the candidate of the Nonpartisan League, a radical party that opposed big industry and was primarily supported by farmers, and of the Republican Party, and once in office, he had made major efforts on behalf of farmers, including by using state funds to significantly subsidize agricultural prices. In 1934, he had been given a prison sentence by a federal court for mismanagement of funds and conspiracy, after which he had been removed from office by the Supreme Court of North Dakota. After a number of appeals, he had eventually been acquitted and re-elected governor in 1936. In 1940, Langer had successfully run for a seat in the US Senate, where after first being denied his seat because he had been considered "unfit," he had served as a committed isolationist. After World War II, the conservative wing of the Republican Party had gained control and the power to govern in North Dakota, Fred G. Aandahl and Milton R. Young being some of their most prominent representatives.[264] Morris seems to have been part of this group, since he had maintained regular contact with Governor Aandahl, but he clearly had not been on similar terms with Senator Langer, who had been a vociferous opponent of the Nuremberg trials.[265] A Presbyterian and a member of a masonic lodge, Morris had had no contact with Bishop Aloysius Muench of Fargo, North Dakota, who had also expressed criticism of the trials during his service as apostolic nuncio to West Germany.[266] And Morris seems not to have been as isolationist, as a good number of North Dakotans were at that time.[267]

His appointment to be a judge in Nuremberg was well received, not least because of the confidence inspired by his long experience and his practical knowledge.[268] The appointment was also a source of pride for Morris: "I am, indeed, fortunate to be assigned to the Farben Case which will be a land mark in international jurisprudence."[269] And as he wrote to the governor of North Dakota at the time: "This case is creating much interest and it is apparently the first time in history that the industrialists and men powerful in business affairs are being charged with violations of international law and crimes against humanity."[270] From early on, however, Morris also expressed his doubts about the legal foundations of the charges. He wrote to a North Dakota general with whom he was acquainted that Control Council Law No. 10 set out, inter alia, that an individual who was acting under government orders or superior orders could nonetheless be held legally responsible in the case of a crime: "I find that many military people are disturbed by this innovation and the impact it may have on military service in the future."[271] He also expressed a high degree of understanding for the Germans in his letters, reporting on the extensive destruction of German cities, which was worse than he had imagined. He was beginning to understand what it meant to be a defeated people, and wished that the Americans understood what it meant to be an occupied country—"even when the victor is as kind-hearted as is our own country."[272] His reservations with respect to the "Russians," who had firmly established themselves in East Germany and were threatening Western Europe, also were clear.[273]

He was not entirely sure about the Germans, but they struck him as rather strange; this reaction was clear, for instance, after his visit to Schloss Linderhof, "built by Bavaria's Mad King Ludwig": "The Germans seem still quite proud of the works of their insane rulers of the past, whether it be those of mad kings or more modern mad men like Hitler. I am beginning to think that one of the greatest obstacles to democracy is history."[274] Morris, himself a freemason, wrote to a lodge brother that one of the first despotic acts of the Nazi regime had been the prohibition of freemasonry, since its principles stood in clear contradiction to despotism and autocracy: "After seeing what happened in Germany one can truly appreciate the freedom of assembly, guaranteed by our own Constitution. … Once the people of Germany lost the privilege of getting together without fear of espionage and reprisal, their basic liberties all soon disappeared and the power to resist on the part of those who would remain free was lost."[275]

Morris was also a decided opponent of the Morgenthau Plan, which he made clear when he spoke of the economic and financial chaos in occupied Germany—which would soon be two Germanys, one East and one West, the latter of which would be rebuilt with the help of the United States: "Back of all this stands the great mistake we made in the first instance of trying to put into effect the Morgenthau plan and reduce Germany to an agrarian state. The plan has now, of course, been abandoned but through it we lost about a year and a half of precious time that could have been used to advantage in rehabilitating Germany."[276] This opinion likely also influenced his position with respect to Josiah DuBois, the lead prosecutor in the I. G. Farben case.

In any case, Morris had a long legal career behind him and was a very experienced judge when he arrived in Nuremberg in 1947. He clearly did not embrace the conspiracy theories popular in North Dakota, nor did he see big business as a force of evil.[277] Nor did Morris embody the widespread stereotype of North Dakotans in the United States, who were described by some as "culturally deprived simpletons, isolated from the mainstream of American life, too unenlightened to seek the good life in easier surroundings."[278]

The third judge of the tribunal was Paul Macarius Hebert, from Louisiana. Born in 1907 in Baton Rouge, Louisiana, he had grown up in what seems to have been a rather ordinary Catholic family, but one which highly prized education. He had attended a Catholic high school, graduating in 1925—after which he had eloped with his high school sweetheart. Hebert had then attended Louisiana State University while working part-time for the Esso company. He had graduated in 1929 and had then gone to Yale Law School with the help of a Sterling Law Fellowship, acquiring a doctorate in 1930. That same year, he had become a law professor at Loyola University in New Orleans, from which Huey Long, the controversial governor and then senator from Louisiana, had received an honorary degree in 1931. Between 1932 and 1936, Hebert had served as the dean of Loyola's law school. Starting in 1937, he had served as the dean of the Louisiana State University Law School in Baton Rouge, which may have been arranged by Governor Huey Long himself, who had been strongly promoting the school at the time.[279]

From 1939 to 1941, Hebert had served as the acting president of the university during the period when it went through what was the biggest scandal in its history up to that point because of grave financial misconduct on the part of its leadership. The background information on the judges at the trial even stated that Hebert had been "in charge of University reorganization and investigations following 'Louisiana Scandals' (1939–41)."[280] His fairly successful efforts as a "Hercules" in the "Augean stables" of Louisiana State University had brought him into conflict with various factions in Louisiana, who had clearly perceived him as too independent. He therefore had not been elected president of the university, returning to his role as dean of the law school after his work was finished. During the war, Hebert had served from 1942 until 1945 as the chief of the Industrial Law Branch in the Industrial Contracts Division of the Army Judge Advocate General's Corps (JAG) with the rank of lieutenant colonel. After the war he had returned to his old position at Louisiana State University until being invited to Nuremberg, apparently on the recommendation of the war secretary. In early July 1947, he traveled, together with his wife, to Nuremberg.[281]

Hebert was a thoroughly decent and very effective jurist and administrator.[282] His professional experience was almost exclusively in higher education, as an academic, as an intellectual, and in administration. In contrast to the other two judges in the I. G. Farben trial, Hebert had no experience as a judge. He seems to have had progressive inclinations as a jurist. In an article in the fall of 1933, he stated that through the New Deal, the role of the US government had changed significantly, increasing substantially in importance: "Powers will be exercised by the federal government which should make John Calhoun, that ardent advocate of states' rights, turn over in his grave." The new role would show itself above all in extensive economic planning: "Our constitutional form of government is elastic enough to permit it. But in order to sustain economic and social planning, the Supreme Court will have to recede drastically from the doctrine which has heretofore characterized many of its decisions and which was tersely stated by Justice Brewer: 'The paternal theory of government is to me odious.' The nineteenth-century concept of law as the absolute expression of the eternal verities is gradually being abandoned."[283]

Like Hebert, Clarence Merrell, who was appointed as an alternate judge in case one of the three judges had to withdraw, also does not seem to have had any experience as a judge. His appointment was most likely due to a recommendation by Judge Shake. Little is known about Merrell: Born in 1887 in Waynestown, Indiana, he had first studied at the prestigious Wabash College in Indiana and then studied law at Columbia University. He had practiced law in Indiana and North Dakota and had been president of the Indianapolis Bar Association in 1939 and vice president of the International Association of Insurance Counsels from 1940 to 1941. Along with the judges Frank Richman and Curtis G. Shake, he was also part of the so-called Indiana group, which enjoyed spending time together and took excursions together. Merrell's stay in Nuremberg was marred by his wife's getting into a serious car accident.[284]

At the start of the proceedings, the mood among the judges was apparently very good. They are pictured working alongside each other in Figure 2.14. Morris wrote in a letter of his fellow judges Shake, Hebert, and Merrell that "[m]y associates on the Tribunal are fine men. I am sure that our association together will be agreeable, and I am looking forward with pleasure to working with them throughout the coming months."[285] He correctly predicted the amount of work entailed. The judges were expecting difficult months and serious responsibilities: "The trial of this case is an interesting and novel experience in jurisprudence. It is also an experience which I am, indeed, grateful to have although it will, undoubtedly, involve months of hard work and tremendous responsibility in determining ultimate justice."[286] Over the course of these months, however, the relationship among the judges would significantly worsen.

Looking back, the former prosecutor William Zeck said in a 1996 interview that the prosecution had put its best people on the industrial trials and that, with this being the case, there should have been a process for selecting judges who were better prepared for them: "Paul Hebert belonged there, Morris of North Dakota, obviously didn't belong there and you know, I'm speaking without knowing any of these people but from what I've heard. That part of the process was faulty."[287] Belle Mayer, whom Zeck had married in the meantime, shared his opinion: "Shake and Morris were very provincial people. I don't know how much they read or how much they studied, but they, from the outset, could not believe that these very respectable former businessmen could be guilty of such perversion."[288]

Figure 2.14. From left to right: Judges James Morris, Curtis G. Shake (presiding judge), Paul M. Hebert, and Clarence Merrell. Source: NARA 238-OMT-VI-T-3; NL Nath; public domain.

The journalist Tom Bower had an even poorer opinion of the judges: the thirty judges of the subsequent trials at Nuremberg had been recruited from the various state court systems and correspondingly had little experience with the topics that were being addressed there. They had, Bower thought, absolutely no knowledge of international law. Some were also fully prejudiced against the trials, especially Judge Morris, from North Dakota, whose wife according to Bower frequently invited the wives of the board members of I. G. Farben, especially Mrs. von Schnitzler, for drinks. And, according to Bower, Drexel Sprecher was accused publicly by a judge's assistant at the bar of the Grand Hotel of being "anti-German." Finally, German newspapers reported on Judge Shake's hospitality in inviting members of the German defense to the Grand Hotel, where they should not have been allowed: "Increasingly Morris and the presiding judge, Curtis Shake, became impatient with the prosecution's presentation of the case, insensitive about the evidence and, according to the prosecutors, noticeably biased in favour of the defence in their decisions during the trial." Bower even wrote that just a few days after the trial started, the members of the prosecution had the feeling that they, and not the managers at I. G. Farben, were in the dock.[289]

DuBois, Mayer, and Zeck's negative assessments of Judges Shake and Morris and Bower's assertions were taken up in the academic literature, most recently, for instance, in Kevin Jon Heller's study.[290] Alberto Zuppi, on the other hand, remained more restrained: "Despite a public allegation that the rest of the Tribunal—Shake and Morris—were sympathetic to the defense, the point was never proved."[291] A report about Judge Shake at the end of the I. G. Farben trial even claimed that the former chief justice of the Supreme Court of Indiana was seen as "one of the ablest jurists at Nurnberg."[292] One must at least scrutinize, therefore, whether the depictions and negative assessments of the two judges, in some cases based only on hearsay or even rumors, were justified.

Notes

1. This is according to the historian of the ancient world Paul Veyne in *Foucault: Der Philosoph als Samurai*, 64.
2. Emanuel Minskoff Papers, RG-10.15*01, Correspondence, Folder 1: Minskoff to his wife, September 13, 1945.
3. Taylor, *Anatomy*, 221–22.
4. Taylor, 61.
5. On the IMT, see Weinke, *Die Nürnberger Prozesse*, 24–56.
6. On this, see Weinke, *Die Nürnberger Prozesse*, 59–98; Ueberschär, *Der Nationalsozialismus vor Gericht*, 73–212; Priemel and Stiller, *NMT*, 67–462.
7. Judt, *Postwar. A History of Europe since 1945*, 86, 89.
8. Judt, 86–88.
9. Unternehmensarchiv BASF, W.1.3/114 and 115: Hans Kugler, "Farben: Chance und Schicksal," [1967], 368 (unpublished manuscript).
10. Judt, *Postwar*, 86.
11. James Morris Papers, Box 1, Folder 1: Morris to George Moses, Associated Press, September 19, 1947; Judt, *Postwar*, 86–87.
12. Judt, *Postwar*, 88–93; Plumpe, *Das kalte Herz*, 398–402; Abelshauser, *Deutsche Wirtschaftsgeschichte*, 129–52.
13. Judt, *Postwar*, 92–93, 125.
14. Judt, 125–26; Herbert, *Geschichte Deutschlands*, 593–601.
15. Taylor, *Anatomy*, 61, 221–22; James Morris Papers, Box 1, Folder 1: Morris to General Heber L. Edwards, October 6, 1947.
16. James Morris Papers, Box 1, Folder 1: Morris to Dr. Peik, September 4, 1947; Morris to General Heber L. Edwards, October 6, 1947.
17. James Morris Papers, Box 1, Folder 1: Morris to Taylor, Supreme Court Librarian, October 6, 1947; for a contrasting view, cf. Priemel, *The Betrayal*, 95–99.
18. James Morris Papers, Box 1, Folder 2: Morris to Mr. Newberry, March 11, 1948.
19. Taylor, *Final Report*, 37.
20. Taylor, *Final Report*, 37–39.
21. Taylor, *Final Report*, 39–43.
22. Telford Taylor Papers, Box 26, TTP-5-1-1-10: NMT-Statistical File: Thomas Hodges, Director Language Division, to Telford Taylor, September 20, 1948: Production of Translation

Branch, Language Division; see also Taylor, *Final Report*, 45 with a typo in the sum because he indicated 133,762 pages instead of the correct number, 133, 262.

23. Telford Taylor Papers, Box 27, TTP-5-1-2-24: NMT-OCCWC: Administrative Division: Strength Report January 31, 1948–April 30, 1949; Taylor, *Final Report*, 43–44.
24. NL Heimerich, 24.1972a-449: Martin Treu to Heimerich, November 20, 1946.
25. Bundesarchiv, AllProz 3/274: Nagel to Rechtsanwalt Siemers, July 14, 1947; Siemers to Dr. Walter Mueller, September 1, 1947; AllProz 3 Siemers/83: Nagel to Siemers, July 14, 1947; cf. also Jung, *Rechtsprobleme*, 35.
26. Bundesarchiv, AllProz 3 Siemers/86: Rudolf Dix to Siemers, January 15, 1947.
27. Bundesarchiv, AllProz 3 Siemers/84: Sekretariat des Militärtribunals Nürnberg, August 2, 1947: Honorierung der Verteidiger; Taylor, *Final Report*, p. 49; NL Heimerich 24/1972a-759: Memo by Heimerich on a meeting with the lawyer Henze, May 3, 1947: There it was said that lunch would be "provided"; in addition, the defense counsels and their assistants received the hard labor card; see also Memorandum by Heimerich of June 23, 1947 on a defense counsels meeting on June 19, 1947; Benjamin B. Ferencz, "Nurnberg Trial Procedure and the Rights of the Accused," 144–51, here 147.
28. Emanuel Minskoff Papers, RG 10.154*01, Correspondence, Folder 2: Minskoff to Joseph Friedman, Treasury Department, February 2, 1948.
29. Cf. Telford Taylor Papers, Box 26, TTP-5-1-1-7: Howard Russell, Secretary General: Tariff Agreement Covering Defense Attorneys, November 18, 1948; on remuneration, cf. Seliger, *Politische Anwälte*, 127–30.
30. Cf. Bundesarchiv, AllProz 3 Siemers/89: Prof. Herbert Kraus to Siemers, September 30, 1947.
31. Interview with Sally Falk Moore, Harvard University, November 3, 2014; cf. USHMM Archives, RG-50.030*0382: Interview with William Zeck and Belle (Mayer) Zeck, September 23, 1996, 24, 27: there one finds concrete remarks about Sally Falk Zeck about how he "went to my first love" and how "I was not very fond of lady lawyers at that particular point in my life." Cf. also Priemel, *The Betrayal*, 94–95; Bush, *New Dealer*, 576–77.
32. Unternehmensarchiv BASF, W.1.3./114 and 115: Kugler, *Farben: Chance und Schicksal*, 375.
33. Drexel Sprecher Papers, Box 54, History File, Prison Operations: Prison Mess, Med. Attention (by D. E. Hauberger), Receiving, Transferring and Discharging of Prisoners (by Gruener), Care of Defendants, n.d.
34. Bayer Archiv, 207/007 Vol. 1: Antrag der Anwälte Aschenauer u.a. an das Militärgericht für den Fall VI, die amerikanische Anklagebehörde, Generalsekretär Colonel Ray, Defense Adminstration, July 11, 1947. At that time, Seidl signed for Dürrfeld and Ambros, Laternser for Ilgner, Berndt for ter Meer and Mann, Henze for Oster, Krauss for Jähne and Lautenschläger, and von Rospatt for Kugler.
35. Bayer Archiv, 207/007 Vol. 2: Rudolf Dix to the military court for Case VI, March 12, 1948.
36. Kempner, *Ankläger einer Epoche. Lebenserinnerungen*, 456.
37. Kempner, 397.
38. Goetz, "Impressions of Telford Taylor at Nuremberg," 669–72, here 669.
39. Bush, "Soldiers Find Wars: A Life of Telford Taylor," 675–92, here 676–81; Taylor, *Anatomy*, ix–xii.
40. Taylor, *Anatomy*, 286–87.
41. Taylor, *Anatomy*, 288–92; Bush, *New Dealer*, 568–71; Gausmann, *Deutsche Großunternehmer*, 192–93.
42. Telford Taylor Papers, Box 26, TTP-5-1-1-11: Office Chief of Counsel Subsequent Proceedings Division, Taylor, Organizational Memo No. 1, May 17, 1946, and Organizational Memo No. 2, June 25, 1946.

43. Drexel Sprecher Papers, Box 54, History File, Public Relations Office: Official Transcript of the Press Conference of Brigadier General Telford Taylor with members of the Soviet Press, Nurnberg, June 25, 1947.
44. Telford Taylor Papers, Box 26, TTP-5-1-1-1x: Invitation from Elfriede Vatte of June 10, 1947, to Taylor for a presentation in the German-American Youth Club on July 23 or 30; Manuscript by Taylor of July 22, 1947: quotation from there.
45. Priemel, "A Story of Betrayal," 70, 104–105; Spicka, "The Devil's Chemists on Trial," 869–70.
46. Priemel, *The Betrayal*, 274.
47. Taylor, *Final Report*, 79; Borkin, *Crime and Punishment*, 135–36.
48. *Trials of War Criminals before the Nuernberg Military Tribunals*, vol. VI, 32.
49. Perels, "Fast vergessen: Franz L. Neumanns Beitrag zur Konzipierung der Nürnberger Prozesse: Eine Erinnerung aus Anlaß seines 100. Geburtstags," 117–25; Lustig, "The Nature of the Nazi State and the Question of International Criminal Responsibility of Corporate Officials at Nuremberg: Revisiting Franz Neumann's Concept of Behemoth at the Industrialist Trials," 965–1044; Pratt, "Quel rôle pour Franz Leopold Neumann en amont et en aval du Procès militaire international de Nuremberg?," 43–57; see also Peter Hayes's introduction to Neumann, *Behemoth: The Structure and Practice of National Socialism 1933–1944*.
50. *Trials of War Criminals before the Nuernberg Military Tribunals*, vol. VI, 114–15.
51. Priemel, *The Betrayal*, 206; a very critical source is Gausmann, *Deutsche Großunternehmer*, 232–36, 360–62; according to Greiner, *Die Morgenthau-Legende*, 356, Pomerantz had "resigned in protest against the appointment of inadequately qualified judges."
52. Priemel, *The Betrayal*, 206.
53. See Gausmann, *Deutsche Großunternehmer*, 208–209, 363–65.
54. Erbelding, *Rescue Board: The Untold Story of America's Efforts to Save the Jews of Europe*, 49.
55. Erbelding, *Rescue Board*, 53, 287.
56. For a benevolent view of DuBois, see Medoff, *Blowing the Whistle on Genocide: Josiah E. DuBois, Jr., and the Struggle for a U.S. Response to the Holocaust*, esp. 20–34; 40–52 (Report), 76–79 (Drew Pearson), 118–30 (War Refugee Board), 131–35 (Epilogue); Greiner, *"IG-Joe"—IG Farben-Prozeß und Morgenthau-Plan*. For critical views of DuBois, see Spicka, "The Devil's Chemists on Trial," 871–72; Gausmann, *Deutsche Großunternehmer*, 345–47.
57. Spicka, "The Devil's Chemists on Trial," 872.
58. Borgwardt, "Re-Examining Nuremberg as a New Deal Institution: Politics, Culture and the Limits of Law in Generating Human Rights Norms," 401–62, here 460.
59. Priemel, *The Betrayal*, 206.
60. Spicka, "The Devil's Chemists on Trial," 872.
61. Taylor, *Final Report*, 66–67; cf. Spicka, "The Devil's Chemists on Trial," 873, and Bush, *Prehistory*, 1201–1204.
62. NARA, RG 238, Entry 159, Box 4, Folder 25: Intra-Office Memorandum by Leo M. Drachsler, July 23, 1946: this contains a copy of the letter of June 11, 1946, from Hyman B. Ritchin to Drachsler. On Harris, see Taylor, *Anatomy*, 289; and for a critical view, see Gausmann, *Deutsche Großunternehmer*, 205–208.
63. Goetz, "Impressions of Taylor at Nuremberg," 670.
64. Taylor, *Anatomy*, 223–24.
65. Cf. on this also Gausmann, *Deutsche Großunternehmer*, 132–33.
66. Sally Falk Moore Interview, Harvard University, November 3, 2014; Sally Falk Moore Interviewed by Kalman Applbaum, August 24, 2008.
67. On Mary Kaufman's experiences, see Marlise James, *The People's Lawyers*, 90–91.
68. NARA, RG 238, Entry 192, Box 1, Folder 6: Letter/Memo from Ben Ferencz to Jim Heath and Drexel Sprecher, June 15, 1946. Gausmann, *Deutsche Großunternehmer*, 224, assesses the letter/memo as cynical; Priemel, *The Betrayal*, 205: long quotation from this letter/memo there.

69. Priemel, *The Betrayal*, 205.
70. Drexel Sprecher Papers, Box 51, Procedure/Press Files, Trial Preparations: Memorandum by Randolph Newman of March 28, 1947; this contains a handwritten note by Sprecher for Taylor.
71. Priemel, "Der Sonderweg vor Gericht: Angewandte Geschichte im Nürnberger Krupp-Prozess," 391–426, here 407–408; Priemel, *The Betrayal*, 204.
72. NARA, RG 238, Entry 159, Box 4, Folder 25: Intra-Office Memorandum by Leo M. Drachsler, July 23, 1946: this contains a copy of the letter from Hyman B. Ritchin of June 11, 1946, to Drachsler.
73. NARA, RG 238, Entry 192, Box 2, Folder 3: "Remarks concerning the Evidence available at present"; a handwritten note on this: "I. G. Farben Summary, D. A. Sprecher" (who could be the author).
74. Greiner, *Die Morgenthau-Legende*, 360.
75. Telford Taylor Papers, Box 32, TTP-5-1-7-118: Pomerantz to M. Touffait, October 29, 1946.
76. USHMM Archives, RG-50.030*0382, Interview with William and Belle Zeck, September 23, 1996, 27–30; Priemel, *The Betrayal*, 206.
77. Priemel, *The Betrayal*, 206.
78. Priemel, *The Betrayal*, 206; Gausmann, *Deutsche Großunternehmer*, 232–36, 360–62; Greiner, *Die Morgenthau-Legende*, 356.
79. Priemel, *The Betrayal*, 205–206; Gausmann, *Deutsche Großunternehmer*, 344–45.
80. Belle Mayer Papers, Nuremberg Related Material, Correspondence, Box 3, Folder 22: Jan Charmatz to Belle Mayer, May 8, 1947. DuBois, *The Devil's Chemists*, 194, reports that Jan Charmatz's brother was murdered in Auschwitz.
81. NARA, RG 238, Entry 159, Box 5, Folder 6: Belle Mayer to General Taylor, November 25, 1946, Re: Personnel for OCCWC.
82. On Dencker, see also Martin, *All Honorable Men*, 64–65: after that, he was one of the Americans' most important helpers at the time as he would have provided them with keys and evidence for many of their assumptions; OMGUS, *Ermittlungen*, introduction by the editor (Karl Heinz Roth), xviii–xix.
83. USHMM Archives, RG-50.030*0382, Interview with William and Belle Zeck, September 23, 1996, 29–30.
84. Interview with William and Belle Zeck, 67. Cf. on this Heine, *Verstand und Schicksal*, 104, indicating that the management of the Works Group Oberrhein had been transferred from Kühne to Haberland, "about which nothing was written in order to avoid Haberland being accused in Nuremberg." This thesis has already been described as unconvincing by Hayes, *Industry and Ideology*, 337, footnote 58.
85. USHMM Archives, RG-50.030*0382, Interview with William and Belle Zeck, September 23, 1996, 29–31; thus, Gausmann, *Deutsche Großunternehmer*, 168, is incorrect in writing that Zeck "was one of the key prosecutors" in the I. G. Farben trial. Zeck was no longer in Nuremberg at that point.
86. Belle Mayer Papers, Nuremberg Related Material, Correspondence, Box 3, Folder 20, H Miscellany Correspondence 1946–49: Cecil Hubbert to William Raugust, Executive Counsel OCCWC, undated (fall 1946?); on Armbruster, who had also published on I. G. Farben, see Greiner, *Die Morgenthau-Legende*, 396–97.
87. Priemel, *The Betrayal*, 206.
88. Emanuel Minskoff Papers, RG-10.154*01, Correspondence, Folder 2: Charles M. LaFollette to William A. Raugust, March 19, 1947.
89. Priemel, *The Betrayal*, 206–207.
90. Belle Mayer Papers, Nuremberg Related Material, Correspondence, Box 3, Folder 22: Jan Charmatz to Belle Mayer, May 8, 1947.

91. Emanuel Minskoff Papers, RG-10.154*01, Correspondence, Folder 2: Minskoff to Joseph Friedman, Assistant General of Counsel, Treasury Department, February 2, 1948 (copy).
92. Priemel, *The Betrayal*, 207.
93. Belle Mayer Papers, Nuremberg Related Material, Nuremberg Trial Material, Box 1, Folder 11: Statements to the Tribunal undated [1947].
94. Priemel, *The Betrayal*, Chapter 6, "Saving Capitalism," above all, 215–20.
95. Priemel, *The Betrayal*, 215.
96. Priemel, *The Betrayal*, 218–20, quote from 220.
97. Gausmann, *Deutsche Großunternehmer*, 137–39.
98. Gausmann, *Deutsche Großunternehmer*, 245–47.
99. OMGUS, *Ermittlungen*, introduction by the editor (Karl Heinz Roth), lv–lvi.
100. Drexel Sprecher Papers, Box 47, Case Files, Case VI, Draft of Press Release (Indictment), n.d.; Gausmann, *Deutsche Großunternehmer*, 343–69: biographical sketches of lawyers for the prosecution; on Kaufman, see also James, *The People's Lawyers*, 88–91.
101. DuBois, *The Devil's Chemists*, 182, 193.
102. Brown-Fleming, *The Holocaust and Catholic Conscience: Cardinal Aloysius Muench and the Guilt Question in Germany*, 6–8.
103. Gausmann, *Deutsche Großunternehmer*, 241–42; claims that the proportion of Jews or return migrants among the lawyers in the prosecution was "quite high overall," which "was, however, more or less shamefully denied then as now." He also assumes that their "often personal desire for revenge" would have been "more than understandable" but would have put a strain on the atmosphere in Nuremberg. He cites a statement from General Lucius Clay as supposed evidence.
104. Emanuel Minskoff Papers, RG-10.154*01, Correspondence, Folder 2: Minskoff to Joseph Friedman, Assistant General of Counsel, Treasury Department, February 2, 1948 (copy).
105. Bower, *Blind Eye*, 351–52.
106. James Morris Papers, Box 1, Folder 2: Morris to Judge Christianson, January 9, 1948.
107. USHMM Archives, RG-50.030*0382, Interview with William and Belle Zeck, September 23, 1996, 45.
108. Belle Mayer Papers, Nuremberg Related Material, Correspondence, Box 3, Folder 12: DuBois to Mayer, November 8, 1947.
109. Belle Mayer Papers, Nuremberg Related Material, Correspondence, Box 3, Folder 12: DuBois to Mayer, April 27, 1948.
110. Taylor, *Final Report*, 31.
111. NARA, RG 238, Entry 192, Box 2, Folder 3: "Legal References Concerning the Crimes against Peace Count," no author or date—according to the IMT ruling, it was probably written in late 1946/early 1947.
112. OMGUS, *Ermittlungen*, introduction by the editor (Karl Heinz Roth), lv.
113. Drexel Sprecher Papers, Box 47, Case Files, Case VI, Draft of Press Release (Indictment), n.d.—contains direct quotes from Taylor when the indictment was announced.
114. Bayer Archiv 207/025: In a folder about Auschwitz, there is a copy of the article from the *Frankfurter Rundschau* of March 22, 1947, "I. G. Farben-Konzern in Auschwitz" by Thomas A. Reedy, Associated Press correspondent.
115. See *Trials of War Criminals*, vol. VII, 10–14.
116. USHMM Archives, RG-50.030*0382: Interview with William and Belle Zeck, September 23, 1996, 32–33.
117. Interview with William and Belle Zeck, 29–30.
118. Drexel Sprecher Papers, Box 47, Case Files, Case VI, Draft of Press Release (Indictment), n.d.
119. Unternehmensarchiv BASF, W.1.3./114 and 115: Kugler, *Farben: Chance und Schicksal*, 425.
120. DuBois, *The Devil's Chemists*, 100, 122–32: Chapter 14 "A Nobel Prizewinner" about Hörlein; then, subsequently, Zuppi, "Slave Labor," 497; Jeffreys, *Hell's Cartel*, 408; Heller,

The Nuremberg Military Tribunals, 94; Suzanne Bellamy, *Hoosier Justice at Nuremberg*, 63. Gattineau, *Durch die Klippen*, 200, reports on the interrogation of Nobel Prize winner Adolf Butenandt as a witness of Hörlein—this may have been the cause of DuBois's error. On Hörlein, cf. Zummersch, *Heinrich Hörlein (1882–1954)*.

121. *Trials of War Criminals*, vol. VII, 14–39.
122. *Trials of War Criminals*, vol. VII, 39–50.
123. *Trials of War Criminals*, vol. VII, 50–54.
124. *Trials of War Criminals*, vol. VII, 54–59.
125. *Trials of War Criminals*, vol. VII, 59.
126. *Trials of War Criminals*, vol. VII, 59–60.
127. Priemel, *The Betrayal*, 204.
128. NL Heimerich, 24/1972a-759: Heimerich: meeting with the lawyer Henze, May 3, 1947.
129. NL Heimerich, 24/1972a-759: Heimerich to Henze, May 8, 1947.
130. Emanuel Minskoff Papers, RG-10.154*01, Correspondence, Folder 2: Minskoff to Joseph Friedman, Assistant General of Counsel, Treasury Department, February 2, 1948 (copy).
131. This is according to Karl Heinz Roth in the introduction to OMGUS, *Ermittlungen*, lv.
132. USHMM Archives, RG-50.030*0382: Interview with William and Belle Zeck, September 23, 1996, 29–30.
133. Interview with William and Belle Zeck, 40–41.
134. Interview with William and Belle Zeck, 42.
135. Martin, *All Honorable Men*, 55–57; OMGUS, *Ermittlungen*, introduction by the editor (Karl Heinz Roth), xix–xx; cf. Hoechst Archiv, Personalakten Lautenschläger: Carl Ludwig Lautenschläger, Erinnerungen, vol. VIII, [75–76].
136. NL Heimerich, 24/1972a-542: Heimerich to the Public Prosecutor at the Heidelberg Spruchkammer, July 12, 1946; note by Ilse Bethge on July 22, 1946.
137. Hoechst Archiv, Personalakten Lautenschläger: Carl Ludwig Lautenschläger, Erinnerungen, vol. VIII, [77–89]; he describes this uncertainty—in these statements he is also trying to explain why he was so talkative with those interrogating him.
138. Unternehmensarchiv BASF, W.1.3./114 and 115: Kugler, *Farben: Chance und Schicksal*, 367–68.
139. Kugler, *Farben: Chance und Schicksal*, 372.
140. USHMM Archives, RG-50.030*0382: Interview with William and Belle Zeck, September 23, 1996, 29–30.
141. Bayer Archiv, 207/007-001: Kühne, Erinnerungen an Nürnberg (undated).
142. Drexel Sprecher Papers, Box 47, Case Files, Case VI—Tribunal Orders: Period and Place (or Nature) of Detention of the Defendants in Case No. VI (Farben) since the Allied Occupation of Germany, Nuremberg May 10, 1948: for prosecution, Sprecher and Taylor, for defense, Dix; "approved and ordered filed": Judge Shake, May 13, 1948. The list is possibly not entirely complete; some period and location of detainment of Fritz ter Meer and Georg von Schnitzler are apparently missing, and possibly also that of Otto Ambros in the US internment camp at Dachau (the former concentration camp)—see DuBois, *The Devil's Chemists*, 65–66; Staatsarchiv Freiburg, T 1 Drischel 54: Klavehn-Berndt to lawyer Drischel, March 5, 1947, on Ambros: "He was likely delivered to Dachau."
143. NARA, RG 238, Entry 192, Box 4, Folder 5: Abe W. Weisbrodt about the Schnitzler interrogation (undated, likely 1947), with the handwritten comment "Return to JEDuBois, Jr." On Weisbrodt, cf. with caution Gausmann, *Deutsche Großunternehmer*, 368–69. Cf. also NARA, RG 238, Entry 159, Box 5, Folder 3: M. L. Kove, Preliminary Outline of Personal Responsibility of Fritz ter Meer, I. G. Farben Trial Team, October 31, 1946: here it was determined that von Schnitzler's comments inculpated ter Meer.

144. Bundesarchiv, N 1814/32: Ter Meer to F.I.A.T., Frankfurt-Höchst, March 30, 1946. Interestingly, these and other documents on this are in the estate of August von Knieriem, who was also imprisoned in Kransberg.
145. Bundesarchiv, N 1814/32: Zusammenfassende Richtigstellung des "Statement by Geheimrat Dr. Hermann Schmitz" vom 17. Sept. 1945 – Draft (Entwurf).
146. Bundesarchiv, N 1814/32: Schmitz Memorandum of August 26, 1946, on his statement of September 17, 1945; attached also is an original version of the statement of September 17, 1945, and a final version on September 17, 1945.
147. Fritz-Bauer-Institut, Archiv, I. G. Farben-Prozess, NI-5187: Affidavit of Hermann [*sic*] ter Meer of April 15, 1947.
148. NI-5187: Affidavit of Hermann [*sic*] ter Meer of April 15, 1947, 1–4.
149. OMGUS, *Ermittlungen*, introduction by the editor (Karl Heinz Roth), lvii–lviii; *Trials of War Criminals*, vol. VII, 1498–1524.
150. Brünger, *Geschichte und Gewinn*, 67; here he also states that all the members of the board had been arrested and interrogated by their respective occupation authorities by winter 1945; this is not entirely correct since some, like Kühne, were not taken in for interrogation.
151. Fritz-Bauer-Institut, Archiv, I. G. Farben-Prozess: Protokoll der Hauptverhandlung deutsch, Militärgericht Nr. VI, 13456–57 (May 3, 1948) (hereinafter: Hauptverhandlung Fall VI—it would be possible to list the individual reels of film, but since page numbers are provided from the first to the last session, this seems like a solution that can be well verified and is clear). Direct quotations are also cited according to the English Transcript of the Proceedings, Case VI, here 13168.
152. Hauptverhandlung Fall VI, 14530–39 (May 10, 1948). English Transcript of the Proceedings, Case VI, quotes from 14156, 14160, 14161–62, 14163–64.
153. Lilly von Schnitzler to Carl Schmitt, November 29, 1946, in Rieß, ed., "Lilly von Schnitzler – Carl Schmitt. Briefwechsel 1919 bis 1977," 113–256, here 171–73.
154. Bayer Archiv, 207/023: Siemers to the defense counsels in the I. G. Farben trial, December 10, 1947.
155. Fritz-Bauer-Institut, Archiv, I. G. Farben-Prozess, NI-5187: Affidavit of Hermann [*sic*] ter Meer of April 15, 1947, 4–5.
156. NI-5187: Affidavit of Hermann [*sic*] ter Meer of April 15, 1947, 6–9.
157. NI-5187: Affidavit of Hermann [*sic*] ter Meer of April 15, 1947, 10.
158. NI-5187: Affidavit of Hermann [*sic*] ter Meer of April 15, 1947, 12.
159. NI-5187: Affidavit of Hermann [*sic*] ter Meer of April 15, 1947, 12–15.
160. NI-5187: Affidavit of Hermann [*sic*] ter Meer of April 15, 1947, 15–17.
161. NI-5187: Affidavit of Hermann [*sic*] ter Meer of April 15, 1947, 18–19.
162. F NI-5187: Affidavit of Hermann [*sic*] ter Meer of April 15, 1947, 19–37.
163. Brünger, *Geschichte und Gewinn*, 70; for his summary of the memorandum, see 67–70.
164. Unternehmensarchiv BASF, W.1.3./114 and 115: Kugler, *Farben: Chance und Schicksal*, 363.
165. Kugler, *Farben: Chance und Schicksal*, 363–64.
166. Kugler, *Farben: Chance und Schicksal*, 370–74. Cf. Georg von Schnitzler to Carl Schmitt, September 9, 1950: According to von Schnitzler, the prosecution had attempted to "bring me and my director Kugler behind bars for life due to Czechoslovakia," in Rieß, ed., "Lilly von Schnitzler – Carl Schmitt," 191–93.
167. Taylor, *Anatomy*, 632.
168. Seliger, *Politische Anwälte*, 110–11.
169. See Jung, *Rechtsprobleme*, 36–37.
170. Bundesarchiv, AllProz 3 Siemers/86: see, inter alia, Dix to Horn, November 26, 1946, including the information about the letter exchange; Siemers to President of the Hamburg Bar Association, December 23, 1946.

171. Bundesarchiv, AllProz 3 Siemers/86: Dix to the Board of the Bar Association in Hamburg, November 8, 1946 (copy).
172. Bundesarchiv, AllProz 3 Siemers/86: Dix to the German Lawyers' Association, c/o Dr. Emil von Sauer, April 19, 1949 (copy); invitation for Dix in Deutscher Anwaltverein to Rudolf Dix, April 12, 1949 (copy). Cf. by contrast Seliger, *Politische Anwälte*, 111, who seems to underestimate the conflict.
173. Bundesarchiv, AllProz 3 Siemers/85: Horn to Siemers, February 24, 1947.
174. Taylor, *Anatomy*, 625: Taylor incorrectly counts the lawyer Otto Nelte among those departing, who, however, represented Heinrich Hörlein in the I. G. Farben case.
175. Drexel Sprecher Papers, Box 62, Publication Project File, Publications—Staff in all cases: Public Information Office OCCWC, January 27, 1949: List of Defense Counsels.
176. Seliger, *Politische Anwälte*, 82–83; on Nazi Party members in the Third Reich, see Benz, "Nationalsozialistische Deutsche Arbeiterpartei," in *Enzyklopädie des Nationalsozialismus*, 601–606, here 604. The unusually high percentage of Nazi Party members among the defense might also have to do with the fact that younger lawyers who were completing their studies under the Nazi regime were generally educated as National Socialists in the community camps of the reformed traineeship education system, which were obligatory at the time—see on this Schmerbach, *Das "Gemeinschaftslager Hanns Kerrl" für Referendare in Jüterbog 1933–1939*.
177. Private Papers of Herbert Nath, Munich/Grünwald (hereinafter: NL Nath), Herbert Nath, Aus der Kulisse des Nürnberger Prozesses, n.d., 83–84.
178. James Morris Papers, Box 1, Folder 19: Taylor, An Outline of the Research and Publication Possibilities of the War Crimes Trials, November 1948, quote from 10.
179. Seliger, *Politische Anwälte*, 226–27; see also Taylor, *Anatomy*, 143–44, 152–58.
180. Seliger, *Politische Anwälte*, 136–38.
181. NL Nath, Nath, Aus der Kulisse des Nürnberger Prozesses, 167.
182. NL Nath, Nath, Aus der Kulisse der Nürnberger Prozesse, 158.
183. Seliger, *Politische Anwälte*, 62–69, 177; see also footnote 496.
184. Seliger, 294–96.
185. Seliger, 112; see also footnote 276.
186. Taylor, *Anatomy*, 385, 133.
187. Taylor, 410, 413.
188. Seliger, *Politische Anwälte*, 268.
189. Bundesarchiv, AllProz 3 Siemers/88: Siemers to his mother, February 3, 1946.
190. NL Nath: various CVs; Seliger, *Politische Anwälte*, 190.
191. Seliger, *Politische Anwälte*, 241.
192. NL Heimerich 24/1972a-449: Note by Heimerich on December 21, 1945, with regard to Prof. Dr. Krauch. Heimerich, *Lebenserinnerungen*, 66–68, about the years 1934–44; Parzer, *Mannheim*, 17, 46–53.
193. Seliger, *Politische Anwälte*, 243. For a detailed biography of Wagner, see Marquet, *Friedrich Wilhelm Wagner*.
194. See Heintzeler, *Im Jahrhundert*, 117; correspondingly, see Seliger, *Politische Anwälte*, 244.
195. Kempner, *Ankläger einer Epoche*, 267.
196. NL Heimerich 24/1972a-449: Note by Ilse Bethge on December 9, 1945, about the discussion on December 9, 1945, in Dr. Heimerich's office. On the work with the press, cf. also his letter to Dr. Helmut Cron, December 19, 1945.
197. NL Heimerich, 24/1972a-449: Philipp Möhring to Heimerich, October 10, 1946; a letter from Dix is quoted in the letter.
198. Unternehmensarchiv BASF, W.1.3./114 and 115; Kugler, *Farben: Chance und Schicksal*, 363.
199. NL Heimerich, 24/1972a-449: Note by Ilse Bethge for Heimerich, November 12, 1946—according to the note, this was the opinion of the lawyer Friedrich Bergold.

200. NL Heimerich 24/1972a-449: Heimerich to the lawyer Pelckmann (Nuremberg), January 7, 1947.
201. NL Heimerich, 24/1972a-449: Pelckmann to Heimerich, January 24, 1947.
202. NL Heimerich, 24/1972a-449: Ilse Bethge to Heimerich, February 22, 1947; Unternehmensarchiv BASF W.1.3./114 and 115: Kugler, *Farben: Chance und Schicksal*, 377; see also Seliger, *Politische Anwälte*, 240–41.
203. Bayer Archiv, 207/023: Henze, Report on meeting of defense lawyers of April 24, 1947 (without a list of those present).
204. Seliger, *Politische Anwälte*, 228–29; on Kraus, see Seliger, *Politische Anwälte*, 177–80, 374–75.
205. Bayer Archiv, 315/091 Silcher: Silcher to Georg von Schnitzler, January 28, 1954; however, Müller had originally worked for Siemers—see Bundesarchiv, AllProz 3/274: Siemers to Employment Office Nuremberg, July 11, 1947: "I intend to hire Dr. Rolf Walter Müller to support my work on the defense in the trial against the managers at I. G. Farben. The aforementioned worked for many years at I. G. Farben on the legal staff." And, in a series of documents from Siemer's office, Müller's signature is present, for instance in Bayer Archiv, 207/006: Rundschreiben Büro Siemers an Verteidiger im Fall VI, November 10, 1947, signed by Dr. Müller; and directly from him, Bayer Archiv, 207/007 vol. 2: Dr. Müller, Administrative Assistant, an die Herren Verteidiger im Fall VI, April 27, 1948.
206. Bundesarchiv, AllProz 3 Siemers/84: Ausgaben (expenses) Nürnberg, October 9, 1946.
207. Bundesarchiv, AllProz 3 Siemers/85: Siemers to Horn, March 11, 1947.
208. Bundesarchiv, AllProz 3 Siemers/85: Horn to Siemers, February 24, 1947.
209. Archiv für Christlich-Demokratische Politik, St. Augustin, Bestand 01-237-051/6: Private Papers of Wahl, Eduard (hereinafter: NL Wahl): Letter from Heimerich to Wahl, June 19, 1947.
210. See Jonathan Wiesen, "Die Verteidigung der deutschen Wirtschaft: Nürnberg, das Industriebüro und die Herausbildung des Neuen Industriellen," 630–52, here 638–39.
211. Staatsarchiv Freiburg, T 1 Friedrich Drischel 52: Aide Memoire [by Ambros] for Dr. Drischel [Ambros's lawyer], Betr.: Prof. Kurt H. Meyer, Nürnberg, June 4, 1947. Here it states that Meyer was "a close friend of Goldschmidt [added by hand: Th. Goldschmidt, Essen, Chem. factory], who as you know is providing me with a lot of help." See also the letter from Drischel to Meyer on July 17, 1947, in which he sends Meyer the piece by Ambros, "not signed, in light of the circumstances."
212. Seliger, *Politische Anwälte*, 270–71; Bayer Archiv, 356/007: Ambros to Silcher, April 14, 1969: "It is a comforting feeling to know that the 'great assistance' that is regularly sent from Leverkusen to us 'Nurembergers' is continuing." Hoechst Archiv, Personalakten Prof. Lautenschläger, Lautenschläger, Erinnerungen, vol. VIII, [81]: mentions packages of donations, in particular from Ludwigshafen and Leverkusen for those detained and their families; Staatsarchiv Nürnberg, KV-Verteidigung, Handakten Sauter 38: handwritten letter from Elisabeth Lautenschläger to lawyer Sauter, May 13, 1947: here it states that she was informed "that the entire management of the factory would stand up for my husband [Carl Ludwig Lautenschläger] and you [Sauter], if you need this, should not hesitate to get in contact with them." Cf., however, Lindner, *Inside IG Farben*, 344.
213. Bayer Archiv, 207/023: Henze to Justizrat Dix, Siemers, Flächsner, Pelckmann, April 26, 1947.
214. Unternehmensarchiv BASF, W.1.3./114 and 115: Kugler, *Farben: Chance und Schicksal*, 376.
215. Bayer Archiv, 207/007-001: Kühne, Erinnerungen an Nürnberg (undated).
216. NL Heimerich, 24/1972a-759: Heimerich: Meeting with the lawyer Henze, May 3, 1947.
217. NL Heimerich, 24/1972a-759: Heimerich to Henze, May 8, 1947; a copy of this letter is also in Unternehmensarchiv BASF, Rechtsanwalt Wagner.
218. Staatsarchiv Nürnberg, KV-Verteidigung, Handakten Sauter 38: Handwritten invitation from Henze to Sauter on May 15, 1948, to a discussion that was to take place that same day of the "gentlemen at Rathenauplatz at the Tuchergaststätte who are interested in I. G. Farben."

219. NL Heimerich, 24/1972a-759: Note by Heimerich from May 18, 1947, about meetings that took place from May 14 to 17, 1947. The discussion with Krauch, in which he stated he would not take on the defense, took place on May 16.
220. Staatsarchiv Nürnberg, KV-Verteidigung, Handakten Sauter 38: Letters from Sauter to Hörlein, Lautenschläger, and Jähne, May 16, 1947. I found the reference to this resignation in Seliger, *Politische Anwälte*, 143.
221. See Seliger, *Politische Anwälte*, 79–80 and 143—he seems to have a positive view of Sauter.
222. Taylor, *Anatomy*, 393.
223. Cf. Staatsarchiv Nürnberg, KV-Verteidigung, Handakten Sauter 38: handwritten letter from Heinrich Hörlein to Sauter, May 25, 1947; handwritten letter from Marie Hörlein to Sauter, June 12, 1947.
224. NL Heimerich, 24/1972a-759: Note by Heimerich from May 18, 1947, in re: Prof. Krauch; Heimerich to Henze, May 19, 1947; Heimerich to Maria Krauch, May 19, 1947; Memo, May 19, 1947: Matter related to Prof. Krauch.
225. NL Wahl, 01-237-055/6: Heimerich to Böttcher, May 27, 1947 (copy for Wahl); NL Heimerich, 24/1972a-759: Heimerich to Henze, May 27, 1947; Note by Heimerich from June 2, 1947, about the meeting at Prof. Wahl's [on May 31, 1947]; Böttcher to Öser, June 2, 1947; Seliger, *Politische Anwälte*, 240–41: According to Seliger, Böttcher was possibly recommended by Silcher, with whom he had published on the ordinance on dividends during the war.
226. NL Heimerich, 24/1972a-759: Note by Heimerich on June 17, 1947, for Böttcher and Wahl on the discussion of the defense that same day; Heimerich to Wahl, June 19, 1947.
227. NL Heimerich, 24/1972a-759: Heintzeler to Heimerich, June 21, 1947.
228. NL Heimerich, 24/1972a-759: Heimerich to Maria Krauch, June 24, 1947.
229. NL Heimerich, 24/1972a-759: Note by Heimerich on July 18, 1947, on the discussion with Böttcher, Wahl, and Fehsenbecker at Prof. Wahl's residence on July 17, 1947; Heimerich to Böttcher, August 18, 1947; Heimerich to Böttcher, September 9, 1947; Note by Heimerich from September 13, 1947, on the discussion with Prof. Wahl in his residence; Wahl to Heimerich, April 20, 1948.
230. NL Heimerich, 24/1972a-759: Böttcher to Heimerich, October 31, 1947.
231. NL Heimerich, 24/1972a-759: Heimerich to Holdermann, November 29, 1947.
232. NL Heimerich, 24/1972a-759: Heimerich to Böttcher, February 6, 1948.
233. NL Heimerich, 24/1972a-759: Böttcher to Heimerich, January 23, 1948.
234. Seliger, *Politische Anwälte*, 238.
235. Staatsarchiv Freiburg, T 1 Nachlass Ernst Bürgin 22: Hermann Schmitz an saemtliche mitangeklagten Kollegen und Mitarbeiter der I.G.-Farbenindustrie AG [undated, likely in spring/summer 1947].
236. *Trials of War Criminals*, vol. VII, 8–9.
237. Drüll, *Heidelberger Gelehrtenlexikon*, vol. 4: *1933–1986*, 644–45; Schroeder, *"Eine Universität für Juristen und von Juristen,"* 566–71. On Wahl, see now Lepej, *Rechtswissenschaft und Rechtspolitik: Eduard Wahl (1903–1985)*; Glahé, *Amnestielobbyismus für NS-Verbrecher: Der Heidelberger Juristenkreis und die alliierte Justiz 1949–1955*, 159, 165–69.
238. NL Wahl, 01-237-055/6: Wahl to Böttcher, February 9, 1948: "By the way, yesterday Dr. Kranzbühler was here and offered me the same position as the one I have for the I. G. Farben trial in the Krupp trial. I see more and more, though, that I cannot add yet a further addition to my many responsibilities and therefore declined, despite the fact that what I am able to determine in our trial would automatically be of assistance in the Krupp trial." See also Seliger, *Politische Anwälte*, 238–39.
239. Seliger, *Politische Anwälte*, 242–43.
240. Seliger, *Politische Anwälte*, 240.

241. Unternehmensarchiv BASF, Privatakten W. Heintzeler, vol. I, von Metzler to Heintzeler, October 29, 1948.
242. Unternehmensarchiv BASF, W.1.3./114 and 115: Kugler, *Farben: Chance und Schicksal*, 377.
243. Seliger, *Politische Anwälte*, 239–41.
244. Cf., e.g., Heintzeler, *Im Jahrhundert*, 126, 132–34.
245. Seliger, *Politische Anwälte*, 225–27.
246. Bayer Archiv, 207/006: Siemers' office, Dr. Müller, to the defense counsels in Case VI, January 30, 1948, and February 6, 1948, on power of attorney for the lawyers Carroll and Foley; Bayer Archiv, 207/017: Copy of a letter from Carroll to General Clay (January 19, 1948). On Carroll, cf. Seliger, *Politische Anwälte*, 231–34, especially footnote 699, which states that the I. G. Farben defense team had wanted to involve him but had not further pursued this. See also Priemel, *The Betrayal*, 182–83.
247. James Morris Papers, Box 1, Folder 1: Morris to Governor Fred Aanda[h]l, August 15, 1947.
248. Zeck, *Nuremberg*, 369.
249. NL Heimerich, 24/1972a-759: Wahl to Heimerich, April 20, 1948.
250. Smith, *The Papers of General Lucius D. Clay: Germany 1945–1949*, vol. 1, 261–62, Document 155: Clay to Echols, September 4, 1946; Taylor, *Final Report*, 34–36.
251. Cf. Taylor, *Final Report*, 34–36; Heller, *The Nuremberg Military Tribunals*, 41–42; Oberndörfer, "Recht und Richter," 537–41.
252. James Morris Papers, Box 1, Folder 1: Morris to George Moses, Associated Press, August 25, 1947; cf. also Morris to Dr. Peik, September 4, 1947. Taylor, *Final Report*, 35–36.
253. Smith, *Lucius D. Clay: An American Life*, 303, 305.
254. *Trials of War Criminals*, vol. VII, 5: Order constituting the Tribunal.
255. Bellamy, *Hoosier Justice*, 17–18.
256. Bellamy, *Hoosier Justice*, 19–24.
257. Bellamy, *Hoosier Justice*, 24–31.
258. Bellamy, *Hoosier Justice*, 31–36; for his biography, see also Drexel Sprecher Papers, Box 52, Procedure/Press File, Press and Nuremberg Trials: Public Relations Office, OCCWC Background Information—Judges of the Six Military Tribunals, [undated]; James Morris Papers, Box 1, Folder 18: List of the judges of the subsequent trials with biographic information.
259. Taylor, *Final Report*, 36; see also footnotes 98 and 100.
260. Kaufman in October 1947, quoted in Priemel, *The Betrayal*, 235; see also footnote 145.
261. On Morris, cf. Meschke and Smith, "The North Dakota Supreme Court: A Century of Advances," 217–310, here 250–62, which also addresses his role in Nuremberg; James Morris Papers, Box 7, Folder 14: Biographic information on James Morris; Box 8, Folder 5: James Morris (Vita); Drexel Sprecher Papers, Box 52, Procedure/Press File, Press and Nuremberg Trials: Public Relations Office, OCCWC Background Information—Judges of the Six Military Tribunals, [undated]. It is therefore not correct when Brünger, in *Geschichte und Gewinn*, 70, writes that the tribunal consisted of two Republicans and one Democrat, since Morris was the sole Republican.
262. James Morris Papers, Box 8, Folder 1: Newspaper clipping "James Morris Announces Candidacy for Justice of N.D. Supreme Court" (March 2, 1934); Box 8, Folder 5: Morris's election letter ("Dear Friend"), October 1, 1934; Box 8, Folder 3: Nuessle to Morris, October 23, 1934, and response from Morris, October 26, 1934. North Dakota had a large number of citizens of Scandinavian and Volga German origin, who traditionally voted Republican—see on this Wilkins and Wilkins, *North Dakota: A Bicentennial History*, 107–109.
263. James Morris Papers, Box 8, Folder 2: Temme to Morris, October 8, 1934; Box 8, Folder 5: Nonpartisan League and Republican Headquarters (Lydia Langer) election letter ("Dear Friend"), October 24, 1934, with written note "Jim—they sure want to beat you."

264. See Robinson, *History of North Dakota*, 403–16, 466–67; Smith, *Langer of North Dakota: A Study in Isolationism 1940–1959*, 23–39; Wilkins and Wilkins, *North Dakota*, 114–20.
265. Smith, *Langer of North Dakota*, 132–54, on the German question.
266. On Muench, cf. Brown-Fleming, *The Holocaust and Catholic Conscience*, 6–8, 26–28, 41–43.
267. Wilkins and Wilkins, *North Dakota*, 153.
268. James Morris Papers, Box 7, Folder 11: Knauf & Knauf (John Knauf) to Morris, July 7, 1947.
269. James Morris Papers, Box 1, Folder 1: Morris to Charles Robertson, Member of Congress, September 15, 1947; cf. Morris to Dr. Peik, September 4, 1947; cf. also Box 1, Folder 2: Morris to Chief Justice Christianson, Supreme Court North Dakota, August 13, 1947.
270. James Morris Papers, Box 1, Folder 1: Morris to Governor Fred Aanda[h]l, August 15, 1947.
271. James Morris Papers, Box 1, Folder 1: Morris to Brigadier General Heber L. Edwards, October 6, 1947.
272. James Morris Papers, Box 1, Folder 1: Morris to Governor Fred Aanda[h]l, August 15, 1947.
273. James Morris Papers, Box 1, Folder 1: Morris to Moses, August 25, 1947.
274. James Morris Papers, Box 1, Folder 1: Morris to Judge Burke, October 2, 1947.
275. James Morris Papers, Box 1, Folder 2: Morris to "Brother Boelter," April 7, 1948.
276. James Morris Papers, Box 1, Folder 2: Morris to Judge Burr, September 15, 1947.
277. Wilkins and Wilkins, *North Dakota*, 122.
278. Wilkins and Wilkins, *North Dakota*, 195.
279. Wade, "Villainy, Virtue, and Louisiana Political Culture: Paul Hebert and the Augean Stables at LSU, 1939–1941," 21–52, 31, on Hebert's biography; see also Williams, *Huey Long*, 489–91 (on honorary doctorate); 492–525 (on LSU); Brinkley, *Voices of Protest: Huey Long, Father Coughlin, and the Great Depression*, 8–35, 263–65.
280. Drexel Sprecher Papers, Box 52, Procedure/Press File, Press and Nuremberg Trials: Public Relations Office, OCCWC Background Information—Judges of the Six Military Tribunals, n.d.; James Morris Papers, Box 1, Folder 18: List of the judges of the subsequent trials with biographic information.
281. Wade, "Villainy," 48–49; Zuppi, "Slave Labor," 500; Drexel Sprecher Papers, Box 52, Procedure/Press File, Press and Nuremberg Trials: Public Relations Office, OCCWC Background Information—Judges of the Six Military Tribunals, n.d.
282. Wade, "Villainy," 50–51.
283. Hebert, "The New Nationalism: Social and Economic Planning under the Constitution," 8–21, here 20.
284. Drexel Sprecher Papers, Box 52, Procedures/Press Files, Press and Nuremberg Trials: Public Relations Office, OCCWC Background Information—Judges of the Six Military Tribunals, n.d.—here on Merrell; DuBois, *The Devil's Chemists*, 94–95, on Merrell; Bellamy, *Hoosier Justice*, 62, 56–58.
285. James Morris Papers, Box 1, Folder 2: Morris to Chief Justice Christianson, Supreme Court North Dakota, August 13, 1947.
286. James Morris Papers, Folder 2: Morris to Mr. and Mrs. Vernon Cooper, August 29, 1947.
287. USHMM Archives, RG-50.030*0382: Interview with William and Belle Zeck, September 23, 1996, 53–54.
288. Interview with William and Belle Zeck, 61.
289. Bower, *Blind Eye*, 357–58.
290. Heller, *The Nuremberg Military Tribunals*, 95–96.
291. Zuppi, "Slave Labor," 511.
292. Telford Taylor Papers, Box 29, TTP-5-1-4-63: From Deane, Nurnberg, to Dave Richardson, *Time Magazine*, July 31, 1948.

Chapter 3

The Trial

The daily court procedure during the trials was relatively strict. The working day began, as Judge Morris reported in fall 1947, with the entry of the judges, upon which, at the direction of the court marshal, all those present were expected to stand up. After everyone sat back down, the court was officially in session, and the marshal announced, "Military Tribunal VI is now in session. God save the United States of America and this Honorable Tribunal. There will be order in the court room." After this, the presiding judge would ask the marshal whether the defendants were present, and the latter would answer correspondingly. If there was no exceptional reason to do otherwise, the tribunal generally began its work at 9:30 a.m. At 11:00 a.m. there was a fifteen-minute break, after which work continued until the lunch break at 12:15 p.m. After lunch the session started up again at 1:30 p.m. At 3:00 p.m., there was a fifteen-minute tea break, after which proceedings continued until 4:30 or 5:00 p.m.[1] Either after these proceedings or interspersed within them, there were also periodic discussions with the prosecution and the defense counsels that were not open to the public.[2]

The daily routine of the tribunal was repeated over the 152 days of proceedings. Toward the end of the trial, the sessions were longer on certain days and occasionally took place on weekends. Not all were always present at them, however. Sometimes so few of the defense counsels were in the courtroom that obligatory sessions had to be set up that certain defense counsels were required to attend. Judge Shake displayed a certain polite irony when, on October 23, 1947, he expressed his pleasure at seeing so many representatives of the defense.[3]

This chapter is not able to recapitulate the trial in its entirety. In light of the large amount of material in the relevant documentation, the many long days of proceedings, and the switches between different charges on different days, this would indeed be very difficult—and would be so extensive that the overall picture would be lost in the details. Instead, this chapter will portray and analyze the most important developments in the four phases of the trial both chronologically and thematically.

In the first phase, that of the taking of evidence, the prosecution presented the indictment and its evidence, brought in witnesses, and explained its theory. In the subsequent second phase of the taking of evidence, the defense had the opportunity to present its view of matters, present its own evidence, and bring in its witnesses. The third phase involved the closing statements by the lawyers on both sides. The fourth and final phase consisted of the pronouncement of the judgment.

The First Phase of the Trial: The Presentation of the Evidence by the Prosecution

The opening session took place on August 14, 1947. First, the names of all the defendants were read. The defendant Max Brüggemann was so sick that Taylor did not object to his lawyer's request to separate his trial from that of the others. Carl Lautenschläger was excused because, as Judge Shake informed the court, his son had died the night prior. Carl Wurster, who had undergone an operation in Ludwigshafen after injuring his shoulder and was unable to travel for multiple weeks, was also excused. According to Taylor, after being presented with the charges in Ludwigshafen, he had suffered a heart attack. Wurster's lawyer had thereupon requested that he be excused or that the trial be separated. US military doctors determined, however, that he could in fact travel, and he was brought shortly thereafter to Nuremberg. These three defendants were therefore not present at the arraignment, at which the defendants were asked whether they had counsel, whether they had received the indictment with enough time to respond, whether they had been able to read the indictment, and whether they pleaded guilty or not guilty in respect of the charges.[4]

After the names of the defendants (many pictured in Figure 3.1) were read, Conrad Böttcher, Carl Krauch's defense counsel—and, as Hermann Heimerich had predicted he would be, now the representative of the defense team as a whole—began by raising two fundamental objections to the trial. First, he argued, the indictment did not correspond to the specifications of Military Ordinance No. 7, according to which accusations of individual defendants had to be made in a concrete and detailed manner; second, he argued that a "fair trial" had not been ensured. On these grounds the defense asked the court to reject the indictment in its current form as inadmissible. Böttcher also requested that the defendants, who, after all, were being tried as a group, be able to confer with each other in the future and that the defense counsels be given more time to prepare for the trial. As the final part of his "principal objections," which he did not want to have understood as a formal motion, Böttcher stated, "There can be no doubt whatever that this trial is destined to write history and to clear up the question how in the future leading industrialists of a country should conduct

Figure 3.1. Defendants and defense counsels—first row, from left: Carl Krauch, Hermann Schmitz, Georg von Schnitzler, Fritz Gajewski; second row, from left: Paul Häfliger, Max Ilgner, Friedrich Jähne, Hans Kühne; among the defense counsels, Friedrich Wilhelm Wagner (in the middle), Alfred Seidl (in the back row, second from the right). Source: Stadtarchiv Ludwigshafen N-25-46; reproduced with permission.

themselves in the event of an international conflagration. This judgment can only, however, make history if it can live up to the scrutiny of the historians."[5]

Walter Siemers, Georg von Schnitzler's defense counsel, also raised an objection to the indictment, which he considered permissible under common law, stating that the charges against the defendants were unspecific and "horrible." In his reply, Telford Taylor described Böttcher's and Siemers's statements as "irrelevant," in the case of the latter even referring to "insurgent remarks."[6] After this exchange of words, the court had the arraignment carried out.[7] Lautenschläger and Wurster had their arraignments in late August and mid-September 1947, respectively, and the charge against Brüggemann was separated from the proceedings by a decision of the court in early September 1947.[8]

At the second session, on August 27, 1947, the actual start of the trial, the judges first rejected the requests of the defense, which in the meantime had been submitted in written form: for one, the court considered the indictment to have standing and to be sufficiently detailed; also, it stated, the defense had had enough time to prepare, and there would therefore be no delay of the trial.[9]

Immediately afterward, Telford Taylor, as the chief of counsel of war crimes, began his opening remarks. At the very outset, he stated that the indictment accused the I. G. Farben managers of "major responsibility for visiting upon mankind the most searing and catastrophic war in modern history." The prosecution was accusing the defendants of "wholesale enslavement, plunder, and murder."[10] The defendants' actions, he further stated, had not been "committed in rage" or "under the stress of sudden temptation," but "with the utmost deliberation." Their goal had been to "turn the German nation into a military machine" and "build it into an engine of destruction so terrifyingly formidable" that by threats of war she could "impose her will and her dominion" on other nations. Taylor predicted that the managers being tried would defend themselves by claiming to have been "merely overzealous, and perhaps misguided, patriots" who were attempting to strengthen their country's army but were not responsible for all the misdeeds of the Nazi regime. He countered that this might sound "plausible" but that it did not correspond to reality, since the defendants had been "eager and leading participants" in the buildup of the war machinery: "They joined in stamping out the flame of liberty, and in subjecting the German people to the monstrous, grinding tyranny of the Third Reich, whose purpose it was to brutalize the nation and fill the people with hate. They marshalled their imperial resourses [*sic*] and focussed [*sic*] their very formidable talents to forge the weapons and other implements of conquest which spread the German terror. They were the warp and woof of the dark mantle of death that settled over Europe."[11]

Taylor also brought up Auschwitz and the role of the I. G. Farben managers in the construction of the factory there, "a revolting story of brutality and murder." Here too, he saw the defendants as having been in roles of leadership and responsibility: "They judged themselves entitled to subjugate and to command. They judged the Jew, the Pole and the Russian to be untouchable. All their judgments sprang from a bottomless vanity and an insatiable ambition which exalted their own power as the supreme and only good."[12]

The rhetorically brilliant start was followed by a detailed overview of the history, the growth, and the organization of I. G. Farben. The prosecution finally stated that each of the defendants had been a "key official in the organizational structure of I. G. Farben"—including the four who had not been members of the board of directors.[13] And the prosecution regretted that it had not been sufficient for the chemists and pharmacists of I. G. Farben to be "workers of beneficent miracles"; instead, they had preferred to become "architects of catastrophe."[14]

As a letter to his family in late August 1947 shows, Judge Morris's outlook at this time was still mostly positive, though he already sensed that problems might arise: "The trial will be very long and the exhibits will number in the hundreds. It is apparent that the attorneys for the defendants, by interposing every objection that they can think of, are trying out the Tribunal to see just how far they can go. At the same time, they are testing the capacity of the attorneys for the prosecution whose experience as trial lawyers is somewhat limited."[15] He also demonstrated a hopeful attitude to the chief justice of the Supreme Court of North Dakota and had only positive things to say about his fellow judges.[16] But Morris quickly became more cautious: "Yesterday and today evidence was received in the form of various exhibits dealing with the early-days of the Hitler regime and its connection with the Farben Organization." He was not yet negative, however: "Most of it seems rather irrelevant at this point but I presume it will be later connected up with some or all of the defendants."[17]

Taylor's opening speech could not cover up the fact that the indictment was highly daring, counts I and V above all, since even leading figures of the Nazi state, such as Reich Ministers Hjalmar Schacht and Albert Speer, had been acquitted by the IMT of nearly the same charges.[18] And thus exactly what a memo of the prosecution had stated as a possible result prior to the trial had happened—that it would take a great effort to plausibly explain that I. G. Farben had played a central role in crimes against peace. It could become necessary, that memo had stated, to paint a full picture of the German system of preparation for the war: "This lengthy method, however, should be chosen only if it will not be possible to prove a good case of crimes against peace on our theory that I. G. Farben planned, prepared and actually waged wars of aggression by producing before and during the war in full knowledge of Hitler's plans to wage wars of aggression."[19]

To do this, in the weeks that followed, the prosecution presented vast quantities of documents and projected maps on the wall to explain in great detail the expansion of I. G. Farben and its various projects. In response to a question from Judge Shake about whether the prosecution was hereby seeking to present something other than "the knowledge and responsibility for the Farben policies on the part of these defendants," Drexel Sprecher answered that this was the "larger purpose," since the intention was to illustrate the functions of the individual defendants.[20] At the end of this session, on September 10, Judge Morris politely—but definitely—criticized the prosecution for the first time. It had presented a long list of minutes, including two on the expansion of I. G. Farben in 1937, to which the prosecution attached "considerable importance." But until the time of attack, I. G. Farben, "so far as the record shows here," had merely been a conglomerate like so many others around the world, if of a greater magnitude. And, Morris added, he did not understand "where documents of this kind are of the slightest materiality to the charges set forth in the indictment." In his personal view, "much wholly irrelevant and unconnected testimony … has gone into this record so far." Morris only wanted his criticism to be understood as a "statement of an individual member of the Court" and asked the prosecution to "consider it a little bit with the idea that if it has any merit perhaps you are going too far into details, and getting too far out into the woods with your proof."[21]

Morris had already expressed his frustration in letters over the complicated method of reading aloud all the documents that were introduced: "The majority of our Court are Middle-Westerners and we decided that entirely too much time was being wasted in the lengthy reading of exhibits to the Court after they had been introduced. We may not know so much law, international or otherwise, but we can at least read and do it faster than can be done in open court where every word must be translated into German and recorded." They even asked the lawyers to point to the most important passages in the documents: "You can realize what time will be saved when I tell you that some of the exhibits were long excerpts from Hitler's speeches and writings and lengthy reports of Farben officials to their board of directors."[22]

At the eleventh session, on September 16, Josiah DuBois explained to the court why, in the opinion of the prosecution, the documents that had been submitted until that point were relevant (see Figure 3.2). It was important to portray I. G. Farben's power in the early 1930s in order to show its leading role in the Third Reich's preparations for a war of aggression. The defendants were not before the court for having had great power but because they had used that power criminally. Proving this required demonstrating that they in fact had held such power

Figure 3.2. Josiah DuBois (standing at the lectern) at the presentation of the indictment. Representatives of the prosecution are at the lower right in the picture. The judges are at the upper right. On the left are the I. G. Farben managers in the dock, and in front of them are their defense counsels. Source: NARA 238-OMT-VI-GV-6; NL Nath; public domain.

and explicating what type of power this was. If someone were to shoot someone else, proof of possession of a pistol was sufficient evidence that the person could kill: "But where, as here, a criminal assault upon a whole world is charged, the proof is more complex. And, unfortunately in some respects, it is often extremely dull. It is nonetheless basic and vitally relevant to show what power it was that the accused commanded." Portraying I. G. Farben's global reach was therefore important, he argued, since the defendants had used it for propaganda and espionage in the preparations for a war of aggression. At the end of his remarks, DuBois emphasized that the prosecution was accusing the defendants of "major responsibility in preparing Germany for an aggressive war and in participating in waging that war. To prove that charge we must show not only the total of power which they collectively commanded. We must also show the place and power of each individual in the collective whole." Without such evidence, DuBois stated, the court would not be able to "properly assess individual guilt or innocence under law." In an attempt to mollify the court, however, DuBois promised to attempt to explain in the future why each document was being introduced.[23]

Nonetheless, the prosecution proceeded to introduce large numbers of documents in order to shed light on I. G. Farben's role, including, in addition to contracts and documents, an article by Major General Löb in the magazine *Vierjahresplan* about the conglomerate's major role in the production of synthetic fuels and excerpts from the popular science book *Wissenschaft bricht Monopole*, by Anton Zischka.[24] In late September Morris asked again whether it was truly necessary to go into such detail about the contracts that I. G. Farben had signed with the state, expressing doubt about whether the details were in fact "necessary." Morris Amchan responded on behalf of the prosecution that he considered them necessary, even if they did seem "irrelevant."[25]

Added to this was a conflict between the prosecution and the defense about how to deal with affidavits and what the legal framework was about cross-examining these affiants—especially in light of the difficulty of traveling in Germany at the time. Since the two sides could not come to an agreement, the court found itself forced to make a procedural decision.[26] It decided that both sides were free to offer any individuals who had submitted affidavits for cross-examination. If someone gave testimony, the cross-examination would follow immediately. However, this was "not practical" when dealing with affidavits. The prosecution therefore could invite the affiants to cross-examination at any time. The defense would be required to give notice if they intended to cross-examine, and the prosecution would have to provide information about when it planned to fit this into the proceedings.[27]

Correspondingly, on October 1, various members of the defense carried out a thorough interrogation of a witness of the prosecution, Werner Hagert, during which Morris finally intervened because he considered a question not to be "fair."[28] The following day he even called for the cross-examination of the witness

Paul Otto Schmidt, a former interpreter for Hitler, to be brought to an end, since it had become "more of a badgering of the witness" by the defense.[29] On October 3, and in light of these experiences, the three judges jointly explained the proper way to carry out a cross-examination and what it should consist of. They also confirmed that declining to cross-examine a witness was not considered equivalent to agreeing with the statements in that witness's affidavit.[30] The day prior, Morris had written to North Dakota with frustration: "Neither the German lawyers nor the German witnesses have the slightest conception of brevity or conciseness. The lawyers' questions are long and involved and the witnesses' answers are still longer and more involved. I am beginning to wonder if there are such words in the German language as 'yes' and 'no.'"[31]

The problems of digression during the trial and of the overburdening of the trial with genuinely irrelevant material led to further sharp criticism by Judge Morris during a hearing on Carl Bosch's role in the Nazi regime. He noted that this was "an excellent example" of "absolutely wasting the time of this Tribunal." In connection with questions about the defendant Krauch, the discussion had switched over to Bosch, and then a member of the prosecution had addressed Fritz Thyssen's attitude toward the Nazi regime: "If we are going to try the attitude of various people throughout Germany, just as a matter of comparison with Bosch or with the defendant or anyone else, then there certainly isn't any limit at all to relevancy as far as this case is concerned." Morris was attempting thereby to make it clear to both the prosecution and the defense how "utterly irrelevant testimony and evidence can become." Judge Shake agreed with these comments.[32]

Toward the end of October, the question of what to do with affidavits whose authors were not available for cross-examination was discussed. On the legal basis of Military Ordinance No. 7, Drexel Sprecher believed that the right to cross-examination existed only if the witness could be brought in. Asked by Shake whether there was a difference between the IMT and the subsequent trials, since the former was international and the latter "an American court constituted under American law," Sprecher responded that he was of the view that the tribunal was engaged in "enforcing international law" and that it was free to apply "any procedure authorized within Ordinance No. 7 which will ensure a fair and just trial." Shake responded that all were in agreement that the legal basis and foundation of the tribunal rested on an international agreement. Probing further, however, he asked whether this meant that jurisdiction should be interpreted, as in the case of the IMT, more freely, or more strictly. Sprecher responded that the procedure should be handled more liberally. The lawyer Otto Nelte, Heinrich Hörlein's defense counsel, responded that the "principle" for the tribunal should be fairness: "It's clear that in a proceeding, that is, this one, which has to be directed according to international law as well as international procedure cannot keep its rules very rigid. However, there must be one limit. This limit means the maintenance of the rights of these defendants." Shake then noted that they would "follow the sound practice" and asked the other judges to take a position. Judge Morris declined to take a position, and Judges Hebert and Merrell agreed with the position of the prosecution with regard to Ordinance No. 7. The lawyer Friedrich Silcher recommended that no immediate fundamental decision on this matter be taken, after which Shake called for both sides, the prosecution and the defense, to attempt to come to an agreement.[33]

At the thirtieth session, which took place on the afternoon of that same day, October 21, 1947, the prosecution began to present the evidence for count II—until then it had only presented the evidence for count I.[34]

By the following day, Judge Morris had already intervened and asked the prosecution to clarify whether spoliation was a war crime or also a crime against humanity, since he was afraid that it would involve "a lot of time wasted on irrelevant evidence and exhibits" which would unnecessarily lengthen the trial. Since the prosecution particularly wanted to address the spoliation in Austria and Czechoslovakia, which constituted invasions but had not taken place during a state of war and therefore did not count as war crimes, Drexel Sprecher and Morris Amchan contended on behalf of the prosecution that it would be possible to pursue spoliation as a crime against humanity, which did not require that it have occurred during a state of war.[35]

That same day, after correcting Randolph Newman, a representative of the prosecution, for making a mistake in the numbering of the evidence materials, Morris again could not hold back from reproaching the prosecution for presenting "a lot of irrelevant evidence." Sprecher, who himself claimed to be the person primarily responsible, countered that the prosecution's task had been difficult. It had made a great effort to present only material that provided conclusive evidence, but, as Control Council Law No. 9 showed, most of the free world saw it as a "fact" that I. G. Farben had, in the law's words, "knowingly and prominently engaged in building up and maintaining the German war potential." While Shake tended to agree with Morris, Hebert expressed his support for the prosecution and called for the court to take on the evidence "with an open mind." It was not possible at that point in the trial, Hebert stated, to say what was or was not of importance. He further stated: "Obviously, with reference to Count 1, on which the major portion of the time has been consumed so far, we are dealing with the very elusive concept of the knowledge of these defendants, the knowledge which would be necessary to charge them with criminal responsibility under the precedents laid down by the IMT, and I can fully appreciate the difficulties which confront the Prosecution in selecting evidence." Hebert also feared that there could be similar problems with the other charges. Merrell agreed with Hebert, criticizing the other two judges, to which Morris responded by once again stating that the trial could not be brought to the intended speedy conclusion if the prosecution and the defense did not cooperate. He argued that "the obligation is primarily that of the Prosecution to not encumber the record with irrelevant material, for irrelevancy breeds and begets irrelevancy, and when something is introduced in the record by the Prosecution that should not be there, the Defense no doubt will feel that they in turn are required to meet it … " If the transcript were to become "too long, too complicated, too cumbersome in its procedure," then the prosecution would be "primarily" responsible. He had hoped to "somewhat guide" the prosecution by indicating what he considered to be irrelevant, and only for that reason had he made comments. Bringing the discussion to a conclusion, Shake stated that he considered it positive that all the judges openly expressed their opinions. Now he wanted, not as the presiding judge, but as a member of the tribunal, to share his opinion, which "differ[ed] from the attitude of two of my colleagues." Shake stated that he did not have "any sympathy whatsoever for the prosecution in this case, or any sympathy for any defendant in this case" and would, as far as possible, make his decision "devoid of sympathy for any person" and "only according to what I understand to be the law and the evidence."[36]

The prosecution noted on this day that Judge Morris had called its claim that I. G. Farben had known about the invasion of Czechoslovakia "an inference upon an inference." Morris had then commented that it seemed that the introduction of irrelevant evidence was continuing. The prosecution responded that it was trying to sort out the evidence. Judge Shake agreed with Morris's criticism that the prosecution was introducing a lot of "purely cumulative" documents. In response, Judges Hebert and Merrell formulated a dissent and emphasized that the complexity of the charge of a war of aggression required that the court be open minded toward the prosecution and its evidence.[37]

For all involved in the trial, this represented a clear moment of fracture on the judges' bench. Josiah DuBois reported on this in a letter to Belle Mayer in early November 1947: "On the whole the case is progressing better than I expected despite another blow-up which occurred shortly after Jan [Charmatz] left for Paris. This blow-up involved another outbreak by Judge Morris concerning the relevance of documents, but this time he was promptly answered by Judge Hebert and Judge Merrell, whereas Judge Shake assumed the role of trying to keep peace in the family. It brought out in the open, however, a clear split in the Court and on the whole I think it is a good thing that it came out." DuBois did not conclude, however, that the prosecution should reconsider how to proceed: "I think that the split within the Court is of such a nature that the brief that we submit on aggressive war may either make or break our case in this respect."[38] This was without a doubt a problematic conclusion to draw, as Kim Priemel has shown, because it implied that the prosecution needed to win Judges Morris and Shake over to their theory and argument instead of betting on Judge Merrell, who was a substitute judge and whose vote therefore did not count if none of the three judges withdrew.[39]

Even though the prosecution had already started on count II, the evidence for count I had not been presented in its entirety. Therefore, there were multiple days when more than one count was addressed in the court proceedings—which also presents difficulties for the descriptions in the present study. In order to portray Max Ilgner's role and the role of his office as a center of espionage for the Nazi regime for the purposes of count I, the prosecution called Rudolf Diels, the first head of the Gestapo, to the stand as a witness. Diels had submitted an affidavit stating that in 1933 Ilgner had offered to work for the Gestapo outside of Germany. During the cross-examination, Ilgner's defense counsel, Herbert Nath, attempted to undermine this claim by describing Ilgner's visit to Diels as a mere introductory conversation, and then got Diels to state that Ilgner's offer did not have any connection to a possible war of aggression.[40]

The prosecution's presentation of evidence went much better for count II than for count I. In late October 1947, it was even able, with the help of the witness Maurycy Szpilvogel, to cast the defendants in a particularly bad light in view of I. G. Farben's acquisitions of Polish companies. Szpilvogel, a Jewish Pole who was by then living in Switzerland, had been the proprietor of the Wola chemical factory. In the course of the occupation of Poland, his company had been seized by employees of I. G. Farben, and Szpilvogel, along with his family, had been sent to the Warsaw ghetto. From there he had sent a letter to Georg von Schnitzler, whom he knew personally and had "met frequently" and with whom he had been on "friendly terms." He had asked von Schnitzler for a position at Wola, and he and his wife had also asked von Schnitzler and Dr. Schwab, the trustee in charge of the factory and an I. G. Farben employee, for support, in particular for his son, who was sick. Von Schnitzler, according to Szpilvogel, "did not comply with my request."[41] In the cross-examination that followed, von Schnitzler's defense counsel, Rupprecht von Keller, attempted first to focus on the nationalization of industry in Poland after 1945, and then to make the company seem like a small piece, in other words attempting to minimize the importance and value of the factory, including by focusing on a fire at Wola and spoliation carried out by Poles. Von Keller also attempted to downplay I. G. Farben's role and to portray Schwab as an official and trustee who was only doing his duty. He finally emphasized his sorrow over the killing of the Jews and asked Szpilvogel whether I. G. Farben had played a role in this, which the latter denied. Szpilvogel emphasized in the cross-examination, however, how sick he and his daughter, who was a survivor of Bergen-Belsen, had become owing to the persecution by the Germans and how he had gone to Sweden and then to Switzerland to stay with relatives after the war in order to find healing from all the traumatic experiences.[42]

While the prosecution's Daily Trial Report only makes a brief mention of this, one of the defendants, Hans Kugler, mentioned after the war that in all three cases of spoliation of chemical factories in Poland—Boruta, Wola, and Winnica—the defense had attempted to "describe I. G. Farben's behavior in an exculpatory way." But this had failed: "If the defense did not succeed in this, this was likely connected with the emotional effect made so tangible by the tragic fate of the former owner of Wola and his family in the handling of the Polish operations, which came to light through the documents and the hearings."[43]

In order not to lose in the duel with the prosecution, the defense therefore made a concerted effort to portray I. G. Farben as a champion of free enterprise, one that did not want to wage a war.[44] I. G. Farben and its managers were, as Kurt Krüger, one of the prosecution's witnesses from I. G. Farben's NW 7 office in Berlin, stated, seen as "the democracy-infested friends of the Jews … the industrial pirates," who had to be put a stop to. The "fear" of the nomination of a commissar for I. G. Farben had led even those who were not sympathetic to the Nazi regime, he claimed, to follow the strategy of "hunting with the great," that is adapting and even bowing to the new rulers.[45] This expression was discussed at length after this statement, and, on questioning by the defense counsel Herbert Nath, Krüger explained in great detail how difficult it had been for leading I. G. Farben managers to follow the policy of "hunting with the great." Nath then asked the purely rhetorical question of whether it was correct that there had been no protests when the workers' movement had gone through the process of *Gleichschaltung*, the Nazi process of coordination of all aspects of society, which Krüger confirmed, calling it a "shocking fact."[46] This was intended to relativize what was clearly very adaptive behavior on the part of the I. G. Farben leadership.

Shake proceeded to criticize the length of the cross-examination and the waste of time it had engendered, a criticism that Nath, who had been primarily responsible for this cross-examination, rejected, emphasizing that the prolonged questioning had been due to the witness and his affidavit—something for which the defense could not be held responsible. Not only did the defense take its responsibilities and duties "very seriously," but it also had a right to ask its own questions in cross-examination.[47] This made it clear that Morris's fears were materializing: The defense was eager to take advantage of the opportunity to laboriously question the excessive evidence submitted by the prosecution.

The evidence taking for count III did not begin until the thirty-eighth session, on October 31, 1947, with the presentation of evidence on slave labor by Virgil van Street, a representative of the prosecution.[48] This approach had earlier been criticized by Emanuel Minskoff, who had argued to Josiah DuBois that the trial should have started with Auschwitz: "We should have started with Auschwitz on the first day." DuBois, however, thought that it was already too late and, moreover, inopportune to change the prosecution's strategy. About Minskoff, he wrote, "Everybody had his baby. With him it was Auschwitz."[49] Therefore, as Taylor and DuBois had planned it, the trial was structured to follow the sequence of the charges, and what Joseph Borkin, too, considered to be the "crucial count in the indictment"—slavery and mass murder—came late, after organizational charts, cartel agreements, patent matters, and other similar subjects had been presented and discussed over long periods of time.[50]

It was clear from early on how nervous at least some of the defendants were about being indicted for Auschwitz. Otto Ambros had already told his lawyer, Friedrich Drischel, in late May 1947 that he found "the acquisition of exculpatory material on the matter of the Auschwitz concentration camp to be of top importance"—while at the same time telling Drischel "that he had chosen the location of the factory without any knowledge of the Auschwitz concentration camp."[51]

In mid-September 1947, a circular letter by Wolfram von Metzler went out to all the defense counsels, who were told to keep it strictly confidential and store it under lock and key upon receipt. Von Metzler stated the following with regard to Auschwitz: "In regard to the Auschwitz matter, which involves just a few people, I consider it best if the defense counsels of those individuals deal with these questions."[52] He thus did not want Auschwitz to be seen as the problem of the entire defense.

But just a few days into the presentation of evidence for count III, the lawyer Böttcher informed all the defense counsels about the comments Rudolf Dix had made at a meeting of the defense on November 11, 1947, including the following: "I would like to draw the attention of the defense to the unusual seriousness of the 'Auschwitz' matter. In order to gain an overview of how the defense should be organized on this charge, it seems necessary that each defendant tests and determines what knowledge he had about the conditions and the events at Auschwitz-Monowitz. These determinations must be made with the greatest conscientiousness." All were to ask themselves whether, when, and for what reason they had been at the camps as well as whether and to whom they had reported about them. Whoever had not been there was to think about when he learned of the relationship between I. G. Farben, Auschwitz, and the SS, what precisely he had learned, and in what way. All the defendants were to ask themselves whether information about Auschwitz-Monowitz was reported at the meetings of the board of directors or in committee meetings, and if so, how and by whom. Finally, all defendants were to ask themselves what they had imagined about the conditions and events at Auschwitz-Monowitz and about the responsibility that I. G. Farben had for what happened there and in the other associated camps.[53]

This nervousness was justified. When the prosecution introduced a whole series of affidavits by *Fremdarbeiter* (foreign workers), forced laborers, concentration camp inmates, and prisoners of war about the living conditions at the various I. G. Farben factories as evidence, the defense complained that there was not "equality of arms" when it came to affiants outside the country and that it would have trouble bringing in witnesses who might exculpate its clients. The court, the defense argued, should ensure that it too could acquire evidence abroad.[54]

Alfred Seidl, the defense counsel for Walter Dürrfeld, who had led the I. G. Farben factory in Auschwitz, turned directly to matters of principle: As a matter of introduction, he remarked that "[a] modern criminal trial should be guided by the principle that the proceedings should be direct and oral." This meant that "on principle witnesses should appear directly before the Court." Now, however, the court "in the case of a large number of cases has made an exception by permitting these witnesses not to be heard in the direct examination before the Tribunal but by submitting affidavits from the Prosecution." Until that point, the subject matter of the statements in the affidavits had in some cases been statistical information, in which cases it was entirely understandable that the witnesses needed to consult documents. But in the affidavits that were now being presented by the prosecution, he argued, the subject matter was "completely different," since the witnesses were making statements about what they themselves had experienced, like the witnesses of a traffic accident. Therefore, these witnesses ought to appear directly in front of the court instead of submitting statements under oath. If the affidavits in their current form were permitted, this would "prejudice the right of the Defense and make it illusory," since they contained "not just statements of facts" but also of occurrences that the witnesses knew of only from hearsay. The writers of the affidavits also drew "a lot of conclusions." According to Seidl, the witnesses' statements on the record would be different from those in the affidavits, since the former would be made under the eye of the court and the defense. Seidl also pointed out that the witnesses in this trial were "ruled by the party system"; they were not witnesses of the court but rather witnesses of the prosecution and witnesses of the defense. As a result, the prosecution had no interest in including "any statements in the affidavits which are favorable for the defendants." This had already disadvantaged the defense in the previous trials, and so far, the prosecution had declined to provide exculpatory material, something that was obligatory under German law. Finally, Seidl argued, it was also hard for a witness to correct previous statements in a cross-examination, since this could lead to a "great danger." It would therefore better serve the pursuit of the truth if the affidavits were not even introduced and the witness only appeared before the court, he claimed. Therefore, Seidl requested that the court "not admit any more affidavits" relating to "the description of working conditions."[55]

During the cross-examinations, the defense also consistently attempted to make the witnesses brought by the prosecution seem untrustworthy. Seidl in particular attempted to discredit witnesses of the prosecution—Arnost Tauber, for example—as untrustworthy communists.[56] The lawyer Friedrich Drischel, who represented Otto Ambros, attempted the same thing when he insinuated that a Jewish former concentration camp inmate who was called as a witness had also been arrested because he was a communist—not just because he was Jewish.[57] This finally led to Emanuel Minskoff anticipating this question and asking, among others, the witness Robert Elie Waitz, who described Monowitz as a death camp, whether he had ever been or was currently a member of the communist party. Waitz stated that he was not, but expressed surprise about the question.[58] Minskoff also asked a series of other witnesses about their political orientations.[59] The court finally announced that it viewed questions about the political orientation of the witnesses to be irrelevant and instructed both sides—the defense and the prosecution—to refrain from making them.[60]

The lawyer Otto Nelte, by contrast, pushed back against an affidavit by Olga Lengyel on the grounds that large parts of it relied on hearsay, namely things she had been told by her husband, who had since died. Judge Shake agreed with this assessment and asked that everything be removed from the affidavit that did not correspond to the criteria of a proper affidavit. He also added: "It seems to me personally that a large percentage of the affidavit is probably not competent at all and I may say the matter concerns the Tribunal."[61]

By mid-October, twenty-one of the twenty-three defendants had requested in writing that their defense counsels carry out prior discussions in all cases in which the interests of other defendants were affected by the cross-examination of an affiant, in order to avoid "conflicts." The defendants Carl Wurster and Heinrich Hörlein did not join the written request at the time.[62]

Only one month later, however, with the Auschwitz-Monowitz issue having become the subject of the proceedings, all twenty-three defendants requested that their defense counsels represent a unified and "solidary" line of defense, something that was "urgently necessary" in this new stage of the trial. "Irrespective of the responsibility of each individual," the signatories had unanimously selected a small committee that would convey the wishes and concerns of the defendants to the defense counsels as a group. The committee consisted of Fritz ter Meer and Walter Dürrfeld, who were both directly responsible for Auschwitz-Monowitz, as well as Max Ilgner, who was responsible for NW 7, and August von Knieriem, the former general counsel. The lawyers were to form a small committee from among their number that would include Carl Böttcher, as the speaker of the defense, and Rudolf Dix, as its future speaker. Böttcher was thus relieved of his duties as speaker and dean of the I. G. Farben defense. The defendants also wanted to have two former I. G. Farben employees from Auschwitz hired as assistants to the defense as soon as possible. Finally, the letter emphasized once again that all defendants sought to ensure, jointly and in solidarity, "irrespective of the individual level of responsibility" with regard to Auschwitz, that all the defense counsels come together "against this infamous attack on the honor of I. G. Farbenindustrie and thus of all the defendants." In the phase of the proceedings during which Auschwitz was addressed as something important for the trial as a whole, the defendants urged the defense lawyers to be present as often and in as complete a number as possible.[63]

The degree to which Fritz ter Meer and the other defendants who were affected by the "Auschwitz matter" put subtle—or not-so-subtle—pressure on the defendants who did not have anything to do with Auschwitz for this letter, is unclear. That they did so is not improbable, however, especially in light of the leading role of ter Meer, who had already put Hermann Schmitz and Georg von Schnitzler under substantial pressure in Kransberg.

A later remark by Hans Kühne, who had been a defendant at the time, to the lawyer Friedrich Silcher about the Wollheim trial is relevant to the question: "By the way, you will certainly remember from Nuremberg the feelings set off among us other board members in Nuremberg when we had to hear about matters for which Mr. Ambros and Mr. Bütefisch were responsible and which we had never heard of nor had been informed about. With the importance that the [Wollheim] trial and subsequent trials have for I. G. Farben and all stakeholders and associates, my opinion is that no consideration should be taken with regard to these two men, who already caused us enough outrage in Nuremberg. In any case, we were all in agreement that such conditions would not have prevailed in any other I. G. Farben factory."[64] But the indictment of all defendants on this charge meant that Kühne and the other defendants who were not in fact involved with Auschwitz were forced into a solidarity that in some cases they clearly did not want. And Wolfram von Metzler had not succeeded in his attempt to argue that Auschwitz should only be the problem of those responsible for the I. G. Farben factory in Auschwitz—all twenty-three defendants were affected equally.

As the prosecution began presenting the evidence for count III, as can already be seen in the remarks by the lawyer Alfred Seidl, the conflicts connected with affidavits and cross-examination became acrimonious. In light of the large amounts of evidence and the impending testimony and cross-examinations on this subject, the judges first had to find a solution to this matter. In order to ensure that the proceedings could proceed with as little delay as possible and because of the need to give the defendants the ability to cross-examine a large number of witnesses, the judges first sought to name a commissioner of the court, John H. E. Fried, who would lead the cross-examinations along with representatives of the prosecution and the defense. Seidl quickly took issue with Fried because he had previously worked for the prosecution.[65] The lawyer Böttcher objected to Fried on the same grounds on behalf of the whole defense team, too—adding that the majority of the witnesses affected were related to count III, which involved the most serious accusations, and that an appointed commissioner would have the power to operate like a judge. Of course, the IMT provided a precedent for such a step, and Ordinance No. 7 made it legally possible, but the defense nevertheless perceived in the appointment of a commissioner a "violation of the basic principle that the evidence must be given directly." Counter to this line of argument, Judge Shake argued that Fried was just a court appointee and not a judge. Judge Morris also stated that the court had the right to name a commissioner in order to "take testimony." He was "unimpressed" by the objections to Fried. Judges Hebert and Merrell agreed with the two other judges, and Judge Shake declared that Fried's appointment was a closed matter.[66]

However, the court later determined that, because of the defense's objections, Fried would not exercise this office, and appointed James G. Mulroy, a legal counsel of the court, as an additional commissioner.[67] On March 18, 1948, because of the many statements and cross-examinations that were still pending, the court also appointed Johnson T. Crawford, who had served as a judge in, among others, the "Doctors' Trial" and then the trial against Ulrich Greifelt (the RuSHA trial).[68]

On the same day the court announced Fried's appointment, the defense raised the fundamental question of whether there was a right to cross-examination and whether affidavits by deceased individuals should even be accepted by the court as evidence. Once again, Seidl, Dürrfeld's defense counsel, was the one to submit the motion. He argued that an affidavit by General Plentipotentiary for Labor Deployment Fritz Sauckel, which had been submitted by the prosecution, should not be used, since he had been sentenced to death and executed under the IMT and therefore could no longer be brought in for cross-examination: "A modern criminal trial should be guided by the principle that the proceedings should be direct and oral." This principle applied under German law and apparently also under American law, he argued—therefore "the submission of an affidavit in evidence is not admissible if the witness cannot be made available for cross examination." Since this affidavit had also been discussed in the IMT, Seidl wanted the debates that had occurred there to at least be taken into account. The same problem applied to a statement submitted by the prosecution by Rudolf Höß, the former commander of the Auschwitz concentration camp, who in the meantime had been sentenced by a Polish court and executed. This statement, moreover, had not been taken under oath—and up until this point, he argued, other Nuremberg military tribunals had not accepted statements that had not been taken under oath.[69] Judge Shake thereupon announced that he had been authorized by the court to state "that the Tribunal has decided upon principle that the affidavits of deceased heretofore offered in evidence will not be admitted in evidence in this proceeding."[70] In its Daily Trial Report, the prosecution commented, "The Tribunal stated that the right to cross examination was a fundamental right and not a mere rule of procedure and that no question of expediency should be allowed to take the place of cross examination."[71] Its request that this pronouncement be reviewed and repealed was denied by the court in early December 1947 after "due consideration." Judge Hebert added for the record, however, that he disagreed with the decision, which was not a correct interpretation of Ordinance No. 7.[72]

Hebert made a statement about another order of the court pronounced that day as well. In this case the court had decided that affidavits of various defendants could be used by the prosecution as evidence. This also related to affidavits that incriminated other defendants. The tribunal had already decided that every defendant had the right to cross-examine the writer of an affidavit. However, a defendant could not be forced to take the witness stand against his will if he would thereby incriminate himself. The need to now apply these two principles led the court to the following conclusion: "One defendant has no right to call another defendant to the witness stand over the latter's objection." However, if a defendant were to take the stand of his own free will, he could become a "witness for all purposes" and could be cross-examined by the prosecution and the other defendants who were incriminated in his affidavit. If the prosecution were to submit an affidavit of a defendant, but that defendant did not take the witness stand, the relevant statement could only incriminate the author of the affidavit, but not the other defendants affected.[73] Hebert concurred with this pronouncement, but with the proviso that it at least made possible the cross-examination of defendants who incriminated other defendants in their affidavits. However, Hebert wanted the statements that affected other defendants still to count as evidence even if a defendant did not agree to be questioned as a witness.[74]

The court as a whole also decreed on December 2, 1947, that it would not grant the defense's request for a postponement of the defense's opening statements. The defense had had plenty of time since the submission of the indictment in early May 1947, it argued. The court met only four days per week and, because of frequent interruptions, had had only fifty-three trial days. The court understood the problems that the defense team was facing but could not give it any concessions, since the court was bound by Military Ordinance No. 7, which called for a "expeditious hearing of the issues" and contained strict measures against "unreasonable delay." The defendants, the court argued, were each represented by a defense counsel and an assistant, each of whom also had access to administrative assistance. In addition, they all shared an expert in international law with an assistant as well as eight special counsels and assistants who had been appointed "to aid the Defense in the preparation of the case." Therefore, "the Tribunal would not be justified in approving any further delay in the trial of this cause."[75]

At the end of their part of the proceedings, the prosecution was expected to draft briefs—short summaries and justifications for the prosecution—for the court. The prosecution rightly took this very seriously. In early November 1947, Josiah DuBois wrote to Belle Mayer that the prosecution had to make a major effort in its briefs, especially in the case of count I, which addressed wars of aggression: "The brief that we submit on aggressive war may either make or break our case in this respect." He asked her to help him in drafting this part of the brief, not least because he was unhappy with Morris Amchan's work.[76]

Part I of the brief, more than one hundred pages long, focused on the planning, preparation, initiation, and carrying out of wars of aggression and invasions of other countries. It stated that CCL No. 10 was not intended to attach criminal guilt automatically to all persons holding high office in Nazi Germany. However, it was also clear that the law did not differentiate between "private persons" and "government officials" and that the "relation between leader and follower" did not preclude responsibility.[77] The individuals accused of crimes against peace in this trial were "those who were responsible for the activities of an organization," I. G. Farben, which the US military government had described as a substantial part of the German war machine in CCL No. 9 and in General Order No. 2.[78]

The evidence presented by the prosecution proved, it argued, that the defendants had taken part in crimes against peace in a number of significant ways and that even if not each of their actions represented participation in these crimes, together they did. The prosecution had sorted the actions of the individual defendants into various categories, such as the creation and armament of the German war machine, counterintelligence and espionage activity, hiding assets, and involvement in the spoliation of Europe and in the slave labor program of the Nazi government. Despite being introduced separately, these activities were not to be viewed individually. They should be seen, it argued, as the US Supreme Court expressed it in its 1946 ruling in *American Tobacco Co. v. United States*, which dealt with a conspiracy to subvert monopoly laws: "It is not the form of the combination or the particular means used, but the result to be achieved that the statute condemns. It is not of importance whether the means used to accomplish the unlawful objective are in themselves lawful or unlawful. Acts done to give effect to the conspiracy may be in themselves wholly innocent acts. Yet, if they are part of the sum of the acts which are relied upon to effectuate the conspiracy which the statute forbids, they come within its prohibition. No formal agreement is necessary to constitute an unlawful conspiracy. Often crimes are a matter of inference deduced from the acts of the person accused and done in pursuance of a criminal purpose."[79] This made it clear how the prosecution was building up its line of argument. It was in fact an antitrust case that was to serve as a model—and it would be beneficial if it were to be accepted by the court.

Unlike Hjalmar Schacht, Carl Krauch and I. G. Farben had never sought to distance themselves from the Nazi regime, the brief argued; rather, starting in June 1936, with Krauch's participation in the Four-Year Plan, it had even taken on a leading role.[80] I. G. Farben had been a significant participant in the creation and armament of the German war machine, it stated further, and in concert with the Nazi regime, it had used international agreements to weaken the enemies of Germany. The defendants had also taken leading roles in Nazi Germany's propaganda and espionage activities. Finally, I. G. Farben had been involved in spoliation and enslavement as part of the preparation and waging of wars of aggression and invasions. It was already clear to any intelligent person in Germany by 1936 that the Third Reich was heading inevitably toward war, even if it was perhaps not clear when it would start.[81] When Generals von Rundstedt and von Bock "were deploying the German legions on the Polish frontier in accordance with their plan of attack, Farben was carefully surveying the Polish chemical industries in anticipation of the benefits to be derived from conquest."

For twelve years, the defendants had supported Hitler and his program "whether for love, or for money, or to protect their positions, or to protect Farben." The defendants' stance had not significantly changed during these twelve years: "They never stopped howling with the wolves. They kept 'hunting with the great.'" Finally, I. G. Farben, in order to be second to none in ratifying and supporting Nazi politics, took more than their share of plunder and forced labor. The defense would most likely attempt to portray this policy as resulting from "superior orders" or "coercion," the prosecution argued. Such justifications should only be seen as attempts, however, to rely on "coercion," "where less active and less willing partnership would have meant a loss to the Farben firm and a loss of personal position and prestige."[82]

Part II of the brief, which dealt with plunder and spoliation, emphasized that these were "committed as an integral part of the planning, preparation, initiation, and waging of wars of aggression and invasions of other countries" and were thus punishable as crimes against peace. This applied to all "acts of spoliation" in occupied Europe, including in Austria and Czechoslovakia. It also quoted Georg von Schnitzler, who had stated that the Nazi regime's primary goal in the occupied countries had been to incorporate the economies of these countries to the purposes of Germany so that they would work for the German war machine. The crime of spoliation had also been "insolubly connected" with persecution on political, racial or religious grounds in all cases.[83] In Poland, Russia, and Alsace-Lorraine, I. G. Farben had taken part in the German confiscations and attempted to get its share, and in Poland, it had become a partner in spoliation. In addition to this open plundering, there also was looting that feigned to take place within the letter of the law. This occurred in Austria, Czechoslovakia, Norway, and France, where "more 'refined' methods" were resorted to.[84] For the methods in France, Georg von Schnitzler and his statements were the prosecution's chief witness.[85]

Part III of the brief, at more than one hundred pages, was even more extensive than the first part. Emanuel Minskoff had put a lot of work into this section since his arrival. It dealt in great detail with I. G. Farben's slave labor program, its delivery of Zyklon B for use in mass murder, its participation in criminal medical experiments, and its role at Auschwitz and at Fürstengrube.[86] According to the prosecution's theory, the slave labor program was part of the waging of wars of aggression and the preparation for further wars of aggression. The main crime charged under this point was "involuntary servitude and the inherent inhumanity, degradation, and maltreatment involved in the enslavement of human beings." A man's freedom was "his most precious possession." Participation in the slave labor system encouraged and condoned its inherent evil, it argued. Even if a participant attempted to slightly improve the lot of the slaves, this was at best a mitigating factor, but one of little meaning in the case of a "principal" in the crime of enslavement. The vast I. G. Farben company had been "one of the most significant markets for slaves in all of Germany"—and the leaders of I. G. Farben bore the responsibility for this.[87]

The prosecution then addressed the delivery of poison gas for the mass murder of "millions of human beings." There was overwhelming evidence, the brief stated, that the defendants knew of the extermination of people in Auschwitz using poison gas. The special sources of knowledge of the defendants made it almost superfluous to address the question of the extent to which the program to murder the Jews and other persecuted peoples was generally known. It was unimaginable that the leadership of the I. G. Farben factory knew nothing about the crimes taking place at Auschwitz concentration camp because the company used "the labor of inmates marked for extermination," had sent "those unfit for work to the gas chambers," had delivered the methanol needed for burning corpses, and "took its share of the clothes taken from the victims."[88] The brief finally focused on medical experiments in the Buchenwald and Auschwitz concentration camps, in which all the members of the board of directors at I. G. Farben had incriminated themselves as primary offenders or participants.[89]

This part also included I. G. Farben at Auschwitz, focusing on how it had taken the initiative to build a factory there using concentration camp inmates who had worked under inhumane conditions and died by the thousands. The prosecution's descriptions were supported by innumerable witness accounts and documents. The responsibility of I. G. Farben's board for the events at the Auschwitz factory, the brief argued, was "clear." Otto Ambros, it stated, had acted in Auschwitz with the approval of Carl Krauch. Most of the members of the Technical Committee shared responsibility for authorizing the funds for construction. Those who carried particular responsibility for the situation in Auschwitz, however, were the defendants Hermann Schmitz, Fritz ter Meer, Otto Ambros, Heinrich Bütefisch and Christian Schneider—and Walter Dürrfeld, who had lived there as head of the factory and had been praised for his work in a letter from Krauch in January 1943.[90]

In the concluding portion, Part VI, the prosecution dealt with its conception of responsibility. It began by stating that it would not attempt to specify the importance of each defendant but rather would address basic general theories relating to the responsibility of these defendants. The taking of evidence had shown that the defendants had participated in the activities not only as managers at I. G. Farben but in some cases "through the high political, civil, or military positions which they held in Germany."[91] With the exception of the defendants Dürrfeld, Gattineau, von der Heyde, and Kugler, all were members of I. G. Farben's board of directors, which, the prosecution stated, determined the fundamental policies of the company and without whose knowledge and authorization "no matter of importance" could happen at the company. It therefore seemed to the prosecution to be unimportant if an individual on the board of directors did not know every detail in the carrying out of a specific program;

more to the point, no one could plead ignorance with regard to a program that had taken place over such a long period of time. I. G. Farben had been a "giant concern," but "not a robot which ran by itself." It would be an "anomalous situation," both legally and factually, if it were claimed that I. G. Farben had become a "Frankenstein" that was no longer governed by humans: "The masters of this concern were the Vorstand members. There could be no other."[92] For the prosecution, there was no doubt that every board member could be "held criminally responsible for all of the activities reviewed in Parts I, II, and III of this brief," since being a member of the board of directors of I. G. Farben meant that the defendants "substantially" took part in I. G. Farben's actions and knew about "any matter of any importance."[93] The brief then addressed the responsibilities of the defendants on both the Technical and the Commercial Committees and their responsibility with regard to plunder, slave labor, medical experiments, and the delivery of Zyklon B.

Observers have drawn a number of conclusions about the prosecution's strategy. Mark E. Spicka hypothesizes that the prosecution had goals in the trials that went beyond the punishment of the defendants, and the public attorneys had organized the trial accordingly: "The prosecution allowed its view of the larger political significance of the I. G. Farben trial to skew its pragmatic considerations of the case. Taylor's wish to use the trial as means to reeducate Germany and Dubois's desire to punish I. G. Farben both resulted in a trial plan that did not stand up in court."[94] In addition, the prosecution, as Joseph Borkin and Raymond Stokes have remarked, had pursued its case in a strategically unfortunate manner: It had written an entirely undifferentiated indictment for four out of five counts, despite it being nearly impossible that all the defendants had in fact committed all the crimes of which they were accused. Borkin also notes, with the benefit of hindsight, that the prosecution had simply set up the wrong sequence for the trial, waiting too long to focus on the most severe accusations—those connected to Auschwitz.[95] One problem, according to Raymond Stokes, was that members of the prosecution coming from the Treasury Department saw I. G. Farben first and foremost as a "trust," whose defining characteristics, such as its attempt to dominate the market or even build up a monopoly, were the logical basis of its crimes and therefore needed to be portrayed to the tribunal. Ultimately, Stokes argues, the prosecution viewed the company as monolithic, and therefore it considered all the accused I. G. Farben managers guilty: "Their strategic mistakes in the case thus probably emerged naturally from a false sense that they 'knew' the concern in its essentials before the trial began."[96]

These diagnoses are surely not incorrect, especially when one considers that many of the leading representatives of the prosecution came from the Treasury Department, with its aversion to trusts. But they also fall short. The essential problem of presenting evidence to the court, especially relating to counts I and V, had already been identified by members of the prosecution, such as Francis

Shea and Sally Falk Zeck: The prosecution had too few concrete, direct pieces of evidence for its case and not infrequently had to make its argument indirectly, through inferences and circumstantial evidence. This was the reason for the prosecution's extensive expositions with their countless documents. Only by using such methods and invoking the legal concept of conspiracy could the prosecution prove its thesis that I. G. Farben had played a particularly important role in the Third Reich. Additionally, the prosecution not only "knew" the company, as Raymond Stokes writes, but was certain of the truth of its accusation that managers at I. G. Farben carried primary responsibility for Germany's wars of aggression. The prosecution saw I. G. Farben's guilt, as determined by Control Council Law No. 9, as already proved. Drexel Sprecher went so far as to state this concretely during the trial. At the same time, however, the prosecution wanted to provide clear proof of the guilt of I. G. Farben and its managers—but could only do so with inferences and indirect and circumstantial evidence.

Therefore, instead of limiting itself in the indictment against the twenty-three I. G. Farben managers to crimes or involvement in crimes that could be relatively well demonstrated, the prosecution put much time and effort into the attempt to prove the defendants' guilt for crimes under counts I and V. Not least among the consequences was the loss of valuable time that could have been used to search for evidence for crimes that were more easily proved, such as plunder or human experiments in concentration camps.

For the line of argument, it was absolutely necessary that the evidence be comprehensible—and Judge Morris was not the only one who had issues with the prosecution's conduct in the trial. Josiah DuBois himself wrote that one of the judges—either Hebert or Merrell—had taken him aside during the trial "to repeat that we would have to 'organize the case a little better.'" With reference to this warning, which had apparently been given multiple times, DuBois told one of his employees that he was worried about the judges: "They've let it be known that we'll have to organize the case some more if we want them to get the picture."[97] Clearly, the prosecution was not entirely successful in organizing itself and conveying the image it desired.

In a letter to DuBois about his book on the I. G. Farben trial, Judge Morris wrote sharply that he was grateful for the work, since despite numerous incorrect details, "It shows that I recognized early in the trial that the tribunal was confronted with an attempted prosecution upon a record that was poorly prepared and was being so haphazardly presented that the entire case would bog down in confusion unless the tribunal exercised reasonable control over the proceedings and restrained the dumping of irrelevant material."[98] Whether one finds this criticism too harsh or not, it is clear that the prosecution could have done a better job in pursuing its goal in the first phase of the trial. The prosecution also faced internal criticism—Emanuel Minskoff only formulated it in a more charitable way in a letter in February 1948, writing about his work on count III, in

Figure 3.3. A full courtroom for the opening of the trial—the lawyer Conrad Böttcher is standing at the lectern. Source: NARA 238-OMT-VI-GV-1; NL Nath; public domain.

particular on the human experiments and on Zyklon B, from the indictment. At the time he wanted to know what evidence there was: "Of course the real answer was that in typical DuBois fashion, enough extra phrases were thrown in to cover evidence that we suspected existed but which we had not quite reduced to possession."[99] (The tribunal in session at the opening, Figure 3.3, and as it wore on, Figure 3.4.)

The Second Phase of the Trial: The Defense

The previously mentioned circular letter from Wolfram von Metzler to all the defense lawyers in Case VI, which was to be treated with strict confidentiality and kept under lock and key upon receipt, was sent around on September 19, 1947. With the prosecution taking so much time, Metzler feared that the defense was going to run out of time "if the preparation of a common plan for the defense is not begun on now." He therefore wanted to present his "personal idea" for such a plan and thereby start a discussion: "In light of the tremendous amount of material that is continuously being presented to the court, it seems

Figure 3.4. The audience in the courtroom, however, was generally smaller—here, Fritz ter Meer is at the lectern. Source: NARA 238-OMT-VI-D-59; NL Nath; public domain.

urgently necessary to me to present our defense to the court systematically, in such a way as to make it easier for the court to gain an overall view of the material of the defense." The defense was correspondingly not just to be guided from the standpoint of the individual defendants. Until that time, he argued, the prosecution had not presented its evidence with a focus on individual defendants. Rather, it had organized the material according to subject matter. Therefore, he argued, the defense should use a series of coordinated opening remarks to address "certain fundamental questions that affect all the defendants," presenting its own documents, too. The defense of the individual defendants would then be linked to this approach.[100]

Von Metzler suggested six general topics to address. First, the defense should lay out the history of I. G. Farben and its development, demonstrating, with an eye to the "fundamental hostility to cartels in American circles," that a hunger for power was not the motive for the cartel agreements that lay in its past. Secondly, it should address the supposed alliance between I. G. Farben and the NSDAP, mentioning, inter alia, Gauleiter Jakob Sprenger's threats to various board members as well as the fact that the company had had "non-Aryan supervisory board members." Third, the "central problem" of the trial, the collective criminal responsibility of the board of directors, was to be given careful treatment: "While the responsibility of individual persons under international law is investigated and affirmed in the IMT verdict, the problem of the responsibility of private individuals for crimes that were the result of government policies seems to me not to have been exhaustively addressed in the IMT verdict, because it should not be forgotten that the persons accused in the IMT were all government functionaries, and therefore holders of political power, through the wielding of which they committed the crimes for which they were tried at that time." Here, von Metzler argued, attention should also be given to the fundamental difference between the civil and criminal responsibility of boards of directors, which the prosecution seemed to be blurring. Then, the defense should make clear that the views expressed in Georg von Schnitzler's statements were not shared by all—and that von Schnitzler himself no longer stood behind them, either. Fourth, it should address the charge of preparing wars of aggression. It was important to emphasize that armament was "not criminal" according to the legal provisions at the time and the IMT verdict. I. G. Farben's participation in armament was "to be seen as irrelevant" as long as the prosecution failed to "prove, at the same time, without a doubt, that the defendants positively knew that this armament served to prepare for a war of aggression, and that they were thereby taking part in a conspiracy to prepare for a war of aggression." The acquittals of Schacht, Funk, Frick, Frank, Streicher, and Kaltenbrunner on this count in the IMT were important, since these figures held important government functions and thus had "without a doubt more intimate knowledge of Hitler's intentions." With this in mind, it was important "to clarify the problem of the W Agency as soon as possible" and to determine the share of war output in total output. Fifth, the defense should address spoliation and plunder, though the role of conspiracy in this matter had mostly been abandoned. Here, the defense counsels of the defendants "who were involved in the various projects" would be in charge of explaining the issues and presenting evidence. Sixth, it should address enslavement. Reference should be made to how the topic had been presented in the Flick trial. There should be an emphasis, he argued, on how well the Fremdarbeiter were treated. And with regard to the "Auschwitz matter," von Metzler stated that "only a few men from the board" had been involved—and that it should be addressed by their respective defense counsels.

Finally, von Metzler drew attention to the fact that it was important to "acknowledge the contributions to scientific achievements and accomplishments I. G. Farben has made for the sake of humanity as a whole, and thereby to counteract the argument the prosecution made at the end of its opening remarks that the defendants were not servants of science, but rather turned science into a criminal alchemy." At the end of his seventeen-page remarks, von Metzler emphasized again, likely also as a swipe at the prosecution: "Finally, it seems important to me to point out that, based on my experience, in monster trials of this type, Anglo-Saxon judges in particular place decisive weight on the clear elaboration of the main thread, and that there is little that they have more distaste for than when the prosecution or the defense loses itself too much in the details and the main thread thereby gets mostly lost."[101]

How right von Metzler was in his final remark is clear in a letter from Judge Morris of early December 1947. He expressed his lack of enthusiasm about the progress of the trial to that point and saw the growing problems that this was causing for the prosecution, though they did not seem to be aware of them. The representatives of the prosecution had finally finished their presentation; the defense wanted to have until March to prepare its argument, but the court had only given it until mid-December: "I am afraid that the defense will be very hard to control and will drag on for a long time. The German attorneys are great for detail. The record, as built up by the prosecution, is loaded with irrelevant and cumulative evidence, much of it in the form of documents. The defense will probably attempt to meet this line by line and word by word. Moreover, the defense has everything to gain by delay. With Congress inclined to curtail expenses and with Russia creating an uncertain international situation, time certainly runs in favor of the defense."[102]

On December 18, the defendants' lawyers presented their opening statements. As had repeatedly occurred in their responses to the prosecution during the first phase, multiple different narratives or defense strategies were employed. On behalf of their clients Krauch and Schmitz, Conrad Böttcher and Rudolf Dix emphasized the tragedy of the historical situation. Böttcher, for instance, stated that Krauch was not the person that Taylor had painted him to be, but rather an "honorable, Christian, simple man" who had cooperated with the Nazi regime merely out of a sense of responsibility toward the German economy and the state of science and for the sake of Carl Bosch, who had been an opponent of the Nazis.[103] The lawyer Ernst Achenbach argued on behalf of Fritz Gajewski that he was only a simple citizen, even if the prosecution attempted to portray the defendants as "sinister persons" who were "worse somehow than Hitler himself." Achenbach added, "I am not of the opinion that the normal decent citizen in any country can be expected to assume that his own government is by definition crooked and that their opponents abroad are always right." He also referred to US committees set up to "investigate into so-called Un-American Activities," which seemed to believe that "a certain loyalty to one's own country and its legitimate government is not a sign of particular stupidity, not even of whole-hearted approval of any governmental decision, but rather a sign of national decency without which no state and no social order could be maintained."[104]

Along the same lines, Hellmuth Dix emphasized on behalf of Christian Schneider that the "average German entrepreneur … never entertained the thought" that the hiring of foreign or forced labor would be seen as illegal, criminal, or inhumane.[105] Karl Hoffmann argued on behalf of the defendant Otto Ambros that he remained a passionate chemist, a "technician," even if he appeared within I. G. Farben "ostensibly as so-called 'Generaldirektor' of the various plants that he founded, developped or took over." He was not in any way responsible for the crimes in Auschwitz, Hoffmann argued.[106] And Herbert Nath, Hans Pribilla, and Helmut Henze emphasized on behalf of their clients Max Ilgner, Carl Ludwig Lautenschläger, and Heinrich Oster that criminal liability was a personal liability that had to be linked to an individual. Henze explained, as Wolfram von Metzler had done before him on behalf of Paul Häfliger, that responsibility given to a member of the board of directors was a civil concept and had "nothing to do with responsibility under criminal law, which can only be a personal one." If the prosecution wanted to argue for the collective responsibility of all the members of the board of directors, "this would imply an attempt to characterize the Vorstand of the I.G. as a criminal organization within the meaning of the Charter." Even then, it would be necessary, based on the IMT verdict, to determine personal guilt.[107]

While these were primarily patterns of argumentation that burdened the prosecution with proving the guilt of each individual defendant, in some cases aggressive accusations were directed toward the prosecution. Fritz ter Meer's and Georg von Schnitzler's lawyers were the most aggressive. Walter Siemers argued on behalf of the latter that the indictment of industrialists irrespective of their political orientation was "pure anti-capitalism," which gave the Communists "great joy." In addition, it coincided with Hitler's attacks on industry and his hatred of "capitalists." On behalf of ter Meer, Erich Berndt argued that "through industrious labor," the prosecution was hoping to "build the steps to the gallows" for the defendants. It was attempting to give proof for this "with a wealth of documents culled from mountains of Farben files, most of which were torn from their natural business contexts, linked together by an apparent systematic design and mixed with excerpts from Hitler's 'Mein Kampf.'" But the defendants' guilt was only being supported by the "theory of alleged common knowledge": "thus has the prosecution tried to prove that these defendants were guilty, for instance, of Hitler's crimes, of wars of aggression, indeed even of the gassings in Auschwitz."[108]

Carl Wurster's defense counsel, the Social Democrat Friedrich Wagner, who had returned from the United States, seems to have argued more cleverly. The Germans, Wagner argued, knew too little about the United States—and the Americans knew too little about the Germans. Few Germans knew, for instance, that Senate sessions began with a prayer. Wagner quoted one of these prayers: "Shed the light of Thy Holy Spirit within our minds and hearts, that all who sincerely seek the truth may find it, and finding it may follow it, whatever the cost, knowing that it is the truth that makes men free." Wagner continued that the truth that was being sought in this trial had to be accompanied by justice: "Truth makes men free: justice is the foundation stone on which is built the communal life of an orderly human society." As Wurster's defense counsel, he wanted to "fight with the sword of truth" to gain Wurster "the liberty, which he expects from your sense of justice."[109]

These opening remarks sketched out the strategy of the defense. In the coming weeks and months, the job of the defense would be to support its arguments with strong evidence and to attempt to counteract, even discredit, the prosecution, as the lawyer Alfred Seidl had already tried to do with the actual or supposed political stance of the Auschwitz survivors. And at first, they disregarded von Metzler's suggestions, choosing to defend their clients individually and on every point for which they were indicted.

In this phase, the trial suffered less from disorganization, as it had during the first phase, than from the strategy and tactics of the defendants and of their counsels. They first made every possible effort to deny individual criminal responsibility for the crimes of which the defendants were accused. The differences between persons, functions, and responsibility were painstakingly addressed, and the role of the individual defendants was portrayed as insignificant. Only in cases in which acts of injustice could not be denied was the argument of "acting under orders" brought to bear. Otto Ambros, for instance, who was on trial for the key role he played in the construction of the I. G. Farben factory in Auschwitz, portrayed himself as a "plain chemist" who wanted to be responsible for practically nothing in Auschwitz.[110] Years later, Judge Shake described the defendants' and their lawyers' strategy: "Every time you got a German defendant in any of the trials in a corner and [*sic*] his final defense was that he was required to do what he had to do, and he knew it was wrong and he regretted it very much but he was under compulsion; he was forced to do it." But in response to the question of who had given the order that had forced him to do it, the answer was always that the relevant person had since died: "He was always dead."[111]

One example from the trial illustrates the defense's approach: when looking at the criminal responsibility for I. G. Farben's involvement in human experiments at concentration camps, Hans Pribilla, Carl Ludwig Lautenschläger's defense counsel, first named Julius Weber, his coworker, as the one responsible. Weber had led the clinical assessment of the drugs developed in the research laboratories, Pribilla explained, receiving guidelines from Lautenschläger, his superior. Pribilla admitted that Lautenschläger, in his function as head of the factory, had the responsibility of exercising due diligence in the selection of those working under him. But Weber had "proved a reliable and impeccable employee" since 1927, one who could be fully trusted: "If Hoechst was responsible for any illegal actions in connection with the examination of the Hoechst typhus remedies, not Professor Lautenschläger, but Dr. Weber would be the person responsible before the law." However, according to the evidence, both Lautenschläger and Weber "proceeded correctly in selecting and supervising the testers," and for the clinical assessment, the assessing doctor finally was the "only person responsible." As a result, I. G. Farben's Hoechst factory was "not responsible for crimes committed by the testers of its nitro acridine preparations." The SS doctor responsible for human experiments at the Buchenwald concentration camp, Dr. Ding-Schuler, was in fact dead—he had committed suicide at the end of the war. And Weber remained in hiding, apparently abroad. Weber, "a fugitive from the American and German authorities," as the indictment noted, was finally to be questioned in March 1948 in Basel through a commissioner.[112] In early April, however, this trip, which was to include Lautenschläger's defense counsel, Pribilla; a representative of the prosecution; and Judge Crawford, as the commissioner of the court, still had not taken place.[113] In late April, Pribilla introduced an affidavit by Weber, expressing his hope that Weber—whether in exile, as the prosecution argued, or suffering from a heart condition, as Pribilla stated—could be questioned in Switzerland. However, Drexel Sprecher, from the prosecution, wanted Weber's affidavit to be stricken from the record if he could not appear before the court; bringing it in would be "much more dangerous" than a statement under oath by someone previously deceased. Weber, who certainly knew about the human experiments and had even helped to organize them for the I. G. Farben Hoechst factory, was not questioned again in the end—and remained in hiding.[114]

The defendants were aided in the matter of responsibility by a question from Judge Morris, who seemed indirectly to be questioning the prosecution's selection of defendants. In the March 22, 1948, session, Morris asked the defendant Max Ilgner whether there were other members of the board of directors of I. G. Farben who were still alive and had not been indicted. Since Ilgner could not think of them on the spot, Morris stated that Ilgner must have been surprised by the question. But he, Morris, was interested, he stated, to know which of the former members of the board had not been indicted, how long they had been on the board, and when they had left it. Morris asked one of the other defendants to convey this information in the witness stand.[115] Two days later, Morris received the information "on the subject of Vorstand responsibility" from the defendant Friedrich Jähne. According to Jähne, a total of nineteen individuals who had been members of the Central Committee or full or substitute members of the board had not been indicted, including Paul Duden, Wilhelm Gaus, and Gustav Pistor. Since the indictment, a number of these nineteen individuals had died—namely, Carl Krekeler, Kurt Oppenheim, and Philipp Ott.[116] This put the responsibility of the board of directors as a whole in perspective, especially in light of the age structure of the board: The older members, including some of those who had retired, could be guilty of counts I and V, whereas counts II and III primarily applied to the younger ones, many of whom had not joined the board until 1938. This raised the burning questions of how the board of directors could bear collective responsibility for all counts except count IV and the role played by the four accused directors, who had only been mid-level managers.

In general, the defense attempted to talk down not just the role of the I. G. Farben managers, but the role of businessmen in general during the Third Reich.

Rudolf Dix made an effort to put words along these lines in the mouth of the defense witness Clemens Lammers, a former politician of the Catholic Center Party and a member of the supervisory board at I. G. Farben. He asked Lammers whether during the Nazi era I. G. Farben was "still master in its own house" and whether the businessman had become "more and more of a government official." Lammers answered these questions in the affirmative—and then spoke about the "consequences of the increasing compulsory economy of the state and trend toward war."[117] The lawyer Walter Siemers even invited Friedrich Flick to be a defense witness; Flick first confirmed that "Farben was at no time considered as a concern which was close to National Socialism" and then stated that "the inner attitudes of the [National Socialist] Party was [*sic*] against such concerns." In response to the question of what happened to industrialists who turned against the NSDAP and its ideas, Flick referred to Professor Junkers, who was subject to forced expropriation. During the war, one had to support the regime and "do his duty as a manufacturer." With the entry of the United States into the war, the material superiority of the other side became apparent, and "scapegoats had to be found." These had been found in industry: "Production demands were made, which, in fact, were unreasonable and could not be met. The well-known Hitler slogan 'The word "impossible" does not exist in my dictionary,' became the slogan for the industry, with which the industrialists were constantly subjected to pressure, bullied and threatened." If production levels were insufficient, "they always threatened people with having them sent into a concentration camp," which was "still a mild threat." Flick closed the session of questioning by Siemers with a saying that Adolf Hitler was said to use in smaller circles: "In order to set an example, one industrialist must at one time be put against the wall and it must be a prominent one."[118]

When he was questioned by his lawyer Günther Lummert during the trial, Hans Kühne, the former manager of the I. G. factory at Leverkusen and of the Niederrhein Works Group, said that he had wanted to go into retirement by 1940 at the age of sixty. However, this had been delayed by the war: "In 1943, however, my psychological opposition against the planned economy that was forced upon Farben and upon all of industry and against the despotism of the regime in Germany at the time became so strong, that I retired." Ulrich Haberland had succeeded him in leading the factory starting in August 1943. On the advice of Hermann Schmitz, Kühne said, he had taken extended leave in order to avoid being mobilized. He officially began his retirement in late June 1945.[119] Kühne emphasized the importance of "decentralized centralization" at I. G. Farben—which meant that one had great responsibility but also significant autonomy. He compared board members who served as factory directors or heads of sales cooperatives with "directors general of independent concerns"—which is how he had seen himself.[120] He had joined the NSDAP in 1933, he stated, because he had been urged to do so by Robert Ley, the leader of the German Labor Front, who had also worked as a chemist in Leverkusen. He was kicked out of the party in the same year for being a freemason, but in 1939 had become a member again through a pardon from Hitler.[121] In his remarks before the court, Kühne emphasized that in his opinion, the accusation that industry, and in particular I. G. Farben, had "supported and brought into being Hitler's aggressive policy" could "only be designated as erroneous and incorrect": "If I could reproach myself and my colleagues with one thing, it would be the fact that we have too little concerned ourselves with politics. We as technical men, scientists and businessmen, devoted our work power to our own enterprises." For this reason, during meetings, "there were never any political discussions." In other countries, by contrast, he argued, industrialists had become involved in politics and had even taken high-level offices, like Baldwin or Chamberlain in Great Britain.[122]

While Kühne therefore accused himself, in a manner irrelevant to the criminal matter at hand, of not having been sufficiently politically involved, the defendant Carl Wurster, when he was questioned by his lawyer Wolfgang Heintzeler, likened the role of German industry in the Nazi state as "more an object than a subject … more the anvil than the hammer." The supposedly passive position of industry with regard to Nazi policy, which there was an effort to convey throughout the trial, especially to the judges, could hardly have been better formulated.[123]

Not least to bring out the main points, the defendants and their defense counsels carefully prepared for their direct examination as well as for possible questions by the prosecution during cross-examination. Hans Kugler later described it this way: "The documents introduced by the prosecution had to be picked to pieces, and those of the defense had to be prepared from the corresponding perspectives. The lawyers had to formulate prompts and the questions they would ask the witnesses of the prosecution during cross-examination. On the other hand, the so-called scripts for the questioning of the witnesses presented by the defense and for our own questionings had to be prepared."[124]

The files of Max Ilgner's lawyer, Nath, show what such a "script" looked like. The questioning with the defense counsel was meticulously rehearsed, and the questions and answers were prepared in great detail and then constantly reviewed and improved.[125] The lawyer Otto Nelte's preparation for his defense of Heinrich Hörlein shows clearly how painstaking the work was—and how helpful the former I. G. Farben employees were for those working on it. Nelte, for instance, turned to Hörlein's coworker, Professor Kikuth, with detailed questions about the charge of human experiments in concentration camps and asked him to carry out in-depth research that would help avoid possible confusion or even contradictions in a cross-examination. Possible uncertainties could, Nelte argued, easily be used by the representatives of the prosecution "to question the credibility of my client, which should be avoided under all circumstances." He therefore asked for photocopies of all relevant pieces of writing: "Of course, I can only make an exhaustive picture of the entire matter, as is required in this trial, if you give me access to all documents, including correspondence and reports about all experiments at locations other than Buchenwald."[126]

Nor did the defense and various defendants, clearly under the leadership of Fritz ter Meer, shy away from pressuring codefendants or witnesses to tell targeted lies, to carry out character assassinations, and to bring in affidavits in which "witnesses" were told almost precisely what they were to say.[127]

Affidavits became an important part of the defense strategy. According to Military Ordinance No. 7, they had originally been intended to support the prosecution. Before the trial, DuBois himself had admitted to being nervous about the fact that the drafters of the Bernstein Report had brought in material in a form that would not have been allowed in a trial: "Some of the statements were unsworn. Some of the most convincing testimony showing Farben's rearmament activities lacked dates. In one form or another about five hundred documents needed fixing." This had then led to a bitter debate among the prosecution, especially about the use of affidavits: "It would be a gigantic task, of course, to produce in open court the hundreds of people who had given us statements. In fact, the drafters of Allied Control Council Law No. 10 had foreseen this dilemma, and had provided that 'affidavits' were admissible as evidence. But the American Constitution provided that the accused must be confronted by his accuser." Despite opposition on his team, DuBois had supported bringing in witnesses, at least in cases in which the defense disagreed with the statements in the affidavits.[128] This was also necessary, as Judge Shake reported with pride years later: "We refused to allow them [the prosecution] to use the affidavits unless they provided means for the defendants to get counter-affidavits from the same parties."[129] The court's decision, however, meant that the defense brought in large quantities of affidavits—the number of sworn statements from the defense, at 2,394 affidavits, exceeded the 419 of the prosecution more than fivefold.[130]

The defense requested affidavits, suggesting what the authors of the affidavits should—or should not—write. Professor Eduard Wahl, for instance, asked the well-respected chemist Alwin Mittasch to review his sworn statement and strengthen aspects related to politics. Wahl stated that he was happy to help with "the necessary adjustment of emphasis."[131] And Ambros's lawyer, Drischel, wrote to Richard Linde with the request that he help Ambros in connection with the use of concentration camp inmates at Auschwitz. The affidavit, written for Linde by Drischel or even by Ambros himself, states how much Linde valued Ambros as a technical expert and how positive Ambros's attitude had been toward employees of Jewish descent and notes that Ambros had criticized the NSDAP. The following was even added in: "Without being able to prove it ourselves, we heard of Dr. Ambros taking a decisive stance on avoiding the use of poison gas in war."[132]

The defense's affidavits contained not only problematic assertions but also known lies, as some examples from the I. G. Farben factory at Hoechst show.

According to information provided by the factory doctor, Adolf Baldus, for instance, only fifty-seven Fremdarbeiter died between 1940 and 1945. The list showed, Baldus stated, "that the number of deaths was still lower than the German mortality rate during the time from 1931 to 1936." This list was not complete, however: Baldus listed six Russians as having died in 1943, but nine Russian children had died in December 1943 alone—these children clearly did not appear in his statistics. In any case, the figure of fifty-seven deaths of Fremdarbeiter deployed at Hoechst, even if it doesn't include children, is very low—in the final analysis, too low.[133] It is also noteworthy how cooperation with the SS and the Gestapo was disputed. In early 1944, the following was stated at a management meeting at Hoechst: "We should request that the SS act against foreigners who do not return from vacation." Hoechst did in fact report employees who had not returned from vacation to the security organs—counter to the claims of a defense witness after the war.[134] And according to the company records, the company management at Hoechst sent no fewer than 264 Fremdarbeiter to jail or to a labor education camp (*Arbeitserziehungslager*). An employee responsible for these workers, Franz Spiess, said in a sworn statement on behalf of the defense that the main punishment of Fremdarbeiter consisted in fines, and that only in cases of "repeated lack of discipline" had they been required, as per an ordinance of the general plenipotentiary for labor deployment, "to report this to the Gestapo in the case of foreign labor." Circumscribing this further, he added that from late 1943 to March 1945, this had "been done in 3 to 4 cases in my memory."[135] While being questioned by Pribilla at the trial, Hans Poehn, the intelligence representative at Hoechst, said that in this role he had "never" reported Fremdarbeiter to the Gestapo for punishment.[136] This statement was untrue, as were the others cited above.

Untruths and lies could be exposed by the prosecution, as was demonstrated in the case of Gerhard Ollendorff, whom the defendant Fritz Gajewski was not too embarrassed to ask for an affidavit in his defense. Ollendorff, a deputy member of the board of directors at I. G. Farben in Wolfen until 1932, had been expelled from his house in Upper Bavaria during the November pogrom of 1938 and then been arrested. He had finally come to Wolfen to speak to Gajewski about his future. In January 1939, he was arrested by the Gestapo in Berlin and brought to the police prison in Halle. His wife shared this information with Gajewski, who then seems to have worked with other leading managers in Wolfen to have Ollendorff released. In June 1939 Ollendorff met with Gajewski on the recommendation of Hermann Schmitz in order to discuss possible emigration to Brazil. Gajewski had been very expressive of his support—and Ollendorff, full of gratitude, had not forgotten this.[137]

Gajewski was, as he told his lawyer, von Metzler, during the trial, a member of the Central Committee, the head of Division III, and the head of the Wolfen film factory. In 1933 he became a member of the NSDAP for professional reasons.

He had problems, however, with the NSDAP's hostile position toward religion as well as with its racist theories. In Wolfen he had difficulties with the local NSDAP, especially with the local district leader. A report on him mentioned in particular his "attitude to the Jewish question." While being questioned by the Gestapo in Bitterfeld, he had been informed that his behavior toward the Nazi party was "absolutely not permissible and that I was known as a friend of Jews. The case of Ollendorff and others demonstrated that." He had also engaged to support Professor Eggert, who was married to a Jewish woman.[138]

In the cross-examination, Morris Amchan referred to his statement that he had rejected racist theories and had proved himself to be a friend of various Jews "at great personal risk." Amchan then asked specifically about Ollendorff, to which Gajewski replied that he had gone personally on his behalf to the Gestapo and had told his sister-in-law that Ollendorff had "no secrets from us" and "could be released." He had even personally sent a letter to the Gestapo in Halle, he stated, on behalf of Ollendorff, "because of certain tragic circumstances in the nature of his arrest." Amchan, who had documents that demonstrated what was meant by "certain tragic circumstances," probed further, stating that Ollendorff had told Gajewski that he wanted to leave Germany because of his "Jewish ancestry." After this, Amchan said, Gajewski had told the Gestapo that they should "arrest him and search his house." Gajewski did not deny this, but justified encouraging the Gestapo to go after Ollendorff by referring to a supposed instruction from Carl Bosch, the chairman of the supervisory board, who had died in 1940, that Ollendorff should not leave the country with company secrets. It was for this reason, Gajewski stated, that "we" decided that Ollendorff's home should be searched. Gajewski also pointed out that it had been "our duty" to do this since Ollendorff had been what he referred to as a "secret bearer of the first rank." In the end, Ollendorff was able to get away, Gajewski stated, "through my efforts." Amchan replied that Ollendorff had not been at I. G. Farben for six years by that point and asked Gajewski whether he had told Ollendorff, who had written an affidavit on his behalf, that he was the one who had instigated his arrest—something Gajewski denied.[139]

Erich von der Heyde and Fritz ter Meer had more success with their lies about the Jewish director Richard May, whom they claimed to have helped, but whom, in fact, as the documents show, they had betrayed to the Gestapo—but May fled to England just in time, without announcing his plan or discussing it with the leadership at I. G. Farben.[140]

What was most dangerous for the defendants, however, was count III, especially the "Auschwitz issue." The defense counsels were well aware of this, as has been previously shown. Nor did Otto Ambros, as previously mentioned, have any illusions about this from the very beginning.[141] Emanuel Minskoff, on the prosecution, also recognized this, while Seidl, on the defense, had attempted to downplay the importance of the Auschwitz-Monowitz camp during the first phase of the trial. It had not been a concentration camp, he argued, as the prosecution had claimed, but "in reality was only one labor camp of which there were 500 throughout Germany, and which were subordinated to 14 large concentration camps."[142]

But this did not make the "Auschwitz issue" less dangerous, as could be seen when Judge Morris asked Ambros whether the factory in Auschwitz was seen as a permanent or temporary installation. His lawyer, Seidl, had already asked him whether Auschwitz was only an improvisation related to the war. Ambros had replied that it was a response to the pressure to produce Buna and high-quality fuel. Ambros added, however, that in the long term, Auschwitz had been planned to be a city with 64,000 inhabitants, two-thirds Polish and one-third German, and that construction had been carried out accordingly. Morris then repeated the question, to which Ambros replied that the factory was to be "a permanent plant": "because of the volume of the plant we could not have it that way [i.e., as a temporary plant]." The factory was intended not just to be in production during the war but to be inserted into the "economic sphere of the East." A firm decision on this question, however, Ambros stated, had not been made.[143]

In light of the crimes connected with the camp, it was not surprising that most of the trial days set aside by the defense for individual defendants were reserved for those primarily responsible for Auschwitz. As the lawyer Böttcher told the defense team on January 21, 1948, ten trial days were set aside for Walter Dürrfeld and eight for Otto Ambros. By contrast, only two each were reserved for the defendants August von Knieriem and Hans Kühne.[144]

The main office for dealing with questions related to Auschwitz for I. G. Farben seems to have been in Ludwigshafen. In order to disguise their own methods and steps, those involved in the defense on this point used code names in their letters, discussions, and telephone calls. On the list, Ambros was called "Bergemann," Dürrfeld was "Heribert," and Oswald Pohl (Figure 3.5), from the SS Main Economic and Administrative Office, was "Haupt." The defense lawyer Wolfgang Heintzeler was referred to as "Heinz" and Wolfgang Alt as "Jozef." Concentration camps were cynically referred to as "Heim," or "home" in English, and inmates as "workers."[145]

Ambros (Figure 3.6), in particular, seems to have become increasingly aware of how problematic the Auschwitz issue could become for him. In early December 1947, he decided to separate from his defense counsel, Friedrich Drischel, accusing him of not sufficiently representing his interests. In his reply, Drischel defended himself against the accusation, but accepted Ambros's decision to be represented by Karl Hoffmann from then on. Drischel also took note, as he wrote, that Ambros, "as a result of the latest events in the trial" (apparently referring to the treatment of Auschwitz in the trial), had "become uneasy, on the one hand toward some of the remaining codefendants and on the other hand with regard to the future development of the defense."[146]

Figure 3.5. Oswald Pohl, SS-Obergruppenführer and general in the Waffen-SS, head of the SS Main Economic and Administrative Office, as a witness for the prosecution on Auschwitz. Source: NARA 238-OMT-VI-W-14; NL Nath; public domain.

In any case, Ambros put great effort into his preparations—and sought to share responsibility with others, or even pass it off or push it away. The relevant preparations for his defense stated that I. G. Farben was aware of the turnover at Monowitz: "Admitted!" But no one, Ambros stated, could have assumed that the "people removed [from Monowitz] were killed, since nothing was known, whether generally or specifically among the leadership at I. G. Farben, about the killing of people, gassing, or incineration of anyone other than those who had died of typhus or other illnesses." Ambros had heard from his colleague Heinrich Bütefisch (Figure 3.7) that a new factory was being built in Upper Silesia. He had also heard that concentration camp inmates would have to be used in the construction: "Order from above." At his first visit to Auschwitz, he had "primarily" visited workshops, he stated—"everything in impeccable shape."[147]

The relationship between Ambros and Fritz ter Meer also seems to have been highly problematic at the time. Ter Meer had seen in Ambros "one of the 'young Nazis' in the company"—the two others had been Bütefisch and Wurster, who, in contrast to the older members of the board, "were more open to the party's efforts and therefore all 3 have the Knight's Cross!" According to ter Meer,

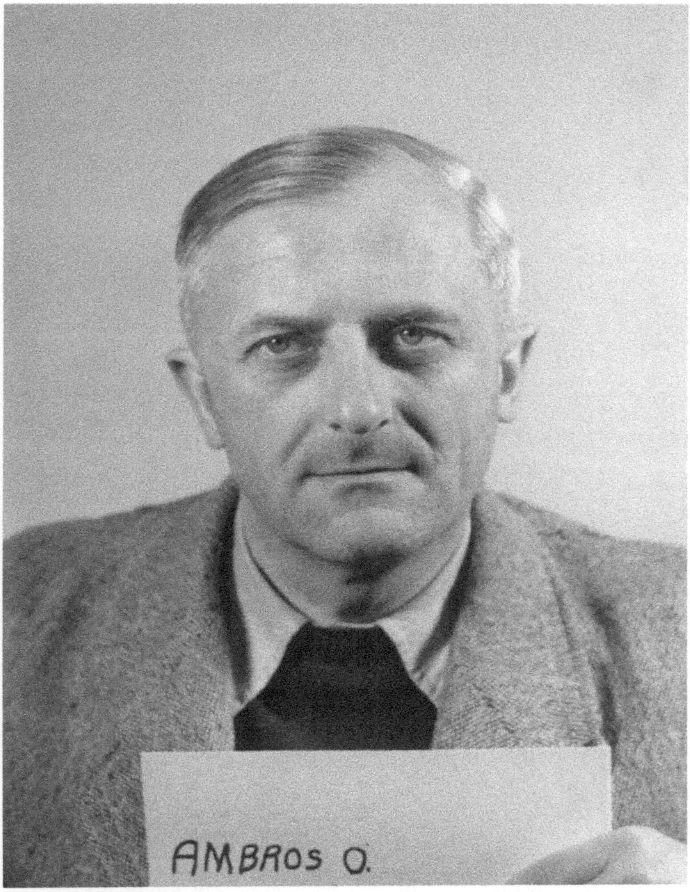

Figure 3.6. Auschwitz-Monowitz—one of the members of the board who was directly responsible, Otto Ambros. Source: NARA 238-OMT-VI-D-9; NL Nath; public domain.

because of their roles, these three had come "necessarily in contact with party offices." Now Ambros strove to distinguish between his own responsibilities and ter Meer's. Until January 1, 1938, Ambros said, it had been "clear as day that I held no responsibility in the big matters of the indictment." Things changed once he became a member of the board of directors. As head of Division II and chairman of the Technical Committee, ter Meer had "not played the role of supervisor with respect to the older men, such as Hörlein, Kühne or Pistor"; "However, it was assumed that he filled this role of Division leader in charge with respect to the younger colleagues." Until that point, there had been differences in opinion between him and ter Meer, but "no reason for disgruntlement."

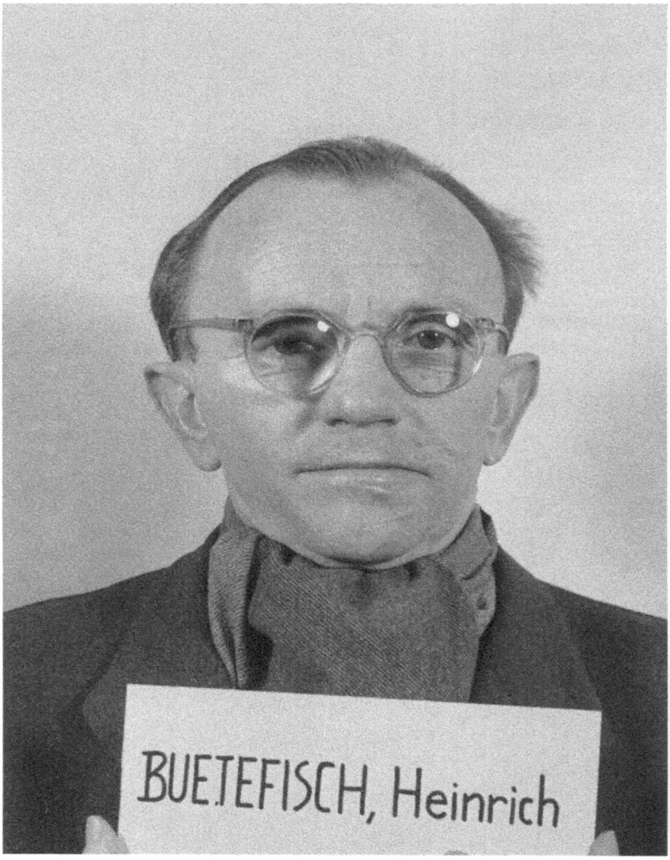

Figure 3.7. Auschwitz-Monowitz—one of the members of the board who was directly responsible, Heinrich Bütefisch. Source: NARA 238-OMT-VI-D-12; NL Nath; public domain.

Ter Meer had agreed to everything that Ambros reported with regard to Auschwitz. Even after 1943, when ter Meer's activities shifted primarily to Italy, he had still regularly met with Ambros.[148] It becomes clear here how big an effort Ambros was making to inculpate his fellow board member ter Meer or even to ascribe to him a greater level of responsibility. However, things were not much better for Ambros, since his former coworker Jürgen von Klenck was apparently testifying against him. In a statement on the factory in Gendorf, Ambros wrote that "the Klenck matter" had to be cleared up: "I don't know where he is; I was just told that he made major statements against me, pushed everything on me, emphasized my interactions with Pohl, etc." He, Ambros, did not believe this, but wanted it to be clarified.[149]

In the well-prepared direct examination by his lawyer, Hoffmann, Ambros finally even claimed that he had had no influence on the decision to build the factory in Auschwitz, since he was only a "technical expert without any rank in the party or in the state or anywhere else."[150] The extensive discussion of reasons for the construction of the Buna factory in Auschwitz—the rivers, the coal, the railroad connection—brought Judge Hebert, in his words, to the "limits of my patience": He simply wanted to know what role the concentration camp played. Hoffmann replied that his client claimed that the concentration camp had played "no role" in the decision to build the factory. Proving this would require a "number of details." This time it was Hebert who complained about the waste of time.[151]

Like Ambros, Heinrich Bütefisch, the second member of the board directly connected with Auschwitz, also sought to minimize his responsibility. Bütefisch stated during the direct examination by his lawyer Hans Flächsner that the Freundeskreis Himmler (Circle of Friends of Himmler), in which he had played an active role, was simply a social gathering. Nor had his participation in the group and his rank in the SS had anything to do with I. G. Farben, he argued; they were, he claimed, something he had done purely for personal reasons.[152] He did not give an answer to Emanuel Minskoff's question during cross-examination as to when he had heard of the planned construction of the Buna factory for the first time, fleeing to the standard response that he and Ambros had just been "technical experts." With regard to the mistreatment of inmates at the I. G. Farben factory in Auschwitz, he argued that I. G. Farben was against violence, even prohibited it—and that he knew of nothing, except in one case.[153]

The Auschwitz topic finally led to major conflicts between the prosecution, the defense, and the judges in the trial. On February 25, 1948, the prosecution made an oral request, and the following day a written request, to be given access to the documents of Camill Santo (codename "Laar") that had been removed by Wolfgang Alt (codename "Jozef"), an employee of the defense, in order to enable them to prepare using the weekly reports from Auschwitz.[154] Apparently this did not happen the way the prosecution had hoped it would. Employees of the prosecution then decided to search Alt's house in Ludwigshafen—and apparently threatened various people with arrest. Some of the I. G. Farben documents that had been brought from Griesheim (near Frankfurt) to Ludwigshafen had apparently been destroyed by Alt—the rest were later given to the court.

On February 28, Rudolf Dix, as speaker of the defense, spoke out against the accusations and measures taken by the prosecution. The accusations were "slander," he argued. Dix protested, instead, that the prosecution "over the course of supposed attempts to determine such claimed violations of the defense, had gained access, with the help of pressure and intimidation and using illegal means, to plans, documents, and evidence (e.g., affidavits) of the defense, which, as is recognized in all civilized nations, are protected by the professional confidentiality of the defenders before their presentation in front of the court." The documents requested by the prosecution, he explained, went beyond the ones in Ludwigshafen. The defense had received a series of documents from the French administration, to which it was returning them; at that point, the prosecution would gain access to them. The defense wanted to get the weekly reports from Auschwitz, which were "particularly urgently desired" by the prosecution, to the general secretary of the military courts without delay. That way, the prosecution could examine them, giving it an opportunity which it did "not have a claim to based on their previous behavior." The defense wanted corresponding access to the material of the prosecution, however—and to have the defense documents that had been seized by Emanuel Minskoff and Benvenuto von Halle returned.[155]

On March 8, the court reprimanded Wolfgang Alt, the assistant to the defense, for his actions, but it also reprimanded the prosecution for its disproportionate, "hasty and ill-conceived action" and criticized it for taking the matter into its own hands, threatening witnesses with arrest, and breaking into the home of a member of the defense without authorization.[156] The prosecution viewed the court's reprimand for its actions to be entirely inappropriate.[157]

Seidl, the defense counsel of Walter Dürrfeld, the ambitious former head of the I. G. Farben factory at Auschwitz-Monowitz, also sought to downplay his client's responsibility in every way. Dürrfeld (Figure 3.8), like ter Meer, Bütefisch, and Ambros, claimed to have known nothing. He too, as he claimed when questioned by his lawyer, had acted under orders. As for Göring's order to use concentration camp inmates for the construction of the factory, he claimed that he had first learned of it from Bütefisch and that the order had come "from the higher level of the Reich, and that it was unchangeable." Therefore, especially in light of the urgent war situation, they had complied.[158] The workers and inmates had been treated and fed very well and had even had clothing arranged for them, he stated. Dürrfeld claimed to have been aided by Oswald Pohl from the SS Main Economic and Administrative Office, who had offered to help when they had trouble finding clothes: "Pohl said 'I don't understand. There must be plenty of old clothing around locally because, as a result of these various resettlement actions, a lot of old clothing was available and was supplied to all these old clothing collection agencies.' He said that he did that himself in the concentration camps. He then suggested to cut all the red tape and help ourselves directly and he would place some old clothing at our disposal." The provision of clothing for the foreign workers had even led to complaints from the German workers, he stated.[159] Dürrfeld's testimony was supported by an affidavit from Pohl, in which he wrote that he had provided sufficient clothing for the I. G. Farben factory for its foreign workers despite the often great difficulties: "I therefore instructed the commander of the concentration camp at Auschwitz to help the factory by delivering available clothing."[160] Left unmentioned was the fact that this clothing

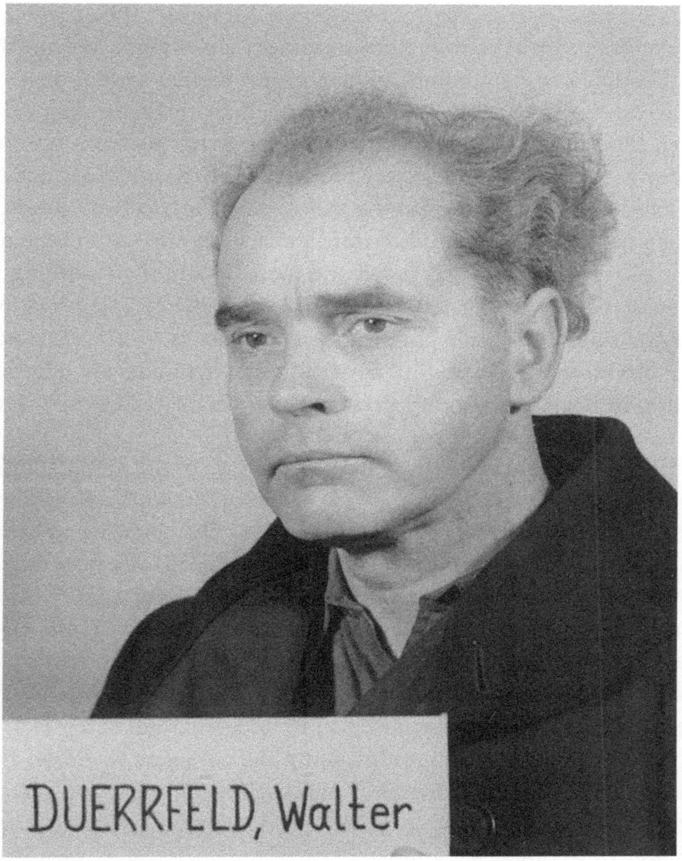

Figure 3.8. Auschwitz-Monowitz—one of the members of the board who was directly responsible, the director Walter Dürrfeld. Source: NARA 238-OMT-VI-D-21; NL Nath; public domain.

came from those who had been murdered at Auschwitz; it was euphemistically referred to as clothing from "resettlement actions."

One of the witnesses brought in by Seidl was Martin Nestler, who described Monowitz as a camp that was properly maintained and more comfortable than others. In cross-examination by Minskoff, however, it turned out that Nestler had been convicted for fraud during the Weimar Republic and, during his time as an inmate, had worn a criminal's green patch and therefore had been denied acceptance by the inmates' organization he had applied to.[161] The witness Adolf Taub admitted to Minskoff during cross-examination that the inmates knew that people were gassed in Auschwitz and that inmates were beaten in Monowitz and worked to death.[162] Nor did Seidl have much luck with another witness, Gerhard

Dietrich, who had been a *kapo*, or overseer, at Monowitz. His statements were entirely taken apart by Minskoff in cross-examination—not in front of the court, however, but in front of a commissioner. Upon further questioning, Dietrich stated that the camp at Monowitz was worse than the camp at Buchenwald, worse even than the main camp at Auschwitz. Inmates had also been executed by hanging at Monowitz. And everyone—inmates, technicians, and those in charge—had known about the gassing in Birkenau. It had been general knowledge among the concentration camp inmates that prisoners who were no longer capable of work were sent to Birkenau and gassed—and their clothing returned to Monowitz. Seidl was angered by Dietrich's statements and brought him in for more questioning—challenging his own witness, as Minskoff noted. In the end, Seidl attempted to destroy his own witness's credibility by referring to his membership in the Association of Persecutees of the Nazi Regime (Vereinigung der Verfolgten des Naziregimes or VVN).[163]

Overall, the defense's strategy of portraying certain of the prosecution's charges as unfounded did not succeed in the case of Auschwitz in the way in which the defendants and their defense counsels had hoped. The defense had been able to cast doubt on witness testimony when the prosecution was presenting its evidence, but during this phase, Emanuel Minskoff stood out among the prosecution because of his success in securing evidence on Auschwitz and his brilliant cross-examinations. However, his cross-examinations most frequently took place in front of a commissioner rather than in front of the court, which likely reduced their effect. The prosecution also successfully addressed the defense of "window dressing," namely deliberate efforts made by the company to mislead the Nazi government. Here, too, the defense's attempt to portray what had been declared war production during the war as civilian production and mere "window dressing," did not truly convince the judges.[164]

Thus, given their need to defend against accusations that could not be denied, it became entirely sensible from the perspective of the defense to follow the initiative of the lawyers Eduard Wahl and Hellmuth Dix and, drawing on a moral-theological evaluation, to introduce the concept of a form of collective pardon—even though it objected to and immediately attacked the idea of collective guilt when it came from the prosecution.[165] The esteemed Jesuit priest Max Pribilla, who had completed his secondary degree in Cologne with Konrad Adenauer and published the well-respected journal *Stimmen der Zeit*, saw, in his reflections on the actions of businessmen in the Third Reich, a "spirit of subordination" in the character of the Germans, who had a "longing" to see their actions legitimized through "orders." He quoted a scene from William's Shakespeare's *Henry V*, in which soldiers reason through whether the king's matter is just—and come to the conclusion that, whether good or bad, their obedience toward the king cleansed them "from all guilt." Most who went to war thought like these soldiers, Pribilla argued, if they thought about it at all. At the end of his reflections, Pribilla, calling for a collective global pardon for the many who had made themselves guilty, quoted a letter from Pope Innocent I to the bishops of Macedonia in 414: "It often happens that when faults are made by entire peoples or a large group, some things remain unpunished, because it is impossible, due to the large number, to put everyone before a tribunal. Then one should leave what happened to God's judgment, but take great care for the future." It was "not likely," Pribilla stated, that "the wisdom of this advice [could be] disproven."[166]

Another major strategy of the defense, from the opening of the trial through the final statements, was to insistently question the legitimacy of the court. They raised the accusation that Nuremberg represented "victors' justice," that the prosecution was contravening the international legal principle of *nullum crimen sine lege, nulla poena sine lege*—no crime without law, no punishment without law—and was relying on inadmissible ex post facto laws. According to the defense, the trial was unfair, and the defense was at a disadvantage with respect to the prosecution. To this was added the argument that an entire German profession was being tried for a form of "collective guilt"—paired, as shown above, with an argument for collective pardon.[167]

In his December 1947 opening statement, Rudolf Aschenauer, speaking on behalf of the defendant Heinrich Gattineau, even argued the "nullity" of CCL No. 10, since the "significance of the German-Russian Secret Treaty of August 23, 1939, for the bringing about of the Law and incidentally for the proceedings instituted here" had not sufficiently been taken into account. After all, he argued, Moscow had wanted Hitler to acquire power, because only after him could Germany become communist. The Russians had financially supported the NSDAP prior to 1933, and the NSDAP had been permeated by people whose allegiance was to Moscow, he added. Aschenauer therefore raised the question of "whether the proceedings, in view of the international history of origin of the norms determining punishment of war criminals, is permissible at all." The London Protocol of August 8, 1945, "with all the rules issued for its supplementation and execution, constitutes a new legal institution, seen from the angle of international law; seen politically, it is an experiment." In order to claim validity and general recognition, these agreements would have had to come into being "with politically loyal partners in a politically loyal manner." But, Aschenauer stated, this had not been the case for the Soviet Union. The German-Soviet secret pact and the division of Poland meant that it plainly counted as a perpetrator and a participant under the charge of a war of aggression. In arguing this, Aschenauer stated, he had no intention of denying the criminal responsibility of the German war criminals, claiming rather that the formal agreement on a form of punishment lost its material basis if the origin of the agreement was faulty in the way described above. If, upon carrying out the review he requested, the court were to confirm this issue in the treaties, then, he argued, an obstacle stood in the way of the continuation of the trial.[168]

In April 1948, Aschenauer made the same request, now backing it up with arguments that were significantly more radical. In his opening statement, he had not sought to question the responsibility of the Nazi leadership from a criminal liability perspective; now he did exactly this. In his request, he argued that the IMT's determinations were not binding for the subsequent trials and called for an immediate striking of counts I and V; he also asked for an immediate termination of the trial. He argued that one could no longer speak of a sole guilt for World War II on the part of leaders of the Third Reich, since the leaders of the Soviet Union not only held significant co-responsibility but, by means of a conspiracy, sought to violently bring about the "Bolshevisation of Europe and Asia": "The responsible German institutions thought they were moving, but they were in fact being moved. They were used as pawns by the USSR, whose end goal was to unleash the so-called 'second imperialist war' (1939–1945). Seen internationally, Goering's objective contribution, among others, to the disruption of world peace became the mere contribution toward a foreign and much more comprehensive plan of destruction. In this regard, therefore, the object becomes not German offense, but German abetting." If the IMT had issued a flawed verdict, in Aschenauer's view, for him the most important basis for the indictment under counts I and V against the managers of I. G. Farben had fallen apart—and the charges could therefore be removed. Aschenauer went even further. He seemed to believe that his arguments had proved that crimes were committed not only on the German side, but also "on the Allied (Soviet) side to the greatest degree." Therefore, the indictment, Aschenauer argued, also ran into the principle of *tu quoque*. He conceded that a defense of *tu quoque* in the "internal laws of a state"—that is, under national criminal law—was "generally agreed to be inadmissible." But in international law, this was not the case, since this was "much more flexible, context-dependent, and less fixed than the internal law of a state." It was "contract law, not legislative law," and even customary international law was "generally more vague and less precisely traceable." This applied in particular to international law, since there was no such thing as universal international law. The London Statute and CCL No. 10, which was based on it, had "major defects": The norms were not universal, since not all states had joined the London agreement; the norms were not reciprocal, since they only foresaw the punishment of war criminals who had been on the losing side of the war; the norms created special courts, and they contravened "substantial aspects of material criminal law, which were recognized in the criminal code of all civilized states," such as the principles of acting under orders and of *nulla poena sine lege*. Aschenauer concluded that the London Statute had created "no new international law," since it was based on "a morbid foundation." The victors' goal as a joint international legal body amounted to "the application of a global criminal justice through the criminal prosecution of the war criminals": "This association's purpose cannot be achieved if the contracting powers show a clear lack of judicial and legislative quality. Already the inclusion of a state recognized to be compromised excludes the possibility of the London Statute being seen as an instrument of global justice. The entire treaty, including Law No. 10, should be seen as invalid from an international law standpoint." Aschenauer added that because of the fact that the "Control Council has ceased to exist as a governing organ, the tribunals no longer have the basis for their jurisdiction."[169]

Aschenauer's request—based less on legal rules or the rules of international law than on a political justification—represented an attempt to deny the court the right to judge the defendants on the basis that its legal framework had originated in an "illegitimate" manner. In Aschenauer's depiction, Nazi perpetrators became the unwilling abettors of a violent seizure of power by the Bolsheviks. This request led historian Hubert Seliger to conclude that Aschenauer was "a radical lawyer"— the other "radical" lawyer, in his estimation, was Alfred Seidl, the author of a similar legal document that had been supported by Aschenauer.[170]

The defendants and their counsels benefitted in this phase from the fact that though the judges still wanted unity, or at the least the appearance of it, the rupture in the tribunal had, since November 1947, become ever clearer—and the majority of the court was not as supportive of the prosecution as the latter had hoped. One cannot argue that Judges Shake and Morris had taken the defendants' side, but they were certainly critical of the prosecution and were showing themselves increasingly well-disposed toward the defendants and their counsels.

In January 1948, Judge Morris wrote a letter to the chief justice of the Supreme Court of North Dakota about the progression of the I. G. Farben trial, describing his attitude toward the prosecution, the other judges, and the defense counsels. He, Morris, had originally had an inkling that the trial would be long-winded and difficult, but, he wrote, it was dragging on inexcusably. The situation in the court itself was unsatisfactory: "The prosecution is being conducted by a group of inexperienced refugees from Washington bureaucracy. They spent about two years assembling a great mass of documentary material, much of which is irrelevant to any real issues in the case. I blew off from the bench a few times about the case bogging down. The presiding judge was inclined to agree with me, but being a good diplomat he, of course, had to try to maintain some semblance of unity in his Tribunal. The Dean of the Louisiana Law School has never tried a case in his life. He served in the Pentagon Building throughout the war and is imbued with the idea that the prosecution can do no wrong, and that whatever the prosecution offers in evidence should be received 'for it might have some probative value.' He is supported in his views by the alternate judge whose prior judicial experience is confined to conducting hearings for the OPA (wherein again the prosecution was always right)." Since the defense had the right to present a similar quantity of evidence, the trial would drag on even longer, Morris stated. According to him the defense counsels were not as familiar with common law legal rights, but very capable: "They undoubtedly realize that time runs in their favor. While they are very diplomatic and suave about it, they are definitely in no hurry to see the case terminated." Morris would therefore be staying in Nuremberg much longer than planned: "That means I will not be home even for the June term unless I could be released from the case and turn my place over to the alternate judge. My conscience, in view of the situation on the Tribunal, would make it difficult for me to do that."[171]

If necessary, Judge Merrell could have stepped in for Judge Morris, which would have been very amenable to the prosecution under Josiah DuBois. For reasons of conscience, however, Morris did not want to step down from the case and remained in Nuremberg. He became increasingly critical of the prosecution and even sympathetic to the major criticism of the trials in Nuremberg voiced by Judge Charles F. Wennerstrum of Iowa. The latter had participated as presiding judge in the trial against generals of the Wehrmacht in Case VII, referred to as the "Hostages Trial," and after his return to the United States had expressed sharp criticism of Nuremberg in the *Chicago Tribune*, provoking a harsh reply from Telford Taylor.[172] Reacting to this, Morris not only wrote of Taylor's "puerile reply" to Wennerstrum's accusations, but even said that the latter's comments, "although somewhat poorly expressed," had some justification. Morris saw problems with achieving just sentences in Nuremberg and with appropriately valuing the work of the prosecution: "There is no question but that the performance of judicial duty is made extremely difficult by the 'prosecution atmosphere' which, like a fog, obscures the perspective of these trials. I don't say that the cause of the defendants is always prejudiced by this atmosphere. It may be that sometimes the resentment that one feels to the constant pressure for conviction may interfere with a fair and just appraisal of the case presented by the prosecution." On this occasion, Morris also made it clear that he no longer expected a unanimous verdict in the I. G. Farben trial: "This will not be easy for I can predict with certainty that it will not be unanimous on all points." The length of the trial and the problems that had arisen in the trial and in North Dakota finally led him to write that he now regretted having gone to Nuremberg. The experience did not make up for the difficulties that had emerged.[173]

In this phase of the trial, however, the court criticized not just the prosecution but also the defense. In early February 1948, Judge Morris noted for the record that Heinrich Hörlein's questioning should be ended. It had reached a point at which he believed "that nothing further can be gained by continuing the examination of this witness in any respect." But the other judges were of the opinion that "the interests of justice" required continuing with the questioning. Judge Shake added, however, that the other members of the tribunal shared Morris's view but hoped that the questioning would be carried out in such a way that it would be of use to the court.[174] In mid-February, Morris once again repeated his criticism of the defense and stated for the first time that the tribunal, in his opinion, should consider giving the defense time limits if it did not hold to the agreed-upon timespans and avoid going into unnecessary detail. That same day, Judge Hebert reprimanded the prosecution for causing the cross-examinations to drag on for too long and for going into details "far beyond the range of pertinent inquiry that the Tribunal is interested in."[175] A few days later, the court drastically limited the time that the prosecution and the defense had for questioning and cross-examination. The defense was also ordered to present all its evidence by May 15—by which time the questioning and cross-examination were also to be concluded.[176]

The court had obviously lost its patience. In response to the defense's objection that the time limitations imposed by the tribunal could prove "very prejudicial" to it, Judges Shake and Hebert jointly stated that the measure was by no means unfair, since the defendants and their defense counsels had been given "the widest latitude" and been allowed "a great deal of repetitious matter" that should have been objected to. The judges stated that they would have open minds if problems arose—but that the rulings of the court were "eminently fair."[177] Judge Morris, who described the trial as "a long drawn out affair," also wanted to limit the defense in order to bring the trial to a quick close: "The attorneys complain bitterly that this is too short, but such arguments as we have had from counsel so far have not been very helpful, so we do not intend to grant more time."[178]

The rupture in the court and the stance of its majority became very clear at the May 11, 1948, session, toward the end of the trial, over the matter of the affidavits by the defendants Georg von Schnitzler and Carl Ludwig Lautenschläger, who had not taken the witness stand and therefore not been cross-examined. The court had to decide on a May 5, 1948, motion by Rudolf Dix on behalf of all defendants, in which he suggested that all these affidavits be stricken with respect to the other defendants but not the authors. Based on the majority decision made by Judges Shake and Morris about the defense as a whole, "the consideration of affidavits by affiants, who did not take the witness stand, was limited to those affiants." These sworn statements would not be used as evidence against other defendants, but "only against the affiants themselves." The Kransberg memorandum, however, including the statements by Schmitz quoted in it, would be allowable as a piece of evidence. Judge Hebert took a strong stance against this decision, though he prefaced it by stating that the decision had been "procedurally proper" and was in keeping with the theory "upon which this case has been tried to date." It was also in keeping with a previous order of the court. Hebert, who had gone along with the decision until then, had decided in the meantime that "the entire series of rulings of the Tribunal, with reference to the admissibility of affidavits, is in error" and that they were not in keeping with Military Ordinance No. 7: "I believe that … affidavits are admissible, even though the affiant cannot be produced for cross-examination, regardless of the reason for which he cannot be produced." In taking this stance, Hebert rejected the interpretation to which all the judges had until that point agreed and affirmed the interpretation of the prosecution. Judge Merrell expressed his full agreement with Hebert's interpretation—with the proviso that he was only a substitute judge. He emphasized that a "thorough study" of the legal bases of the trial had convinced him that "in keeping with the expressed intent of the law to avoid technical rules of evidence and to admit any evidence deemed to have probative value, affidavits should be received in evidence without regard to whether the affiant is available for cross-examination." Merrell admitted that "in a search for truth, cross-examination is an important help," but that an affidavit that carried the possible penalty of perjury had "even without cross-examination … a certain weight" that should be recognized by the court.[179]

At this point the trial was reaching its end. All that was missing were the concluding briefs by the prosecution and the defense, the closing statements of both parties, and the defendants' final words.

The Closing Arguments

By the end of the trial, all sides were weary, exhausted, and even in some cases sick. The lawyer Christian Tuerck, the assistant counsel of Fritz ter Meer, expressed his disappointment in a mid-April 1948 letter to the Leverkusen jurist Hugo Schramm that he would have to cancel his trip to Leverkusen because he had a "bad flu with fever, chills, and other bad side effects."[180] And Erich Berndt, ter Meer's chief defense counsel, wrote in a letter to Schramm in early June, "Over the past while we have had to work a hell of a lot." And since in Nuremberg, as Berndt stated, "everyone is pretty weary, in some cases also sick with colds," he asked for an entire pharmacy's worth of medications: Novalgin-quinine, Priovit, dextrose, and "some Adalin, since the working up of the nerves sometimes causes sleeplessness."[181]

The defendants were haggard, too. As Rudolf Dix described it in March 1948, they lacked time for personal hygiene, in particular for cleaning their cells, because of the length of the court sessions, including those on weekends. Because they did not have Saturdays off and did not have the chance to take showers throughout the week, there was no opportunity for bathing. The busy schedule also meant that they had to speed through meals. The defendants felt the schedule to be an "unbearable physical and psychological burden," not least since many were beginning their fourth year of imprisonment, and asked that the old schedule be reinstated. The letter was signed by twenty of the defendants—not including Otto Ambros, Paul Häfliger, and Heinrich Oster. Attached to the letter was also a listing of the defendants by age group, which was intended to show the relatively advanced age of many of the defendants. Oster, Jähne, Kühne, Schmitz, and Hörlein were sixty-five to seventy years of age; von Schnitzler, ter Meer, Bürgin, Gajewski, Häfliger, Krauch, Schneider, von Knieriem, and

Lautenschläger were sixty to sixty-five years of age; and Mann, Bütefisch, Ilgner, Dürrfeld, Wurster, von der Heyde, Ambros, Kugler, and Gattineau were younger than sixty.[182]

Judge Morris expressed his frustration multiple times during the final phase of the trial. By this point, it was clear that he was not only highly displeased but also exhausted. In May 1948 he touched on his decidedly mixed feelings in a letter: "The case is very interesting in that it involves many novel questions of law and international law. On the other hand, the long-drawn out presentation of the evidence became very trying and monotonous. The documents alone that were presented as exhibits run well into the thousands." And, Morris added, "I have never worked so hard in my life. This is a wonderful experience but one which I would not care to repeat."[183] Formulating his mood in another way, he wrote, "While this experience has been most interesting, it has also been the most difficult in which I ever became involved."[184]

But both sides had to focus once again and mobilize all available resources to ensure that their closing statements would convey their theories and arguments as effectively and convincingly as possible. The briefs and the closing statements, some of which were very long, took much time and effort, in particular because both sides were attempting to position themselves quickly with respect to the arguments of the other side.

The September 1947 recommendations by Wolfram von Metzler had clearly found a hearing in the defense, since they were taken up in this phase. Professor Eduard Wahl (Figure 3.9), who served as the special counsel of all defendants, started.

In his closing letter on behalf of all defendants, entitled "Fundamental Questions of Law," Wahl first argued that the court in Case VI was not an international or a German court, but rather "an American Military Tribunal deriving its authority from the Control Council."[185] Next, he took the position that an American court was bound, for legal reasons, "to acquit the defendants in the industrial trials at least." This was because the legal basis of the IMT judgment had been the London Statute—and thus, for an American court, an ex post facto law. The circumstances were also different with regard to the charge of a war of aggression: "If, in the IMT, leaders of the state or other political figures in leading positions were concerned, this time it is a question of the punishment of private persons." It was, Wahl stated, "not of minor importance" that the IMT was about "leaders of the State or other political figures in leading roles" while now "private individuals" were to be punished. Because while in the punishment of Nazi leadership there was "an idea of retaliation rejecting the objection *nulla poena sine lege*," this idea must cease to apply in the case of the accused businessmen. Even if one accepted the idea that in light of the "depravity of the German Fuehrer clique," legal objections to their punishment were to be seen as pointless, the question remained: "What have those businessmen and industrialists, none of whom took part in the Fuehrer's conferences which are so critical according to the IMT judgment, to do with the policy of the highest Nazi government clique?"[186]

Despite the good faith of the initiators of the Nuremberg trials, these trials had to some extent developed "precisely as special courts, for which a special law has been created ex post facto." This was "the sore point which explains the unusually sharp condemnation of the Nuernberg trials, in Anglo-Saxon quarters," where one representative voice even spoke of a "travesty of justice" and stated that "lynching [would have been] more honorable and legitimate."[187] The Kellogg-Briand Pact had not provided for sanctions against private persons. Overall, the criminal prosecution of private individuals from an international law standpoint was a "novum" that should raise the strongest doubts. Even members of governments had not been criminally liable as individuals until that point. In addition, individuals who acted on the orders of their government could not generally be held criminally liable: "This peculiarity of international law is based on good reasons. How could government function if any citizen could make himself a judge on the political measures taken by his government? Who would protect him if he violated the law of his country, invoking the provisions of international law?" The "criminal responsibility of the private person" could play no role, Wahl stated, either for the initiation or the waging of a war, since the "decisions involved are of a highly political nature and must, of necessity, remain outside the judgment of the individual citizen." There was a right to resist dictatorships, but there "has never been a duty."[188]

Wahl also claimed that the charges of plunder and spoliation and the use of forced labor should be dropped, because the Allies had also committed corresponding violations of international law, not least over the course of "total warfare."[189]

With reference to crimes against humanity, Wahl emphasized that until then international law had declined to hold "private individuals responsible for the misdeeds of the political organs of the State." Moreover, the Nazi regime had woven "a fine net of steel" over Germany and had shaped its power apparatus "into a man-eating Moloch which left the people no choice." In Germany, a criminal state had emerged that had used the entire people for its purposes. It was obvious that these misdeeds should be criminally prosecuted—but in a "total criminal state," the possible offenses included not only crimes against humanity involving murder or personal injury, but also persecution for racial, religious, or political reasons, making the total numbers of people responsible very high. The IMT had already "opposed the theory of collective guilt," however. The fact that necessity could limit criminal liability also came into play. In the Flick trial, this had been largely used in defense of the defendants. They had lived in the "reign of terror" of the Nazi state, where enforcement agents and the Gestapo had always been present "ready to go into instant action and to mete out savage and immediate punishment against anyone doing anything that could be construed as obstructing or hindering the carrying out of governmental regulations or decrees." It did not make sense, Wahl argued, "to ignore the fact that the individual is inextricably tangled in the meshes of the State, or to postulate from the point of view of international law that the individual be liable to punishment as an accomplice to the crimes committed by the totalitarian state."[190] Beyond the argument that the defendants had been acting under orders, Wahl even called for the recognition that they had faced a "conflict of duties": It had been their tragic fate to search in vain for an escape from the inner conflict between their patriotism and their desire to "have done with the criminal tyranny of Nazism." The defendants had finally seen "a higher duty" in "remaining at their posts" ensuring that "a worse evil is prevented."[191]

Finally, Wahl expressed his rejection of the charge of conspiracy, which contravened "the recognized principles of the civilized nations." He asserted that the "concept of 'plot'" had been gotten rid of on the European continent in the 19th century; courts no longer sentenced conspirators in a "mass condemnation" but sought to hold individuals responsible "only for what he has consciously contributed to the accomplished crime." Wahl did admit that in the case of the persecution of political opponents, whether for high treason or attempted assassination, most recent developments in Germany had gone back to that idea of "plot."[192]

In his closing arguments on June 2, 1948, which he later published with the provocative title "Eine deutsche Verteidigung" (A German Defense) in the journal *Der Ruf*, Eduard Wahl once again employed the ideas discussed above.[193] He began his argument by emphasizing the influence of the Russian Professor Trainin on the London Statute, with the aim of making the trials of the industrialists seem like a Soviet-concocted travesty. In particular, Professor Trainin had proposed "to attribute personal guilt for crimes against peace not only to members of armies and governments, but also to propagandists, capitalists and industrialists." This cast a "significant light" on the definition in CCL No. 10, Article II, point 2(f), of criminal responsibility of representatives of private industry, Wahl said, which, according to the text, was sufficient in itself to justify conviction, even if the prosecution only suspected guilt. Wahl concluded, "Thus it is this trial in particular which is overshadowed by the Russian ideology and by the fight against the old and revered legal traditions of the civilized world, which is stigmatized as an outcome of the capitalist an imperialist ideology."[194] With regard to count I, Wahl repeated the substance of his arguments from the closing letter. He wanted the charge of crimes against peace for "private persons" such as the I. G. Farben managers to be made invalid and attacked them as "retroactive criminal law." At the same time, he emphasized with regard to counts II and III that the waging of a "total war" had rendered the previously applicable rules of war largely obsolete. To punish German managers would be to employ a double standard, since in the total war against Germany, the Allies had committed the

Figure 3.9. Professor Eduard Wahl, special counsel of all defendants. Source: NARA 238-OMT-VI-DC-9; NL Nath; public domain.

same crimes as the Germans. In practice, states had been "inclined to act in accordance with what was called military necessity" during war more than in accordance with international law. Though Wahl admitted that the Allies had not committed these offenses to the same degree as the Germans, he clearly saw the actions of the Germans as not particularly severe: "The use of civilians for labor is a minus quantity compared to their killing, just as exploitation of foreign plants is a lesser incursion on private property than their violent destruction by bombing." To conclude, Wahl once more argued strongly for the recognition of the concept of superior orders with reference to individuals in a totalitarian state, the contradictory obligations of the German managers, and the pressure that had been placed on them.[195]

Wahl clearly made an impression with his closing argument—some of his formulations appeared in the verdict. Moreover, he motivated his colleagues. The following day, the lawyer Erich Berndt wrote to Leverkusen, "The introductory closing statement by Professor Wahl was very good, and I think it helped us a lot."[196]

On June 2 and 3, Wolfram von Metzler (Figure 3.10) delivered his closing statement. While it is infrequently quoted, it was also important, especially in light of the verdict. He addressed two essential points for the defense as a whole: the evidence as presented for counts I and V of the indictment and the general theory of the responsibility of the defendants. According to von Metzler, the court had to examine whether the evidence presented by the prosecution

Figure 3.10. The lawyer Wolfram von Metzler. Source: NARA 238-OMT-VI-DC-8; NL Nath; public domain.

and the defense was substantial and convincing. In so doing, the judges should, if needed, "take control of the scales of Justice and … throw into them a few grains of mercy so as to give the defendant the benefit of a reasonable doubt." The defense had already submitted a request on December 17, 1947, to have the defendants acquitted on counts I and V of the indictment and from the charge of plunder in Austria and Czechoslovakia. According to von Metzler, the evidence as a whole was irrelevant with respect to count I of the indictment—just as had been the case in the trial against Krupp, in which the court had acquitted the defendants on the same charge. Von Metzler linked his approach to the IMT verdict and asked about the defendants' knowledge of Hitler's goals, a key element in the commission of a crime against peace. I. G. Farben's share of German armaments had been "of no interest," he stated. Rather, the question was whether the defendants were personally responsible for the furtherance of Hitler's attack plans and thus knew of his intentions. Seen from the standpoint of the IMT verdict, however, this knowledge was not identical with the so-called common knowledge of what Hitler might do or not do but meant the "special knowledge of specific aggressive plans which Hitler revealed to a certain limited circle of his closest advisors," specifically in four particular secret conferences. Otherwise, there would "hardly be any sensible limitation of the circle of men responsible for such crimes in Germany," which, in the end, would lead to "mass punishments," something the IMT wanted to avoid. The defendants in the IMT had been "government and army officials," whereas the defendants in this trial were businessmen, for whom there could be "undoubtably adopted no stricter standard than in the case of the top representatives of the Nazi system." The defendants Schacht and Speer were both substantially responsible for German armament but had been acquitted, since armament of itself was no crime against peace. The prosecution would therefore argue, he stated, that the defendants had not just been businessmen but had held official positions in the administration, remaining vague, however, about what this meant concretely. If the prosecution claimed, von Metzler stated, that the defendants were involved in the preparation and waging of the war of aggression to a greater degree than a Reich minister or a high-level Reich official, then "such a theory clearly shows that the Prosecution has no knowledge at all what influence, as compared with even a prominent businessman, a top-ranking government official had and exercised in the Third Reich in synchronizing the efforts and activities of the German nation with the aims of the Nazi policy."[197]

In a criminal trial, von Metzler argued, the following rules applied for proving the guilt of a defendant: first, there should be no conviction without the proof of personal guilt. Second, guilt had to be proved beyond a reasonable doubt. Third, innocence must be presumed throughout the trial. Fourth, the burden of proof lay on the prosecution. Fifth and finally, the rule *in dubio pro reo* applied in cases of doubt for the defendants. From the perspective of the defense, the material presented by the prosecution for a war of aggression "[did] not constitute a circumstantial evidence" according to these rules. To infer knowledge of Hitler's attack plans from financial support for Hitler and the NSDAP would be out of discussion. In general, it would not be sufficient to prove that the defendants knew that Hitler wanted to wage a war. They had to know that Hitler was preparing an aggressive war, since his actions could have been "merely measures of precaution in the case of a defensive." Since the prosecution had failed to provide evidence for count I, the defendants also had to be acquitted of count V, since there could not have been a corresponding conspiracy. In direct contrast to the principles presented in the IMT verdict, the prosecution had presented "a vague and ambiguous theory" and had pulled together "a lot of irrelevant evidence."[198]

In the second part of his remarks, von Metzler went into great detail on a general theory of the responsibility of the defendants for the acts under discussion, the "key problem of this trial." The prosecution had only presented an "incredibly small amount of evidence" about the personal responsibility of the individual defendants. It had completely failed, von Metzler argued, to fulfil the evidentiary obligation mentioned above—to prove beyond reasonable doubt the personal guilt of each of the defendants. In criminal law, guilt was personal. There was no collective responsibility or guilt deriving from membership in a certain organization or body. However, the indictment alleged the collective guilt of all defendants on the basis of their position on the board of directors or other committees of I. G. Farben, which apparently served as a "dragnet to draw in all defendants." The line of argument in the prosecution's trial briefs had been, in some cases, "a classic example of a complete misconception of the burden of proof." The prosecution was taking the position that to prove the defendants' guilt, it was not necessary "to prove that each defendant had knowledge of each specific crime covered by the Indictment respectively of any details of such crime, nor that each defendant actively participated in the commission of such crime." The prosecution argued, he stated, that all the crimes had occurred "in execution of an alleged general policy and program" that the defendants had set into motion and authorized. This position of the prosecution was, von Metzler stated, "in flat contradiction" to the theory he defended—"that criminal guilt is personal, that there exists no collective criminal guilt and that therefore it is up to the Prosecution to prove beyond any reasonable doubt on the part of each defendant his personal participation in and knowledge of each specific crime charged under the different Counts of the Indictment." As presented, the prosecution's interpretation "in substance [was] not a theory of criminal guilt under Count I, II, and III of the Indictment," but "rather a theory of criminal guilt under the conspiracy charge." But on the basis of the determination of the court, for counts II and III "no conspiracy [could] be assumed from a legal point of view."[199]

Thus, for Wolfram von Metzler, the "only legally sound approach" to adequately deal with the problem of responsibility was "dividing the responsibility among the different members of the Vorstand in accordance with the special tasks which were assigned to them." The basis for this had to be the "principle of decentralization" that applied at I. G. Farben. It would have been impossible for the members of the board of directors to deal with all the affairs of this large company. A division of fields of work and responsibilities was a "cogent necessity" and had led to "considerable autonomy" of the individual works and sales divisions. The decentralization and the related "principle of individual responsibility of the members of the board" would also have been in agreement with the 1928 statutes of I. G. Farben and the corresponding German legal requirements.[200] In fact, the division of labor had been particularly marked at I. G. Farben—the defendants had no obligation to do a "constant check" on the work of their colleagues, not least because these colleagues were more familiar with the relevant topics. The prosecution had established in "no case a violation of the duty to supervise and intervene." Negligence was not punishable. And for failing to take an action that would have opposed measures of the Nazi regime, they could claim the "plea of necessity." Finally, von Metzler argued on behalf of the defense that "even if—contrary to their opinion—certain activities of one or several defendants directly involved therein should be considered criminal, in none of such cases can a criminal responsibility of the other defendants be assumed on the basis of all the afore-mentioned observations."[201]

This made it clear that some defense counsels and their clients wanted to distance themselves from the actions of other defendants. This related in particular to the "Auschwitz matter," which was considered particularly dangerous. Correspondingly, the individual closing arguments of the defense counsels focused on the criminal responsibility of the defendants and the fundamental questions that Wahl and von Metzler had raised. The lawyers left few stones unturned in the effort to exonerate the I. G. Farben managers.

In his closing remarks on behalf of Hermann Schmitz, Rudolf Dix called for a collective pardon, quoting from the document by the Jesuit Max Pribilla cited above: if so many people had committed faults, it was not possible to have a criminal procedure, even though this meant that some things might remain unpunished—the judgment could be left to God. Dix also expressed his general skepticism about the trial. He had no inhibitions about describing the accused managers as scapegoats who had been put on the dock owing to the "Prosecution legend of the 'unholy trinity' ": "When Hitler suffered reverses, the cry went up 'The Jews are to blame.' The place of the Jews as scapegoat has now been taken by the 'bloated capitalists,' which is the term of abuse now publicly bestowed upon the industrialist. Every age has its own scapegoats."[202]

Walter Siemers addressed the fundamentals on behalf of defendant Georg von Schnitzler, emphasizing the difference between the state and private individuals with regard to count I. There was the tendency to "make private individuals responsible under international law," which the IMT itself had approved: "It must however be taken into consideration that the Trial before the International Military Tribunal did not concern private people, as the present trial does, but responsible officials of the state, that is to say persons who by virtue of their office acted *for* the State." To theorize such a responsibility was not unjustified, but could not be applied to the I. G. Farben managers, he argued: "But it is on no account permissible to make a private individual, namely an industrialist, legally answerable, as long as he is not acting on behalf of the state, and is not a government official or functionary, and who, in view of the described legal theories hitherto applied, could not possibly, and actually did not, imagine that he, as well as his government had the duty to ensure that international law is observed."[203] The prosecution had been able to provide neither direct nor indirect evidence that the defendants had known about Hitler's plans of attack and had taken part in the preparations: "They therefore resolved to furnish proof by submitting statements by Schnitzler, made during his stay at the Preungesheim prison in 1945." The prosecution had taken the "enormous trouble of giving new form" to von Schnitzler's statements from that period and presenting them as affidavits in 1947, "hoping in this way that Schnitzler would incriminate himself and the other representatives of the I.G." He, Siemers, could prove that the statements of 1945 and 1947 had been created "under heavy physical and psychological duress" and therefore could not be used as evidence.[204]

The lawyer Werner Schubert also emphasized the distinction between official role and private individual, stating with regard to count I that the defendants were "not even credited with idealistic or commendable motives" such as patriotism by the prosecution, which instead had argued that "greed and lust for power motivated their actions." He countered that "if such a monstrous charge has been raised against men who were no political leaders, no military commanders nor holders of high government offices, then it is necessary to apply the strictest standards of evidence in order to prove the offense."[205]

The defense also emphasized that I. G. Farben and its managers had already essentially been prejudged by CCL No. 9. The lawyer Otto Nelte, for instance, in his closing statement on behalf of Heinrich Hörlein, questioned whether the prosecution was "trying just as hard to find the truth as I am." Anyone who was setting out "to prove a certain thesis is not a seeker of the truth," because the search for truth was "incompatible with the desire to prove correct a decision which has already been made." This was the position of the prosecution, Nelte alleged, when it argued that the preamble of CCL No. 9 showed that I. G. Farben had taken part in armament "knowingly and prominently" and that the majority of the free world assumed this to be the case. Political decisions aimed at a specific purpose, but decisions of the court "must not be predicated on a purpose" but should only serve the law and justice. For Nelte, therefore, the trial of the I. G. Farben managers stood "under the singular handicap of the Control Council Law No. 9, especially in regard to Counts 1 and 5 of the Indictment."

If the IMT had acquitted Hjalmar Schacht, Nelte argued, how could his client Hörlein, "whose activities precluded any contact with politically important or oriented personalities," be found guilty of count I? It was easy to establish that Hitler could not have waged war without I. G. Farben. But before a verdict was rendered, the objective facts and *mens rea* had to be examined—the production of evidence must always include "the desire for the criminal occurrence." Therefore, the "seemingly so convincing statement" that Hitler's war would not have been possible without I. G. Farben was "as true as it is irrelevant for the judgment under criminal law."[206]

The lawyer Horst Pelckmann also emphasized the problems with the Allied ordinances for his client August von Knieriem, referring to General Order No. 2 of the US military government for carrying out Law No. 52, in the preamble of which I. G. Farben was described as a knowing participant in Germany's efforts for world conquest. Pelckmann asked rhetorically, "Do not these words already anticipate all that should only be decided by your verdict, Your Honors?" The court, Pelckmann stated, was "not bound by these words;" the formulation did not establish *res iudicata* and was "legally irrelevant." In any case, he said, this legal measure had been overtaken by CCL No. 9 and other developments. It was still based on the directive JCS 1067, which had been influenced by Henry Morgenthau. In the meantime, however, Pelckmann argued, "the Morgenthau plan has been recognized as a great and even tragic historical error."[207]

Finally, as in the closing statement on behalf of Fritz Gajewski, the concept of superior orders was cited. In order to fulfill state production goals, an industrialist had no choice but to exploit forced laborers and concentration camp inmates that had been "allocated by the labor distribution agencies." Otherwise, he would have risked "his personal freedom or even his life." As Military Tribunal IV had determined in the Flick trial, the Gestapo had been ever-present in Germany, ready at any time to mete out gruesome punishment if it got the scent of sabotage or anything similar.[208]

Owing in large part to von Metzler's clarification of the matter of individual guilt, each defendant who had any connection with Auschwitz attempted to emphasize that he was in no way responsible for the construction of the I. G. Farben factory there and the crimes tied up with it. Fritz ter Meer's lawyer, Erich Berndt, described Auschwitz as a dilemma, a matter of acting under orders. The construction of the factory in Auschwitz had been determined by the Reich Ministry of Economics and the Reich Office for Economic Development and had been forced on I. G. Farben, and the use of concentration camp inmates "had not been the original intention of Farben" but had been "forced upon Farben by the state authorities." Göring's decree had given the I. G. Farben managers no other choice, since the factory was considered important for the war effort and they would otherwise have made themselves guilty of sabotage. However, Berndt distanced himself from the consequences of the use of concentration camp inmates, since his client had had no responsibility for their "management ... in particular on the social welfare of the workers employed in the plant." "Neither in his capacity of chairman of the Technical Committee, nor in his capacity of chief of Sparte II was ter Meer concerned with the construction of the plant. This was the exclusive task of the local plant management." Had ter Meer heard about it, he would have had to act. But he had "never heard" that inmates had been poorly treated, nor had he heard before 1945 of the "killings and cremations in the Auschwitz concentration camp ... not even rumors."[209] This distancing was even more surprising considering that it had been Fritz ter Meer who had originally brought all the lawyers and defendants "in line" with regard to the "Auschwitz matter." As a result of what, from the perspective of the defense, was a failed presentation of evidence when it came to Auschwitz, he was now clearly seeking to distance himself from the conditions and crimes there.

Otto Ambros's lawyer, Karl Hoffmann, also sought to deny his client's responsibility by emphasizing that he had planned the Auschwitz factory, like the other Buna factories, but had not built it. This had to be said very clearly, Hoffmann stated, even if Ambros had not done so, since he "feared to give the suspicion of being a coward by shifting the blame from his own shoulders" and also feared "losing his self-respect." He, Hoffmann, was required as his defense counsel to make note of this. Ambros had not been the factory head, he stated—therefore he was not responsible for what had occurred at the factory or in the concentration camp: "Not Otto Ambros, but others are responsible for the deaths of the victims of Auschwitz."[210]

The lawyer Friedrich Wagner, who put his personal fate and his entire reputation on the line for Carl Wurster, argued along entirely different lines. Wagner began his remarks by referring to the fact that he could not have imagined returning to his country after fourteen years of exile to argue on behalf of a man who was accused of war crimes: "If I am doing so, nevertheless, it is because I am firmly convinced that I am thus serving a just cause." Wagner emphasized the important and weighty role of the judge, on whose words honor, freedom, and often even life depended. This power had to be exercised within the framework of the law and "with the high aim of realization of justice for all." This was especially well guaranteed in advanced countries such as the United States, which had brought forth many great and independent-minded judges. The path toward truth was by its essence "not always easy to find," but it was especially difficult in this trial, in which the judges were led into "deep underbrush which is formed by interests, over-zealousness, misunderstanding and mistake." The judges had even been led "too far" into the weeds, but "with the help of the Defense," they had found their way onto the path "which leads to the truth." And, simply put, the truth looked "entirely different" from how the prosecution had depicted it. For Wagner, the Fremdarbeiter in Ludwigshafen had been "forced workers in a double sense": "The Nazi authorities forced them to come to Germany to work, and these same authorities compelled the Plant Manager, Dr. Wurster, to accept them." One could hardly come up with a better justification of the concept of superior orders—both for the Fremdarbeiter and for Wurster. Wagner described resistance under Nazi tyranny in this case as "completely senseless and therefore impossible." Instead of a "wave of hatred" toward Wurster, Wagner said, the forced laborers had in the end felt gratitude. The American and French occupation authorities had also respected Wurster, and when he had been arrested, the employees at Ludwigshafen had even organized a "sympathy strike." Wagner therefore expressed his hope that Wurster, a "conscientious man," be acquitted—in fact, this was demanded by the principle of justice. "At the same time," Wagner argued, an acquittal would "be a contribution so necessary to the moral reconstruction since it will restore to many that without which men cannot live together in peaceful communities; the faith in justice."[211]

Finally, on June 9, 1948, Friedrich Silcher, the in-house counsel at Leverkusen, made a closing statement about I. G. Farben on behalf of all defendants. Hermann Heimerich had suggested before the trial—and Wolfram von Metzler had echoed him in September 1947—that the positive sides of I. G. Farben be more strongly drawn out in the defense in order to counter the image that Taylor and other members of the prosecution had painted of the company, its managers, and its scientists and technical experts. Friedrich Silcher now took up this task.[212]

He began his remarks by commenting that in the trial formally only the twenty-three defendants in the dock were indicted, not the I. G. Farben company. "However this firm from a moral point of view is the invisible defendant who in addition to those twenty three men has been mentioned time and again in this trial. Your Honors only need to read the indictment in order to gather therefrom this inescapable impression." Therefore, the defense considered it necessary, Silcher stated, to speak about the company, which had been so falsely depicted by the prosecution, as well: "The Prosecution gives a picture of I. G. Farben black in black, pretending it to be an overall canvas. This picture is false for a double reason; not only does the Prosecution present as black points, which are in fact white. Apart from this it leaves unmentioned numerous white points which lie in between." In his attempt to "draw the true picture of Farben," Silcher started by pointing out that scientific and technical achievements could be misused: "industry and technology are man's servants and instruments which he may utilize to make them either a blessing or a curse. The instrument is innocent; man's mind alone decided." Chemistry, in particular, was a raw-material industry, most of the products of which could be used both for peace and for war.[213]

Silcher enumerated I. G. Farben's numerous products, praised the scientific achievements made in its laboratories, mentioned its high investment in research, and came to the conclusion that "it was an alliance of research, science, technology, and true enterprise, typical of Farben and the only one that Farben concluded and not, as the Prosecution maintains, an alliance with Hitler."[214]

Silcher emphasized I. G. Farben's social attitudes toward its employees and its good treatment of them—and interpreted a supposed lack of acts of sabotage in the I. G. Farben factories as evidence of the fact that the company had treated the many Fremdarbeiter as well as the "considerable number of concentration camp inmates" in Auschwitz-Monowitz fairly.[215]

Silcher mentioned that the I. G. Farben managers had succeeded in their careers not primarily because of relationships, but because of their hard work and their personalities. He remarked that the company had "ceased to belong to any individual persons or groups but had become the property of the general public." It was not the property of the defendants, but of everyone who had decided to invest their money in I. G. Farben stock—from a percentage standpoint, there had been no more controlling shareholders. The distributed profits had been relatively small, because, owing to the necessity to be highly innovative in chemistry, a good portion of the money brought in was reinvested in research and development, as well as in social services for the employees. The founding of I. G. Farben in the wake of the merger of the founding companies, Silcher argued, was the result of a recognition of the "necessity of a better regulation and reasonable distribution of working fields within their scope of production." The owners of the founding companies had not completed a "concentration of power on a gigantic scale," but had rather declined power "due to considerations of a higher order."[216]

Finally, Silcher expressly rejected the prosecution's theory that I. G. Farben had substantially profited from an alliance with Hitler and from the wars of aggression. In fact, Silcher argued, it entailed two different subtheories: on the one hand, the I. G. Farben managers had yearned for conquest and prepared the machinery of war—had even been "the real top war criminals, the real initiators of the aggressive war," while the leading Nazi figures had been "only meaningless puppets." This theory was similar to the one that underlay the Morgenthau Plan. The prosecution's second theory, Silcher continued, was that the defendants knew about and approved of Hitler's plans of attack. The I. G. Farben managers were thus the "guardians of the State's secrets of the Third Reich." During the trial, however, the two theories had "not [been] mentioned with one single word anymore." Silcher asked himself whether "they will perhaps rise up tomorrow in the final plea of the Prosecution. We wonder whether the stinky corpse of both these theories will once again be presented to us after having done its duty against Farben outside this trial." All that remained had been a third theory, according to which I. G. Farben had to have known "that Hitler planned and prepared aggressive wars and that therefore they had participated deliberately therein by their industrial achievements."[217]

The prosecution overlooked, Silcher argued, that the development of I. G. Farben after the global economic crisis had been similar to that of companies such as DuPont, Standard Oil, General Motors, United States Steel, and ICI—and not so strongly influenced by the Four-Year Plan or armament. Further, I. G. Farben's share of the chemical industry and of industry in Germany in general had also not been as large as had been claimed, he argued. It had not been "this surpassing and overwhelming giant." Among international companies, too, I. G. Farben ranked "modestly." I. G. Farben was also "of international and worldwide standard" not only in its business dealings but "also in its bearing."[218]

Even under the Nazi regime, Silcher stated, I. G. Farben had succeeded in its strategy of pursuing the path of "evasive resistance in order to maintain its main position and thus save the economic reason." I. G. Farben had always been perceived as a foreign body in the Third Reich, however, and for important actors in the Nazi regime, it had even been "the most hated enterprise." According to Silcher, I. G. Farben was not an ally of Hitler, as the prosecution painted it, but rather a "prisoner."[219] Silcher knew, he stated, that "Farben [was] dead" and that he was holding "a funeral sermon in this respect." But the importance of what he was saying, Silcher ended dramatically, went far beyond the immediate context—it related to the saving of Europe and the future of the world, for which I. G. Farben and its employees could still do much—if its managers were not thrown in jail.[220]

On the following day, June 10, 1948, Telford Taylor and his team delivered the prosecution's closing plea. A few days prior, on June 1, the prosecution had submitted its closing brief to the court. In the introduction, it once again focused on the personal responsibility of the defendants and went into detail with regard to the role of the members of the board. For the prosecution, drawing on the verdict from *American Tobacco Co. v. United States* of 1946, all the members of the board of directors ought to be held criminally responsible owing to their participation in and their shared knowledge of criminal acts that took place at I. G. Farben. The fact that a defendant was a member of the board meant, for one, that he had participated substantially in the actions carried out by I. G. Farben. It also meant, for the prosecution, that he knew about "any matter of any importance in the affairs of Farben even though he may not have known (although he could have found out with the slightest investigation) of many details in connection with the administration of such matters." At the same time, the prosecution emphasized that it was not of the opinion "that membership in the Vorstand of Farben automatically makes a person responsible for the criminal activities carried on through Farben during the period in which he was a member." Each of the defendants was "being tried for his individual participation in the crimes charged." Nor was the claim being made that CCL No. 10 provided for "vicarious criminal responsibility." Rather, the prosecution was of the opinion "that the evidence which has been introduced concerning the activities and organization of Farben [established] beyond a reasonable doubt" that each board member accused had made himself guilty of the crimes listed under counts I, II, III, and V. The evidence proved the individual guilt of each individual member of the board—the accused directors and their responsibility were not addressed here.

Finally, the prosecution emphasized that I. G. Farben's crimes were "not the acts of a soulless, lifeless legal entity" but the acts of the managers responsible. Special responsibility for a certain area of the company also in no way absolved each individual member of the board from responsibility for all actions that they had authorized. The prosecution even came to the following conclusion: "The fact that each defendant had a special role to perform increases rather than lessens the responsibility of each defendant for the over-all program. For if it were not for the activities carried on by any particular defendant, the whole program might have failed."[221]

Again and again, the final brief named the company instead of individually assigning criminal responsibility—something that Kim Priemel has drawn attention to.[222] In the very detailed Part IV of the prosecution's concluding brief, however, under the heading "Certain activities in the field of slave labor and mass murder," the prosecution became very precise, attaching criminal responsibility above all to the defendants Carl Krauch, Fritz ter Meer, Otto Ambros, Heinrich Bütefisch, and Walter Dürrfeld. That said, it also viewed the members of the Technical Committee—the entire I. G. Farben board, in fact—as responsible for Auschwitz.[223]

In the fifth part, the prosecution addressed the arguments of the defense, such as the claim of duress, armament for defense, and "window dressing" under the Nazi regime, and investigated the credibility of the defense and the defendants. This involved another look at the abovementioned case of Ollendorff and Fritz Gajewski's behavior toward him.[224] In the sixth and final part—the longest, at more than six hundred pages—each of the twenty-three defendants was assigned individual criminal responsibility, including the four directors. This was not without its problems, since the latter, in some cases, had not been involved until 1938 and often only indirectly, and saw themselves, like Erich von der Heyde, charged as "an accomplice in the execution of a common plan or conspiracy" that aimed to further the Nazi expansion policy "to take from the peoples of other countries by force their land, their property, and their personal freedom."[225]

After the defense's closing statements, it was important for the prosecution's closing statement to counter not just the briefs but also the core statements and theories of the defense as convincingly as possible.[226] Telford Tayler began by saying that everything essential had already been addressed and debated over the course of the trial. Both sides, the prosecution as well as the defense, had clearly explained their stances. The court had "dedicated itself to the conduct of the trial with manifest devotion to the task at hand." The defense had represented the defendants, Taylor argued, "most ably." However, Taylor now argued: "The proven facts in this case, we submit, present a compelling claim to a firm and meaningful judgment." The court was not being asked for "a declaratory judgment on naked questions of law," since this was a criminal trial. But a "meaningful" sentence, Taylor stated, was "doubly necessary": "The issues in this case travel far beyond the confines of Nurnberg, and the impact of their solution here will be felt thousands of miles away and for many years to come. In a very deep sense, Nurnberg is the world in microcosm."[227]

Responsibility for I. G. Farben's criminal record lay, the prosecution argued, with a few men: "The Farben record was written by men, and somewhere exists the guilt for the crimes in that record. Such guilt may indeed be attributable in part to persons not present in the dock, but it can profit those defendants nothing that we have charged too few rather than all, and it is far better that we punish too few rather than too many." The board of directors carried the major share of responsibility, the prosecution argued. I. G. Farben had been "a cohesive organization with coherent policies and a well-disciplined organization for carrying out those policies." As much as the various fields of the company differed from each other, there was still central management. The prosecution compared I. G. Farben to a ship "under the captain's control." The captain did not control the individual tasks on the ship, for which he had ship's engineers or navigators, "but a ship is commanded from the bridge, and Farben was commanded by the Vorstand." This was aimed at von Metzler's closing statement, in which he had sought to limit the criminal responsibility of the defendants to their individual fields in light of I. G. Farben's decentralized structure. According to the prosecution, however, while the board of directors gave individual members areas of responsibility, "it did not and it could not relinquish or shift the responsibility for overall management." Individuals bore the responsibility not only for their actions, but also for their omissions. Many of the crimes of which the I. G. Farben managers had been accused were clear actions, as could be seen in the example of Auschwitz. The responsibility of a member of the board for the crimes of another was certainly not unlimited, as von Metzler had pointed out. But the idea that each person was responsible only for his area of the business made "a complete mockery of the whole concept of management responsibility." It was an "abdication of responsibility," the prosecution argued, to allow men with a high level of responsibility in a company to be protected from punishment by "pleading ignorance of the most fundamental policies and activities of the corporation" or by "tearing the mantle of responsibility into individual shreds."[228]

Along these lines, the prosecution, summarizing counts I and V, called for the court to "enforce the doctrine of international penal law … that the deliberate planning and waging of aggressive war is a crime." The prosecution did not want thousands of ordinary people to feel condemned under this charge, but only those I. G. Farben managers who had been proved to have known "that the military machine which they helped build would be used to launch a German program of military conquest." Von Metzler's arguments, "an able piece of advocacy," changed nothing about that. He seemed to be of the view that it was not sufficient that the I. G. Farben managers knew that Germany's military might be used to launch a program of military conquest. The prosecution apparently had to prove that they had detailed knowledge of it: "According to this theory, a man who joins with and supports a group of gangsters in an undertaking to rob a series of banks cannot be held criminally responsible unless he knew which bank would be robbed first, and precisely what time the robbery was scheduled to occur." The agenda of conquest of the Nazi regime, however, had been "highly flexible and opportunistic." The choice of timing and goals had been primarily based on assessments that were not directly connected to "long term economic preparation for conquest." Qualifying criminal responsibility in the way von Metzler had suggested would be "completely unrealistic, and [would reduce] the whole concept of the crime against peace to an academic shibboleth." Nor did von Metzler's mention of the men who had been acquitted on this charge at the IMT, the prosecution claimed, help to determine what the I. G. Farben managers did or knew: "During the period when these aggressive wars were being planned and launched, Speer was a government architect and functionary in the Labor Front, Fritsche, a junior official in the Propaganda Ministry, and Sauckel and Streicher were provincial political bosses."[229]

The prosecution then went into plunder and spoliation and what they meant for those affected—as in the case of Szpilvogel, for example. It addressed Auschwitz in great detail. The defendants claimed ignorance to avoid responsibility for the conditions there. But millions of people had been "put to death in the very backyard of one of Farben's pet projects"—with I. G. Farben's gas used to kill them and its methanol used to incinerate their bodies. The clothing of those murdered had even been collected. In light of the close cooperation between I. G. Farben and the SS, it was "utterly inconceivable that the responsible officials of Farben did not know what was happening there."[230]

The prosecution finally addressed the defense's objections, which related to all the defendants, but especially to Eduard Wahl's closing letter and statement. Wahl emphasized, the prosecution claimed, that crimes against peace did not constitute a criminal offense. The unleashing of a war of aggression was "sinful," but not a crime. This perspective was based, the prosecution stated, "on a totally erroneous conception of the true nature of international penal law" and of its recent developments. The IMT's verdict on crimes against peace had nowhere been elucidated with "greater clarity and precision" than by former Minister of War Stimson. According to Stimson, it had been a new judicial ruling that had reinforced a moral conviction that was a generation old—but not a retrospective law. Wahl, however, not only opposed the charge of a war of aggression; because of the new way in which war was waged—the "new pitch in violence" in war—he opposed the prosecution of war crimes, which would have forfeited their character as crimes. Thus, while for Wahl, a war of aggression "[had] not yet attained the status of a criminal concept," war crimes for him were "the outmoded offspring of nineteenth century liberalism." The prosecution considered it very important to "note that Dr. Wahl, having endeavored to erase the first half of the indictment by crying 'too soon!', now endeavors to expunge the second half with the admonition 'too late!'" The "twin impact" of Wahl's "too soon" and "too late" called international law in its entirety into question—destroyed it, even.[231]

Finally, the prosecution addressed the defenses of "window dressing" and superior orders. Here, the prosecution criticized the judges in the Flick case, which had allowed the appeal to superior orders to a degree "which stretches, if indeed it does not exceed, the appropriate limits." But even the Flick trial had determined a state of irresistible compulsion did not exist if it was clear "that their criminal action was taken on their own initiative, or transcended what was required of them, or that fear and coercion in fact played no part in their decision to take such action." This had clearly been the case with I. G. Farben. It had taken the initiative, and its success in spoliation had been due to "persistence and perseverance." Nor had there been compulsion in Auschwitz, the prosecution argued—the actions had been taken voluntarily. The defendants' deeds had not been carried out "under duress or fear."[232]

By way of conclusion, the prosecution emphasized that in the end, the trial depended on whether one believed in the validity and effectiveness of international law. The defense had sowed the seeds of doubt, it argued, especially in most recent weeks. There was only a small step between Eduard Wahl's theory of "too soon" and "too late" to "a desperate if not cynical conclusion that the world is a ruthless and unmoral pasture in which the wolves fare better than the sheep." In the unfortunate developments that had led up to World War II, Stimson had seen a lack of courage—an indecisiveness on the part of the United States and other countries to enforce decisions on behalf of the international world. There were parallels now: Local wars were raging, and in the United States, there were fears of a renewed arms race and talk of a "cold war." But even if the conditions were not encouraging, they represented, according to the prosecution, "the shortcomings of the police force, but not of the law." The definition of a war of aggression as a crime could no longer seriously be called into question, "any more than there was doubt about the law against murder or robbery" in the time of Henry de Bracton. Taylor closed his remarks with the words: "I am sure that all of us in the court room want to see this torn land once again 'ready to bloom and grow fruits,' as Dr. Silcher put it yesterday, but we do not want to reap another harvest of dragons' teeth. Nor can a healthful and peaceful European community be restored by drawing a shroud over the dead without benefit of inquest. Solemn as is the obligation that the defendants be given every benefit of a full and fair trial, equally solemn is the obligation to the millions on whose behalf these charges are brought that they be given the protection of law and order in a war-weary world."[233]

After the final words by the individual defendants that followed, which will not be addressed in further detail here, the judges withdrew to prepare their verdict. In late June, as the judges brooded over the decision, Judge Morris wrote with frustration to Congressman Karl Mundt of South Dakota (later a senator) that when he had been called by the War Department, he had originally assumed that he would only be in Nuremberg for six months. Now, he was finally working on a verdict after the presentation of evidence and the exchange of arguments: "We are confronted with a record consisting of about 15,000 pages of transcript and 6,570 exhibits, mostly documentary. Only a fraction of this record is of any value in determining the case but, under the practice indulged in at these war crimes trials, the Tribunal is practically powerless to control the amount of so-called evidence presented by people who have very poor judgment as to what real evidence is. I started my judicial career thirty-four years ago as a Justice of the Peace and after ten months as a War Crimes Judge I feel that I am right back where I started from."[234]

However, the court had ensured that for all those involved—the prosecution, the defendants, and their counsels—uncertainty about the outcome of the trial reigned until the end. As Josiah DuBois wrote to Belle Mayer in late April 1948, "There is still a terrific job to be done on selling our whole theory of aggressive war to the Court. Recent developments have indicated that there is possibly still considerable doubt in the minds of some if not all of the members of the Court." Since Mayer was to prepare an initial draft of the closing statement, DuBois encouraged her to portray the arguments of the prosecution as best she could: "Nothing can be more important in terms of a possible successful conclusion of the trial."[235]

The defense also had doubts about the coming verdict, as a letter from Eduard Wahl to Hermann Heimerich of April 1948 shows: "Unfortunately, it is still to hard to get a sense of how the matter will end. Though everything in the presentation of the evidence went according to the wishes of the defense up to this point, strong currents can still be felt today that might help the prosecution."[236] Wolfgang Heintzeler was more optimistic when he spoke in mid-June 1948 of "a dignified and remarkably impressive finale" to the trial, adding, "On the whole, we can, I believe, be very satisfied with how the defense and the closing statements went. The court maintained its exemplary fairness until the last minute. Hopefully the verdict reflects that."[237]

How uncertainly—and yet self-righteously—some of the defendants waited for the verdict is clear in a letter from Heinrich Bütefisch to his friend Walter Gerlach, the rector of the University of Munich, of early July: "We all hope now that the court will free itself from the unbelievable accusations that the prosecution wants to pin on us; if you knew the details, you would throw up your hands—it is simply unimaginable the degree to which the facts have been twisted or motives have been ascribed to our work and our efforts that are simply outside our mindsets. You, too, have helped me and all of us to fight against the prosecution's devilish ideas. The result must now show whether we have succeeded or whether this is simply a political trial."[238]

In fact, over the course of the trial, Judge Shake had clearly come closer and closer to being an ally of the defense. The lawyer Karl Hoffmann later attested: "Judge Curtis G. Shake of Vincennes, Indiana, in the Farben Trial so often explicitly ruled in favor of the Defense that Mr. Drexel A. Sprecher from Washington D.C., our antagonist of the Prosecution—as I learnt later on—got grey hair by seeing the President disregard the rules he had learned on [*sic*] Harvard University."[239]

Shake also generously granted the defendants "vacation on word of honor." The son of the defendant Lautenschläger had died the night before the arraignment, causing him to break down entirely since he had not been allowed to visit him.[240] If Shake had already been responsible for Lautenschläger at the time, he likely would have allowed him to visit his sick child, since over the course of the trial Shake was exceptionally friendly toward the defendants on matters such as these. In late August 1947, he enabled Hans Kugler to hurry to the sickbed of his seriously ill son "on word of honor" and then to travel to his funeral in November. In June 1948, Kugler was allowed once again, along with Paul Häfliger, to take a trip to Frankfurt on parole to deal with financial matters. Heinrich Gattineau was also given the opportunity to visit his father-in-law.[241] Much to the consternation of the prosecution, Shake even allowed Fritz ter Meer to travel to Frankfurt with his lawyer in order to look at documents there.[242] Finally, in July 1948, while he and Judges Morris and Hebert were still writing the verdict, Shake allowed Carl Krauch to take a "vacation on word of honor" to recuperate from an illness—though when it became public, the vacation had to end early.[243]

Judge Shake's generosity toward the defendants, especially in the final months before the issuance of the verdict, could speak for a favorable verdict. Thus, the lawyer Wagner was likely not mistaken when he attempted to reassure Carl Wurster's wife, who was very nervous about the upcoming verdict—and did not like when Wagner praised the Americans to her. As she wrote, "May it be what it is, but in truth: In this case, I am too personally affected and have little to thank them for. It is therefore much better in the future if you don't praise these brothers too much in my presence. Of course, the judge may be an excellent person, but whether he also has the power to let justice prevail will be shown in the outcome of the trial."[244]

The Verdict and Its Reasoning

In June 1948, Judge Morris was very worried about whether the court would be able to come to a unified verdict: "It would be comparatively easy to do that if all the members could agree upon the principles to be applied and the results to be obtained. This, however, is scarcely possible."[245] But the judges were working on an agreement. In early July, Morris wrote to the chief justice of the Supreme

Court of North Dakota, Adolph M. Christianson, that the final briefs had been submitted, the final arguments spoken, and the closing words of the defendants heard: "Since then the members of the Tribunal have been working diligently and trying to solve the issues and write a just judgment on a record, which can only be described by the somewhat elegant word 'mess.'" Each judge was working long and hard, as the verdict had to be ready by early August. He would still like to visit his relatives in Wales, he said, but that depended on when the verdict was pronounced—and "whether or not at that time the Russians are headed for Nurnberg."[246]

For the defendants, the pronouncement of the verdict, which finally occurred on July 29 and 30, 1948, represented the end of what Hans Kugler described as a "nerve-wracking wait time."[247] The previous day, July 28, a devastating explosion at the factory in Ludwigshafen had killed more than two hundred people and injured thousands. At the start of the session, and before the reading of the verdict, Judge Shake commemorated those who had died and expressed his sympathies, touching, Kugler stated, more than just the defendants.[248]

Starting with the discussion of counts I (the planning and waging of wars of aggression) and V (conspiracy against peace), the court immediately sought to make it absolutely clear that the principles of Anglo-American common law applied in the case of its judgment. First, there could be no conviction "without proof of personal guilt." Second, the guilt had to be "proved beyond a reasonable doubt." Third, each defendant had to be presumed innocent throughout the entirety of the trial. Fourth, the burden of proof was always "upon the Prosecution." Fifth and finally, if "from credible evidence two reasonable inferences may be drawn, one of guilt and the other of innocence, the latter must prevail."[249]

Under counts I and V, the prosecution had relied on the same facts and referred to the same evidence, the court stated, so it would address the two charges together.[250] Since both counts had been addressed in detail by the IMT, the court stated, "That well-considered Judgment is basic and persuasive precedent as to all matters determined therein."[251] Here, the IMT had affirmed the question of guilt "only where the evidence of both knowledge and active participation was conclusive." No defendant had been convicted, the court argued, "unless he was, as was the Defendant Hess, in such close relationship with Hitler that he must have been informed of Hitler's aggressive plans and took action to carry them out or attended at least one of the four secret meetings at which Hitler disclosed his plans for aggressive war."[252]

The precedent of the IMT and the strict interpretation of the abovementioned principles led to all defendants' being acquitted under counts I and V. Even in the case of Carl Krauch, the chairman of the supervisory board of I. G. Farben and the plenipotentiary general for special questions of chemical production under the Four-Year Plan, the court came to the "definite conclusion" that he "did not knowingly participate in the planning, preparation or initiation of an aggressive war."[253] The prosecution, the judges stated, had had the difficult task of proving that he knew not only about Germany's rearmament, but also about the plans for a war of aggression that lay behind it. It had not succeeded in doing so, however; the material provided was conflicting.[254] In the case of Georg von Schnitzler, whose statements had strongly incriminated himself and the other members of the board under these charges, the court also concluded that the evidence beyond his statements did "not approach that required to establish guilty knowledge." If one were to summarize von Schnitzler's actions, it would seem that he "was not even remotely connected" with the planning and unleashing of Nazi Germany's wars of aggression and that his participation in the war "did not exceed that of the normal, substantial German citizen and businessman."[255]

According to the court, and contrary to the view of the prosecution, the accused I. G. Farben managers were followers rather than leaders in the Nazi state: "The defendants now before us were neither high public officials in the civil government nor high military officers. Their participation was that of followers and not leaders." The court added that, despite all its efforts, it had not been able to "find, once we have passed below those who have led a country into a war of aggression, a rational mark dividing the guilty from the innocent." In order to convict defendants of the crime of a war of aggression, the court would have had to move the line of separation that the IMT had drawn, without having any reference points for how to do so. The judges therefore concluded, "We leave the mark where we find it."[256]

After having long considered accepting the prosecution's views, as his comments show, Judge Hebert also decided on acquittal for these charges.[257] According to Alberto Zuppi, Hebert had not decided to follow Judges Shake and Morris on this question after an "awful struggle of conscience," as DuBois portrayed it in his book. Rather, his decision was based on a precise analysis of the IMT's verdict on Speer and Schacht, on the implications of the French zone tribunal's verdict on Röchling, and on the article about the IMT verdict by Leventhal et al.[258] However, Hebert did not want to go along with the statements of the majority of the court, as he wrote in his concurring opinion on the two counts: "I cannot express agreement with factual conclusions of the Tribunal which, in my opinion, misread the record in the direction of a too complete exoneration and an exculpation even of moral guilt to a degree which I consider unwarranted." I. G. Farben had, Hebert stated, an "ugly record." He supported the ruling in light of the cases of precedent available; the acquittals under the corresponding charges in the IMT, especially those of Speer and Schacht; and the acquittals in the Krupp and Röchling trials. He expressed concern, however, that the evidence could also have led to another conclusion: "I do not agree with the majority's conclusion that the evidence presented in this case falls so far short of sufficiency as the Tribunal's opinion would seem to indicate."[259]

Therefore, it was not just two of the judges who were not convinced by the prosecution on these two charges, as Telford Taylor insinuated in his 1949 *Final Report to the Secretary of the Army on the Nuernberg War Crimes Trials Under Control Council Law No. 10*. The three judges decided jointly to acquit all the defendants under counts I and V.[260] On count IV of the indictment—membership in a criminal organization, the SS—the three judges also jointly decided to acquit the three accused SS members. And all three judges were also willing to follow the argumentation of the prosecution for counts II and III if the accusations were proved beyond a reasonable doubt.

Under count II (plunder and spoliation), the verdict first established that it did not concur with the prosecution in treating the offenses committed under the charge not only as war crimes but also as crimes against humanity. CCL No. 10, the basis of the military tribunal, did not provide, the court unanimously agreed, for treating property crimes as crimes against humanity. The court in the Flick trial had ruled the same way. The court treated this verdict as a precedent, assessing the alleged plunder, exploitation, and spoliation only as possible war crimes. Nor, basing itself on the applicable international law and CCL No. 10, did the court see itself as responsible for offenses committed during the annexation of Austria or the incorporation of the Sudetenland under the Munich Agreement, since no "state of actual warfare" existed at the time.[261]

The offenses of plunder, spoliation, and exploitation, the court stated, did not originate under the IMT, but had already been defined as war crimes beforehand: "The offense of plunder of public and private property must be considered a well-recognized crime under international law."[262] The Hague Conventions were relevant here: their most important determinations were generally sufficient to fairly assess the alleged offenses to property of which the defendants were accused. Based on the Hague Conventions, the court found that "the essence of the crime of plunder or spoliation [is] that the owner be deprived of his property involuntarily and against his will."[263] These provisions were, as had been shown in the Flick trial, also applicable to individuals, and they applied to occupied, annexed, or integrated territories—and were, contrary to Eduard Wahl's closing argument, by no means outdated in the context of a total war. It went, the court argued, "beyond the authority of any nation to authorize its citizens to commit acts in contravention of international penal law." Despite changing customs and practices in international law, "the basic concept of respect for property rights during belligerent occupation" had not changed so much that "the widespread acts of plunder and spoliation" by Nazi Germany could be given "any legal protection."[264]

The court emphasized that when I. G. Farben was spoken of, the name did not refer to the legal entity; rather, the use of the term was "descriptive": corporations acted "through individuals," and it was the task of the prosecution to convey "beyond a reasonable doubt" that a defendant had been involved in, authorized, or approved an offense. The judges refused to convict a defendant solely because that person held a high office: "Responsibility does not automatically attach to an act proved to be criminal merely by virtue of a defendant's membership in the Vorstand."[265]

But there was no question for the court that multiple I. G. Farben managers had carried out punishable actions under count II. The formulations in this section of the verdict were the same, or similar, to those of the prosecution: "One cannot condone the activities of Farben in the field of spoliation. If not actually marching with the Wehrmacht, Farben at least was not far behind."[266] The course of its actions, the court stated, "clearly indicate[d] a studied design," and in "most instances the initiative was Farben's." Therefore, the actions of the I. G. Farben managers should not be treated any differently from the actions of German officers and officials who had committed property offenses. I. G. Farben had also operated using the threat of the "power of the military occupant": "The result was enrichment of Farben and the building of its greater chemical empire through the medium of the military occupancy at the expense of the former owners. Such action on the part of Farben constituted a violation of the Hague Regulations." For these criminal offenses, the court argued, I. G. Farben had used varied and complicated contracts, but "the objective of pillage, plunder, and spoliation stands out, and there can be no uncertainty as to the actual result."[267]

For each individual case under this count, the principles of common law referred to above were rigorously applied—and therefore, the judges did not always follow the indictment. Overall, however, a large succession of property crimes in Poland, Norway, and France, including Alsace-Lorraine, were listed as criminal offenses. It was determined that I. G. Farben already had "far-reaching plans to participate" in Nazi acts of plunder and spoliation in the Soviet Union but had not been able to carry them out because of the German defeat.[268] Only because there had been no "completed act of spoliation" in the Soviet Union was Otto Ambros acquitted.[269] Nine I. G. Farben managers, however, were found guilty of having carried out plunder and spoliation measures: Hermann Schmitz, the chairman of the board; Fritz ter Meer, the chairman of the Technical Committee; Georg von Schnitzler, the chairman of the Commercial Committee, who according to the court had "a major responsibility for Farben's spoliative activities in Poland and in France"; board members Max Ilgner, Ernst Bürgin, Paul Häfliger, Heinrich Oster, and Friedrich Jähne; and Hans Kugler, who was a director but not a member of the board.[270]

Under count III, the defendants were charged "individually, collectively, and acting through the instrumentality of Farben" of having committed "war crimes and crimes against humanity" as set out under Article II of CCL No. 10. This included I. G. Farben's participation in the slave labor program, the supply of poison gas (Zyklon B) for the extermination of concentration camp inmates, participation in criminal medical experiments on concentration camp inmates, and "the unlawful and inhumane practices of the defendants in connection with Farben's plant at Auschwitz."[271]

The court ruled that Degesch, a subsidiary of I. G. Farben and Degussa, had unquestionably delivered large amounts of Zyklon B to concentration camps, including Auschwitz. It was not evident, however, the court stated, that the poison had been used to murder people. The court therefore determined that the evidence for a criminal action was insufficient.[272]

With regard to the charge that I. G. Farben and its managers had participated in human experiments in concentration camps, the court also ruled for acquittal. It was unconvinced by the evidence that the defendants were criminally liable: "The inference that the defendants connived with SS doctors in their criminal practices is dispelled by the fact that Farben discontinued forwarding drugs to these physicians as soon as their improper conduct was suspected. We find nothing culpable in the circumstances under which quantities of vaccines were shipped by Farben to concentration camps, since it was reasonable to suppose that there was a legitimate need for such drugs in these institutions." The question of whether the responsible offices at I. G. Farben had to have determined from the doctors' reports that their medications were being used for illegal purposes depended on whether the German word "*Versuch*" were interpreted as the English word "experiment," as the prosecution argued, or as "test," as the defendants argued. The defendants insisted that with their precautionary measures in place, the tests, or experiments, had not only been permitted, but had even served a purpose. Following the legal principle of *in dubio pro reo*, the court came to the following conclusion: "Applying the rule that where from credible evidence two reasonable inferences may be drawn, one of guilt and the other of innocence, the latter must prevail, we must conclude that the Prosecution has failed to establish that part of the charge here under consideration."[273]

The prosecution was more successful with the charge of participation in the slave labor program and the crimes at Auschwitz, in particular in connection with the construction of the I. G. Farben factory there. The court determined that there had been slave labor under the Nazi regime involving involuntary Fremdarbeiter, prisoners of war, and concentration camp inmates: "It is enough to say here that the utilization of forced labor, unless done under such circumstances as to relieve the employer of responsibility, constitutes a violation of that part of Article II of Control Council Law No. 10 which recognizes as war crimes and crimes against humanity the enslavement, deportation, or imprisonment of the civilian population of other countries."[274] To counter this, the defendants had invoked conditions that exempted them from responsibility, namely, coercion: "The defendants who were involved in the utilization of slave labor have testified that they were under such oppressive coercion and compulsion that they cannot be said to have acted with that intent which is a necessary ingredient of every criminal offense."[275] The court had recognized coercion in the verdict at the

IMT, which referred to the Nazi regime as a dictatorship "with all its methods of terror," in which the justice system was controlled and instrumentalized, and in which any form of criticism could have led to severe punishment. Judges Shake and Morris were therefore unable to determine whether the defendants were telling the truth, "when they asserted that in conforming to the slave-labor program they had no other choice than to comply with the mandates of the Hitler Government." The sympathy of these two judges for the defendants went so far as to lead them to accept the assertions of Friedrich Flick, among others: "There can be but little doubt that the defiant refusal of a Farben executive to carry out the Reich production schedule or to use slave labor to achieve that end would have been treated as treasonous sabotage and would have resulted in prompt and drastic retaliation. Indeed, there was credible evidence that Hitler would have welcomed the opportunity to make an example of a Farben leader."[276]

Despite this exceptionally sympathetic position, however, the court saw a basic limitation for the recognition of coercion. The IMT had ruled, the court stated, that the fact that someone was acting on the orders of the government did not exempt them from punishment but could be the grounds for a reduced punishment. In this case, the decisive factor was not the order itself but whether a "moral choice" had actually been possible for the person in question.[277] For the application of this principle the court used as a precedent the verdict from the Flick trial, which had been so vilified by William Zeck and Telford Taylor: The judges in the Flick trial had recognized coercion in the case of four of the defendants, but not in the case of two others, who were proved to have taken personal initiative that went beyond following orders—and were convicted accordingly. The tribunal also recognized the French trial of Hermann Röchling, who had also been convicted for his participation in the slave labor program, as another important precedent. It had been determined that the actions of the individuals convicted in these trials had not been due to the impossibility of acting differently—rather, they had "embraced the opportunity" to gain every possible advantage from the slave-labor program. "Indeed, it might be said that they were, to a very substantial degree, responsible for broadening the scope of that reprehensible system." Therefore, the court concluded that "an order of a superior officer or a law or governmental decree will not justify the defense of necessity unless, in its operation, it is of a character to deprive the one to whom it is directed of a moral choice as to his course of action."[278]

This position of the court came into play with regard to the "Auschwitz issue": "The evidence is sharply conflicting as to the importance of the concentration camp in deciding upon the location of the plant. We are satisfied, after a thorough consideration of the evidence, that while the camp may not have been the determining factor in selecting the location, it was an important one and, from the beginning, it was planned to use concentration-camp labor to supplement the supply of workers." Those at I. G. Farben responsible for Auschwitz were, according to the court, the board members Otto Ambros and Heinrich Bütefisch, and the director of I. G. Farben's Auschwitz factory, Walter Dürrfeld.[279]

The court determined that these three individuals had made themselves criminally liable. The inmates provided by the Auschwitz concentration camp "lived and labored under the shadow of extermination." The defense had emphasized, "not wholly without merit," that the inmates were under the authority of the SS. It was also "clear that Farben did not deliberately pursue or encourage an inhumane policy with respect to the workers." It was even true that "some steps were taken by Farben to alleviate the situation." However, this did not acquit the three defendants from shared responsibility, because, the court ruled, they bore "great responsibility with respect to the workers" since they had requested and accepted the concentration camp inmates as workers: "Responsibility for taking the initiative in the unlawful employment was theirs and, to some extent at least, they must share the responsibility for mistreatment of the workers with the SS and the construction contractors."[280]

The construction of the I. G. Farben factory in Auschwitz was connected, the court stated, with the acquisition of coal mines there. The factory and the coal mines had been "wholly private projects" operated by I. G. Farben. Those in charge had had "considerable freedom and opportunity for initiative." Nor had the construction of a factory in Auschwitz been due to coercion: "The site was chosen after a survey of many factors, including the availability of concentration-camp labor for construction work. As an adjunct of Auschwitz, the controlling interest in the Fuerstengrube an[d] Janina Mines was acquired under circumstances that impute knowledge of the fact that they could not be operated successfully by voluntary labor." In the view of the court, the use of prisoners of war in the coal mines, especially in light of the conditions there, had been a war crime. The use of concentration camp inmates and foreign forced labor in Auschwitz was, the court stated, a crime against humanity, since it showed "the initiative displayed by the officials of Farben in the procurement and utilization of such labor." In the case of foreign nationals this was also a war crime—"to which the slave-labor program of the Reich will not warrant the defense of necessity." The court also considered it to be proved that "the employment of concentration-camp labor was had with knowledge of the abuse and inhumane treatment" by the SS—and that the work on the construction site in Auschwitz had worsened the fate of the inmates.[281]

From the perspective of the court, however, beyond the three defendants already mentioned, two other leading managers were criminally responsible for the crimes at Auschwitz. The court considered Carl Krauch, chairman of the supervisory board, to share in the responsibility for the acquisition of slave labor. It was not of the opinion that Krauch was involved in the slave labor program at the beginning of recruitment of forced labor. However, he had later taken part in the program from a technical standpoint—though possibly without knowing about the maltreatment that was taking place. If one considered, however, "what he clearly must have known about the procurement of forced labor and the part he voluntarily played in its distribution and allocation, his activities were such that they impel us to hold that he was a willing participant in the crime of enslavement."[282]

Finally, the court was convinced that the board member responsible for the construction of all new factories, Fritz ter Meer, was also guilty. The court described him as the immediate supervisor of Otto Ambros. The evidence "clearly establishes," the court stated, that one of the main problems in the construction of the factory in Auschwitz had been acquiring workers, and "the availability of concentration-camp labor figured in the planning of the Auschwitz construction." Ambros had regularly informed his supervisor about everything. And, aiming itself directly against ter Meer's defense strategy, the verdict stated: "The overall field of new construction was one in which ter Meer was both active and dominant. It is indeed unreasonable to conclude that, when Ambros sought the advice of and reported in detail to ter Meer, the conferences were confined to such matters as transportation, water supply, and the availability of construction materials and excluded that important construction factor, labor, in which the concentration camp played so prominent a part." The court also added: "Ter Meer's visits to Auschwitz were no doubt as revealing to him as they are to this Tribunal." The commander of the Auschwitz concentration camp, Rudolf Höß, had also disliked sending his inmates outside the camp; the workers were "not forced upon" I. G. Farben. Therefore, the "inference is strong that Farben officials subordinate to ter Meer took the initiative in securing the services of these inmates on the plant site." This inference, the court stated, was "further supported by the fact that Farben at its own expense and with its own funds appropriated by the TEA, of which ter Meer was chairman, built Camp Monowitz for the specific purpose of housing its concentration-camp workers." The court therefore came to the clear conclusion that ter Meer was guilty of criminal charges.[283]

The court acquitted other members of the Technical Committee, which had been led by Fritz ter Meer, and of the board of directors of I. G. Farben, however, since the majority of the judges did not believe it had been proved beyond a reasonable doubt that they had been fully informed about the slave-labor program at Auschwitz.

Judge Hebert registered two main disagreements in his dissent to the majority opinion on charge III. He agreed with the conviction of the five managers with regard to Auschwitz, but wanted criminal responsibility for Auschwitz to be extended to the entire board of directors and, in contrast to the majority opinion, did not want to accept the defense of superior orders for the slave labor program: "In my view all the members of the Farben Vorstand should be held guilty under count three of the indictment, not only for the participation by Farben in the crime of enslavement at Auschwitz, but also for Farben's widespread participation and willing cooperation with the slave-labor system in the other Farben plants."[284]

To summarize, ten of the twenty-three accused I. G. Farben managers were acquitted of all charges, while thirteen were sentenced to between one-and-a-half and eight years of prison time for crimes under counts II and III, from which the time that they had already been under arrest was deducted. Two managers who were seen as directly responsible for the "Auschwitz issue," Otto Ambros and Walter Dürrfeld, received the most serious punishments: eight years each. The top managers of I. G. Farben also received relatively serious punishments, with six years for Carl Krauch, four years for Hermann Schmitz, five years for Georg von Schnitzler, and seven years for Fritz ter Meer, who was the only defendant to be sentenced under both counts.

Though Judge Morris had expressed sympathy for Charles F. Wennerstrum, he did not do the same as him and criticize the criminal prosecution of Nazi crimes in Nuremberg after his return to the United States.[285] All three judges in the I. G. Farben trial saw their responsibility for the prosecution and punishment of the crimes addressed by the Nuremberg courts as justified, as they stated clearly during the pronouncement of the verdict in reaction to the protests of the defense—and they continued to think so after the trial.[286] Shake, who not only was the presiding judge in the I. G. Farben trial but also served in the important role of chairman of the Supervisory Committee of Presiding Judges from November 1947 until his departure in the summer of 1948,[287] continued to express this view years later. He knew, Shake said, that the Nuremberg trials had been the subject of controversy and that some had considered them a mistake and thought that the United States had practiced ex post facto law. In light of the indictments handled by the tribunals, he had never had major concerns in this regard, however. In some cases, the accusations had been covered by existing conventions, but more than anything, they were justified by a "common law of civilization, that it doesn't take a statute or a treaty to make it unlawful to put five or six million people through gas chambers, burn them up, knock their teeth out for the gold fillings, cut the hair of the women and use it to pad mattresses, burn them and take the ashes out for fertilizer on the farms."[288] Shake referred to American legal traditions: "All crimes in Indiana, for example, now are statutory. That hasn't always been true. … Murder from time immemorial under American and British jurisprudence has been a common law crime. And back in the early history of the state before the Constitution of 1851 it didn't take an act of the legislature to make murder a crime." In addition to these legal traditions, he referred to impressions from his visits to former concentration camps: "We took the view that so far as trying to destroy people in concentration camps as they did over there in the ovens and burning them, it didn't require a law. It didn't require a formal statute or an international law to say that that's criminal and that's the theory we proceeded on and I'll say this that you can go to all the movies you want to, you can read all the books you want to, you can read the magazine and the newspaper articles, you just can't have any conception whatever of the horror of those places unless you've been to Buchenwald or Dachau or Auschwitz or those places; and I've been to all three of those and just seen how they were run."[289]

The self-perception of all the judges in the I. G. Farben trial, according to which the worst of crimes were being brought to justice in Nuremberg, was tempered in the case of Shake and Morris by the awareness that the tribunals in Nuremberg were those of victors over the defeated, to whom they wanted to and felt obligated to show a correspondingly generous amount of fairness. In the comments cited above, Shake also added: "I do say this that I never was very proud of the setup we had over there. We were an American Tribunal; ... We represented the victor. The defendants were citizens of the loser of the war." It would be better, Shake argued, to conduct such trials in front of international courts with judges from neutral states, so his view of the Nuremberg trials was critical. Shake emphasized, however, that for these reasons, all the courts in Nuremberg had put tremendous effort into ensuring the defendants a fair and just trial—"the tribunals actually leaned over backwards to give those defendants a fair trial."[290]

The effort of the court in the I. G. Farben trial to ensure the defendants a fair trial based on common law legal principles was also emphasized by Judge Morris in an article from 1949: "These principles, the majority of the tribunal felt, included the burden of proof of the prosecution, the rule of reasonable doubt, immunity from compulsory self-incrimination, and the right of a defendant to interrogate witnesses who testified against him either from the witness stand or through ex parte affidavits, the use of which was provided by Military Government Ordinance No. 7." However, Morris warned, "The greatest stumbling blocks to the just administration of international criminal law are the desire of the victor to sit in judgment on the vanquished and the temptation to tarnish justice with vengeance."[291]

That said, Morris defended the Nuremberg trials from what he perceived as too radical a criticism. In a 1953 letter to Heinrich Kronstein he wrote, "I am inclined to agree with you that the Nurnberg trials, taken as a whole, lack uniformity, both in procedure and in the concept and application of substantive law. That is a natural result of a dearth of statutory law and a lack of precedent. But it does not mean that the Nurnberg trials should never have been held, or that the result was, in general, not an approximation of justice." Morris shared Kronstein's criticism of the theory that individuals who followed the orders of the government or pursued its policies were criminally responsible: "That theory which was strongly pressed by the prosecution gave me great concern, for it involved the setting of a highly dangerous precedent." Therefore, he and Judge Shake had recognized and used the defense's argument of necessity, he argued, and justified it in detail in the verdict—much to the disappointment of Chief Counsel Taylor: "The majority of the Farben tribunal tried to adhere to the proposition that guilt is personal and must be established beyond a reasonable doubt with respect to each individual, and that his acts must be judged in the light of the circumstances and under the conditions surrounding and affecting their performance."[292]

The tribunal had therefore treated the defendants far from unfairly. Even in his book criticizing the Nuremberg trials, the former defendant August von Knieriem could not avoid recognizing the fairness of the court in the I. G. Farben trial.[293] It should be noted that the majority of the judges had exceptional, if not excessive, sympathy for opportunism, necessity, and misguided patriotism. They did not see the defendants as leaders or important decision makers, but as followers and average businessmen who should be punished as such.[294] Judge Shake wrote years later that in his opinion, "almost every intelligent German was a Nazi," that this had even been necessary to survive.[295] Such a large amount of sympathy for opportunism might find its foundation in Shake's own background—it seems that as a young man in Indiana, he himself had been a member of the Ku Klux Klan, which was very strong at the time, before he turned against the secretive racist association.[296]

Thus, Judges Shake and Morris saw the argument of necessity as "a good defense," one that, unlike the prosecution and Hebert, they fully accepted, probably not least with an eye to possible future conflicts that the United States might be involved in: "Now, we took the view that if a defendant could show that he was acting in compliance with a positive governmental order it was a good defense, took the view that if your country was at war whether you were a German, American, English or whatever else, that a law-abiding citizen is going to comply with directives and regulations that he gets."[297] Accordingly, the portion of the verdict on counts I and V, which was written by Judges Shake and Morris, stated, after it was determined that the accused managers had been neither high-level officials nor high-level officers, "We cannot say that a private citizen shall be placed in the position of being compelled to determine in the heat of war whether his government is right or wrong, or, if it starts right, when it turns wrong. We would not require the citizen, at the risk of becoming a criminal under the rules of international justice, to decide that his country has become an aggressor and that he must lay aside his patriotism, the loyalty to his homeland, and the defense of his own fireside at the risk of being adjudged guilty of crimes against peace on the one hand, or of becoming a traitor to his country on the other, if he makes an erroneous decision based upon facts of which he has but vague knowledge."[298]

Citing this part of the verdict, Judge Morris defended the Nuremberg trials in late 1958 to an American general—and judged the conviction of Admiral Dönitz in the IMT as entirely justified: "It is my view that the Nuernberg trials were completely justified to the extent that they dealt with the policy makers of Germany who participated in planning and carrying out Hitler's decrees and orders and that military personnel who so participated were entitled to no different consideration than civilians." This did not apply, however, as Morris added, to those receiving orders.[299]

Another factor contributing to the mildness of the verdict on the I. G. Farben managers was the fact that Judge Morris was staunchly anti-Soviet. It can also be shown that Judge Shake was critical toward the Soviet Union. One cannot forget that shortly before the pronouncement of the verdict, the Soviet Union had toppled the Czechoslovak government and installed a puppet regime and had blockaded Berlin, inspiring the organization of the Berlin Airlift and suddenly turning Berlin from the capital of the Nazi enemy into a symbol of freedom from Soviet oppression.[300]

Finally, Judge Shake had been friendly toward the Germans in a way that went beyond normal American politeness. In his response to Lilly von Schnitzler, for example, who seems to have written to him on the occasion of her husband's release, Shake stated, "I entertain the deepest sense of sympathy for the German people, generally, and trust that the new experiment in government will result in better and happier times for all." Shake also found the actions of the defendants in the I. G. Farben trial to be less iniquitous than the actions of other defendants: "The offenses for which they were convicted are clearly distinguishable from many of the others who were found guilty at Nurnberg."[301] Shake later remarked that the cases dealt with in the I. G. Farben trial were not as horrible as those handled in the Doctors' Trial, for instance; thus, the punishments had also been less severe.[302] In reference to a letter from the defendant Paul Häfliger, who had thanked him for the court's good treatment of the defendants, Shake wrote to Max Ilgner that his judicial role in Nuremberg was "not a pleasant responsibility for us."[303] And when Shake heard from the lawyer Rolf Müller about the early release of the last imprisoned defendant in the I. G. Farben trial, Otto Ambros, he wrote to Müller that he welcomed the news: "This action meets with my hearty approval and I feel that the ends of justice have been fully served." And about all the defendants, he had this to say: "I have always entertained the very highest regard for the abilities and capacities of the Farben defendants. They are men who are equipped to render valuable service to Germany and the world. It was unfortunate that any of them should have been involved in the matters that resulted in a part of them being convicted of international crimes."[304]

It thus seems hardly surprising that in May 1949, the lawyer Wolfram von Metzler wrote a form of thank-you note to all the judges in Case VI for their exceptional friendliness and the consideration that they had given to the defense counsels: "Please do not consider me a flatterer if I say that never in my professional career—and I have defended in not a few big cases—I have had such a stisfactory [*sic*] experience as in this trial. No doubt you and your colleagues were in a difficult position in face of the enormous bulk of evidence placed before you and the comparatively short time available for deliberating the judgment. All the more I sincerely admire the way in which you have overcome all these difficulties."[305]

Nor is it surprising that the chief prosecutor in the I. G. Farben trial, Josiah DuBois, had an entirely different opinion from von Metzler about Judge Shake. In late 1948, he wrote with bitterness to the journalist Drew Pearson that Judge Merrell had told him and at least two other members of the prosecution that even before the I. G. Farben trial, Shake had expressed the opinion that industrialists should never be tried for planning and waging a war of aggression. Pearson was to keep it confidential, however, that Merrell had been the source from which the prosecution had learned this. Judge Shake had become a very disagreeable person to DuBois in the meantime: "Judge Shake was a very vain man and especially sensitive to criticism ... Throughout the trial the German lawyers (numbering over 60 as compared with the 8 lawyers on the prosecution staff) were very adept at the game of kissing Shake' ___, [*sic*] with the result that, in the words of Judge Merrell, all that a German attorney had to do to have his way, was to appeal to Judge Shake. The basic ignorance on the part of Judge Shake (as well as Judge Morris) as to Germany, combined with his being treated over a period of a year by the German attorneys as almost God, produced a result which (though Shake may have finally convinced himself was just) was nevertheless objectively a shocking piece of business."[306]

Judge Shake himself viewed the trial, his role, and the verdict, which he had written with the other two judges, in a different light. In a letter to Drew Pearson, Shake went into detail about the motives and self-perception of the judges, which had played a role in their verdict. He was fully aware, Shake wrote, that there were people who were of the opinion that every important German who was tried should have been promptly convicted and executed. The court, however, had represented the view that the defendants should receive a fair trial based on the American standard: "We tried, as best as we knew how, first, to interpret international law in the terms that might justly be applied to our own countrymen, if we should be so unfortunate as to lose some future war; and, secondly, to conduct the trials with due regard for those fundamental rights that enlightened jurisprudence throws around a human being charged with crime. I think we would have rendered a positive disservice to our country and to the cause of law and order if we had resorted to so-called vindictive justice upon a defeated people. The progress that the human race has already made in the development of the orderly administration of law is too valuable and cost too much in blood and tears to be frittered away in a spirit of vengeance. If the American people had desired to align themselves with that kind of policy they did not need to send judges to Germany. Firing squads would have sufficed."[307]

Notes

1. Cf. on this James Morris Papers, Box 1, Folder 1: Morris to Taylor, Supreme Court Librarian, October 6, 1947.
2. See, for example, Staatsarchiv Freiburg, T 1 Drischel 52: Boettcher to the defense counsels in the I. G. Farben trial, October 8, 1947: after a discussion with Drexel Sprecher, there was a request that the court have "a closed meeting, without minutes and without the public in attendance, of all the defendants and all their chief defense counsels" in order to discuss various matters related to the trial.
3. Hauptverhandlung Fall VI, 2581 (October 23, 1947)—Shake; Staatsarchiv Nürnberg, KV-Prozesse Fall 6, Nr. ZF 11/II: Circular letter Siemers office, signed by Dr. Müller, on January 28, 1948, obligatory sessions: "In light of the fact that the court took the opportunity to complain about insufficient participation of the defense counsels in the sessions, obligatory sessions, like in the case of the prosecution, are going to be established again." This did not seem to work well, though; see Bayer Archiv, 207/023: Rudolf Dix to the defense counsels in Case VI, March 23, 1948: "In the last discussion among the defense counsels we were in agreement that the obligatory sessions had to be respected in order to avoid unpleasantness with the court. We were also in agreement that it was clear that recently most people were not even thinking about obligatory sessions. This agreement made little difference." According to Dix, on March 22, 1948, six of eight who were expected to attend the obligatory sessions were absent, thus resulting in his request that they meet their responsibilities in order not to find themselves in a "very awkward situation" with the tribunal. See also Bayer Archiv, 207/006: Siemers/Müller office to the defense counsels in Case VI, March 25, 1948, on obligatory sessions.
4. Hauptverhandlung Fall VI: August 14, 1947, 1–5.
5. Hauptverhandlung Fall VI, 5–15. Quotes from US Military Tribunal VI; English Transcript of the Proceedings of Case No. VI, United States v. Carl Krauch et al., August 14, 1947–July 30, 1948, hereinafter: English Transcript of the Proceedings, Case VI, 13.
6. Hauptverhandlung Fall VI, 15–23, here Taylor 22–23. Quotes from English Transcript of the Proceedings, Case VI, 19 and 22–23.
7. Hauptverhandlung Fall VI, 23–34.
8. Lautenschläger had his arraignment on August 27, 1947, and Wurster's was on September 17, 1947; the decision on Brüggemann was made on September 9, 1947. See Hauptverhandlung Fall VI, 35, 819–20, 519–21.
9. Hauptverhandlung Fall VI, 36–39.
10. Hauptverhandlung Fall VI, 40.
11. Hauptverhandlung Fall VI, 42–43; cf. also *Trials of War Criminals*, vol. VII, 100–101. Quotes from English Transcript of the Proceedings, Case VI, 41–42.
12. Hauptverhandlung Fall VI, 44–45. Quotes from English Transcript of the Proceedings, Case VI, 44.
13. Hauptverhandlung Fall VI, 60–61.
14. Hauptverhandlung Fall VI, 65. Quotes from English Transcript of the Proceedings, Case VI, 59–60.
15. James Morris Papers, Box 1, Folder 2: Morris to Mr. and Mrs. Vernon Cooper, August 29, 1947.
16. James Morris Papers, Box 1, Folder 2: Morris to Judge Christianson, August 13, 1947.
17. James Morris Papers, Box 1, Folder 2: Morris to Judge Christianson, August 29, 1947.
18. Cf. Bush, *Prehistory*, 1160–68, 1200–15.
19. NARA, RG 238, Entry 192, Box 2, Folder 3: "Legal References Concerning the Crimes against Peace Count," no author, undated—written after the IMT sentence, most likely in late 1946/early 1947.

20. Hauptverhandlung Fall VI, 650–52 (September 10, 1947). Quotes from English Transcript of the Proceedings, Case VI, 687.
21. Hauptverhandlung Fall VI, 689–90. Quotes from English Transcript of the Proceedings, Case VI, 723–24. With regard to Morris's statements, cf. also DuBois, *The Devil's Chemists*, 82: "Speaking for myself only, I am at a complete loss to comprehend where documents of this kind are of the slightest materiality to the charges."
22. James Morris Papers, Box 1, Folder 2: Morris to Judge Nuessle, September 5, 1947.
23. Hauptverhandlung Fall VI, 766–71 (September 16, 1947). Quotes from English Transcript of the Proceedings, Case VI, 800–802. Cf. also NARA, RG 238, Entry 159, Box 6, Folder 4: *Daily Trial Report* [of the prosecution], Report No. 6, September 16, 1947, and DuBois, *The Devil's Chemists*, 82–83, claiming his reply to Morris was the next day, so on September 11; however, this is not correct.
24. Hauptverhandlung Fall VI, 949 and 953–55 (September 18, 1947).
25. Hauptverhandlung Fall VI, 1218–19 (September 25, 1947). Quotes from English Transcript of the Proceedings, Case VI, 1243.
26. Hauptverhandlung Fall VI, 1229–35 (September 26, 1947).
27. Hauptverhandlung Fall VI, 1360–61 (September 30, 1947).
28. Hauptverhandlung Fall VI, 1492 (October 1, 1947).
29. Hauptverhandlung Fall VI, 1573 (October 2, 1947). Quotes from English Transcript of the Proceedings, Case VI, 1593.
30. Hauptverhandlung Fall VI, 1591–601 (October 3, 1947).
31. James Morris Papers, Box 1, Folder 1: Morris to Judge Burke, October 2, 1947.
32. Hauptverhandlung Fall VI, 2044–46 (October 14, 1947). Quotes from English Transcript of the Proceedings, Case VI, 2054–55.
33. Hauptverhandlung Fall VI, 2394–404 (October 21, 1947). Quotes from English Transcript of the Proceedings, Case VI, 2403–6.
34. Hauptverhandlung Fall VI, 2485–89 (October 21, 1947).
35. Hauptverhandlung Fall VI, 2498–504 (October 22, 1947). Quote from English Transcript of the Proceedings, Case VI, 2502.
36. Hauptverhandlung Fall VI, 2546, 2559–67. Quotes from English Transcript of the Proceedings, Case VI, 2564, 2566–68, 2570, 2572.
37. NARA, RG 238, Entry 159, Box 6, Folder 3: *Daily Trial Report* by the prosecution, Report No. 12 (13 is in fact correct—see NARA, RG 238, Entry 159, Box 6, Folder 4: *Daily Trial Report*, Report No. 14: correction), October 22, 1947; this states that Hebert and Morris dissented, which, however, is a misstatement.
38. Belle Mayer Papers, Nuremberg Related Material, Correspondence, Box 3, Folder 12: DuBois to Mayer, November 8, 1947.
39. Priemel, *The Betrayal*, 235.
40. Hauptverhandlung Fall VI, 2843–57 (October 27, 1947). Quotes from English Transcript of the Proceedings, Case VI, 2630–60.
41. Hauptverhandlung Fall VI, 2625–31 (October 23, 1947). Quotes from the English Transcript of the Proceedings, 2632–33.
42. Hauptverhandlung Fall VI, 2632–60 (October 23, 1947).
43. NARA, RG 238, Entry 159, Box 6, Folder 3: *Daily Trial Report* by the prosecution, Report No. 12 (13 is correct): October 23, 1947; Unternehmensarchiv BASF, W1.3./114 and 115: Kugler, *Farben: Chance und Schicksal*, 402.
44. Hauptverhandlung Fall VI, 2965–66 (October 28, 1947)—as put by the lawyer Silcher during cross-examination of Kurt Krüger.
45. Hauptverhandlung Fall VI, 2989–90 (October 29, 1947)—the witness Krüger in cross-examination by the lawyer Nath. Quote from English Transcript of the Proceedings, Case VI, 2971.

46. Hauptverhandlung Fall VI, 3049–50 (October 29, 1947)—the witness Krüger in cross-examination by the lawyer Nath. Quote from English Transcript of the Proceedings, Case VI, 3029.
47. Hauptverhandlung Fall VI, 3057–59 (October 29, 1947). Quote from English Transcript of the Proceedings, Case VI, 3035.
48. Hauptverhandlung Fall VI, 3209 (October 31, 1947).
49. DuBois, *The Devil's Chemists*, 99; cf. also Borkin, *Crime and Punishment*, 141; Stokes, *Divide and Prosper*, 153; Jeffreys, *Hell's Cartel*, 386–87.
50. Borkin, *Crime and Punishment*, 137–38; Stokes, *Divide and Prosper*, 153.
51. Staatsarchiv Freiburg, T 1 Drischel 54: Report [of Drischel] about the trip to Nuremberg from May 27 to June 4, 1947.
52. Staatsarchiv Nürnberg, KV—Verteidigung Handakten Hoffmann, Nr. 9, Dr. W. von Metzler, September 19, 1947: Circular letter to the defense counsels in Case No. VI, quote from 16 (Document also in Bayer Archiv, 207/023).
53. Bayer Archiv, 207/023: Conrad Böttcher to all defense counsels in Case VI, November 13, 1947.
54. See, for example, Hauptverhandlung Fall VI, 3297–99 (November 4, 1947)—Heintzeler.
55. Hauptverhandlung Fall VI, 3300–02 (November 4, 1947). Quotes from English Transcript of the Proceedings, Case VI, 3236, 3277–78.
56. Hauptverhandlung Fall VI, 3616–18 (November 12, 1947).
57. Hauptverhandlung Fall VI, 3677–78 (November 12, 1947)—the witness Ludwig Hess.
58. Hauptverhandlung Fall VI, 3806 (November 14, 1947).
59. Hauptverhandlung Fall VI, 3835 (Kai Feinberg), 3841 (Frederick Davison), 3855 (Robert W. Ferris), 3881 (Gregoire Afrine) (November 14, 1947).
60. Hauptverhandlung Fall VI, 3932 (November 17, 1947).
61. Hauptverhandlung Fall VI, 3770–74 (November 13, 1947). Quote from English Transcript of the Proceedings, Case VI, 3750.
62. Bayer Archiv, 207/023: Carl Krauch et al. to our defense counsels, October 19, 1947.
63. Bayer Archiv, 207/023: All defendants to all defense counsels and assistants in Case VI, November 16, 1947; the two assistants from Auschwitz named were Dr. Karl Häseler and Dr. Stradal.
64. Bayer Archiv, 315/053 (Silcher): Kühne to Silcher, August 14, 1953 (copy).
65. Hauptverhandlung Fall VI, 3256–58, 3306–308 (November 4, 1947).
66. Hauptverhandlung Fall VI, 3492–501 (November 7, 1947). Quotes from English Transcript of the Proceedings, Case VI, 3475–81.
67. Hauptverhandlung Fall VI, 3955 (November 18, 1947).
68. Hauptverhandlung Fall VI, 9685 (March 18, 1948); see also Heinemann, "Rasse, Lebensraum, Genozid," 110–11; Oberndörfer, "Recht und Richter," 531.
69. Hauptverhandlung Fall VI, 3258–61 (November 4, 1947). Quote from English Transcript of the Proceedings, Case VI, 3236.
70. Hauptverhandlung Fall VI, 3502–503 (November 7, 1947). Quote from English Transcript of the Proceedings, Case VI, 3484.
71. NARA, RG 238, Entry 159, Box 6, Folder 4: *Daily Trial Report* by the prosecution, Report No. 15, 4, on November 7, 1947.
72. Hauptverhandlung Fall VI, 4553–54 (December 2, 1947); cf. also NARA, RG 238, Entry 159, Box 6, Folder 4: *Daily Trial Report* by the prosecution, Report No. 18: 6–8, on December 2, 1947. Quote from English Transcript of the Proceedings, Case VI, 4532.
73. Hauptverhandlung Fall VI, 4513–14 (December 2, 1947). Quotes from English Transcript of the Proceedings, Case VI, 4493–94.

74. Hauptverhandlung Fall VI, 4553–4 (December 2, 1947); NARA, RG 238, Entry 159, Box 6, Folder 4: *Daily Trial Report* of the prosecution, Report No. 18, 6–8, on December 2, 1947.
75. Hauptverhandlung Fall VI, 4514–16 (December 2, 1947). Quotes from English Transcript of the Proceedings, Case VI, 4494–95.
76. Belle Mayer Papers, Nuremberg Related Material, Correspondence, Box 3, Folder 12: DuBois to Mayer, November 8, 1947.
77. Staatsarchiv Nürnberg, KV-Prozesse, Fall 6, Nr. B-112: Vereinigte Staaten von Amerika gegen Krauch und andere (Fall VI), Vorläufiges Memorandum und Schriftsatz der Anklagebehörde, I. Teil, December 6, 1947, 2, 7–8, 12.
78. Staatsarchiv Nürnberg, I. Teil, December 6, 1947, 10.
79. Staatsarchiv Nürnberg, I. Teil, December 6, 1947, 13–14.
80. Staatsarchiv Nürnberg, I. Teil, December 6, 1947, 21–25.
81. Staatsarchiv Nürnberg, I. Teil, December 6, 1947, 89.
82. Staatsarchiv Nürnberg, I. Teil, December 6, 1947, 102–106.
83. Staatsarchiv Nürnberg, KV-Prozesse, Fall 6, Nr. B-113: Vereinigte Staaten von Amerika gegen Krauch und andere (Fall VI), Vorläufiges Memorandum und Schriftsatz der Anklagebehörde, Anklagepunkt II Raub und Spoliation, [undated], 1, 14.
84. Staatsarchiv Nürnberg, Anklagepunkt II Raub und Spoliation, 16, 22, 24.
85. Staatsarchiv Nürnberg, Anklagepunkt II Raub und Spoliation, 37.
86. Staatsarchiv Nürnberg, KV-Prozesse, Fall 6, Nr. B-114: Vereinigte Staaten von Amerika gegen Krauch und andere (Fall VI), Vorläufige Denkschrift und Schriftsatz der Anklagebehörde, Teil III, December 13, 1947.
87. Staatsarchiv Nürnberg, Teil III, December 13, 1947, 5, 28–29.
88. Staatsarchiv Nürnberg, Teil III, December 13, 1947, 32, 37–38, 57.
89. Staatsarchiv Nürnberg, Teil III, December 13, 1947, 85–86.
90. Staatsarchiv Nürnberg, Teil III, December 13, 1947, 87, 102–106.
91. Staatsarchiv Nürnberg, KV-Prozesse, Fall 6, Nr. B-117: Vereinigte Staaten von Amerika gegen Krauch und andere (Fall VI), Vorläufige Denkschrift und Schriftsatz der Anklagebehörde, Teil VI, December 13, 1947, 1.
92. Staatsarchiv Nürnberg, Teil VI, December 13, 1947, 2–3.
93. Staatsarchiv Nürnberg, Teil VI, December 13, 1947, 8–9.
94. Spicka, "The Devil's Chemists on Trial," 869–72, 878–80, quote from 879.
95. Borkin, *Crime and Punishment*, 2–4, 140–42; Stokes, *Divide and Prosper*, 153–54.
96. Stokes, *Divide and Prosper*, 153–54.
97. DuBois, *The Devil's Chemists*, 97–98; see also 103.
98. James Morris Papers, Box 1, Folder 4: Letter Morris to DuBois, March 26, 1953; also in Telford Taylor Papers, Box 298, Correspondence: Morris to DuBois, March 26, 1953, (copy) as attachment to a letter from DuBois to Taylor, March 31, 1953.
99. Emanuel Minskoff Papers, RG-10.154*01, Folder 2: Letter from Minskoff to Joseph B. Friedman, February 2, 1948.
100. Staatsarchiv Nürnberg, KV-Verteidigung Handakten Hoffmann, Nr. 9, W. von Metzler, September 19, 1947: Circular letter to the defense counsels in Case No. VI, quotes from 1.
101. Staatsarchiv Nürnberg, Nr. 9, Dr. W. von Metzler, September 19, 1947, quotes from 3, 4, 9, 11, 14–17.
102. James Morris Papers, Box 1, Folder 1: Morris to Judge Thomas Burke, December 9, 1947.
103. Hauptverhandlung Fall VI, 4725–29 (December 18, 1947). Quote from English Transcript of the Proceedings, Case VI, 4712.
104. Hauptverhandlung Fall VI, 4758–62 (December 18, 1947). Quote from English Transcript of the Proceedings, Case VI, 4746–51.

105. Hauptverhandlung Fall VI, 4798–99 (December 18, 1947). Quote from English Transcript of the Proceedings, Case VI, 4790.
106. Hauptverhandlung Fall VI, 4804–10 (December 18, 1947). Quotes from English Transcript of the Proceedings, Case VI, 4795–98.
107. Hauptverhandlung Fall VI, 4878–79 (Nath) (December 19, 1947), 4832–35 (von Metzler) (December 18, 1947), 4910 (Henze) (December 19, 1947). Quote from English Transcript of the Proceedings, Case VI, 4896.
108. Hauptverhandlung Fall VI, 4744 (Siemers), 4790 (Berndt) (December 18, 1947). Quotes from English Transcript of the Proceedings, Case VI, 4732 (Siemers), 4782 (Berndt).
109. Hauptverhandlung Fall VI, 4914–15 (Wagner) (December 19, 1947). Quotes from English Transcript of the Proceedings, Case VI, 4899–900.
110. Cf. DuBois, *The Devil's Chemists*, 205–207, 219–33, 298–306.
111. Curtis Grover Shake: Transcript of Taped Interview, 1968: Indiana State Library, Indiana Division, Oral History Project 1972, 74 (hereinafter: Shake Interview).
112. Hoechst Archiv, IG/54: IG-Prozessakten, Hans Pribilla, Trial Brief für den Angeklagten Carl Ludwig Lautenschläger, June 1948, quotes from 59–60; Hauptverhandlung Fall VI, 9685 (March 18, 1948); NARA, RG 238, Entry 159, Box 6, Folder 4: *Daily Trial Report* by the prosecution, Report No. 30, here on March 17, 1948. Cf. Lindner, *Inside IG Farben*, 309–10, 331–33.
113. Hauptverhandlung Fall VI, 11050 (April 8, 1948).
114. Hauptverhandlung Fall VI, 13057–3060 (April 29, 1948). For more detailed information on the human experiments at Hoechst, see Lindner, *Inside IG Farben*, 307–36.
115. Hauptverhandlung Fall VI, 9896–97 (March 22, 1948).
116. Hauptverhandlung Fall VI, 10066–7 (March 24, 1948). Jähne also mentioned Gerhard Ollendorff, stating that he had also already died—according to Heine, *Verstand und Schicksal*, 115, however, he did not die until December 15, 1949, in Rio de Janeiro.
117. Hauptverhandlung Fall VI, 5683–5685 (January 20, 1948); on C. Lammers, see Heine, *Verstand und Schicksal*, 210–12. Quotes from English Transcript of the Proceedings, Case VI, 5644–45.
118. Hauptverhandlung Fall VI, 9137–45 (March 12, 1948). Quotes from English Transcript of the Proceedings, Case VI, 9041–49.
119. Hauptverhandlung Fall VI, 10220–22 (March 25, 1948).
120. Hauptverhandlung Fall VI, 10233–36 (March 25, 1948). Quotes from English Transcript of the Proceedings, Case VI, 10096–10099.
121. Hauptverhandlung Fall VI, 10239–44 (March 25, 1948).
122. Hauptverhandlung Fall VI, 10288 (March 30, 1948). Quotes from English Transcript of the Proceedings, Case VI, 10151–52.
123. Hauptverhandlung Fall VI, 11083 (April 9, 1948); this formulation might have referred to a 1941 sermon by Clemens August von Galen, bishop of Münster, who said at the time that people were not hammers but anvils—cf. Johannes Neuhäusler, *Amboss und Hammer: Erlebnisse im Kirchenkampf des Dritten Reiches*, 11. Quote from English Transcript of the Proceedings, Case VI, 10923.
124. Unternehmensarchiv BASF, W 1.2./114 and 115: Kugler, *Farben: Chance und Schicksal*, 425–26.
125. Staatsarchiv Nürnberg, KV-Verteidigung Nr. 4, Handakten Nath: New structure of questioning Dr. Ilgner; KV-Verteidigung Nr. 5, Handakten Nath: For example, "C.S.R. /Aussig – Falkenau," here written by hand on top "Bad!" or on the margins "Frank-Fahle again and more precise!"
126. Bayer Archiv, 207/028: Nelte to Prof. Kikuth, June 26, 1947; quotes are from this source; Reply Kikuth to Nelte on July 7, 1947; see, for example, also Bayer Archiv, 207/023: Note

by Dr. Goth on November 3, 1947, about the discussions of Dr. Nelte with, inter alia, Prof. Domagk and Prof. Kikuth in Elberfeld on October 30 and 31, 1947.

127. Cf. Wagner, *IG Auschwitz*, 300–304; DuBois, *The Devil's Chemists*, 166–67; shows in the example of Dr. Hans Braus that German witnesses were often unwilling to speak on behalf of the prosecution or later wanted to withdraw their statements because they had to continue to live "with these people" after the trial in Germany.
128. DuBois, *The Devil's Chemists*, 67–68.
129. Shake Interview, 37; Judge Hebert was apparently against this decision: see Paul Hebert Papers, "Procedural errors," https://digitalcommons.law.lsu.edu/nuremberg_docs/11/ (last retrieved on July 22, 2025).
130. *The Judgement in the Farben Trial*, 3.
131. NL Wahl, 01-237-055/6: Eduard Wahl to Alwin Mittasch, November 6, 1947.
132. Staatsarchiv Freiburg T 1 Drischel 52: Rechtsanwalt Drischel to Richard Linde, August 12, 1947, with the draft of an affidavit.
133. Hoechst Archiv, IG/50: Jähne Dokument Nr. 60: Affidavit of Adolf Baldus on March 9, 1948; Lindner, *Inside IG Farben*, 245–46, 248–49.
134. IG/50: IG-Prozessakten, Jähne Dokument Nr. 54: Affidavit of Karl Gebhardt on March 4, 1948; Lindner, *Inside IG Farben*, 236.
135. Hoechst Archiv, IG/50: IG-Prozessakten, Jähne Dokument Nr. 21: Affidavit of Franz Spiess on January 16, 1948; Lindner, *Inside IG Farben*, 236–38.
136. Hauptverhandlung Fall VI, 10197 (March 25, 1948).
137. Fritz-Bauer-Institut, Archiv, I. G. Farben-Prozess, Reel 85, Document Book I for Dr. Fritz Gajewski, submitted by Defense Counsel Dr. Ernst Achenbach: Gajewski Nr. 4, Affidavit by Dr. Gerhard Ollendorff, April 24, 1947.
138. Hauptverhandlung Fall VI, 8246–54 (March 2, 1948). Quotes from English Transcript of the Proceedings, Case VI, 8180–81.
139. Hauptverhandlung Fall VI, 8408–10 (March 3, 1948). Quotes from English Transcript of the Proceedings, Case VI, 8325–27. For the documents putting Gajewski in a bad light, see Reel 33, Prosecution Exhibits, Document No. NI-13522, Prosecution Exhibit No. 1957 (March 3, 1948); cf. also Karlsch, "Fritz Gajewski (1885–1965)—charismatischer Manager in einem multidivisionalen Konzern? Ein Beitrag zur Unternehmensführung der IG Farbenindustrie AG, 1928–1939," 91–130, here especially 122–24; in my opinion, Karlsch casts Gajewski in far too positive a light.
140. On May, cf. Lindner, *Inside IG Farben*, 183; Hauptverhandlung Fall VI, 12724–25, with regard to false statements by von der Heyde on May and ter Meer (April 26, 1948). Cf. on this also Löhnert, "Richard May, Theodor Mariam, Oskar Falek: Schicksale jüdischer Chemiker in der Farbenfabrik Wolfen nach 1933," 137–73, here 139–59.
141. Staatsarchiv Freiburg, T 1 Drischel 54: Report [by Drischel] about his visit to Nürnberg from May 27 to June 4, 1947: At the time, Ambros had already told Drischel that he found "the acquisition of exculpatory material on the matter of the Auschwitz concentration camp to be of top importance."
142. Hauptverhandlung Fall VI, 3427 (November 6, 1947)—Seidl. Quote from English Transcript of the Proceedings, Case VI, 3408.
143. Hauptverhandlung Fall VI, 8126–28 (March 1, 1948). Quotes from English Transcript of the Proceedings, Case VI, 9052–53.
144. NARA, RG 238, Entry 159, Box 6, Folder 4: *Daily Trial Report* by the prosecution, Report No. 22, January 21, 1948—Developments outside the court.
145. Unternehmensarchiv BASF, A 866/1: Decknamen/Code names (Liste).
146. Staatsarchiv Freiburg, T 1 Drischel 55: Ambros to Drischel, December 3, 1947; Hoffmann to Major Schaefer, Defense Center, December 8, 1947; Drischel to Ambros, December 9, 1947;

the quote is from here; see in addition Drischel to Dr. Klavehn-Berndt (who had acquired Otto Ambros as a client for him), December 12, 1947, in which he reported on Ambros's major mood swings; Dr. Klavehn-Berndt to Drischel, December 16, 1947. DuBois stated that the relationship between Hoffmann and Ambros was also tense. DuBois even wrote, in *The Devil's Chemists*, 181: "Dr. Hoffman's distaste for his client had grown so obvious that he let him go on at great length alone (which Ambros did not mind at all); then Hoffman asked a few questions apathetically."

147. Unternehmensarchiv BASF, A 866/1: Ausarbeitungen A-D, May 17/18/21, 1947 (Verteiler May 27, 1947)—Quotes from Ausarbeitung A and B, both on May 17, 1947.
148. Unternehmensarchiv BASF, A 866/1: Discussion with ter Meer on June 7, 1947 (by Ambros, but not signed).
149. Unternehmensarchiv BASF, 866/1: Anorgana GmbH—Werk Gendorf, Nachtrag May 12, 1947; for Klenck's or even Krauch's statements to the prosecution inculpating Ambros, see NARA, RG 238, Entry 192, Box 1, Folder 6: Mr. H. Thayer, Memorandum for Mr. Heath, Subject Slave Labor—I. G. Farben—Interim Report, December 6, 1946.
150. Hauptverhandlung Fall VI, 7900–901 (February 27, 1948).
151. Hauptverhandlung Fall VI, 7907–909 (February 27, 1948). Quotes from English Transcript of the Proceedings, Case VI, 7835.
152. Hauptverhandlung Fall VI, 8910–20 (March 10, 1948). Quotes from English Transcript of the Proceedings, Case VI, 8828–34. See on this Vogelsang, *Der Freundeskreis Himmler*.
153. Hauptverhandlung Fall VI, 9001–16 (March 11, 1948). Quote from English Transcript of the Proceedings, Case VI, 8911.
154. Hauptverhandlung Fall VI, 7720–21 (February 25, 1948).
155. Staatsarchiv Nürnberg, KV-Prozesse, Fall 6, Nr. C 30, 31: Rudolf Dix on behalf of the defense team, February 28, 1948, in the case United States vs Krauch et al (Case VI), Response of the defense to the prosecution's requestion for documents of February 26, 1948.
156. Hauptverhandlung Fall VI, 8711–12 (March 8, 1948). Quote from English Transcript of the Proceedings, Case VI, 8628.
157. For the prosecution's view on the conflict, see DuBois, *The Devil's Chemists*, 189–93; 201–204.
158. Hauptverhandlung Fall VI, 11852–56 (April 16, 1948). Quote from English Transcript of the Proceedings, Case VI, 11643. On Dürrfeld's ambition, assertiveness, and position, see Wagner, *IG Auschwitz*, 60.
159. Hauptverhandlung Fall VI, 11883–86 (April 16, 1948). Quote from English Transcript of the Proceedings, Case VI, 11673.
160. Fritz-Bauer-Institut, Archiv, I. G. Farben-Prozess, Reel 65, 389–91: Defense Exhibit Dürrfeld, Doc-No. Dü-93, Dürrfeld Exhibit No. 66, Affidavit by Oswald Pohl on July 17, 1947.
161. Hauptverhandlung Fall VI, 12176–202—Seidl, 12202–207—cross-examination by Minskoff (April 20, 1948).
162. Hauptverhandlung Fall VI, 13752–60 (Commissioner session on May 4, 1948).
163. Hauptverhandlung Fall VI, 14049–67 (Commission II, Commissioner session on May 6, 1948). With regard to Minskoff's success in the cross-examinations on Auschwitz in this phase of the trial, see also DuBois, *The Devil's Chemists*, 228–31, here 228: "Without exception, the witnesses changed their stories under withering cross-examination, or were shown to have been the type of criminals whose word was worthless in any court."
164. Hauptverhandlung Fall VI, 8136 (March 1, 1948)—Ambros being cross-examined by Amchan. Quote from English Transcript of the Proceedings, Case VI, 8064.
165. NL Wahl 01-237-055/6: Letters from Wahl to Father Pribilla, SJ, September 28, 1947, December 27, 1947, and January 31, 1948; NL Wahl 01-237-056/1: Hellmuth Dix to Father Pribilla, September 1, 1948, seeking to have his role as promoter of Pribilla's opinion recognized; Wahl to Count Ballestrem, Archepiscopal Bishopric of Cologne, September 2, 1948;

Pribilla to Wahl, September 7, 1948. On the further involvement of Father Pribilla, SJ, and his argument for "propagandistic work" with respect to the Americans, see Unternehmensarchiv BASF, Privatakten W. Heintzeler vol. II: Pribilla to Dr. Müller, March 31, 1949 (copy).

166. Published as Max Pribilla, S.J., "Das Verhalten der Unternehmer im Dritten Reich. Moraltheologisches Gutachten," Freiburg im Breisgau, n.d. (special edition of *Stimmen der Zeit* 143, no. 3 [Dec. 1948])—quotes from 5, 8–9, 14. The opinion was taken up as a document of the defense and later quoted many times, inter alia by Rudolf Dix, the defense lawyer, and Hermann Schmitz, in his closing statement. *Trials of War Criminals*, vol. VIII, 935–52, here 950–51; by Professor Wahl in the foreword of the book by August von Knieriem, Nürnberg, xiv and xviii; cf. also Müller, "Nürnberg und die deutschen Juristen," 257–77, here 257–58.
167. Cf. Wagner, *IG Auschwitz*, 305–9; see on this also von Knieriem, *Nürnberg*, 205–207.
168. Staatsarchiv Nürnberg, KV-Verteidigung, Nr. 5 Handakten Aschenauer: Opening Statement (Original, deutsch) für den Angeklagten Gattineau (Fall VI), überreicht von Rudolf Aschenauer, Verteidiger.
169. Staatsarchiv Nürnberg, KV-Prozesse, Fall 6, Nr. C 29: Antrag von Rudolf Aschenauer an den Generalsekretär am Amerikanischen Militärgericht (Fall VI), April 6, 1948; quotes from 1, 9, 10, 11, 12, 15, 17, 18, 24.
170. See Seliger, *Politische Anwälte*, 350, who suspects that Prof. Reinhart Maurach had helped to write this legal document. Cf. also James Morris Papers, Box 1, Folder 19: Telford Taylor, "An Outline of the Research and Publication Possibilities of the War Crimes Trials," November 1948, 10, where he writes about German defense counsels who had taken "very extreme positions"—Aschenauer and Seidl surely counted among them.
171. James Morris Papers, Box 1, Folder 2: Morris to Judge Christianson, January 9, 1948. "OPA" presumably refers to the Office of Price Administration.
172. See Priemel, *The Betrayal*, 348–49, here also footnote 154.
173. James Morris Papers, Box 1, Folder 2: Morris to Judge Nuessle, March 3, 1948. Morris also discussed Wennerstrum with another judge: Morris to Judge Burr, February 28, 1948: "It was a rather unfortunate incident—and the most unfortunate thing about it is that most of the charges made by Judge Wennerstrum seem to be well founded."
174. Hauptverhandlung Fall VI, 6485–86 (February 5, 1948). Quotes from English Transcript of the Proceedings, Case VI, 6427–28. See also NARA, RG 238, Entry 159, Box 6, Folder 4: *Daily Trial Report* by the prosecution, Report No. 24: February 5, 1948 (Law and Procedure).
175. Hauptverhandlung Fall VI, 7232–33, 7251–52 (February 17, 1948). Quote from English Transcript of the Proceedings, Case VI, 7191. See also, NARA, RG 238, Entry 159, Box 6, Folder 4: *Daily Trial Report* by the prosecution, Report No. 26: February 17, 1948 (Law and Procedure).
176. NARA, RG 238, Entry 159, Box 6, Folder 4: *Daily Trial Report* by the prosecution, Report No. 27: February 24, 1948 (Law and Procedure, in chambers conference).
177. Hauptverhandlung Fall VI, 8776–81 (March 9, 1948). Quotes from English Transcript of the Proceedings, Case VI, 8698–703.
178. James Morris Papers, Box 1, Folder 2: Morris to Frank Rowley, Dean of Law, University of Cincinnati, Ohio, April 19, 1948.
179. Hauptverhandlung Fall VI, 14599–603 (May 11, 1948). Quotes from English Transcript of the Proceedings, Case VI, 14251–54.
180. Bayer Archiv, 207/007-002: Tuerck to Schramm, April 16, 1948.
181. Bayer Archiv, 207/007-002: Berndt to Schramm, Leverkusen-Bayerwerk, June 3, 1948.
182. Bayer Archiv, 207/007 vol. 2: Rudolf Dix to the Military Tribunal, Case VI, March 12, 1948—"Altersklasse Reihenfolge nach Alter."

183. James Morris Papers, Box 1, Folder 2: Morris to Lillian W. Kamplin, May 13, 1948.
184. James Morris Papers, Box 1, Folder 2: Morris to Ruth Guthrie, May 1, 1948.
185. Staatsarchiv Nürnberg, KV-Prozesse, Fall 6, Nr. C 26: Prof. Dr. Eduard Wahl, Closing Letter about "Grundsätzliche Rechtsfragen" im Namen aller Angeklagten (Fundamental Questions of Law in the Name of all the Defendants), May 21, 1948, 5–6; on the closing letter, see also Lorenz, "Eduard Wahl," 9–45, here 24–26.
186. Staatsarchiv Nürnberg, KV-Prozesse, Fall 6, Nr. C 26: Prof. Dr. Eduard Wahl, Closing Letter about "Grundsätzliche Rechtsfragen" im Namen aller Angeklagten (Fundamental Questions of Law in the Name of all the Defendants), May 21, 1948, 13–18. Quotes from Defense Closing Statements, Trial and Closing Briefs, and Final Pleas for Case No. 6, United States v. Carl Krauch, et al., Closing Brief, Wahl, Case VI, 13–18, hereinafter: Closing Brief, Wahl, Case VI (English).
187. Closing Brief, Wahl, Case VI (English), 28–31: The representative quoted here on 30 is the journalist Felix Morley, mentioned as president of Haverford College, though he only served 1940–45.
188. Closing Brief, Wahl, Case VI (English), 38–40.
189. Closing Brief, Wahl, Case VI (English), 46–61.
190. Closing Brief, Wahl, Case VI (English), 62–75.
191. Closing Brief, Wahl, Case VI (English), 76–81.
192. Closing Brief, Wahl, Case VI (English), 82–88.
193. Hauptverhandlung Fall VI, 14818–873. Published later as "Eine deutsche Verteidigung: Das Plaidoyer von Prof. Dr. E. Wahl im Nürnberger Prozeß gegen die Angeklagten der deutschen Wirtschaft," *Der Ruf: Unabhängige Blätter für unabhängige Leser* 4 (February 15, 1949): title page, 4–7, and 10–12. On the journal *Der Ruf*, in particular, as the inspiration for Group 47, see Gallus, " 'Der Ruf' – Stimme für ein neues Deutschland," 32–38.
194. Quoted from Wahl, "Eine deutsche Verteidigung," 4. On the Soviet role, see Hirsch, "The Soviets at Nuremberg: International Law, Propaganda, and the Making of the Postwar Order," 701–30.
195. For quotes, see Wahl, "Eine deutsche Verteidigung," 10.
196. Bayer Archiv, 207/007-002: Berndt to Schramm, Leverkusen-Bayerwerk, June 3, 1948.
197. Closing statement by von Metzler, see Hauptverhandlung Fall VI, 14942–15007; quoted here from Staatsarchiv Nürnberg, KV-Prozesse, Fall 6, C 27: Wolfram von Metzler, Abschließende Ausführungen über die allgemeinen Themen I. Die Erheblichkeit des Beweismaterials der Anklagebehörde bezüglich der Punkte I und V der Anklageschrift, II. Die allgemeine Theorie der Verantwortlichkeit der Angeklagten an den zur Klage stehenden Verbrechen, here on I, 1–16. Quotes from English Transcript of the Proceedings, Case VI, 14663–75.
198. Staatsarchiv Nürnberg, Part I, 18–27. Quotes from English Transcript of the Proceedings, Case VI, 14676–83.
199. Staatsarchiv Nürnberg, Part II, 1–8. Quotes from English Transcript of the Proceedings, Case VI, 14687–94.
200. Staatsarchiv Nürnberg, Part II, 8–18.
201. Staatsarchiv Nürnberg, Part II, 29–31. Quotes from English Transcript of the Proceedings, Case VI, 14694–716.
202. Hauptverhandlung Fall VI, 14938–940 (June 2, 1948)—Rudolf Dix. Quotes from English Transcript of the Proceedings, Case VI, 14661.
203. Hauptverhandlung Fall VI, 15014–15 (June 3, 1948)—Siemers. Quotes from English Transcript of the Proceedings, Case VI, 14717–22.
204. Hauptverhandlung Fall VI, 15035 (June 3, 1948)—Siemers. Quotes from English Transcript of the Proceedings, Case VI, 14741.
205. Hauptverhandlung Fall VI, 15299–300 (June 7, 1948)—Schubert for Bürgin. Quotes from English Transcript of the Proceedings, Case VI, 14982.

206. Hauptverhandlung Fall VI, 15109–13 (June 3, 1948)—Nelte for Hörlein. Quotes from English Transcript of the Proceedings, Case VI, 14805–808.
207. Hauptverhandlung Fall VI, 15160–15163 (June 4, 1948)—Pelckmann for von Knieriem. Quotes from English Transcript of the Proceedings, Case VI, 14850–52.
208. Hauptverhandlung Fall VI, 15096–97 (June 3, 1948)—Carl Mayer for Gajewski. Quotes from English Transcript of the Proceedings, Case VI, 14792–93.
209. Hauptverhandlung Fall VI, 15202–207 (June 4, 1948)—Berndt.
210. Hauptverhandlung Fall VI, 15284–95 (June 4, 1948)—Hoffmann. Quotes from English Transcript of the Proceedings, Case VI, 14969–77.
211. Hauptverhandlung Fall VI, 15593–15610 (June 8, 1948)—Wagner for Wurster. Quotes from English Transcript of the Proceedings, Case VI, 15257–73.
212. Hauptverhandlung Fall VI, 15747–90 (June 9, 1948)—Silcher for all defendants. For greater detail on these remarks and this exculpation topic of the defense, see Brünger, *Geschichte und Gewinn*, 75–84.
213. Hauptverhandlung Fall VI, 15747–15751. Quotes from English Transcript of the Proceedings, Case VI, 15400–402.
214. Hauptverhandlung Fall VI, 15757. Quote from English Transcript of the Proceedings, Case VI, 15410.
215. Hauptverhandlung Fall VI, 15760–63. Quotes from English Transcript of the Proceedings, Case VI, 15415–16.
216. Hauptverhandlung Fall VI, 15766–70. Quotes from English Transcript of the Proceedings, Case VI, 15418–21.
217. Hauptverhandlung Fall VI, 15772–78. Quotes from English Transcript of the Proceedings, Case VI, 15428–30.
218. Hauptverhandlung Fall VI, 15778–82. Quotes from English Transcript of the Proceedings, Case VI, 15433.
219. Hauptverhandlung Fall VI, 15783–86. Quotes from English Transcript of the Proceedings, Case VI, 15434–36.
220. Hauptverhandlung Fall VI, 15788–90.
221. Staatsarchiv Nürnberg, KV-Prozesse, Fall 6, B 118, 119, 120: Abschliessender Schriftsatz der Anklagebehoerde, Teil I: Allgemeine Bemerkungen bezueglich der persoenlichen Verantwortung der Angeklagten, June 1, 1948, 9–13. Quotes from Final Brief of the Prosecution, United States v. Carl Krauch, et al., Case VI, 10–13.
222. Staatsarchiv Nürnberg, KV-Prozesse, Fall 6, B 118, 119, 120: Abschliessender Schriftsatz der Anklagebehoerde, Teil III: Gewisse Betaetigungen auf dem Gebiete von Pluenderung und Kriegsbeute, June 1, 1948, see, for example, 27, 33, 35—cf. on this Priemel, *The Betrayal*, 204–205.
223. Staatsarchiv Nürnberg, KV-Prozesse, Fall 6, B-121, 122: Schluss-Brief der Anklagebehoerde, Teil IV: Gewisse Taten auf dem Gebiet der Sklavenarbeit und des Massenmordes—of the 113 pages of this part of the brief, around 70 were devoted to Auschwitz alone, while the rest addressed Zyklon B and the human experiments at concentration camps.
224. Staatsarchiv Nürnberg, KV-Prozesse, Fall 6, B-121, 122: Schluss-Brief der Anklagebehoerde, Teil V: Beurteilung gewisser Aspekte der Verteidigung—on Gajewski, see 18.
225. Staatsarchiv Nürnberg, KV-Prozesse, Fall 6, B-123a: Abschliessender Schriftsatz der Anklagebehoerde Teil VI: Besondere Kommentare und Vorschlaege fuer den Tatbestand bezueglich der Einzelverantwortlichkeit jedes Angeklagten, here 638–49; quote from 649.
226. Staatsarchiv Nürnberg, KV-Prozesse, Fall 6, B 125: Abschließender Schriftsatz fuer die Vereinigten Staaten von Amerika, June 10, 1948; see also Hauptverhandlung Fall VI, 15791–903 (June 10, 1948)—Closing statements by Taylor and other members of the prosecution.
227. Staatsarchiv Nürnberg, KV-Prozesse, Fall 6, B 125: Abschließender Schriftsatz fuer die Vereinigten Staaten von Amerika, June 10, 1948, 1–2. Quotes from English Transcript of the Proceedings, Case VI, 15443.

228. Staatsarchiv Nürnberg, KV-Prozesse, Fall 6, B 125: Abschließender Schriftsatz fuer die Vereinigten Staaten von Amerika, June 10, 1948, 45–55. Quotes from English Transcript of the Proceedings, Case VI, 15485–96.
229. Staatsarchiv Nürnberg, KV-Prozesse, Fall 6, B 125: Abschließender Schriftsatz fuer die Vereinigten Staaten von Amerika, June 10, 1948, 4–15. Quotes from English Transcript of the Proceedings, Case VI, 15483–84.
230. Staatsarchiv Nürnberg, KV-Prozesse, Fall 6, B 125: Abschließender Schriftsatz fuer die Vereinigten Staaten von Amerika, June 10, 1948, on spoliation und plunder, 22–33; on Auschwitz, 39–42.
231. Staatsarchiv Nürnberg, KV-Prozesse, Fall 6, B 125: Abschließender Schriftsatz fuer die Vereinigten Staaten von Amerika, June 10, 1948, 66–74. Quotes from English Transcript of the Proceedings, Case VI, 15512–17.
232. Staatsarchiv Nürnberg, KV-Prozesse, Fall 6, B 125: Abschließender Schriftsatz fuer die Vereinigten Staaten von Amerika, June 10, 1948, on "window dressing," 75–80; on necessity, 81–92. Quotes from English Transcript of the Proceedings, Case VI, 15521–32.
233. Staatsarchiv Nürnberg, KV-Prozesse, Fall 6, B 125: Abschließender Schriftsatz fuer die Vereinigten Staaten von Amerika, June 10, 1948, 93–95. Most of this part of the closing remarks is also printed at the end of the book by Taylor, *Die Nürnberger Prozesse*, 139–40. Quotes from English Transcript of the Proceedings, Case VI, 15532–34; and from Taylor, *Final Report*, 237.
234. James Morris Papers, Box 1, Folder 2: Morris to Karl Mundt, Member of Congress, June 21, 1948.
235. Belle Mayer Papers, Nuremberg Related Material, Correspondence, Box 3, Folder 12: DuBois to Mayer, April 27, 1948.
236. NL Heimerich, 24/1972a-759: Wahl to Heimerich, April 20, 1948. Cf. also Staatsarchiv Freiburg, T 1 Drischel 52: Heintzeler to Drischel, April 27, 1948: Wolfgang Heintzeler wrote at the time to Otto Ambros's former defense counsel, Friedrich Drischel, about the trial, which was coming to a close: "The atmosphere is generally good, but it is impossible to predict the verdict."
237. Staatsarchiv Freiburg, T 1 Drischel 52: Heintzeler to Drischel, no date—end of trial referred to as "the day before yesterday," so likely June 13, 1948; the letter got to Drischel on June 16, 1948.
238. Deutsches Museum Archiv, NL 080/290/1 A-C: handwritten letter from Bütefisch to Gerlach, July 8, 1948.
239. Drexel Sprecher Papers, Box 59, Publication Project File, Military Government of Germany: Dr. Karl Hoffmann, The Nuernberg Trials. Cf. also DuBois, *The Devil's Chemists*, 356, which cites Judge Shake's recommendation on November 10, 1948—after the trial—of the defendant Max Ilgner to General Bishop, which states at the end: "I have said to many convicted defendants in the Farben case that they have an unusual opportunity to perform good services for Germany and the world by reason of their unfortunate and tragic experience. I firmly believe that all of these men can and will make good citizens of the new and better Germany."
240. Hoechst Archiv, Personalakten Carl Ludwig Lautenschläger, Lautenschläger, Erinnerungen, vol. VIII [86–87], where he writes with great sorrow that his request to leave the jail in Nuremberg in order to be at the sickbed of his dying son was not authorized by the prison administration and his court officer; cf. also Lindner, *Inside IG Farben*, 344.
241. Unternehmensarchiv BASF, W.1.3./114 and 115: Kugler, *Farben: Chance und Schicksal*, 432–36; Gattineau, *Durch die Klippen*, 199; Drexel Sprecher Papers, Box 47, Case Files, Case VI-Tribunal Orders, inter alia: Order for Christian Schneider on January 27, 1948 (permission to visit his sick mother); Order for Georg von Schnitzler on February 28, 1948 (permission to visit his sick mother) and on March 29, 1948 (permission to attend his mother's funeral);

Order for Otto Ambros on March 31, 1948 (permission to attend his daughter's first communion); Order for Heinrich Gattineau on June 17, 1948 (permission to visit his sick father-in-law); Order for Hans Kugler on June 22, 1948 (permission to deal with family matters and "business affairs").

242. DuBois, *The Devil's Chemists*, 132–34.
243. NL Wahl, 01-237-056/1: Ilse Bethge to Eduard Wahl, July 14, 1948, where she writes that Böttcher had delivered the "patient"—in other words, Krauch—that day to Nuremberg since the "vacation on word of honor," as she wrote, was "unfortunately ended" "after the press took an interest." See also Bethge to Wahl, June 28, 1948: Krauch had to take a cure in the prison sick ward after examination, she stated.
244. Stadtarchiv Ludwigshafen, N25/161 Nachlass Wagner (hereinafter: NL Wagner): handwritten letter from Margarete Wurster to Wagner, May 9, 1948.
245. James Morris Papers, Box 1, Folder 2: Morris to Judge Nuessle, June 9, 1948.
246. James Morris Papers, Box 1, Folder 2: Morris to Judge Christianson, July 2, 1948.
247. Unternehmensarchiv BASF W.1.3./114 and 115: Kugler, *Farben: Chance und Schicksal*, 413.
248. Kugler, *Farben: Chance und Schicksal*, 413; Hauptverhandlung Fall VI, 16009 (July 29, 1948). See also Stokes, "From the IG Farben Fusion to BASF AG," 351.
249. *The Judgement in the Farben Trial*, 30.
250. *The Judgement in the Farben Trial*, 18.
251. *The Judgement in the Farben Trial*, 19.
252. *The Judgement in the Farben Trial*, 23–24.
253. *The Judgement in the Farben Trial*, 40.
254. *The Judgement in the Farben Trial*, 37–39.
255. *The Judgement in the Farben Trial*, 43.
256. *The Judgement in the Farben Trial*, 49–50.
257. Paul Hebert Papers, https://digitalcommons.law.lsu.edu/nuremberg_docs/index.html (last retrieved on July 22, 2025): cf. on this Crimes against Peace [1947]; Economic Support [1947–1948]; Jottings 10 [1947]; Less Culpable on September 8, 1947; Jottings on January 12, 1948; No Immunity [1948]; Perfectly Obvious [no date]; Plough New Ground [1948].
258. Zuppi, "Slave Labor," 512–14; DuBois, *The Devil's Chemists*, 347, 352–53.
259. *Trials of War Criminals*, vol. VIII, Concurring Opinion of Judge Hebert on the Charges of Crimes against Peace, 1211–1306, here 1211–12.
260. Taylor, *Final Report*, 197–99.
261. *The Judgement in the Farben Trial*, 52–54, quote from 54.
262. *The Judgement in the Farben Trial*, 55.
263. *The Judgement in the Farben Trial*, 58.
264. *The Judgement in the Farben Trial*, 61–62.
265. *The Judgement in the Farben Trial*, 77–78.
266. *The Judgement in the Farben Trial*, 78.
267. *The Judgement in the Farben Trial*, 64.
268. *The Judgement in the Farben Trial*, 77.
269. *The Judgement in the Farben Trial*, 86.
270. *The Judgement in the Farben Trial*, 78–94, quote from 81.
271. *The Judgement in the Farben Trial*, 94.
272. *The Judgement in the Farben Trial*, 94–96. Historical research has come to this conclusion in the meantime; cf. Hayes, *From Cooperation to Complicity. Degussa in the Third Reich*, 272–300; Joly, "L'implication de l'industrie chimique allemande dans la Shoah: le cas du Zyclon B," 368–400.
273. *The Judgement in the Farben Trial*, 98–99. According to the current state of historical research, at least some of those responsible at I. G. Farben had known about the experiments on humans

in the concentration camps and had authorized them and thereby made themselves criminally liable—cf. Lindner, *Inside IG Farben*, 307–36.

274. *The Judgement in the Farben Trial*, 101.
275. *The Judgement in the Farben Trial*, 101.
276. *The Judgement in the Farben Trial*, 102.
277. *The Judgement in the Farben Trial*, 103.
278. *The Judgement in the Farben Trial*, 105–106.
279. *The Judgement in the Farben Trial*, 107.
280. *The Judgement in the Farben Trial*, 111–12.
281. *The Judgement in the Farben Trial*, 113–14.
282. *The Judgement in the Farben Trial*, 116.
283. *The Judgement in the Farben Trial*, 117–19.
284. *Trials of War Criminals*, vol. VIII, Dissenting Opinion of Judge Hebert on the Charges of Slave Labor, 1307–25, here 1308. On the basis of the current state of knowledge, there would be agreement with Hebert that I. G. Farben had independently sought out slave labor and that "superior orders" by no means existed to such a degree as the majority of the court accepted at the time. However, research has confirmed the majority opinion of the court in that, owing to the centrifugal forces in the company, the entire board of directors should not have been held criminally responsible for Auschwitz. Cf. on this Hayes, *Industry and Ideology*, 206, 343–47; on Auschwitz, 348–68; Lindner, *Inside IG Farben*, 224–30, 248–49.
285. Buscher, *The U.S. War Crimes Trial Program in Germany, 1946–1955*, 34–36.
286. *The Judgement in the Farben Trial*, 131–32.
287. Taylor, *Final Report*, 36; Shake Interview, 35.
288. Shake Interview, 35–36.
289. Shake Interview, 53–56; cf. on this Bellamy, *Hoosier Justice*, 63–64. In contrast to this was the expressed suspicion in DuBois, *The Devil's Chemists*, 195, that Shake and Morris had not once checked out their surroundings in Nuremberg.
290. Shake Interview, 36–38.
291. Morris, "Major War Crimes Trials in Nurnberg," 108–9.
292. James Morris Papers, Box 1, Folder 5: Letter Morris to Kronstein (copy), March 25, 1953, with excerpts from the I. G. Farben verdict.
293. See von Knieriem, *Nürnberg*, 515, 543.
294. Cf. on this DuBois, *The Devil's Chemists*, 355–56; Stokes, *Divide and Prosper*, 153: "the mild punishments fit with the American judicial tradition of light sentences for 'white-collar crime.'"
295. Shake Interview, 74–75.
296. Cf. Bellamy, *Hoosier Justice*, 27–31.
297. Shake Interview, 64.
298. *The Judgement in the Farben Trial*, 49.
299. James Morris Papers, Box 7, Folder 13: Morris to Major General Heber L. Edwards, October 20, 1958.
300. Cf. on this DuBois, *The Devil's Chemists*, 95, 338, 357; anti-Soviet comments can be found in the letter from Morris to DuBois; Meschke and Smith, 256; Shake Interview, 52–53, on his experience with Soviet justice. Cf. on this also Wagner, *IG Auschwitz*, 304–305; Greiner, *Die Morgenthau-Legende*, 384–86; DuBois, *The Devil's Chemists*, 355, even concluded that the developments over the course of 1948 and the resulting anxiety on the part of Judges Shake and Morris had had a significant effect on the verdict.
301. Bayer Archiv, 207/007-001: Shake to Lilly von Schnitzler, March 27, 1950 (Response to her letter from March 10, 1950).

302. Shake Interview, 63–65: though he incorrectly remembered having given about fifteen years of prison time as the maximum penalty, the maximum penalty in the I. G. Farben trial had been only eight years; cf. also Stokes, *Divide and Prosper*, 153: "white-collar crime."
303. Bundesarchiv, AllProz 3/281: Shake to Ilgner, January 25, 1949 (copy—part of the attachment of a letter from the lawyer Martin Johannsen to Dr. Nagel, April 5, 1949, in which the correspondence between Ilgner and Shake is attached in copy—"with the request that it be treated confidentially").
304. Bayer Archiv, 207/007-001: Shake to Dr. R. W. Muller, February 22, 1951. Cf. also the letter from Shake for Ilgner to General Bishop, Military Governor in Düsseldorf, printed in DuBois, *The Devil's Chemists*, 356.
305. James Morris Papers, Box 1, Folder 4 Correspondence: von Metzler to Morris, May 9, 1949—containing reference to the fact that similar letters had gone to Shake and Hebert.
306. Belle Mayer Papers, Nuremberg Related Material, Correspondence, Box 3, Folder 12: DuBois to Drew Pearson, December 7, 1948.
307. Byron R. Lewis Historical Collection Library, Vincennes University, Indiana, Curtis G. Shake Papers, RHC 38, 1–2: Shake to Drew Pearson, November 12, 1948 (hereinafter: Curtis G. Shake Papers).

Chapter 4

The Posthistory of the Trial

Controversies over the Judges

The extent to which the judgment in the I. G. Farben trial personally affected Telford Taylor can be seen in the strong words he applied to the judgment in a description of the subsequent trials in Nuremberg published shortly after their conclusions had been made public: "In the prosecution's mind, the evidence against the Farben defendants was the strongest of all the industrialist trials." However, all the evidence presented had led to no convictions under the charges of wars of aggression or conspiracy, which had been seen as a mere suspicion: "Whatever the impact of this evidence may be on the writing of history, it made little impression on two of the judges."[1] It was to be regretted, Taylor argued, that the judgments in the I. G. Farben and the High Command trials "bypassed the problems raised by the specific evidence relating to the individual defendants, and relied chiefly on such general phrases as 'followers and not leaders' and 'policy-making level.'"[2] Taylor closed his publication with a long quote from his closing statement in the I. G. Farben trial about the value of the Nuremberg trials. He was sure, Taylor stated at the time, that "all of us in the court room want to see this torn land once again 'ready to bloom and grow fruits.'" But, he added, "we do not want to reap another harvest of dragons' teeth." It would not be possible to build up a healthy and peaceful Europe again by "drawing a shroud over the dead without benefit of inquest." There was an obligation that the defendants "be given every benefit of a full and fair trial," but "equally solemn" was the obligation with respect to the millions of victims "in whose behalf these charges are brought that they be given the protection of law and order in a war-weary world."[3]

The dissenting opinion that he submitted after the judgment was not the only place in which Judge Hebert clearly distanced himself from Judges Shake and Morris's judgment. On the trip back, he and Judge Merrell apparently sought out the company of the members of the prosecution who were traveling on the same ship.[4] He also expressed his great appreciation for the members of the prosecution by writing personally to Belle Mayer about what a good job she had done.[5] And he arranged for a position at the Law School of Louisiana State University for Jan Charmatz, who did not want to return after the trial to what had now become Communist Czechoslovakia and had emigrated to the United States via Cuba.[6]

It was not only the prosecution and the two other judges who criticized and even showed hostility to Judges Shake and Morris for the judgment. Substantial parts of the American press commented negatively on the verdict. The well-known journalist Sylvia Field Porter, for instance, gave free rein to her outrage over the judgment. The tribunal had acquitted all twenty-three defendants of the charge of waging wars of aggression and of conspiracy against peace: "But my mind and heart have returned another verdict against these men, a verdict of guilty on every count. My judgment is they are guilty of plotting and waging war, guilty of plunder and spoliation, guilty of espionage and exploitation." The judges had explained that the defendants had not been high-level state officials or officers—not leaders but followers. This was artificial, she argued, because the truly dangerous and treacherous ones more often hid behind the scenes; they claimed not to be leaders, but they pulled the strings: "Had Farben wanted to crush Hitler, it could have. It did not want to crush him. It wanted him as 'front man.'" The twenty-three defendants had not been low-level employees, but rather the leaders of the "most powerful economic organization of all time." The truth was that they had been the "heart of the guilt": "Despite all the white-wash in the world, to me they are and always will be—guilty."[7]

Though this was a highly critical reaction to the judgment, Porter did not question the authority of the tribunal or of the judges. The journalist Drew Pearson did so, however. In his column, entitled "Washington Merry-Go-Round," he accused the judges, under the title "Nuremberg's Social Season," of having fraternized with the defendants and their lawyers. Specifically, he accused Judge Morris's wife of having frequently invited Mrs. von Schnitzler to the American cafeteria and to have happily spoken with her "as if they were bosom friends." And Judge Shake had had the "brilliant idea" of inviting a number of lawyers of the defense to eat at the Grand Hotel, where Germans normally would not have had access: "It's significant that the I. G. Farben defendants got off with lenient sentences." Mrs. Morris immediately refuted the comments about her to the press—and in Bismarck, North Dakota, her statement was published jointly with the column.[8] Thus began the first confrontation between Drew Pearson and Judges Shake and Morris.

That same day, Judge Shake sent a letter to Pearson in which he wrote that the accusations in the article had no basis, and that he had never fraternized with the defense lawyers. He also considered the accusation against Mrs. Morris to be unjustified. Anyone was free to criticize the tribunal's judgment—"so long as they do not misquote it or unfairly reflect upon the integrity of the members of the court that rendered it." Shake correspondingly demanded that Pearson publicly rescind his claims.[9] Judge Morris and his wife also sent a telegram to Pearson in which they denied the accusations and demanded their full retraction. In addition, Morris wrote a letter in which he denied Pearson's accusations and demanded a public apology.[10]

But Drew Pearson dug in his heels. He replied to Morris that he was sorry that he thought he was unjustly accusing his wife. But he had a witness who had seen her with Lilly von Schnitzler, he said. And another witness confirmed, he claimed, that Mrs. Morris had told her that the prosecution would have to try hard to prove the guilt of the I. G. Farben managers, because her husband thought that such men should never be accused of war crimes. This was, as Pearson wrote, "rather an amazing statement" from the wife of a judge. Pearson also asked Morris a series of questions that he sought clarification for: whether it was true that he viewed the I. G. Farben managers like other managers; whether he had not said multiple times that too many Jews were working for the prosecution; why he had not given a more severe punishment to those responsible for Auschwitz, and why he, in contrast to Judge Hebert, had come to the conclusion that I. G. Farben had been forced into taking slave labor.[11]

To Shake's letter, Pearson replied that two witnesses had seen him in a very friendly conversation with the lawyer von Metzler and another member of the defense in the lobby of the Nuremberg Grand Hotel. Since the I. G. Farben trial had been "one of the most important trials in postwar history," Pearson, as he had done with Morris, asked Shake a series of questions: why he did not want to convict industrialists for the charge of waging a war of aggression; why he reprimanded the prosecution when they drew his attention to hidden and destroyed documents related to Auschwitz; why he supported the defendants in collecting evidence on the accusations of plunder; why he, along with Judge Morris, devalued Georg von Schnitzler's statements against the will of Judge Hebert; whether it was true that Judge Hebert was stricken when he saw the final judgment, as formulated by Shake and Morris; why Judge Merrell refused to be in attendance at the pronouncement of the judgment; and whether it was true that he did not want journalists to report on the trial and I. G. Farben's activities in Auschwitz—and that he would have wanted to have some of them in his jurisdiction.[12]

Judge Shake took the time to respond to Pearson's letter in detail. He started by emphasizing that he would like to know the identity of Pearson's informants. If it had been a member of the prosecution, which Pearson's letter had implied, he would be shocked: "I can only say that I would be very greatly shocked to learn that a member of the group for whom I have heretofore entertained such a high regard would stoop so low as to instigate a criminal libel on a national scale against a judge before whom he had practiced: merely because the lawyer did not agree with the court's decision." Then Shake explained that in his function as executive presiding judge of all the tribunals, he had met not just once, but multiple times with German defense lawyers about administrative matters in the hotel lobby. He described the meeting with von Metzler in detail: it had been about the fact that a defendant needed clothing for his statement the following day. Then Shake pointed out that the prosecution had once put him and the other judges in a difficult situation when they invited "a group of 'distinguished British Jurists' " on their request, one of whom turned out to be a witness for the prosecution. And with regard to the judgment, he stated that he had no claim to call it "perfect." However: "I do assert that it represents the honest effort of three conscientious judges to reach a safe and sound solution of a novel, perplexing and far-reaching problem. We did not all see eye-to-eye as to all aspects of the case—as to most of them we did—but I can say on behalf of my associates, as well as myself, that we tried as best we knew how to do our duty as we saw it. This is the reason why the false charges and inuendos [*sic*] contained in the article appearing in your column, reflecting upon my personal integrity as an American citizen and a judge, affected me so keenly." Shake also went into detail on Pearson's individual questions: he had not assumed the post of presiding judge, but rather had been appointed by General Clay. He had never said that industrialists should not be tried, and he had never discussed the case in hotel lobbies, but rather only with the other judges on the tribunal. He had the highest regard for those who had a different opinion and would have wanted to see another judgment—"but I feel that I am entitled to my views on this extremely controversial subject, without being maligned and pictured as a rogue." With regard to the Auschwitz documents, the relevant employees of the defense had been severely reprimanded by the tribunal, but the prosecution had also been reprimanded owing to the illegal house search. It ought to have turned to the tribunal instead of taking the law into its own hands. Nor did he see it as problematic to help the defense to communicate with possible witnesses abroad—most of this had also been discussed in front of the tribunal. Georg von Schnitzler's affidavits had been very much worth discussion, and he was willing to call into question the soundness of the tribunal's decision. However it was important to consider, he argued, that von Schnitzler had been sentenced by all three judges jointly for a prison term of five years. On Judge Hebert he finally stated that they had met nearly daily for more than one month and had discussed the verdict sentence by sentence. Hebert had written important parts of the verdict himself. And according to Shake, Hebert would not claim that he had not been treated with respect and tact. Finally, with regard to the judgment, Judge Merrell had no longer had an official function and therefore had wanted to deal with personal matters at the time. The final point, that he would have liked to have the journalists under his jurisdiction, confused him, Shake stated, because he had never said such a thing to the media covering Auschwitz. He could imagine, however, where the accusation came from. Shake closed the letter with a reference to a thank-you letter from all judges for the work he carried out in Nuremberg on the occasion of his departure—and attached a copy of it.[13]

That same day Shake also wrote to Morris in order to discuss his view of things with him. He believed that the source of Pearson's "misinformation" had to be someone who was on close terms with the tribunal, presumably a member of the prosecution, though there were also indications that some of the information must have trickled from their conference room, which had already been a source of concern for him and Morris during the trial. Shake did not believe that Taylor would have been the source, and he doubted it was DuBois either: "I could hardly bring myself to believe that DuBois would do such a thing." Shake had not heard much from Judge Hebert for a longer time, but Judge Merrell had written to him that the column with the accusations expressed against him was absurd and could not do damage to a man of his reputation. In any case, he had sent a detailed response to Pearson, he wrote, since the accusations affected him directly. "This whole incident comes as a disgusting anti-climax to a most trying public service, but I guess that we must endure such things to protect free speech." Shake closed the letter with the suspicion that the person presumed to be Mrs. von Schnitzler had been a friend of Mrs. Morris, Mrs. Lorena Hahn.[14]

In early December Morris also wrote to Pearson, but in less detail than Shake. He explicitly referred to the fact that his wife had stayed away from a luncheon after she heard that Mrs. von Schnitzler would be in attendance. The accusations against her were absurd, he stated. Pearson was also the first person, he wrote, to criticize him for the judgment since his return from Nuremberg. This was fine, but not in the form of the accusations made against his wife and the way they were expressed in Pearson's letter. Moreover, Morris added, "You even ignore or fail to realize that the sentences imposed, which you criticize, were the unanimous decision of all three members of the tribunal."[15]

Shake tried to think of who could have been the source for Pearson's article: "I wish to heavens I knew who it was." He also perceived the recently initiated work on an edition of the documents from the Nuremberg trials under the leadership of Drexel Sprecher as dangerous, since not only the indictment and the judgment were to be published: "If they undertake summarizing evidence and selecting documents, there is grave danger that this may not be impartially done and it may well result that the judgments themselves will thereby be undermined, if they are not made contrdictory [*sic*] and ridiculous."[16]

Morris replied to Shake's letter from late November that he had responded to "Drew Pearson's tirade" in a fair and complete manner. He addressed the interaction with von Metzler, which Judge Hebert could also have witnessed, as well as the accusation with regard to von Schnitzler. Pearson did not want, Morris argued, to truly know the whole story. He was satisfied with the statements of someone who had been very disappointed about the judgment. But the accusations, and the public nature of them, rankled Morris: "It is certainly disappointing and disgusting to have a year of honest effort criticized in such an irresponsible manner and in a way that does not give us a fair opportunity to present the truth." Morris repeated a criticism that he had already expressed during the trial about the atmosphere in Nuremberg. There, the camaraderie among the prosecution and the tribunal in the Röchling trial had been praised, and articles had been hung up on the bulletin board near the restaurant for the judges that disparaged defendants and criticized tribunals for excessively small punishments: "The entire atmosphere of the Palace of Justice was one of guilt and conviction." Therefore, Shake had done the right thing, he stated, by attaching the letter from the judges, which proved his "high standing among the judges for both your ability and integrity." They would have to see how it continued, he wrote: one never knew with Pearson. In an effort to reassure himself, Morris concluded, "In the meantime we can take great satisfaction in rendering a judgment that will some day be considered a landmark in international justice."[17]

Drew Pearson then seems to have wanted to confirm with Josiah DuBois whether his accusations against Judge Shake and Mrs. Morris had been correct—upon which DuBois replied, inter alia, that his information source had been Judge Merrell.[18] In the end, it would be impossible to determine for certain who told the truth, to what degree DuBois's statement relied on hearsay, and whether Shake and Morris's claims were primarily a means of protection, justifying their behavior. It seems that Judge Merrell and possibly also members of the prosecution played a rather ignoble role in this story. In any case, Judge Hebert wrote to Judge Morris that he considered the published rumors to be unfair: "Judge Shake tells me that adverse criticism of our case was in Drew Pearson's column. I did not see it but this week saw something similar in its unfairness in the Society for Prev. of War III."[19]

The rumors about Judges Shake and Morris, which Drew Pearson had set off, did not end—he even renewed them in January 1960 in connection with a resurgence of antisemitism in West Germany at the time. Shake heard about this the day before publication and attempted to stop it, in which he succeeded only partly.[20] He wrote angrily to Pearson that the published piece implied that he had acted highly unethically when he fraternized with the German lawyers and that he was partly guilty for the resurgence of antisemitism in West Germany: "This is a most serious charge to make against one who has spent a life-time in establishing and maintaining a good reputation for professional probity, and I do not propose to let the matter pass unnoticed. The re-publication of this charge with knowledge of its falsity and a warning not to do so, is wholly inexcusable and is nothing less than a deliberate and malicious libel on your part."[21] Pearson only replied coolly that he had asked Shake a series of questions in November 1948 which he had not answered. During a time of resurgence of National Socialism and antisemitism, it seemed important to him to revive his thoughts about the I. G. Farben trial.[22]

The accusations against Shake and Mrs. Morris that had been spread by Pearson finally were picked up in Tom Bower's portrayal and, beyond this, even in the important work by Kevin Jon Heller; in both cases these rumors were presented as fact.[23] Even if one does not want to lend credibility to the statements in the correspondence between Judges Shake and Morris, this exchange of letters does raise substantial doubt as to whether the accusations hit the mark. Interestingly, these accusations were not mentioned in Josiah DuBois's book about the I. G. Farben trial, in which the prosecution, supported by Judges Hebert and Merrell, sought to ensure the interpretative control over the trial—which it mostly succeeded in doing.

In early July 1952, Judge Shake heard from his colleague Clarence Merrell that DuBois was writing a book about the I. G. Farben trial—and that Merrell and Hebert had corresponded with him and had proofread the manuscript.[24] Merrell praised DuBois for having done "a very difficult job surpassingly well" with the book. The book would, Merrell stated, hopefully make the I. G. Farben trial more understandable to a larger number of Americans: "While the result in the Farben case was not all that many persons familiar with the evidence and international law thought should have been reached, the trial nevertheless was a worthwhile effort as another step in the forward progress toward making law supreme over war."[25]

Shake thanked Merrell for the information and sent a letter to DuBois in which he wrote that he was waiting with anticipation for the book. It was surely a difficult undertaking, he stated, even if DuBois was very familiar with the case—but there was much to say "with respect to both sides of the controverted issues."[26] In mid-October 1952, Shake wrote to Morris after reading the book with the warning "If you have not read it, I recommend it to you providing you are suffering from low blood pressure. If you are not, you should take it in small doses."[27]

Morris then became active and acquired the address of Josiah DuBois from Drexel Sprecher in order to be able to send him his reaction to the book.[28] In late March 1953, he wrote to DuBois that he was happy that he had written the book, because he no longer had to excuse his participation in the trials: "You have, perhaps unwittingly, done me a great favor by furnishing a written record which, though erroneous and misleading in many details, presents an over-all picture which I regard as highly complimentary. It shows that I recognized early in the trial that the tribunal was confronted with an attempted prosecution upon a record that was poorly prepared and was being so haphazardly presented that the entire case would bog down in confusion unless the tribunal exercised reasonable control over the proceedings and restrained the dumping of irrelevant material." He also thanked DuBois for showing his sense of being threatened by the Russians, though he had interpreted this incorrectly. At the start of the trial, he had expressed his discomfort with the fact that the Russians would overrun the courtroom: "I had already become alarmed over the Moscow influence that was then so visibly present in Nurnberg." The Russians had, in fact, practically on the request of the prosecution, stormed the courtroom against the will of the tribunal—Russian observers, journalists, photographers, and others whose identity was unclear. Morris closed his letter with great confidence—and entirely counter to his statement about the "Nuremberg nightmare" in Fall 1948: "I know that you were greatly disappointed in the judgment and the sentences meted out. It would seem, however, that your disappointment was not well grounded since the defendants receiving the longer sentences were released long before those sentences expired and, as you point out in your book, pardon had terminated all sentences by 1951. It would seem, therefore, that the tribunal was entirely in step with the progress of history in the making and that we were wise in not creating dangerous precedents which would have been an impediment to the future foreign policy of our country. I have always had confidence in the correctness of the views and acts of the majority of the tribunal. The intervening years have proved that the Farben judgment was wise and just."[29]

Morris also wrote a letter to Heinrich Kronstein in which he defended the Nuremberg trials and went into greater detail on the judgment in the I. G. Farben trial, emphasizing its correctness. He then sent both letters, addressed to DuBois and Kronstein, to General Lucius D. Clay, informing him that DuBois had written a book about the I. G. Farben trial, in which he dealt with the majority of the tribunal in a manner "somewhat less than complimentary." Clay responded quickly that he generally agreed with Morris. He made it clear, however, that the different actors had had different roles to play at the time: "Obviously, our prosecuting staff, assembled with difficulty and lacking in established procedure, had to be zealous in its efforts to convict; and, equally obviously, our courts had to exercise an unusual degree of control to insure fair trials." The tribunals had done a "splendid job," he added. Clay also added that neither he nor the tribunals had been expected to judge the wisdom of the international treaties on which the trials were based: "It was their duty and my duty, in review, to determine that under these policies the defendants had reasonable opportunity to defend and that findings of guilt were sustained by the evidence under the policies which had been fixed." Clay closed his response with the statement that he did not believe that either of them had to apologize for their participation in the Nuremberg trials, either then or in the future.[30]

Josiah DuBois found the content of the letter from Morris, in particular his phobia of the Russians, notable and malapropos—because they had had full access since the tribunal was open to the public. After first planning a response consisting only of two lines, DuBois decided to send a detailed reply to Morris.[31] He had, as DuBois wrote to Morris, written the story as he had seen it, but was aware of the fact that it could have been seen in other ways. DuBois then responded ironically to Morris's irony: "Since I believe that you have always been sincere in your attitudes and convictions, both during the trial as well as now, I am not surprised that you find that the book 'presents an overall picture' which you regard 'as highly complimentary.' I am sure that having decided the various issues of the trial as you did, you would necessarily feel complimented by this overall picture." In DuBois's opinion the fear of Russia and Communism had weighed so heavily on Morris that he had incorrectly interpreted many events in good faith. Perhaps the Soviet leaders, who were currently conquering countries and treating people as machines, would hold a different position if they had observed a court that had effectively punished such actions, DuBois argued. He also criticized Morris's statement that the judgment had been aligned with historical developments and that the judges had wanted to avoid a dangerous precedent: "Assuming that you are correct in your fundamental premise that these factors should be taken into consideration by a court of law (a premise which many jurists might challenge), I wonder to what extent we can be proud of the foreign policy of our country as it was administered during the seven years following the end of World War II. In my judgment, the execution of our foreign policy during that period was the most tragic failure in the history of our Nation." DuBois added that it was clear to him that Morris did not share his analysis, but that he had received numerous positive reviews and comments which he wanted to make Morris aware of and therefore had included in his letter.[32]

It would be impossible to list all the attached reviews at this point and to quote them, but some should be briefly addressed. Quentin Reynolds, for instance, wrote in *United Nations World* that DuBois had conclusively proved that I. G. Farben had made Hitler's war of aggression possible. His book had been written "in white hot anger," but DuBois always remained a lawyer—who in this case wrote a damning indictment against the "generals in grey suits." The judges, however, had failed to follow his argument: "Bewildered, heartsick, disillusioned, DuBois could only bow to the decision of the Tribunal but his indignation was too great to be kept within himself and The Devil's Chemists is the result." According to DuBois, the "brilliant and evil men" would make themselves heard again; owing to their affinity with totalitarian regimes, they would fight for the Soviet Union, however. Reynolds concluded bitterly, "During the last war Noel Coward wrote a brilliantly satirical song 'Don't Let's Be Beastly to the Hun.' We laughed at it in London but now it develops that Noel's little song wasn't satire at all—it was sheer prophesy." The well-respected historian Gordon A. Craig, who was based at Princeton at the time, reviewed the book also positively. He agreed with most of DuBois's arguments and recommended the book despite a few historical inaccuracies: "Mr. DuBois argues his case passionately and, for the most part, effectively." DuBois even found the support of Albert Einstein for his book: "He [DuBois] regards it as his duty to enlighten the public on those threatening forces which represent the centralized super organizations of modern industrialism. Exclusively dominated by the motive of maximal rentability, they are absolutely amoral and are not responsible to anybody except their stockholders. Whether they manufacture dyes for textiles or contraptions for mass extermination of innocent people, whether they use war prisoners for cheap labor and work them to death—their only guide post is always the balance sheet. This modern apocalyptic monster knows no frontiers and the State is in danger to become his docile tool or his partner."[33]

The Defendants after the Judgment

A few days prior to the pronouncement of the judgment, a tailor visited the twenty-three defendants in order to take measurements of—as Hans Kugler wrote—"the black garb that would be worn at the war criminals' prison in Landsberg."[34] After the pronouncement, those sentenced were separated from those being released. While one group prepared to return home and received information about the procedures for release, the other group already wore "the clothes that had been made to measure for us."[35] A series of cars was then waiting at the Nuremberg court building for those I. G. Farben managers who were being released because they had been acquitted or had already served their time in prison, in order to take them home—these had been ordered by the factories at Leverkusen and Ludwigshafen or from the Behring factory in Marburg.[36]

The former defendants also differed in the way they experienced their prison time. Carl Wurster returned to Ludwigshafen and took over the management of the factory there. Dieter Ambros, the son of Otto Ambros, reported in early October 1948, "Dr. Wurster has now been back in office for around 3 weeks and it is truly a pleasure to see the old spirit and new momentum everywhere, because a strong personality is leading the factory alone."[37] In late 1948 he wrote that Ludwigshafen was being built up again "in a big way": "The ship that had tottered through the sea for three years is back on a firm course due to the return of the helmsman. Wurster knows the factory."[38] Wurster did not forget, however, to whom he primarily owed his acquittal. Ten years later, on July 29, 1958, he sent a telegram to his former defense counsel Wagner that on vacation he and his wife had just been thinking back to that day ten years prior: "We connect this memory with lots of thoughts of sincere thanks for you."[39]

Only very few looked back on this positively. Hans Kühne, who had also been acquitted, remembered that the substitute judge and one of the judges had likely been "leftist democrats," who had been "noticeably hostile" to them from the beginning. By contrast, the "excellent president of the court and his immediate associate" had already been convinced from early on that "we were not criminals, but respectable people." And they had treated the defendants "with full objectivity, even with noticeable sympathy." Judge Shake had also provided them with a certain amount of relief. They had been able to meet on Saturdays in order to discuss their defense, which had been absolutely necessary, "because many of us—myself included—had only been indicted due to the overall responsibility of the board of directors." The conviction of a portion of the defendants had been due to "supposed violation of the Hague Conventions." It had been welcome news that the court had believed the defendants when they said that they believed Hitler's assertions of wanting peace and that they had not taken part in human experiments or murder with Zyklon B. The sentences had only been due to CCL No. 10 and against the principle of *nulla poena sine lege*. The judgment was, Kühne stated, "apparently a compromise between the perspective of two objective judges and the third judge, who clearly was biased." Overall, however, it had been a success for clearing I. G. Farben and the entire people of serious accusations, such as knowledge of Hitler's intention to attack, and of collective guilt. He even saw himself as a martyr: "We members of the board of I. G. Farben, who in some cases were under arrest for more than 3 years, are of the opinion that our battle and our plight had not been for naught in the judgment of I. G. Farben and on behalf of the entire German people."[40]

Carl Ludwig Lautenschläger, despite being acquitted, never fully recovered from his time in prison. Filled with hatred and self-pity, he remained a broken man who saw himself as cheated of his life's work. In his memoirs, full of antisemitic tirades, he claimed that during his arrest he had been interrogated "almost exclusively" by "Jews of the worst kind," who had underhandedly tricked him.[41] He considered the judgment to be a "gross injustice and miscarriage of justice." The defendants had had the impression that the judges appeared before them "with a very bad conscience" and were not in agreement about the reasoning for their ruling: "But here unfortunately it was the dark forces, the international Jew clique, that achieved their goal from the very beginning and with bought-out abettors; they were seeking prey."[42]

As might be expected, the mood among the I. G. Farben managers who had been convicted was not much better. Hans Kugler wrote a memorandum in August 1948, shortly after his release, as an "attempt to personally justify himself" with regard to the Nuremberg judgment on the Francolor agreement. He laid out his view of the historical background and of the agreement—and closed with the hope that the reader would "gain at least a human understanding for my subjective feeling not to have been involved in any transaction which, with scant valuation of all the circumstances and aspects deserves the description of 'plunder and spoliation.'"[43]

The atmosphere among the I. G. Farben managers that were moved to the Landsberg prison after the judgment was even more bleak. Carl Krauch suffered "heart trouble" due to all the agitation in Nuremberg. When he was transferred to the Landsberg prison, he was, as his secretary reported, immediately sent to the sick ward, where he shared a room for the first days with an inmate who was about to be executed. He was clearly not equal to the conditions there, and his health deteriorated significantly. His secretary claimed, "He suffers from serious stomach and intestinal disorders that he had not had before. He was particularly affected by the fact that an inmate who had attempted suicide and another inmate who had been shot in the legs when attempting to flee were hung after being moved straight from the stretcher to the gallows."[44]

Dieter Ambros also described the conditions at Landsberg, where his father Otto now lived, very negatively. The largest group of inmates there were "recidivist criminals," followed by the second-largest group, consisting of "former, re-arrested concentration camp inmates and SS guards." These were then followed by officers of the Luftwaffe and the army who had killed Allied pilots. The "smallest portion" of the inmates was "our Nurembergers," among whom "industrialists are also minimally represented." The demoralizing conditions included "miserable hygiene (no pajamas, a large scarf for the morning ablutions and emptying of the chamber pot for 250 men, the like with only one toilet, etc.) and not particularly good food." To this was added, Dieter Ambros wrote, "the horrifying image of weekly executions."[45]

Paul Häfliger also described the depressing situation for the inmates every Friday, when, because of the executions, "in Landsberg a heavy cloud of depression [lay] over the entire prison." However, he described the situation differently from Ilse Bethge or Dieter Ambros. Häfliger wrote that he could "not complain for the most part about the treatment at Landsberg in any way." He considered the "involuntary stay" in Landsberg even to be "much more tolerable" than the one in Nuremberg. And Häfliger estimated the group of criminals in Landsberg, for the most part according to him "kapos [inmates serving as overseers] from the concentration camps," to be, in contrast to Dieter Ambros's estimate, only "approx. 10 percent of the inmates."[46]

Fritz ter Meer, who was sentenced to seven years, wrote on August 4, 1948—that is, four days after the judgment, in which he had been the only one sentenced for plunder and crimes against humanity—that in "political judgments" such as these, a time would come "when a calmer view would prevail, and it was time to prepare for this." He personally had adjusted to the conditions in prison and would also survive Landsberg, he stated, especially because he was assuming that he would not have to sit through the entire sentence: "After the first shock, I quickly regained my peace of mind and will be able to deal with things." After introducing in this way, he began to interpret the judgment as "an overwhelming victory of our matter," "even if a few soldiers remained on the field of honor." He saw himself in this as a martyr and hero: "I stood at the front lines in this battle and therefore get to say that I had a substantial part in the results." They had carefully reduced *ad absurdum* what he called "the worst charge of the indictment," the war of aggression in alliance with Hitler, so "that this part of the judgment provides clear exculpation for I. G. Farben, for German industry, and for the German people." Ter Meer added, "We had good judges. What they have to say in the relevant chapter in the judgment will make history." With regard to the second count, they had become "victims of the new interpretation of international law," according to which individuals could also be considered criminally liable. Ter Meer also added, untruthfully, "But the 'misdeeds' committed are not of a criminal nature. Here there is a purely technical judgment that does not affect us morally." For the third count, ter Meer also created his own reality: "In the case of Auschwitz we succeeded 90 percent." They had been acquitted, he stated, of the serious allegations of gassing, experimenting on, and mistreating inmates. It had even been recognized that the defendants—himself especially—had tried to improve their fate: "Here too, no moral condemnation! The tribunal had not been able to get away from the long shadow of the word Auschwitz and finds us guilty in the initiative or participation, despite the fact that it was explicitly stated that the evidence was contradictory." Ter Meer only saw personal guilt in the fact that he had been the chairman of the Technical Committee, but even those "directly involved in Auschwitz," Ambros, Bütefisch, and Dürrfeld, were "not morally incriminated": "Thus, here too the matter is more an exoneration of wild charges, rather than the recognition of personal guilt. Anglo-Saxon legal principles play into the causality here too, in a way that is different from European law." Ter Meer concluded that the judgment had been "a meager return and a clear failure" for the prosecution: "All in all, one should not be too heavily affected by what was stated in the judgment—this lies in the realm of feelings."[47]

If one views this letter in isolation, one likely comes, like Sebastian Brünger, to the conclusion that "Here no one defended themselves with their backs to the wall, but rather offensively expressed the unambiguous claim of interpreting the recent Nazi past on one's own terms, counter to any resistance."[48] However, ter Meer apparently fell apart in Landsberg. His defense counsel, Karl Bornemann, reported to Struss that ter Meer, "who had acted brilliantly in Nuremberg, suffered from a complete nervous breakdown as a result of the severe sentence (6 years) [*sic*] in Landsberg." Ter Meer declared, he stated, that he had been overrun by the younger members of the board, especially by Otto Ambros "with regard to the Auschwitz matter." He had been against the construction of the factory in Auschwitz and had also had this in writing—however, the written document had not been found in the files and the revision of his sentence, which he had sought at the time, was thus impossible.[49] Otto Ambros's son also wrote about ter Meer's problems and the eventual manner of dealing with this, in late 1948. None of those convicted had "decidedly broken down," Dieter Ambros stated; on the contrary, "those hard hit by the judgment, like ter Meer, had gathered themselves together."[50]

Nearly one year later, Fritz ter Meer, writing to his former colleague on the board, August von Knieriem, sounded entirely different than he had on August 4, 1948: "Our trial and the judgment are considered by people à la

Dix I [Rudolf] to be a 'fair trial.' Häfliger also supposedly sent a letter along these lines to Shake, which had become well known. The fact is that a horrible misjudgment put us in jail!" The judges might have "pushed aside certain obstacles in the pre-examination (for example in the case of v. Schnitzler) and not judged these against us." But these obstacles had to be mentioned, because they had shown the methods of the prosecution: "The personal fairness of our tribunal is given, though from a purely objective perspective a lot was entirely 'unfair.'" Therefore, the "one-sided digging through the files by the prosecution over years" had had as much influence over the outcome of the trial as the prevention of the defendants from accessing the files and the possible destruction of exculpatory material—such as ter Meer's Auschwitz files. Finally, Struss, a "main witness of the prosecution," had also "been comparable with Kugler, inter alia, because he could easily have been on the dock." Struss therefore had advantages with regard to denazification and reinstatement; in Nuremberg he had always lived with Virgil van Street, who had been on the prosecution: "His statement about the selection of Auschwitz for the Buna factory and his statement about certain knowledge of events in the concentration camps might have been decisive in the judgment." The prosecution had also had the advantage, he stated, of being able to bring in a number of former concentration camp inmates "as witnesses from the East," whereas the defense had not had a single witness. And, ter Meer concluded, "Even a fair tribunal can make mistakes!"[51]

A memorandum that Otto Ambros wrote, apparently along with his son Dieter and other assistants, and also sent to the judges in the I. G. Farben trial, was much along the same lines. In it, he emphasized his complete innocence. The fourth Buna factory had been built on the order of the Reich. The provision of the workforce had not been a problem of I. G. Farben, since the authorities had been responsible for this. And the selection of the location had been due to the natural factors. According to his assessment, his situation had been misconstrued. He had been a "victim" of the tribunal, since "likely only a technical expert could correctly assess all the questions related to choice of location for a large modern chemical factory in its entirety." The use of concentration camp inmates in the construction of the factory had occurred on the initiative of the authorities, Ambros stated, and not on his own initiative. They had then been well treated, however—the construction site in Auschwitz had "top-rate in its application of social conditions in I. G. Farbenindustrie." Ambros even went further and claimed to have seen, in the statements of the witnesses of the prosecution with regard to their treatment, "shocking evidence of human weakness": "It sometimes seems as if a circle of former inmates of the work camp at Monowitz got together in Nuremberg with the goal of putting the blame for all the sufferings of their imprisonment on I. G. Farbenindustrie." Full of self-righteousness, he emphasized again at the end of the memorandum that he had only acted on orders and had fulfilled his obligations. He had not known about the horrors at Auschwitz, he claimed, but now had "to carry the heavy weight of being suspected of having known about the horrifying events at this camp." However, he awaited "with confidence, the final judgment of history about I. G. Farben's actions in Auschwitz and of my involvement with it."[52]

Paul Häfliger had written a letter to Judge Shake, to which ter Meer had referred, shortly before Christmas 1948 in order to express gratitude for the correction to his term of imprisonment, which had been incorrectly calculated, and due to which he was released earlier. He had suffered in Landsberg, where he spent three months in the hospital, as a result of feeling robbed of his freedom, despite being of the opinion that he had lived an honest life. He suffered especially from the weekly executions that took place in the close vicinity of the hospital. He had assumed he would be acquitted, since he could never have imagined, he stated, that the transactions over Nordisk Lettmetal would be interpreted as plunder and that he would be convicted for this. However, he could understand, he stated, that political circumstances had made it impossible to acquit all the defendants. This would even not have served their interests, even if this sounded paradoxical, he argued, because it would have been hard for public opinion, and likely also the opinion of those in government, to accept in light of the years-long accusations of I. G. Farben. Finally, the "ex-convict" wanted to wish Judge Shake, "without bitterness," a merry Christmas: "I have been a great admirer of the fair and impartial way you conducted this trial and I am more and more convinced that we owe it to you and your high sense of justice solely that the sentences were kept within limits which may be termed as lenient when compared with the verdicts of other Nuernberg trials."[53]

Judge Shake was touched by Häfliger's letter and therefore departed, as he wrote, from the rule of not discussing a case in which he had served as judge. He assumed that Häfliger was already familiar with the concurring opinion and the dissenting opinion by Hebert: "When you consider it in the light of the majority of opinion with which Judge Morris and I concurred, you will have some idea of the trouble we experienced in trying to bring our views into harmony. I do not claim infallibility for the Judgment of the Tribunals, but I do know that it represents the honest efforts of three men to arrive at a proper result."[54]

Shake explained repeatedly that those imprisoned could be granted clemency. In a discussion with the lawyer Achenbach he had said, for instance, that every "offender against law" could have a portion of their punishment forgiven, and that it was right and just also to forgive at least a third of the prison time for the Farben people, who had not taken part in the atrocities and who could not be accused of turpitude.[55]

Nor did the managers of the various successor firms of I. G. Farben forget their former leading figures. Ulrich Haberland wrote a letter to all the leading employees of the successor companies with an attached obligatory statement of support for the defendants and those convicted in the Nuremberg I. G. Farben trial: Thirteen of the defendants had been convicted, and ten had been released. The latter had not received a compensation, however, for the years-long arrest or for the removal from their economic and social position. Their assets, as far as they existed, had been devalued and seized; most of them, and especially their families, needed aid. Therefore, Haberland concluded: "Our Nuremberg defendants were accused, and in some cases convicted, on behalf of I. G. Farben as a whole. The hands of the company, which is dissolved by order of the control council and all of which is under Allied control, are tied. I consider it a duty of honor and the prerogative of the former leading I. G. Farben employees—insofar as they are able—not to abandon their colleagues who are accused in Nuremberg and their families and to at least protect them from harm."[56]

In addition, Ulrich Haberland (as chairman of the board of directors at Bayer) and Karl Winnacker (as the new chairman of the board of directors at Hoechst) jointly and actively supported those who had been sentenced in Nuremberg in the years that followed—whether by installing Fritz ter Meer or Friedrich Jähne as chairman of the supervisory board in Leverkusen and Frankfurt-Höchst, or by generously providing for Walter Dürrfeld and Max Ilgner.[57]

In the months after the sentencing there were also a series of solidarity campaigns carried out by West German industry for the convicted managers, demanding their release.[58] The former defense counsels and a number of former defendants made an effort to formulate a counter-position to the judgments and to gain amnesty for those convicted. In early February 1949 Rudolf Dix wrote to various of the defense counsels from Case VI. At least the defense counsels for those convicted under count III, Dix argued, should take a position against Judge Hebert's dissenting opinion, in which he viewed the entire board of directors as criminally responsible for the slave labor.[59] However, August von Knieriem, one of those acquitted, quickly refused to participate in such a position statement, since a possible second authority could by all means lead to a stricter verdict. He saw the danger that the involvement of those acquitted in such a position statement "could lead to the impression that they saw the trial, even for themselves, as not definitely decided." A circle of I. G. Farben defense counsels had carried out a discussion and decided "that it would be dangerous—also for the men convicted—to call in another authority in the various processes taking place (as improbable as it might be) and that it would be better to take the path of 'clemency.'"[60]

However, von Knieriem—as former chief legal counsel of I. G. Farben—also began writing a treatise on I. G. Farben and the Nuremberg trials. To do this, he had the assistance from the beginning of Krauch's former chief secretary, to whom he dictated the treatise.[61] This treatise, about CCL No. 9 among others and written with the goal of justifying the actions of the I. G. Farben managers as well as to clear them of all accusations,[62] did not proceed as von Knieriem had wished. Friedrich Silcher, one of the I. G. Farben in-house counsels who had been involved at the time, encouraged him to finish the memorandum: "This matter is of very great importance. This work must be done for I. G. Farben and this task has fallen on our circle and can only be done by our circle."[63] The piece was continued under the aegis of Rolf W. Müller, who thought that they "owed it to the old store, that it has a good obituary and in a certain way it is our right to write this obituary."[64] By 1951 the text was mostly finished and was apparently to be published.[65] At this point Fritz ter Meer intervened against publication, however, as August von Knieriem wrote, "Ter Meer is now decidedly of the opinion that the publication of those parts that relate to the Nuremberg trial are entirely inopportune, it seems highly undesirable to him to roll back out all of these now practically forgotten events in the public eye." Von Knieriem agreed with these concerns and informed Müller in closing that ter Meer was currently considering publishing an essay himself about I. G. Farben from 1918 until 1945.[66] Nor did a protest from Müller against this development, his declared will "that we are the interpreters of the I. G. Farben story and not others," change the decision from the former top echelons at I. G. Farben. The manuscript was archived—and ter Meer published a short book the following year about I. G. Farben.[67]

In addition to ter Meer's short book, August von Knieriem also published his book about the Nuremberg trials in 1953. Professor Eduard Wahl should, in fact, have written this book. The lawyer Otto Kranzbühler had approached Wahl about this, but he later limited his involvement to merely writing a foreword to the book that August von Knieriem had already written.[68]

Kranzbühler also hoped for the support of the law departments of West German universities in his "fight against the Nuremberg trials." The public was prepared to support it, he argued, in contrast to the "view of Dr. Adenauer that Nuremberg was a problem that no longer interested people."[69] Kranzbühler expressed his disappointment in general with Federal Chancellor Konrad Adenauer. He referred to a discussion with Adenauer in which he asked the latter, on the occasion of the founding of the West German state "to speak to the Allies about generous pacifying actions." This was not to be the responsibility of the Catholic Church and the Protestant Church or of associations, but of "the German politicians responsible." He noted with frustration: "Adenauer for the most part very reticent. Expresses no opinion on the matter, but only expresses considerations of what other might think. Asks primarily about the reaction of the Allies." Nor did Adenauer want to bring the issue into the election and asked about the mood in the SPD about the question. Kranzbühler should, Adenauer said, seek out the discussion with Schumacher. Kranzbühler noted in closing: "The discussion in which Adenauer's repeated expression of resentment about his own fate in the Third Reich resonated—'the 12 best years of my life, eliminated'—lasted for more than an hour. Thereafter a discussion with Blankenhorn, who had a much more positive stance."[70] Kranzbühler wrote to Herbert Blankenhorn, a close collaborator of Adenauer, correspondingly a few days later that he hoped to be able to convince Adenauer that "the thoughts about amnesty that I presented to him truly are in the air."[71]

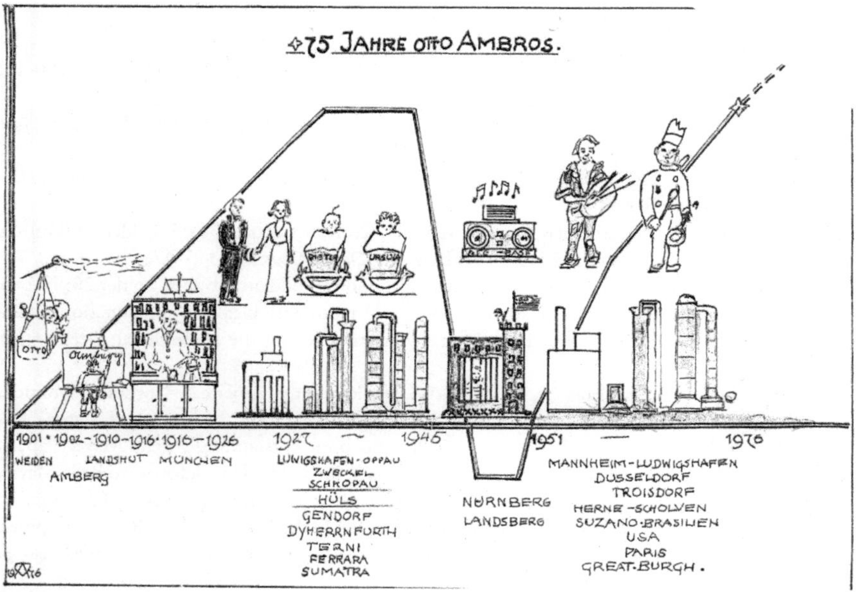

Figure 4.1. Drawing by Otto Ambros on May 19, 1976, on the occasion of his seventy-fifth birthday. The drawing suggests that Ambros achieved everything in his career at I. G. Farben before 1933; however, he did not become a member of the board until 1938. Notably, many places where he worked are mentioned—but not Auschwitz. Source: Evonik Archiv Marl: Bestand B.00.02.01; reproduced with permission.

As outlined, Fritz ter Meer clearly shared Adenauer's perspective, however, that the Nuremberg trials were no longer interesting and also did not need to be brought back into public consciousness. All of those convicted from I. G. Farben had also been released by early 1951—and therefore were not affected by John McCloy's pardons.[72] They also did not see themselves abandoned by their colleagues at I. G. Farben at the time; they were even mostly successfully reintegrated from a social and a business perspective. Even Otto Ambros always knew himself to be supported by the successor firms of I. G. Farben, as he gratefully remarked in the late 1960s to Friedrich Silcher: "It is a relief to know that the 'great aid' that was repeatedly given to us 'Nurembergers' from Leverkusen continues."[73] However, the I. G. Farben trial and the involvement of I. G. Farben with Auschwitz haunted not just the former I. G. Farben managers, even if they tried to conceal the facts (see, for example, Figure 4.1). It also haunted the successor companies of the I. G. Farben conglomerate—BASF, Bayer, and Hoechst. Wolfganz Heintzeler's hope, formulated in summer 1980 "that the tirades against I. G. Farben and its 'successor companies' is finally dying out," remained an illusion.[74] I. G. Farben's connection to Auschwitz did not allow for this.

Notes

1. Taylor, "Nuremberg Trials: War Crimes and International Law," 241–371, here 314–15; Taylor, *Die Nürnberger Prozesse*, 91–93.
2. Taylor, "Nuremberg Trials: War Crimes and International Law," 340; Taylor, *Die Nürnberger Prozesse*, 121.
3. Taylor, "Nuremberg Trials: War Crimes and International Law," 354–55; Taylor, *Die Nürnberger Prozesse*, 138–40.
4. Belle Mayer Papers, Nuremberg Related Material, Correspondence, Box 3, Folder 12: DuBois to Drew Pearson, December 7, 1948; DuBois, *The Devil's Chemists*, 346–47.
5. Belle Mayer Papers, Nuremberg Related Material, Correspondence, Box 3, Folder 20: Hebert to Belle Mayer, March 7, 1949, where he writes: "I recall with pleasure your superior professional work at Nurnberg, and I know that you are enjoying the professional success your attainments merit."
6. Telford Taylor Papers, Box 26, TTP-5-1-1-5: Taylor to the American Consulate Munich, February 9, 1948: Letter of recommendation for his emigration to the United States: "His professional work, both as lawyer and scholar, has been outstanding"; Belle Mayer Papers, Nuremberg Related Material, Correspondence, Box 3, Folder 22: Jan Charmatz to Belle Mayer, July 18, 1948, from Havana; Telford Taylor Papers, Box 189, TTP-14-4-4-73: Charmatz to Taylor, October 23, 1953, with the request for a review in the Louisiana Law Review; response from Taylor on October 26, 1953. On Charmatz, see also Landon, *The University of Mississippi School of Law: A Sesquicentennial History*, 87.
7. Drexel Sprecher Papers, Box 47, Case VI: Article by Sylvia F. Porter, "They Are Guilty," *New York Post*, August 2, 1948.
8. James Morris Papers, Box 1, Folder 3 1948: *The Bismarck Tribune*, November 12, 1948: Drew Pearson, "The Washington Merry-Go-Round" with Editor's Note stating that Mrs. Morris denied the accusations.
9. Curtis G. Shake Papers, RHC 38, 1–2: Shake to Drew Pearson, November 12, 1948.
10. James Morris Papers, Box 1, Folder 3 1948: Morris to Pearson, Telegram Western Union, November 13, 1948; Morris to Pearson, November 13, 1948.
11. James Morris Papers, Box 1, Folder 3 1948: Pearson to Morris, November 23, 1948.
12. James Morris Papers, Box 1, Folder 3 1948: Pearson to Shake, November 23, 1948 (copy).
13. James Morris Papers, Box 1, Folder 3 1948: Shake to Pearson, November 29, 1948 (copy). Also attached is the letter from Judge Hebert and all the other judges to Shake, July 30, 1948 (copy).
14. James Morris Papers, Box 1, Folder 3 1948: Shake to Morris, November 29, 1948. Lorena Hahn was a friend of Mrs. Amelia Morris. She was from Nebraska and was stationed at the time in Berlin—and was the former president of the American Legion Auxiliary. On this, see James Morris Papers, Box 1, Folder 1: Morris to Lenora Swanson, December 16, 1947.
15. James Morris Papers, Box 1, Folder 3 1948: Morris to Pearson, December 2, 1948; see also the letter from Mrs. Morris to Pearson, December 2, 1948, in which she personally takes issue with the accusations Pearson had made against her.
16. James Morris Papers, Box 1, Folder 3 1948: Shake to Morris, December 2, 1948.
17. James Morris Papers, Box 1, Folder 3 1948: Morris to Shake, December 4, 1948.
18. Belle Mayer Papers, Nuremberg Related Material, Correspondence, Box 3, Folder 12: DuBois to Drew Pearson, December 7, 1948: "Judge Merrell told me (and at least two other members of the prosecution) that Judge Shake had expressed the view prior to the commencement of the Farben trial that he (Judge Shake) did not believe that it was ever intended that industrialists should be brought to account for preparing and waging aggressive war."
19. James Morris Papers, Box 1, Folder 2: Copy of Hebert to Dr. Russell, December 20, 1948, below, handwritten note from Hebert to Morris.

20. Curtis G. Shake Papers, RHC #38, 23–26: Telegram from Shake to Pearson, January 15, 1960; Copies of article, January 16, 1960; Shake to Mr. List, *Chicago's American*, January 26, 1960.
21. Curtis G. Shake Papers, RHC #38, 27–28: Shake to Pearson, January 26, 1960.
22. Curtis G. Shake Papers, RHC #38, 29–32: Pearson to Shake, February 1, 1960.
23. Bower, *Blind Eye*, 357–58; Heller, *The Nuremberg Military Tribunals*, 95. See also Jeffreys, *Hell's Cartel*, 382.
24. Curtis G. Shake Papers, RHC #17 18: Merrell to Shake, July 1, 1952. See on this DuBois, *The Devil's Chemists*, 369, in which he writes about "invaluable suggestions" from Judges Merrell and Hebert.
25. Curtis G. Shake Papers, RHC#38, 21: Merrell to DuBois, June 24, 1952 (copy).
26. Curtis G. Shake Papers, RHC#38, 20, 22: Shake to Merrell, July 2, 1952, and Shake to DuBois, July 2, 1952.
27. James Morris Papers, Box 7, Folder 12: Shake to Morris, October 13, 1952.
28. James Morris Papers, Box 7, Folder 12: Sprecher to Morris, March 5, 1953.
29. James Morris Papers, Box 1, Folder 4 Correspondence: Morris to DuBois, March 26, 1953; a copy is also in Telford Taylor Papers, Box 298, General Correspondence.
30. James Morris Papers, Box 1, Folder 4 Correspondence: Morris to Kronstein, March 25, 1953 (copy); Morris to Clay, March 28, 1953; Clay to Morris, March 31, 1953.
31. Telford Taylor Papers, Box 298, General Correspondence: Sprecher to Taylor, March 30, 1953; DuBois to Taylor, March 31, 1953 (handwritten note: "note that Morris is now Chief Justice"); DuBois to Taylor, April 1, 1953; Taylor to Sprecher, April 20, 1953; Taylor to DuBois, April 20, 1953.
32. James Morris Papers, Box 1, Folder 5 Correspondence The Devil's Chemists: DuBois to Morris, April 9, 1953, along with all attachments—including the cited reviews; copy of letter in Telford Taylor Papers, Box 298, General Correspondence.
33. James Morris Papers, Box 1, Folder 5 Correspondence The Devil's Chemists: DuBois to Morris, April 9, 1953, with the entire attachment, including: Quentin Reynolds in United Nations World, November 1952; Gordon A. Craig, *New York Herald Tribune*, October 5, 1952; copy of a statement by Professor Albert Einstein [undated].
34. Unternehmensarchiv BASF, W.1.3./114 and 115: Kugler, *Farben: Chance und Schicksal*, 413.
35. Kugler, *Farben: Chance und Schicksal*, 437. See also Hoechst Archiv, Personalakten Carl Ludwig Lautenschläger: Lautenschläger, Erinnerungen, vol. VIII, [131].
36. Unternehmensarchiv BASF, W.1.3./114 and 115: Kugler, *Farben: Chance und Schicksal*, 437; Hoechst Archiv, Personalakten Carl Ludwig Lautenschläger: Lautenschläger, Erinnerungen, vol. VIII, [135].
37. Unternehmensarchiv BASF, A 866/6: Dieter Ambros to Gebhard Wilhelmi, October 1, 1948.
38. Unternehmensarchiv BASF, A 866/6: Dieter Ambros to Gebhard Wilhelmi, November 22, 1948.
39. NL Wagner N 25/161: Telegram from Margareta and Carl Wurster to Justizrat Friedrich Wilhelm Wagner, July 29, 1958.
40. Bayer Archiv, 207/007-001: Dr. Kühne, Erinnerungen an Nürnberg [undated].
41. Hoechst Archiv, Personalakten Carl Ludwig Lautenschläger: Lautenschläger, Erinnerungen, vol. VIII, [85].
42. Lautenschläger, Erinnerungen, [131]; cf. Lindner, *Inside IG Farben*, 344–45; Lindner, "Wissenschaftler und Manager im 'Dritten Reich': Carl Ludwig Lautenschläger, Vorstandsmitglied der I. G. Farben," 53–68.
43. Bayer Archiv, 207/007-001: Hans Kugler, Die Nürnberger Entscheidung über das Francolor-Abkommen. Ein Urteil und eine persönliche Rechtfertigung, Frankfurt, August 1948; quotes from 1, 16.

44. NL Wahl, 01-237-056/1: Affidafit of Ilse Bethge from November 30, 1948—whether this story from Ilse Bethge is correct cannot be determined.
45. Unternehmensarchiv BASF, A 866/6: Dieter Ambros to Wilhelmi, November 22, 1948; see here also Privatakten Wolfgang Heintzeler, vol. I: Der Aufenthalt im Landsberger Gefängnis, eine Schilderung aus Eindrücken von Besuchern und Auszüge aus einem Affidavit, December 6, 1948—likely a mixture of Bethge and D. Ambros; it also includes a letter from Bethge to Heintzeler, December 4, 1948, and, attached, a copy of the affidavit from November 30, 1948, by Ilse Bethge.
46. NL Wahl, 01-237-056/1: Häfliger to Wahl, December 7, 1948.
47. Bayer Archiv, 374/209: Transcription from a letter from Dr. Fritz ter Meer, Nürnberg, August 4, 1948. Not the draft of a letter, as stated in Brünger, *Geschichte und Gewinn*, 9, footnote 1.
48. Brünger, *Geschichte und Gewinn*, 9, 92–93.
49. Hoechst Archiv, WIN 653, Büro Winnacker: Akten zu Struss, including on the I. G. Farben trial in Nuremberg a note by Struss about ter Meer's attempt for a revision, written on May 31, 1952; see also Lindner, *Inside IG Farben*, 345–46.
50. Unternehmensarchiv BASF, A 866/6: Letter from Dieter Ambros to Gebhard Wilhelmi, November 22, 1948.
51. Unternehmensarchiv BASF, Privatakten W. Heintzeler, vol. II: Knieriem/Ilse Bethge to Heintzeler, September 15, 1949, along with an attached copy of a letter from ter Meer to von Knieriem, September 5, 1949.
52. Unternehmensarchiv BASF, A 866/1: Otto Ambros, Gedanken zu meiner Verurteilung durch das Nuernberger Gericht am 29./30. Juli 1948, in October 1948, especially 9–10, 16, 19, 21, 23, 25, 27–28, 37–39; A 866/6: Dieter Ambros to Wilhelmi, November 22, 1948. Cf. Stokes, "From the IG Farben Fusion to BASF AG," 343–44.
53. Bayer Archiv, 207/007-001: Häfliger to Shake, December 21, 1948 (copy).
54. Bayer Archiv, 207/007-001: Shake to Häfliger, January 25, 1949 (copy). A copy is also in Unternehmensarchiv BASF, Privatakten W. Heintzeler, vol. II.
55. See Unternehmensarchiv BASF, Privatakten W. Heintzeler, vol. II, Brief Ilse Bethge to von Knieriem, October 21, 1949; Bundesarchiv, N 1814/43: Carl Weyer to von Knieriem, October 25, 1949; see also Bayer Archiv, 207/007-001: Shake to R. W. Müller, August 18, 1950, on the petition for a reduction in the sentence for ter Meer and Ambros; Shake to R. W. Müller, February 22, 1951, on the release of Ambros.
56. Unternehmensarchiv BASF, Privatakten W. Heintzeler, vol. I: Ulrich Haberland Brief (Vorlage, i.e., template), December 27, 1948, with declaration to be signed attached—funds were to be submitted via Bayer.
57. See Lindner, *Inside IG Farben*, 346–60.
58. Bundesarchiv, AllProz 3/280: Gesellschaft Deutscher Chemiker to General Clay, September 1, 1948 (copy); Wirtschaftsvereinigung Eisen- und Stahlindustrie to General Clay, November 3, 1948 (copy); Arbeitsgemeinschaft Chemische Industrie des Vereinigten Wirtschaftsgebietes, Das Nürnberger Urteil gegen die I. G. Farbenindustrie. Eine Stellungnahme (here also an announcement on October 14, 1948, by Theo Goldschmidt); Vereinigung der Industrie- und Handelskammern des Landes Nordrhein-Westfalen (IHK, Chamber of Industry and Commerce of North-Rhine Westphalia) to the Presidents of the IHK of North-Rhine Westphalia, November 4, 1948; Stellungnahme zu den Urteilen in den Industrieprozessen; Bayer Archiv, 207/007-001: Dr.-Ing. S. Balke, Der IG-Farben-Prozeß in Nürnberg; cf. also Wiesen, "Overcoming Nazism: Big Business, Public Relations, and the Politics of Memory, 1945–50," 201–26, esp. 221–24, on the I. G. Farben judgment and the Krupp judgment.
59. NL Wahl, 01-237-056/1: Two letters from Rudolf Dix on February 7, 1949, as copies.
60. Bundesarchiv, N 1814/9: von Knieriem to Pelckmann, February 16, 1949; see also von Knieriem to Wilhelm R. Mann, February 23, 1949: Wurster and Wagner were alleged to have had the same opinion.

61. Unternehmensarchiv BASF, Privatakten Wolfgang Heintzeler, vol. I: Ilse Bethge to Heintzeler, December 12, 1948.
62. Bundesarchiv, N 1814/38: von Knieriem to Heintzeler, August 18, 1949, attachment about CCL No. 9, third draft.
63. Bundesarchiv, N 1814/43: Silcher to von Knieriem, November 4, 1949.
64. Unternehmensarchiv BASF, A 866/27a: Müller to Heintzeler, August 21, 1949.
65. Unternehmensarchiv BASF, A 866/27a: Die IG Farbenindustrie Aktiengesellschaft. Schicksal eines deutschen Unternehmens; letter draft from Müller to the Rechts- und Wirtschaftsverlag H. Gruber, Munich, July 14, 1951.
66. Unternehmensarchiv BASF, A 866/27a: von Knieriem to Müller through Heintzeler, March 20, 1952.
67. Unternehmensarchiv BASF, A 866/27a: Müller to von Knieriem, March 24, 1952; ter Meer, *Die I.G Farbenindustrie Aktiengesellschaft*, 1953.
68. NL Wahl, 01-237-056/6: Kranzbühler to Wahl, September 7, 1949: "Now the DM 5,000, which we had considered the necessary starting funds for academic treatment of the Nuremberg trials that you had intended, are ready. The work can now start."; 01-237-055/2: Knieriem to Wahl, May 15, 1952: sending of the manuscript entitled "Nürnberger Rechtsprobleme" for Wahl to prepare a foreword.
69. NL Wahl, 01-237-051/3: Kranzbühler to Wahl, July 30, 1949.
70. NL Wahl, 01-237-051/3: Note by Kranzbühler on July 11, 1949, about the discussion with Adenauer in Bonn.
71. NL Wahl, 01-237-051/3: Kranzbühler to Deputy Secretary Blankenhorn, July 15, 1949.
72. Unternehmensarchiv BASF, W.1.3./114 and 115: Kugler, *Farben: Chance und Schicksal*, 420–21, where he reports on Shake's letter of February 22, 1951, in which he expressed his satisfaction, upon receiving the information from Müller, that Ambros, the last to still be in prison, had been released, that justice was thereby fully served. None of the convicted I. G. Farben managers therefore had to be later pardoned—cf. on this Schwartz, "Die Begnadigung deutscher Kriegsverbrecher. John McCloy und die Häftlinge von Landsberg," 375–414.
73. Bayer Archiv, 356/007: Ambros to Silcher, April 14, 1969.
74. Unternehmensarchiv BASF, A 866/25: Heintzeler to Prof. Seefelder, July 11, 1980.

Conclusion

The entire I. G. Farben trial is so significant
that the older participants, and most likely
the younger ones too, will live
in the shadow of this trial.

—August von Knieriem

The Nuremberg trials, including both the IMT and the subsequent trials, had their justification and cause in the fact that Germany's war crimes in World War II had to be atoned for. On the basis of the "Lesson of Leipzig"—the observation that German war crimes in World War I had essentially not been prosecuted by the Reichsgericht after 1919—the Allies did not want to leave the punishment of war criminals to the German courts again. That this stance was well justified is shown not least by Eduard Wahl's article "A German Defense," which Hans Lamm described in a memorandum to Telford Taylor as the most significant and pointed critique of the Nuremberg trials that had yet been published in a widely read journal.[1] According to Wahl, as explained in greater detail above, crimes against peace were not yet punishable, and hitherto recognized war crimes were no longer punishable owing to the novel situation of "total war." And potential criminally relevant offenses should be forgiven through a general amnesty, as had been called for by the Jesuit Priest Pribilla. Thus, if there was to be a punishment of German crimes, then the Allies did in fact need to arrange for this themselves.

The Soviets, French, and Americans wanted to see German representatives of private industry on the dock in Nuremberg, while the majority of the British were not convinced. For Telford Taylor, the American chief prosecutor in the subsequent trials at Nuremberg, the representatives of private industry were one of the pillars of the Nazi regime and part of the "unholy trinity" of National Socialism, militarism, and economic imperialism. He wanted to prove criminal and moral guilt in the three trials of leading representatives of the companies Krupp, Flick, and I. G. Farben—and thereby bring them to justice. The indictment in the I. G. Farben trial, like the one in the Krupp trial, did not limit itself to easily demonstrable war crimes, such as slave labor. Taylor and his deputy counsel, Josiah DuBois, not only extended the indictment to the crimes of planning and carrying out a war of aggression (count I) and conspiracy against peace (count V); they even focused their efforts on these two charges.

The legal scholar Alberto Zuppi later criticized the prosecution's strategy of devoting so much time and effort to counts I and V: "Regardless of the overwhelming evidence of the Board's liability for the criminal decision to build up a factory in the most notorious camp of extermination, stubbornly the Prosecution engaged itself in a meaningless pursuit of a conspiracy of industrialists with the German war machine, undoubtedly weakening the accusation."[2] The prosecution had believed, Zuppi argued, that it had a clear and simple case against a conglomerate that had even built its own concentration camp in Auschwitz, a place that would be associated with "absolute evil." It had considered the charge of participation in a war of aggression and conspiracy against peace to be easy to prove.[3]

The prosecution's strategy, with its focus on counts I and V, was in fact tactically mistaken, and Alberto Zuppi was not the first to determine this. The prosecution knew from early on that it would have trouble finding evidence for these two charges and knew also how difficult it would be to prove individual criminal responsibility. Nonetheless, the leading representatives of the prosecution—Telford Taylor, Josiah DuBois, and Drexel Sprecher—thought it would be possible to provide evidence by drawing inferences or by showing evidence against the institution—in other words, against I. G. Farben as a whole. This seemed to them to be a problem that they could solve—and to some degree they saw it as already solved, since CCL No. 9, as Drexel Sprecher once explicitly stated in the trial, for them, already provided the proof.

Taylor, DuBois, and Sprecher apparently did not see that their strategy in the I. G. Farben trial was counterproductive. For one, they lost time that they urgently needed to search for evidence for counts II (plunder and spoliation) and III (slave labor and mass murder). For another, they also thereby delayed the trial, which according to Military Ordinance No. 7 was to take place expeditiously, while the memory of the crimes was still fresh. Because of its choice of emphasis and approach, the prosecution needed too much time, and it brought in too much evidence, including evidence that was of little or no relevance.[4] The defense used this, as Judge Morris had feared, to delay the trial with its own excessive material and testimony. After all, time ran in favor of the defendants. The longer the trial took, as Morris once correctly noted, the better the defendants' position was, since with the rise of the Cold War, the defeated Germans were turning into possible future partners.

It was also a mistake, as Raymond Stokes and Peter Hayes have shown, to word the indictment so broadly and, in counts I, II, III, and V, to formulate it in so undifferentiated a manner against all the defendants—it was impossible that all twenty-three defendants were responsible in the same way for all the charges. The prosecution's situation would have been greatly improved by focusing on crimes with sound evidence that could be incontrovertibly linked to the individual defendants, in particular with regard to the "Auschwitz matter" and the forced expropriations. How much could be achieved in this manner was proven by Emanuel Minskoff, who in a relatively short amount of time collected a large amount of evidence on Auschwitz and used this knowledge to dissect the testimony of the witnesses of the defense in cross-examination, to tie them up in inconsistencies, and in some cases even to turn them into witnesses for the prosecution.

Finally, the prosecution was far from having the advantages that were generally ascribed to it by the defendants and their counsels. It did not have unlimited support, for instance, from the American occupation authorities—in some cases, the opposite was the case. Moreover, many of the lawyers of the prosecution, not a few of whom came from the US administration, lacked trial experience. In many cases, they also lacked necessary knowledge about Germany and German industry, which made their work more difficult. The members of the prosecution were therefore not so much obstinate (as Frank Gausmann writes) but rather unexperienced. However, because a number of them also worked themselves to the point of exhaustion or beyond, by the end of the trial they had nonetheless fully earned Taylor's praise that their work had continuously been of an "exceedingly high standard."[5]

It bears emphasizing that the defense in the I. G. Farben trial always had a significant advantage. A large number of highly qualified lawyers were facing a smaller number of lawyers who in many cases were less experienced. The defense received substantial personal and material support from the former I. G. Farben factories, especially from Ludwigshafen and Leverkusen. The lawyers and their assistants, whom they had recruited from the I. G. Farben factories, had an invaluable advantage in knowledge over the prosecution, both with regard to the I. G. Farben company and because of their experience with German tribunals and other courts in the Nuremberg trials. The defense in many cases used every possible means to pursue its case, and it played to its advantages increasingly skillfully, not least in that defense counsels were often very obliging to the judges—in contrast to the defense in the Krupp trial, which did not shy away from severe conflict.[6]

This brings us to the procedural aspect of the trial. Emanuel Minskoff's effectiveness with regard to Auschwitz in particular had led to a certain change in the prosecution's strategy. His work also led to changes on the defense. Fritz ter Meer's Kransberg memorandum had in fact provided an initial defense strategy, as Karl Heinz Roth and Sebastian Brünger have shown. During the trial, however, the various defense counsels also pursued their own strategies for their defendants, though the overarching charges against all twenty-four, or twenty-three, I. G. Farben managers in counts I, II, III, and V did not make this easy. With regard to the "Auschwitz issue" in particular, over the course of the trial, the defense counsels of the defendants who were not directly affected increasingly sought to distance them from those responsible—including, by the end, ter Meer, who had been the prime mover in imposing a joint, unified strategy for the defendants.

Judge Morris developed, as shown above, an increasingly negative stance toward the prosecution. He expressed his opinion particularly strongly in late April 1948 to Adolph Christianson, the chief justice of the North Dakota Supreme Court: "To sum it all up, may I say that it is a grand lawsuit, prepared and tried with supreme ignorance and incompetence."[7] However, Morris was not the only one to adjust, or even change, his stance over the course of the trial. As we have seen, Judge Shake seems to have increasingly tended toward Morris's views—though perhaps he shared them from the beginning. In any case, he did not express them publicly for some time. Judge Hebert, by contrast, grew in sympathy for the prosecution, especially with regard to counts II and III. However, he increasingly disagreed with its positions on counts I and V—despite seeming to have shared them at first. In the end, however, Hebert did not want to diverge from the precedent set by the IMT. At the same time, he was wary of the formulations and further remarks in the majority opinion of the tribunal, finally writing a concurring opinion that clearly distanced itself from them.

In the end, none of the judges in the I. G. Farben trial accepted the prosecution's analysis of Nazi Germany and the role of big industry—not even Judge Hebert. In the Flick trial, the charges of planning a war of aggression (I) and conspiracy against peace (V) were not even part of the indictment. And in the Krupp trial, the tribunal dismissed these points in the indictment over the course of the trial. For the majority of the judges in the I. G. Farben trial, too, the accused managers were not, as Taylor and DuBois held, a pillar of the Nazi regime, the highest representatives of the state, or individually responsible "leaders." For Shake and Morris, the defendants were just "followers," simple citizens. But in the end, all three judges came to hold the defendants not guilty of these two counts.

However, there was plenty of evidence for war crimes as recognized by international law, and these could be assigned to individuals; there were clear divisions of responsibility. This resulted in a series of convictions that all judges supported. Despite this, Judges Shake and Morris generally saw the defendants in these cases as accomplices who shared responsibility with others: with the SS in the case of Auschwitz, for instance. This reduced criminal responsibility—and, accordingly, the degree of punishment.

In contrast to the other two judges, Judge Hebert saw all board members as criminally responsible with regard to count III, in reference in particular to slave labor and Auschwitz. On this, he took a decidedly different position than did Shake and Morris, who wanted to rule on guilt based only on individual actions, not on the role a defendant held in the company. With regard to count III,

Hebert called not only for all members of the board to be punished, but for more stringent punishments. Hebert agreed, however, with the sentences of the managers convicted under count II (plunder and spoliation).

Alberto Zuppi writes that Hebert was deeply concerned by the criminal responsibility of the I. G. Farben managers who had built a factory in Auschwitz out of greed and inhumanity. He adds, "The lenient decision of the majority, without consistent legal reasoning, should be seen as a blind bowing to the American decision to bring to an end the prosecution of German war criminals." Only the "lonely voice" of Judge Hebert stood against this, Zuppi argues.[8] Alberto Zuppi's assumption that the majority of the judges had bent to political pressures was and is widespread—and casts the entire trial in a primarily political light. Hans Kugler wrote in the 1960s, for instance, that the defendants had hoped in late 1947 that counts I, II, and V would be removed from the indictment: "It could be, the optimists among us thought, that the presiding judge would have discussions in Washington during his Christmas vacation and bring back new instructions."[9] As shown above, the prosecutor Mary Kaufman also considered the verdict to be political. And Grietje Baars wrote recently that even Judge Hebert adapted his dissent on counts I and V (war of aggression, conspiracy against peace) out of the fear of communism and amid the broader developments of 1948.[10]

But the idea—one could even say the accusation—that the judges had been given instructions or had bent to political pressure implies that the Nuremberg trials were purely political trials in the end—and that the results corresponded to the convictions of those politically responsible. This idea does not hold up, however, as hopefully has been clearly shown in this book. Of course, the judges did not work in a political vacuum, and they had political convictions and values like all those involved. But however much a given judge disliked the Soviets or opposed the Morgenthau Plan, such considerations were, as should be clear, by no means solely definitive for the verdict.

In early 1947, former War Secretary Henry Stimson expressed his disapproval of Hjalmar Schacht's acquittal, describing it as a weakness of the verdict that the legal concept of conspiracy was so narrowly interpreted. A broader construal would have led to a different verdict. But, Stimson added, "We may regret that some of the charges were not regarded as proven and some of the defendants not found clearly guilty. But we may take pride in the restraint of a tribunal which has so clearly insisted upon certain proof of guilt. It is far better that a Schacht should go free than that a judge should compromise his conscience."[11]

What Stimson accepted, even against his will, was ultimately the caution of the judges, who were open to new juridical paths, but did not want to depart entirely from the course of what they knew and were familiar with, despite the possibilities offered by the special legal foundations of the IMT.

In the I. G. Farben trial, too, the majority of the judges did not want to use all the options against the defendants that, in principle, the London Statute, CCL No. 10, and Military Ordinance No. 7 put at their disposal. They shied away from denying the defendants the right to cross-examination and allowed the defense of coercion when they thought it appropriate. Judges Shake and Morris, who made these decisions, were experienced judges. Judges Hebert and Merrell, who likely would have made greater use of the new legal possibilities, clearly had less experience in the courtroom. Hebert, as a university lecturer, was perhaps more open to legal novelties—but even he concluded that the defendants should be acquitted under counts I and V. The not so infrequent dissenting opinions and concurring opinions in Nuremberg are a sign that the judges thought carefully about their decisions and discussed them thoroughly—and nonetheless simply sometimes could not come to an agreement. If judges came to different conclusions, this did not mean that their judgments were political, arbitrary, or "incorrect." It meant, rather, that the judges had come to different judgments according to how they weighed the evidence and against the background of their convictions. None of this would have been necessary if there had been a politically predetermined verdict.

For the analysis of the I. G. Farben trial and its judgment, a report by the journalist Rebecca West about the Nuremberg trials provides helpful insights. At the time, she noted that public accusations that the judgment was too mild and even that the judges were "pro-Nazi" did not serve civilizing aims. As she pointed out, "When those criminals were brought to trial there often turned out to be no legal proof that they were guilty of the graver among the charges brought against them. There was usually good ground for suspecting that their guilt had been as black as that, but no evidence of the sort which our pernickety courts required; and we went to war to preserve just such pernicketiness. The criminals were then charged with the lesser offences which could be proved, and if their judges found them guilty they gave them appropriate sentences."[12]

Exactly this occurred in the I. G. Farben trial—it was not always possible to assign criminal responsibility to the defendants unambiguously and clearly. Thus, for instance, the charge of human experiments in concentration camps had resulted in acquittal; the judges, faced with evidence that was not fully convincing, ruled "in doubt for the defendants." Therefore, the judgment was not "worse" than the Krupp verdict, which was in fact much harsher.[13] When Kevin Jon Heller comes to the conclusion that some of the defendants in the I. G. Farben trial were "wrongly acquitted" because the judges had shown "excessive credulousness toward defense claims," it in certain ways contradicts his own call for the highest degree of fairness toward the defendants. An unjustified judgment would have robbed them of their freedom and possibly even their lives. Heller also sees the frequent use of statements made by the defendants themselves in interrogations without lawyers present as highly problematic—the judges had barred exactly this in the I. G. Farben trial.[14]

In January 1949, Judge Shake wrote the following to one of the convicted I. G. Farben managers about the judgment: "I do not claim infallibility for the Judgment of the Tribunals, but I do know that it represents the honest efforts of three men to arrive at a proper result."[15] However, as has been shown, the judgment was mostly viewed negatively. Belle Mayer even described it as "pretty shattering emotionally."[16] One may criticize the leniency of the judges in the I. G. Farben judgment, as Alberto Zuppi has: "An aura of impunity pervaded the judgment of the case."[17] But it is surely an exaggeration to contend, like Bernd C. Wagner, that "as for broad swathes of the German population, it apparently was difficult for Judge Shake, only three-and-a-half years after the end of the war, to clearly demarcate the victims from the perpetrators."[18] Dietrich Eichholtz's stance on what he perceived as a scandalous I. G. Farben judgment was more problematic still: For him, "the behavior of I. G. Farben in the Auschwitz matter alone called for the death penalty for all members of the board of directors and those directly involved."[19]

In the end, thirteen of the twenty-three I. G. Farben managers, including the top leadership, were convicted and given relatively long prison terms of up to eight years for plunder, spoliation, and participation in the inhumane slave labor program at Auschwitz. The accused I. G. Farben managers were not, therefore, as DuBois argued in his book, punished as if they had been chicken thieves or had committed traffic violations.[20] They were also by no means acquitted of all charges, as Karl Winnacker claimed on the occasion of Hoechst's first extraordinary general meeting in 1953.[21] The convicted managers also for the most part had to serve the entirety of their prison terms, in contrast to most of the others convicted in Nuremberg, as Judge Morris correctly noted. There was therefore a proportionality between verdict and punishment, which, as Kevin Jon Heller has noted, must be the goal of any court judgment.[22] And acquittal by the court, in some cases based only on the principle of "in doubt for the defendant," by no means absolved them of moral guilt, for which, however, the court was not responsible.[23]

It was surely frustrating for prosecutors to watch as some of the defendants, of whose guilt they were convinced, got off without any punishment whatsoever. And it was surely no less frustrating to see how, after their release from Landsberg prison, even those who were convicted returned to affluence, finding rank and recognition in postwar West German society. In mid-December Carl Schmitt wrote to Lilly von Schnitzler that her husband would shortly be free again: "Then he will have to explain a lot to us. Misfortune and suffering are the only things that ennoble us. I felt this recently when I visited Ernst Jünger, whose disadvantage consisted in the fact that he was never in a prisoner's cell."[24] For Carl Schmitt, a criminal conviction for plunder and spoliation thus turned into an "ennobling" experience. Georg von Schnitzler was released in late 1949 and clearly felt himself to be somewhat ostracized because of his role in the trial. But in 1954, he received birthday greetings not just from "all I. G. Farben companies," but even from the federal minister for economics, Ludwig Erhard.[25]

In November 1948, Telford Taylor wrote that the Nuremberg trials would be of great interest for historians. Studying the trials against Krupp, I. G. Farben, Flick, and Röchling would bring out the nature of the relationship between Hitler and leading German industrialists with the necessary amount of clarity, he argued. However, Taylor also saw those who were deeply disappointed, who had hoped in vain that the revelation of the conditions in the concentration camps and the disclosures in the trials of the war criminals would serve a purificatory function in Germany and pave the road for democracy.[26]

Benjamin Ferencz was also chagrined about developments after the war in West Germany. Using Nazi terminology sarcastically, he wrote to Taylor in summer 1951 that the "master race" knew that it had prevailed through denazification, prosecution of war crimes, decartelization, industrial dismantlement, and demilitarization—and still demanded more. Ferencz described the scene in Germany, where, he said, 1,300 people had done the Hitler salute at the grave of the war criminal Otto Ohlendorf, as "highly depressing."[27] But he did not let himself be brought low. At a meeting of the Jewish Claims Conference in mid-November 1954 with representatives of I. G. Farben in liquidation, Ferencz commented that the prosecution in Nuremberg had been of the opinion "that the defense of the IG Farben had been very successful and the prosecutors more or less lost the case."[28] However, he stated, he now aimed to have the damage done to victims of the Nazis at least paid back through the Jewish Claims Conference. He therefore asked former members of the prosecution to support him in his negotiations with representatives of I. G. Farben in liquidation, who were polite, but, Ferencz stated, were not willing to pay: "With the convicted IG Farben criminals now living in luxurious retirement or again prospering in German Industry and with the IG Farben stocks at al [*sic*] all-time high, there is a very strong desire to forget that these distinguished gentlemen were ever involved in that sort of business or exploiting human lives for their advantage. Since I am aware of the misery in which almost all of the former IG Farben slaves must now live, I somehow have not been able to give up the fight."[29]

This time, Benjamin Ferencz was successful—and the compensation payments that he played a key role in negotiating were also somewhat satisfactory.[30] If one is faced with the problem, described by Rebecca West, of lacking sufficiently unambiguous and individually assignable evidence against the defendants, then compensation payments for the victims and their surviving family members perhaps present an at least halfway satisfactory solution to make amends.[31]

Such payments would also have corresponded with Telford Taylor's call, in his closing arguments, not to simply cover the corpses with a shroud. For the prosecution, there was no doubt that the criminal guilt of the accused I. G. Farben managers justified conviction—however, as we have seen, for a variety of reasons, they succeeded in this only at times and unsatisfactorily. One may be unhappy with the judgment and consider the compensation payments too small, but the latter helped at least 5,855 former Jewish concentration camp inmates in forty-two countries.[32] Nor can one argue that the judgment represented revenge against the vanquished; no innocent person was convicted after the extremely fair trial that the tribunal carried out. Nonetheless, despite the undeniable leniency of the majority of the judges, thirteen of the accused I. G. Farben managers were ultimately convicted for being what they had become in the Third Reich: criminals.

Notes

1. Drexel Sprecher Papers, Box 52, Procedures/Press File, Press and Nuremberg Trials: Hans Lamm for Telford Taylor, February 17, 1949: Inter alia, Lamm explained: "At any rate, it is my humble opinion that one should not allow those who saw to it that Wahl's attacks would be spread over 8 pages of *Der Ruf* to get away with it." See also Taylor's memorandum for Sprecher, February 19, 1949, and Kempner's memorandum for Sprecher, February 23, 1949. The quote of August von Knieriem at the beginning of this chapter is from Bundesarchiv, NL 1814/9, Knieriem to Wilhelm R. Mann, September 23, 1949.
2. Zuppi, "Slave Labor," 525.
3. Zuppi, "Slave Labor," 521–22.
4. USHMM Archives, RG-50.030*0382: Interview with William and Belle Zeck, September 23, 1996, 66–67: On DuBois it should be added, however, that in spite of all the mistakes for which he was responsible as chief prosecutor, William Zeck's words—that one could not forget the good he had done during the war for Jewish refugees through his involvement in the establishment of the War Refugee Board—should not be forgotten: "My little set-to with DuBois about von der Hyde [*sic*] and Haberland pales into nothingness against the totality of Joe DuBois's contribution that I know of, to the good part of the war effort and Nuremberg."
5. Telford Taylor Papers, Box 26, TTP-5-1-1-5: Thank-you letter from Taylor to DuBois, Sprecher, Amchan, Newman, Kaufman, Charmatz, Van Street, Minskoff, June 15, 1948.
6. This even led, after the defense showed the tribunal very little deference, to a blow-up in the Krupp trial, after which the defense counsels had to spend a weekend under arrest; see Priemel, "Tradition und Notstand: Interpretations- und Konfrontationslinien im Fall Krupp," 434–63, here 453–55.
7. James Morris Papers, Box 1, Folder 2: Morris to Judge Christianson, April 23, 1948.
8. Zuppi, "Slave Labor," 525–26.
9. Unternehmensarchiv BASF, W.1.3./114 and 115: Kugler, *Farben: Chance und Schicksal*, 385–86.
10. Baars, *Capitalism's Victor's Justice*, 186–87.
11. Stimson, "The Nuremberg Trial," 187–88.
12. West, *A Train of Powder: Six Reports on the Problem of Guilt and Punishment in Our Time*, 238.

13. Cf. NL Wahl, 01-237-051/3: Kranzbühler to Assistant Secretary Blankenhorn, July 15, 1949: When one compares the I. G. Farben judgment to the Krupp judgment, which was supposedly much better and more stringent, reference is often made to the dispossession of Alfried Krupp. However, the degree to which this was enacted is unclear, as one can see from written material by Alfried Krupp's lawyer, Kranzbühler. He wrote in a letter to Herbert Blankenhorn, one of Adenauer's closest associates, that not only had Alfried Krupp von Bohlen been given prison time, but his assets had also been confiscated, to be transferred to the Control Council: "General Clay did not confirm this part of the judgment, but rather replaced it with an ordinance, according to which each zone commander was authorized to seize the assets of Alfried Krupp that were in that respective zone. No zone commander has done so as of yet, surely not least because of the serious legal concerns about such a measure. Therefore, for the time being the assets of Alfried Krupp have not been confiscated."
14. Heller, *The Nuremberg Military Tribunals*, 399–400.
15. Bayer Archiv, 207/007-001: Shake to Häfliger, January 25, 1949 (copy).
16. See USHMM Archives, RG-50.030*0382: Interview with William and Belle Zeck, September 23, 1996, 69–71.
17. Zuppi, "Slave Labor," 518.
18. Wagner, *IG Auschwitz*, 309.
19. Eichholtz, "Der IG-Farben-Prozess in Nürnberg 1948," 41–52, here 50.
20. DuBois, *The Devil's Chemists*, 339.
21. Karl Winnacker in a speech on March 27, 1953, quoted in Bäumler, *Ein Jahrhundert Chemie*, 112–13.
22. Heller, *The Nuremberg Military Tribunals*, 400.
23. Cf. on this Jaspers, *Die Schuldfrage: Von der politischen Haftung Deutschlands*, who differentiates between crimes—in other words, criminal guilt—and political guilt, moral guilt, and metaphysical guilt.
24. Carl Schmitt to Lilly von Schnitzler, December 17, 1949, in Rieß, ed., "Lilly von Schnitzler – Carl Schmitt," 187–88.
25. Lilly von Schnitzler to Carl Schmitt, November 9 [1954], in Rieß, ed., "Lilly von Schnitzler – Carl Schmitt," 211–12.
26. James Morris Papers, Box 1, Folder 19: Taylor, An Outline of the Research and Publication Possibilities of the War Crimes Trials, November 1948, in particular, 7, 9.
27. Telford Taylor Papers, Box 188, TTP-14-4-3-54: Ben Ferencz to Telford Taylor, July 24, 1951.
28. USHMM Archives, Benjamin B. Ferencz Collection, RG-12.004.12*02: Minutes on the discussion in the office of the Conference on Jewish Material Claims against Germany, November 13, 1954, 8–9.
29. USHMM Archives, RG-12.004.12*02: Ferencz to Sprecher (cc: Amchan, Minskoff, Uiberall, Zeck, Ormond, Kagan, Reichmann), December 23, 1954.
30. Lindner, *Inside IG Farben*, 364: The total sum was thirty million DM; see on this also Rumpf, *Der Fall Wollheim gegen die I. G. Farbenindustrie AG in Liquidation.*
31. Cf. on this Claus Roxin, "Beihilfe zum Mord durch Dienst im Konzentrationslager Auschwitz," 83–92.
32. Wagner, *IG Auschwitz*, 313–14: Thanks to pro bono assistance, nearly 28 million DM could be distributed to 5,855 former Jewish concentration camp inmates in forty-two states.

Bibliography

Archives

Archiv des Deutschen Museums, Munich
NL 080 Nachlass Gerlach, Walther
Archiv für Christlich-Demokratische Politik, Sankt Augustin
01–237–051 Nachlass Wahl, Eduard
Bayer Archiv, Leverkusen
Bundesarchiv Berlin/Koblenz
– AllProz Alliierte Prozesse
– N 1814 Nachlass von Knieriem, August
Byron R. Lewis Historical Collection Library, Vincennes University, Vincennes, Indiana
– Curtis G. Shake Papers
Columbia University, Rare Book and Manuscript Library, New York
– MS 1684 Telford Taylor Papers
Evonik-Konzernarchiv, Marl
Fritz-Bauer-Institut, Frankfurt a. M., Archiv und Bibliothek
– IG Farben-Prozess: Protokoll und Dokumente
Harvard University, Harvard Law School Library, Cambridge, Mass.
– Zeck, Belle Mayer Papers (accessible online)
Hoechst Archiv, Frankfurt a. M. (now the Sanofi Archiv)
Indiana State Library, Indianapolis
– Transcript of Taped Interview with Curtis G. Shake, taped 1968; Indiana State Library, Indiana Division, Oral History Project, 1972
John F. Kennedy Presidential Library and Museum, Boston
– Drexel A. Sprecher Papers
Louisiana State University Law Center, Library, Archival Collections, Baton Rouge, Louisiana
– Paul Macarius Hebert Papers (accessible online)
National Archives and Records Administration, College Park, Maryland (NARA)
RG 238 Office of Chief of Counsel for War Crimes
RG 122 Record of the Federal Trade Commission
Marchivum – Stadtarchiv Mannheim
– 24/1972 Nachlass Heimerich, Hermann
Privater Nachlass Dr. Herbert Nath, Munich/Grünwald
Staatsarchiv Freiburg (Landesarchiv Baden-Württemberg)
– T 1 Drischel, Friedrich
– T 1 Bürgin, Ernst
Staatsarchiv Nürnberg
– KV-Prozesse, Fall 6

– KV-Verteidigung
Stadtarchiv Ludwigshafen
– N 25 Nachlass Wagner, Friedrich Wilhelm
State Archives / State Historical Society of North Dakota, Bismarck, North Dakota
– MSS 10154 James Morris Papers
United States Holocaust Memorial Museum Archives, Washington, DC
– RG-10.154 Emanuel E. and Dorothy G. Minskoff collection
– RG-12 Benjamin B. Ferencz collection
– RG-50.030*0382 Interview with William and Belle Zeck, September 23, 1996
– RG-50.030*0219 Interview with Drexel Sprecher, June 8, 1990
Unternehmensarchiv BASF, Ludwigshafen

Interviews

Dubois, Josiah E. Interview by Richard D. McKinzie, Camden, New Jersey, June 29, 1973. https://www.trumanlibrary.gov/library/oral-histories/duboisje (last retrieved on July 23, 2025).

Moore, Sally Falk. Interview by Kalman Applbaum, August 24, 2008. http://www.alanmacfarlane.com/ancestors/moore.htm (last retrieved on April 29, 2019). This interview can be viewed now on https://sms.cam.ac.uk/media/1126787/ (Cambridge University site, last retrieved on July 23, 2025).

Moore, Sally Falk. Interview by the author, Harvard University, November 3, 2014.

Secondary Sources

Abelshauser, Werner, "Rüstungsschmiede der Nation? Der Kruppkonzern im Dritten Reich und in der Nachkriegszeit 1933–1951." In *Krupp im 20. Jahrhundert: Die Geschichte des Unternehmens vom Ersten Weltkrieg bis zur Gründung der Stiftung*, ed. Lothar Gall, 267–472. Berlin, 2002.

Abelshauser, Werner, Wolfgang von Hippel, Jeffrey Allen Johnson, and Raymond G. Stokes. *German Industry and Global Enterprise. BASF: The History of a Company*. Cambridge, 2004.

Abelshauser, Werner. *Deutsche Wirtschaftsgeschichte: Von 1945 bis zur Gegenwart*. 2nd revised and extended edition. Munich, 2011.

Ahrens, Ralf. "Der Exempelkandidat: Die Dresdner Bank und der Nürnberger Prozess gegen Karl Rasche." *Vierteljahrshefte für Zeitgeschichte* 52, no. 4 (2004): 637–70.

Aschenauer, Rudolf. *Zur Frage einer Revision der Kriegsverbrecherprozesse*. Nürnberg, 1949.

——. *Landsberg: Ein dokumentarischer Bericht von deutscher Seite*. Munich, 1951.

Ausschuss zur Untersuchung der Erzeugungs- und Absatzbedingungen der deutschen Wirtschaft, Verhandlungen und Berichte des Unterausschusses für allgemeine Wirtschaftsstruktur (I. Unterausschuß), 3. Arbeitsgruppe: Wandlungen in den wirtschaftlichen Organisationsformen. Erster Teil: Wandlungen in den Rechtsformen der Einzelunternehmungen und Konzerne. Berlin, 1928.

Baars, Grietje. "Capitalism's Victor's Justice? The Hidden Stories Behind the Prosecution of Industrialists Post-WWII." In *The Hidden Histories of War Crimes Trials*, ed. Kevin Jon Heller and Gerry Simpson, 163–92. Oxford, 2013.

Bähr, Johannes, Axel Drecoll, Bernhard Gotto, Kim C. Priemel, and Harald Wixforth. *Der Flick-Konzern im Dritten Reich*. Munich, 2008.

Bäumler, Ernst. *Ein Jahrhundert Chemie*. Düsseldorf, 1963.

Bellamy, Suzanne S. *Hoosier Justice at Nuremberg*. Indianapolis, 2010.

Benton, Wilbourn E., and Georg Grimm, eds. *Nuremberg: German Views of the War Trials*. Dallas, 1955.

Benz, Wolfgang. "Nationalsozialistische Deutsche Arbeiterpartei." In *Enzyklopädie des Nationalsozialismus*, 3rd edition, ed. Wolfgang Benz, Hermann Graml, and Hermann Weiß, 601–06. Munich, 1998.

Biddle, Francis. "The Nurnberg Trial." *Virginia Law Review* 33, no. 6 (Nov. 1947): 679–96.

Biedenkopf, Kurt. "Heinrich Kronstein." In *Deutschsprachige Zivilrechtslehrer des 20. Jahrhunderts in Berichten ihrer Schüler: Eine Ideengeschichte in Einzeldarstellungen*, ed. Stefan Grundmann and Karl Riesenhuber, 187–205. Berlin, 2007.

Bishai, Linda S. "Leaving Nuremberg: America's Love/Hate Relationship with International Law." *Review of International Studies* 34, no. 3 (July 2008): 425–43.

Bloxham, Donald. "'The Trial That Never Was': Why There Was No Second International Trial of Major War Criminals at Nuremberg." *History* 87, no. 285 (January 2002): 41–60.

——. *Genocide on Trial: War Crimes Trials and the Formation of Holocaust History and Memory*. Oxford, 2003.

Blum, John Morton. *Deutschland ein Ackerland? Morgenthau und die amerikanische Kriegspolitik 1941–1945: Aus den Morgenthau-Tagebüchern*. Düsseldorf, 1968.

Boll, Bernd. "Fall 6: Der IG-Farben-Prozess." In *Der Nationalsozialismus vor Gericht: Die alliierten Prozesse gegen Kriegsverbrecher und Soldaten 1943–1952*, 3rd edition, ed. Gerd R. Ueberschär, 133–43. Frankfurt am Main, 2008.

Boot, Machteld. *Genocide, Crimes against Humanity, War Crimes: Nullum Crimen Sine Lege and the Subject Matter Jurisdiction of the International Criminal Court*. Antwerp, 2002.

Borgwardt, Elizabeth. "Re-Examining Nuremberg as a New Deal Institution: Politics, Culture and the Limits of Law in Generating Human Rights Norms." *Berkeley Journal of International Law* 23, no. 2 (2005): 401–62.

——. *A New Deal for the World: America's Vision for Human Rights*. Cambridge, Massachusetts, 2005.

Borkin, Joseph. *The Crime and Punishment of I. G. Farben*. London, 1978.

——. *Die unheilige Allianz der I. G. Farben: Eine Interessengemeinschaft im Dritten Reich*. Frankfurt am Main, 1990.

Borkin, Joseph, and Charles A. Welsh. *Germany's Master Plan: The Story of Industrial Offensive*. London and New York, 1943.

Bower, Tom. *Blind Eye to Murder: Britain, America and the Purging of Nazi Germany—A Pledge Betrayed*. London, 1981.

Boylan, John. *Sequel to the Apocalypse. The Uncensored Story: How Your Dimes and Quarters Helped Pay for Hitler's War*. Foreword by Rex Stout. New York, 1942.

Brecht, Bertolt. *Poems 1913–1945*. Ed. John Willett and Ralph Manheim. New York, 1998.

Brinkley, Alan. *Voices of Protest: Huey Long, Father Coughlin, and the Great Depression*. New York, 1982.

Brown-Fleming, Suzanne. *The Holocaust and Catholic Conscience: Cardinal Aloysius Muench and the Guilt Question in Germany*. Notre Dame, Indiana, 2006.

Broszat, Martin. "Siegerjustiz oder strafrechtliche 'Selbstreinigung'. Vergangenheitsbewältigung der Justiz 1945–1949." *Vierteljahrshefte für Zeitgeschichte* 29, no. 4 (1981): 477–544.

Brünger, Sebastian. *Geschichte und Gewinn: Der Umgang deutscher Konzerne mit ihrer NS-Vergangenheit*. Göttingen, 2017.

Buscher, Frank M. *The U.S. War Crimes Trial Program in Germany, 1946–1955*. New York, 1989.

Bush, Jonathan A. "Soldiers Find Wars: A Life of Telford Taylor." *Columbia Journal of Transnational Law* 37, no. 33 (1999): 675–81.

——. "'The Supreme ... Crime' and Its Origins: The Lost Legislative History of the Crime of Aggressive War." *Columbia Law Review* 102, no. 8 (Dec. 2002): 2324–424.

——. "The Prehistory of Corporations and Conspiracy in International Criminal Law: What Nuremberg Really Said." *Columbia Law Review* 109, no. 5 (2009): 1094–262.

——. "New Dealer, Flüchtlinge und Radikale? Die Nürnberger Ankläger im Profil." In *NMT: Die Nürnberger Militärtribunale zwischen Geschichte, Gerechtigkeit und Rechtschöpfung*, ed. Kim C. Priemel and Alexa Stiller, 547–85. Hamburg, 2013.

"Cartels and National Security: Report from the Subcommittee on War Mobilization to the Committee on Military Affairs, United States Senate, Pursuant to S. Res. 107, a Resolution Authorizing a Study of the Possibilities of Better Mobilizing the National Resources of the United States." Washington, DC, 1944.

Carter, Edward F. "The Nurnberg Trials: A Turning Point in the Enforcement of International Law." *Nebraska Law Review* 28 (1948–49): 370–86.

Clay, Lucius D. *Entscheidung in Deutschland*. Frankfurt am Main, n.d. [after 1950].

Conot, Robert E. *Justice at Nuremberg*. New York, 1983.

Dinstein, Yoram. *The Defence of 'Obedience to Superior Orders' in International Law*. Leiden, 1965.

Dix, Hellmuth. "Die Urteile in den Nürnberger Wirtschaftsprozessen." *Neue Juristische Wochenschrift* 2, no. 17 (1949): 647–52.

Drecoll, Axel. "Flick vor Gericht: Die Verhandlungen vor dem alliierten Militärtribunal 1947." In *Der Flick-Konzern im Dritten Reich*, ed. Johannes Bähr et al., 559–645. Munich, 2008.

Drüll, Dagmar. *Heidelberger Gelehrtenlexikon* 4: *1933–1986*. Berlin, Heidelberg, 2009.

DuBois, Josiah E. *The Devil's Chemists: 24 Conspirators of the International Farben Cartel Who Manufacture Wars*. Boston, 1952.

Earl, Hilary. *The Nuremberg SS-Einsatzgruppen Trial, 1945–1958: Atrocity, Law, and History*. Cambridge, 2009.

Ehard, Hans. "Der Nürnberger Prozess gegen die Hauptkriegsverbrecher und das Völkerrecht." *Süddeutsche Juristen-Zeitung* 3, no. 7 (July 1948): 353–68.

Eichholtz, Dietrich. "Der IG-Farben-Prozess in Nürnberg 1948." *Bulletin für Faschismus- und Weltkriegsforschung* 10 (1998): 41–52.

Erbelding, Rebecca. *Rescue Board: The Untold Story of America's Efforts to Save the Jews of Europe*. New York, 2018.

Ferencz, Benjamin B. "Nurnberg Trial Procedure and the Rights of the Accused." *Journal of Criminal Law and Criminology* 39, no. 2 (July/August 1948): 144–51.

Fischer, Wolfram. "Dezentralisation oder Zentralisation—kollegiale oder autoritäre Führung? Die Auseinandersetzung um die Leitungsstruktur bei der Entstehung des

I.G.-Farben-Konzerns." In *Recht und Entwicklung der Großunternehmen im 19. und frühen 20. Jahrhundert*, ed. Norbert Horn und Jürgen Kocka, 476–88. Göttingen, 1979.

Frei, Norbert. *Vergangenheitspolitik: Die Anfänge der Bundesrepublik und die NS-Vergangenheit.* Munich, 1996.

——, ed. *Transnationale Vergangenheitspolitik: Der Umgang mit deutschen Kriegsverbrechern in Europa nach dem Zweiten Weltkrieg.* Göttingen, 2006.

——, Ralf Ahrens, Jörg Osterloh, and Tim Schanetzky. *Flick: Der Konzern, die Familie, die Macht.* Munich, 2009.

Freyer, Tony A. *Antitrust and Global Capitalism 1930–2004.* Cambridge, 2006.

Gall, Lothar, ed. *Krupp im 20. Jahrhundert: Die Geschichte des Unternehmens vom Ersten Weltkrieg bis zur Gründung der Stiftung.* Berlin, 2002.

Gallus, Alexander. "'Der Ruf'—Stimme für ein neues Deutschland." *Aus Politik und Zeitgeschichte* 25 (June 18, 2007): 32–38.

Gattineau, Heinrich. *Durch die Klippen des 20. Jahrhunderts: Erinnerungen zur Zeit- und Wirtschaftsgeschichte.* Stuttgart, 1983.

Gausmann, Frank. *Deutsche Großunternehmer vor Gericht: Vorgeschichte, Verlauf und Folgen der Nürnberger Industriellenprozesse 1945–1948/51.* Hamburg, 2011.

Glahé, Philipp. *Amnestielobbyismus für NS-Verbrecher: Der Heidelberger Juristenkreis und die alliierte Justiz 1949–1955.* Göttingen, 2024.

Glueck, Sheldon. "By What Tribunal Shall War Offenders Be Tried?" *Harvard Law Review* 56, no. 7 (June 1943): 1059–89.

Goetz, Celia. "Impressions of Telford Taylor at Nuremberg." *Columbia Journal of Transnational Law* 37, no. 3 (1999): 669–72.

Greiner, Bernd. *Die Morgenthau-Legende: Zur Geschichte eines umstrittenen Plans.* Hamburg, 1995.

——. *"IG-Joe" – IG Farben-Prozeß und Morgenthau-Plan.* Frankfurt am Main, 1996.

Haensel, Carl. "Der Ausklang von Nürnberg." *Neue Juristische Wochenschrift* 2, no. 10 (1949): 367–70.

——. *Das Gericht vertagt sich: Tagebuch eines Verteidigers bei den Nürnberger Prozessen.* 2nd ed. Wiesbaden, 1980.

Haffner, Sebastian. *Geschichte eines Deutschen: Die Erinnerungen 1914–1933.* Stuttgart, 2000.

Hankel, Gerd. *Die Leipziger Prozesse: Deutsche Kriegsverbrechen und ihre strafrechtliche Verfolgung nach dem Ersten Weltkrieg.* Hamburg, 2003.

Hayes, Peter. "IG Farben und der IG Farben-Prozeß: Zur Verwicklung eines Großkonzerns in die nationalsozialistischen Verbrechen." In *Auschwitz: Geschichte, Rezeption und Wirkung*, ed. Fritz Bauer Institut, 99–121. Frankfurt am Main, 1996.

——. *Industry and Ideology: IG Farben in the Nazi Era.* 2nd ed. New York, Cambridge, 2001.

——. *From Cooperation to Complicity: Degussa in the Third Reich.* Cambridge, 2004.

Heberer, Patricia, and Jürgen Matthäus, eds. *Historical Perspectives on the Politics of Prosecuting War Crimes.* Lincoln, Nebraska, 2008.

Hebert, Paul. "The New Nationalism: Social and Economic Planning under the Constitution." *Southwest Review* 19, no. 1 (October 1933): 8–21.

Hébert, Valerie Geneviève. *Hitler's Generals on Trial: The Last War Crimes Tribunal at Nuremberg.* Lawrence, Kansas, 2010.

Heimerich, Hermann. *Lebenserinnerungen eines Mannheimer Oberbürgermeisters.* Stuttgart, 1981.

Heine, Jens Ulrich. *Verstand und Schicksal: Die Männer der I. G. Farbenindustrie AG in 161 Kurzbiographien*. Weinheim, 1990.

Heinemann, Isabel. "Rasse, Lebensraum, Genozid: Die nationalsozialistische Volkstumspolitik im Fokus von Fall 8 der Nürnberger Militärtribunale." In *NMT: Die Nürnberger Militärtribunale*, ed. Kim C. Priemel and Alexa Stiller, 100–26. Hamburg, 2013.

Heintzeler, Wolfgang. *Der rote Faden. Fünf Jahrzehnte: Staatsdienst, Wehrmacht, Chemische Industrie, Nürnberg, Marktwirtschaft, Mitbestimmung, Kirche*. Stuttgart, 1983.

——. *Was war mit IG Farben? Der Nürnberger Prozess und der Fernsehfilm "Väter und Söhne."* Herford, 1987.

——. *Im Jahrhundert extremer Turbulenz: Erlebtes und Perspektiven*. Herford, 1988.

Heller, Kevin Jon. *The Nuremberg Military Tribunals and the Origins of International Criminal Law*. Oxford, 2012.

Henke, Klaus-Dietmar. *Die amerikanische Besetzung Deutschlands*. Munich, 1995.

Herbert, Ulrich. *Geschichte Deutschlands im 20. Jahrhundert*. Munich, 2014.

Hirsch, Francine. "The Soviets at Nuremberg: International Law, Propaganda, and the Making of the Postwar Order." *American Historical Review* 113 (2008): 701–30.

Hörner, Stefan. *Profit oder Moral: Strukturen zwischen I. G. Farbenindustrie AG und Nationalsozialismus*. Bremen, 2012.

Irons, Peter H. *The New Deal Lawyers*. Princeton, 1982.

James, Harold. *Krupp: Deutsche Legende und globales Unternehmen*. Munich, 2001.

James, Marlise. *The People's Lawyers*. New York, 1973.

Jeffreys, Diarmuid. *Hell's Cartel: IG Farben and the Making of Hitler's War Machine*. New York, 2008.

Jaspers, Karl. *Die Schuldfrage: Von der politischen Haftung Deutschlands*. 2nd ed. Munich, 2016 [orig. 1965].

Jeßberger, Florian. "Die I. G. Farben vor Gericht: Von den Ursprüngen eines 'Wirtschaftsvölkerstrafrechts.'" *JuristenZeitung* 64, no. 19 (Oct. 2009): 924–32.

Joly, Hervé. "L'implication de l'industrie chimique allemande dans la Shoah: le cas du Zyklon B." *Revue d'histoire moderne et contemporaine* 47, no. 2 (April–June 2000): 368–400.

The Judgement in the Farben Trial: The Complete Wording with an Appendix of Documents. Offenbach, 1948 (English version of *Das Urteil im I.G.-Farben-Prozess: Der vollständige Wortlaut mit Dokumentenanhang*. Offenbach, 1948).

Judt, Tony. *Postwar: A History of Europe Since 1945*. New York, 2005.

Jung, Susanne. *Die Rechtsprobleme der Nürnberger Prozesse dargestellt am Verfahren gegen Friedrich Flick*. Tübingen, 1992.

Karlsch, Rainer. "Fritz Gajewski (1885–1965)—charismatischer Manager in einem multidivisionalen Konzern? Ein Beitrag zur Unternehmensführung der IG Farbenindustrie AG, 1928–1939." In *Studien zur Geschichte der Filmfabrik Wolfen und der IG Farbenindustrie AG in Mitteldeutschland*, ed. Rainer Karlsch and Helmut Maier, 91–130. Essen, 2014.

Kempner, Robert M. W. *Ankläger einer Epoche: Lebenserinnerungen*. Frankfurt am Main, 1983.

Knieriem, August von. *Nürnberg: Rechtliche und menschliche Probleme*. Foreword by Prof. Dr. Eduard Wahl. Stuttgart, 1953.

Kochavi, Arieh J. *Prelude to Nuremberg: Allied War Crimes Policy and the Question of Punishment*. Chapel Hill, 1998.

Kraus, Elisabeth. *Ministerien für das ganze Deutschland? Der Alliierte Kontrollrat und die Frage gesamtdeutscher Zentralverwaltung*. Munich, 1990.

Kraus, Herbert, *Kontrollratsgesetz Nr. 10*. Hamburg [1948].

——. "The Nuremberg Trial of the Major War Criminals: Reflections after Seventeen Years." *DePaul Law Review* 13, no. 2 (Spring/Summer 1964): 233–59.

Kress, Claus. "Versailles-Nuremberg-The Hague: Germany and International Criminal Law." *The International Lawyer* 40, no. 1 (Spring 2006): 15–39.

Kronstein, Heinrich. *Briefe an einen jungen Deutschen*. Munich, 1967.

Kunze, Rolf-Ulrich. *Ernst Rabel und das Kaiser-Wilhelm-Institut für ausländisches und internationales Privatrecht 1926–1945*. Göttingen, 2004.

Landon, Michael de L. *The University of Mississippi School of Law: A Sesquicentennial History*. Jackson, Mississippi, 2006.

Latour, Conrad, and Thilo Vogelsang. *Okkupation und Wiederaufbau: Die Tätigkeit der Militärregierung in der amerikanischen Besatzungszone Deutschlands 1944–1947*. Stuttgart, 1973.

Laudani, Raffaele, ed. *Secret Reports on Nazi Germany: The Frankfurt School Contribution to the War Effort*. Princeton, 2013.

Lawrence, [Geoffrey], Lord Justice. "The Nuremberg Trial." *International Affairs* 23, no. 2 (April 1947): 151–59.

Lepej, André. *Rechtswissenschaft und Rechtspolitik: Eduard Wahl (1903–1985)*. Baden-Baden, 2023.

Leventhal, Harold, Sam Harris, John M. Woolsey, Jr., and Warren F. Farr. "The Nuernberg Verdict." *Harvard Law Review* 60, no. 6 (July 1947): 857–907.

Lindner, Stephan H. *Inside IG Farben: Hoechst during the Third Reich*. Cambridge, 2008.

——. "Wissenschaftler und Manager im 'Dritten Reich': Carl Ludwig Lautenschläger, Vorstandsmitglied der I. G. Farben." In *Gesichter der Zeitgeschichte: Deutsche Lebensläufe im 20. Jahrhundert*, ed. Theresia Bauer et al., 53–68. Munich, 2009.

——. "Das Urteil im I.G.-Farben-Prozess." In *NMT: Die Nürnberger Militärtribunale*, ed. Kim C. Priemel and Alexa Stiller, 405–33. Hamburg, 2013.

Lingen, Kerstin von. "Setting the Path for the UNWCC: The Representation of European Exile Governments on the London International Assembly and the Commission for Penal Reconstruction and Development, 1941–1944." *Criminal Law Forum* 25, no. 1 (June 2014): 45–76.

Lippman, Matthew. "Conundrums of Armed Conflict: Criminal Defenses to Violations of the Humanitarian Law of War." *Penn State International Law Review* 15, no. 1 (1996): 1–111.

Löhnert, Peter. "Richard May, Theodor Mariam, and Oskar Falek: Schicksale jüdischer Chemiker in der Farbenfabrik Wolfen nach 1933." *Mitteilungen der Gesellschaft Deutscher Chemiker, Fachgruppe der Geschichte der Chemie* 20 (2009): 137–73.

London International Assembly. *Reports on Punishment on War Crimes*, n.d. [December 1943].

Lorenz, Werner. "Eduard Wahl." In *In memoriam Eduard Wahl: Gedächtnisfeier der Juristischen Fakultät der Universität Heidelberg am 4. Februar 1987*, ed. Juristische Fakultät der Universität Heidelberg, 9–45. Heidelberg, 1988.

Luhmann, Niklas. *Legitimation durch Verfahren*. Berlin, 1969.

Lustig, Doreen. "The Nature of the Nazi State and the Question of International Criminal Responsibility of Corporate Officials at Nuremberg: Revisiting Franz Neumann's Concept of Behemoth at the Industrialist Trials." *Journal of International Law and Politics* 43, no. 4 (2011): 965–1044.

Lüthy, Herbert. "Die Verheerungen des Krieges (1945)." In *Nach dem Untergang des Abendlandes: Zeitkritische Essays*. 2nd ed., 50–79. Cologne, 1965.

Maguire, Peter. *Law and War: International Law and American History*. Revised edition. New York, 2010.

Mai, Gunther. *Der Alliierte Kontrollrat in Deutschland 1945–1948: Alliierte Einheit—deutsche Teilung?* Munich, 1995.

Marquet, Andreas. *Friedrich Wilhelm Wagner 1894–1971: Eine politische Biografie*. Bonn, 2015.

Martin, James Stewart. *All Honorable Men*. Boston, 1950.

Matthäus, Jürgen. "The Lessons of Leipzig: Punishing German War Criminals after the First World War." In *Historical Perspectives on the Politics of Prosecuting War Crimes*, ed. Patricia Heberer and Jürgen Matthäus, 3–23. Lincoln, Nebraska, 2008.

Mausbach, Wilfried. *Zwischen Morgenthau und Marshall: Das wirtschaftspolitische Deutschlandkonzept der USA 1944–1947*. Düsseldorf, 1996.

Medoff, Rafael. *Blowing the Whistle on Genocide: Josiah E. DuBois, Jr., and the Struggle for a U.S. Response to the Holocaust*. West Lafayette, Indiana, 2009.

Merkel, Reinhard. "Nürnberg 1945, Militärtribunal: Grundlagen, Probleme, Folgen." *Merkur: Deutsche Zeitschrift für europäisches Denken* 50, nos. 9/10 (Sept./Oct. 1996): 918–36.

Meschke, Herbert L., and Ted Smith. "The North Dakota Supreme Court: A Century of Advances." *North Dakota Law Review* 76, no. 2 (2000): 217–310.

Morgenthau, Henry. *Germany Is Our Problem*. New York and London, 1945.

Morris, James. "Major War Crimes Trials in Nurnberg." *North Dakota Bar Briefs* 25, no. 2 (April 1949): 97–109.

Mouralis, Guillaume. "Outsiders du droit international: Trajectoires professionnelles et innovation juridique à Londres, Washington et Nuremberg, 1943–1945." *Monde(s)* 7, no. 1 (2015): 113–34.

Müller, Ingo. "Nürnberg und die deutschen Juristen." In *Gegen Barbarei: Essays Robert M. W. Kempner zu Ehren*, ed. Rainer Eisfeld and Ingo Müller, 257–77. Frankfurt am Main, 1989.

Neave, Airey. *Nuremberg: A Personal Record of the Trial of the Major Nazi War Criminals in 1945–46*. London, 1989.

Nelte, Otto. *Die Generale: Das Nürnberger Urteil und die Schuld der Generale*. Hannover, 1947.

Neuhäusler, Johannes. *Amboss und Hammer: Erlebnisse im Kirchenkampf des Dritten Reiches*. Munich, 1967.

Neumann, Franz. *Behemoth: The Structure and Practice of National Socialism 1933–1944*. Chicago, 2009 [orig. 1942].

Niethammer, Lutz. *Entnazifizierung in Bayern: Säuberung und Rehabilitierung unter amerikanischer Besatzung*. Frankfurt am Main, 1972.

Oberndörfer, Ralf. "Recht und Richter: Verfahrensrechtliche Aspekte der Nürnberger Prozesse." In *NMT: Die Nürnberger Militärtribunale*, ed. Kim C. Priemel and Alexa Stiller, 525–46. Hamburg, 2013.

OMGUS. *Militärregierung der Vereinigten Staaten für Deutschland: Amerikanische Gruppe des Kontrollrats—Finanzabteilung, Ermittlungen gegen die I. G. Farbenindustrie AG—September 1945*. Translated and edited by the Dokumentationsstelle zur NS-Sozialpolitik Hamburg, with an introduction by the editor, Karl Heinz Roth. Nördlingen, 1986.

Osterloh, Jörg, and Clemens Vollnhals, eds. *NS-Prozesse und deutsche Öffentlichkeit: Besatzungszeit, frühe Bundesrepublik und DDR*. Göttingen, 2011.

Parzer, Sebastian. *Mannheim soll nicht nur als Stadt der Arbeit neu erstehen … Die zweite Amtszeit des Mannheimer Oberbürgermeisters Hermann Heimerich (1949–1955)*. Ubstadt-Weiher, 2008.

Pendas, Devin O. "Seeking Justice, Finding Law: Nazi Trials in Postwar Europe." *The Journal of Modern History* 81, no. 2 (June 2009): 347–68.

Perels, Joachim. "Fast vergessen: Franz L. Neumanns Beitrag zur Konzipierung der Nürnberger Prozesse. Eine Erinnerung aus Anlaß seines 100. Geburtstags." *Kritische Justiz* 34 (2001): 117–25.

Phillips-Fein, Kim. *Invisible Hands: The Businessmen's Crusade against the New Deal*. New York, 2010.

Plumpe, Gottfried. *Die I. G. Farbenindustrie AG: Wirtschaft, Technik und Politik 1904–1945*. Berlin, 1990.

Plumpe, Werner. *Das kalte Herz. Kapitalismus: Die Geschichte einer andauernden Revolution*. Berlin, 2019.

Pomerance, Michla. *The United States and the World Court as a "Supreme Court of the Nations": Dreams, Illusions and Disillusion*. The Hague and London, 1996.

Pratt, Valéry. "Quel rôle pour Franz Leopold Neumann en amont et en aval du Procès militaire international de Nuremberg?" *Comparativ: Zeitschrift für Globalgeschichte und vergleichende Gesellschaftsforschung* 26, no. 4 (2016): 43–57.

Pribilla, Max. *Das Verhalten der Unternehmer im Dritten Reich: Moraltheologisches Gutachten*. Freiburg i. Br.: Herder, n.d. (Special edition of *Stimmen der Zeit* 143, no. 3, December 1948).

Priemel, Kim C. *Flick: Eine Konzerngeschichte vom Kaiserreich bis zur Bundesrepublik*. Göttingen, 2007.

——. "Der Sonderweg vor Gericht: Angewandte Geschichte im Nürnberger Krupp-Prozess." *Historische Zeitschrift* 294 (2012): 391–426.

——. "'A Story of Betrayal': Conceptualizing Variants of Capitalism in the Nuremberg War Crimes Trials." *Journal of Modern History* 85 (March 2013): 69–108.

——. "Tradition und Notstand: Interpretations- und Konfrontationslinien im Fall Krupp." In *NMT: Die Nürnberger Militärtribunale zwischen Geschichte, Gerechtigkeit und Rechtschöpfung*, ed. Kim C. Priemel and Alexa Stiller, 434–63. Hamburg, 2013.

——. *The Betrayal: The Nuremberg Trials and German Divergence*. Oxford, 2016.

Priemel, Kim C., and Alexa Stiller, eds. *Reassessing the Nuremberg Military Tribunals: Transitional Justice, Trial Narratives, and Historiography*. New York, 2012.

——, eds. *NMT: Die Nürnberger Militärtribunale zwischen Geschichte, Gerechtigkeit und Rechtschöpfung*. Hamburg, 2013.

Raithel, Thomas. *Die Strafanstalt Landsberg am Lech und der Spöttinger Friedhof (1944–1958): Eine Dokumentation im Auftrag des Instituts für Zeitgeschichte*. Munich, 2009.

Rebentisch, Dieter. *Führerstaat und Verwaltung im Zweiten Weltkrieg: Verfassungsentwicklung und Verwaltungspolitik 1939–1945*. Stuttgart, 1989.

Reuther, Thomas. *Die ambivalente Normalisierung: Deutschlanddiskurs und Deutschlandbilder in den USA, 1941–1955*. Stuttgart, 2000.

Rieß, Rolf, ed. "Lilly von Schnitzler—Carl Schmitt: Briefwechsel 1919 bis 1977." In *Schmittiana, Neue Folge: Beiträge zu Leben und Werk Carl Schmitts*, Vol. 1, 113–256. Berlin, 2011.

Robinson, Elwyn B. *History of North Dakota*. Lincoln, Nebraska, 1966.

Röpke, Wilhelm. *Die deutsche Frage*. Erlenbach-Zürich, 1945.

Rosen, Elliot A. *The Republican Party in the Age of Roosevelt: Sources of Anti-Government Conservatism in the United States*. Charlottesville, Virginia, 2014.

Roxin, Claus. "Beihilfe zum Mord durch Dienst im Konzentrationslager Auschwitz." *Juristische Rundschau* 2017, no. 2 (2017): 83–92.

Rumpf, Joachim Robert. *Der Fall Wollheim gegen die I. G. Farbenindustrie AG in Liquidation: Die erste Musterklage eines ehemaligen Zwangsarbeiters in der Bundesrepublik Deutschland—Prozess, Politik und Presse*. Frankfurt am Main, 2010.

Safferling, Christoph. "Die Strafbarkeit wegen 'Conspiracy' in Nürnberg und ihre Bedeutung für die Gegenwart." *Kritische Vierteljahresschrift für Gesetzgebung und Rechtswissenschaft* 93, no. 1 (2010): 65–82.

Sasuly, Richard. *IG Farben*. New York, 1947.

Schmerbach, Folker. *Das "Gemeinschaftslager Hanns Kerrl" für Referendare in Jüterbog 1933–1939*. Tübingen, 2008.

Schroeder, Klaus-Peter. *"Eine Universität für Juristen und von Juristen": Die Heidelberger Juristische Fakultät im 19. und 20. Jahrhundert*. Tübingen, 2010.

Schwartz, Thomas Alan. "Die Begnadigung deutscher Kriegsverbrecher: John McCloy und die Häftlinge von Landsberg." *Vierteljahrshefte für Zeitgeschichte* 38, no. 3 (1990): 375–414.

——. "John McCloy and the Landsberg Cases." In *American Policy and the Reconstruction of West Germany, 1945–1955*, ed. Jeffry M. Diefendorf, Axel Frohn, and Hermann-Josef Rupieper, 433–54. Cambridge, 1999.

Schwerin von Krosigk, Lutz Graf. *Die großen Schauprozesse: Politische Justiz*. Munich, 1981.

Seliger, Hubert. *Politische Anwälte? Die Verteidiger der Nürnberger Prozesse*. Baden-Baden, 2016.

Shklar, Judith N. *Legalism*. Cambridge, Massachusetts, 1964.

Sliedregt, Elies van. *The Criminal Responsibility of Individuals for Violations of International Humanitarian Law*. Den Haag, 2003.

——. *Individual Criminal Responsibility in International Law*. Oxford, 2012.

Smith, Bradley F. *Reaching Judgment at Nuremberg*. New York, 1977.

——. *The Road to Nuremberg*. London, 1981.

——, ed. *The American Road to Nuremberg: The Documentary Record 1944–1945*. Stanford, 1982.

Smith, Glenn H. *Langer of North Dakota: A Study in Isolationism 1940–1959*. New York, 1979.

Smith, Jean Edward, ed. *The Papers of General Lucius D. Clay: Germany 1945–1949*. 2 volumes. Bloomington, 1974.

——. *Lucius D. Clay: An American Life*. New York, 1990.

Später, Jörg. *Vansittart: Britische Debatten über Deutsche und Nazis 1902–1945*. Göttingen, 2003.

Spicka, Mark E. "The Devil's Chemists on Trial: The American Prosecution of I. G. Farben at Nuremberg." *The Historian* 61, no. 4 (June 1999): 865–82.

Sprecher, Drexel A. *Inside the Nuremberg Trial: A Prosecutor's Comprehensive Account*. 2 volumes. Lanham, 1999.

Stimson, Henry L. "The Nuremberg Trial: Landmark in History." *Foreign Affairs* 25, no. 2 (Jan. 1947): 179–89.

Stokes, Raymond G. *Divide and Prosper: The Heirs of I. G. Farben under Allied Authority 1945–1951*. Berkeley, 1988.

——. "From the IG Farben Fusion to the Establishment of BASF AG (1925–1952)." In *German Industry and Global Enterprise. BASF: The History of a Company*, by Werner Abelshauser et al., 206–361. Cambridge, 2004.

Stoltzfus, Nathan, and Henry Friedlander, eds. *Nazi Crimes and the Law*. Cambridge, 2008.

Taylor, Telford. *Final Report to the Secretary of the Army on the Nuernberg War Crimes Trials under Control Council Law No. 10*. Washington, DC, 1949.

——. "Nuremberg Trials: War Crimes and International Law." *International Conciliation*, no. 450 (April 1949): 241–371.

——. *Die Nürnberger Prozesse: Kriegsverbrechen und Völkerrecht*. With forewords by James T. Shotwell and Robert M. W. Kempner. Extended special edition. Zürich, 1951.

——. *The Anatomy of the Nuremberg Trials: A Personal Memoir*. New York, 1992.

ter Meer, Fritz. *Die I. G. Farbenindustrie Aktiengesellschaft: Ihre Entstehung, Entwicklung und Bedeutung*. Düsseldorf, 1953.

Trials of War Criminals Before the Nuernberg Military Tribunals Under Control Council Law No. 10, Vol. 6: *The Flick Case*. Washington, DC, 1952.

Trials of War Criminals Before the Nuernberg Military Tribunals Under Control Council Law No. 10, Vol. 7: *The I. G. Farben Case*. Washington, DC, 1953.

Trials of War Criminals Before the Nuernberg Military Tribunals Under Control Council Law No. 10, Vol. 8: *The I. G. Farben Case*. Washington, DC, 1952.

Tusa, Ann, and John Tusa. *The Nuremberg Trial*. New York, 1985.

Ueberschär, Gerd R., ed. *Der Nationalsozialismus vor Gericht: Die alliierten Prozesse gegen Kriegsverbrecher und Soldaten 1943–1952*. 3rd edition. Frankfurt am Main, 2008.

Das Urteil im I.G.-Farben-Prozess: Der vollständige Wortlaut mit Dokumentenanhang. Offenbach, 1948.

Veyne, Paul. *Foucault: Der Philosoph als Samurai*. Stuttgart, 2009.

Vogelsang, Reinhard. *Der Freundeskreis Himmler*. Göttingen, 1972.

Wade, Michael G. "Villainy, Virtue, and Louisiana Political Culture: Paul Hebert and the Augean Stables at LSU, 1939–1941." *Louisiana History: The Journal of the Louisiana Historical Association* 49, no. 1 (Winter 2008): 21–52.

Wagner, Bernd C. *IG Auschwitz: Zwangsarbeit und Vernichtung von Häftlingen des Lagers Monowitz 1941–1945*. Munich, 2000.

Wahl, Eduard. "Eine deutsche Verteidigung: Das Plaidoyer von Prof. Dr. E. Wahl im Nürnberger Prozeß gegen die Angeklagten der deutschen Wirtschaft." *Der Ruf: Unabhängige Blätter für unabhängige Leser* 4 (February 15, 1949): 4–7, 10–12.

——. "Grundfragen der Nürnberger Prozesse: Ein Vortrag, gehalten am 12.12.1947 im Rahmen der Professoren-Vorträge der Universität Heidelberg." In *Aus Leben und Forschung der Universität 1947/48*, ed. Wolfgang Kunkel, 76–98, Berlin, 1950.

Weinberg, Gerhard L. "The Setting and the Significance of the Nuremberg Trials: A Historian's Perspective." In *Nazi Crimes and the Law*, ed. Nathan Stoltzfus and Henry Friedlander, 35–41. Cambridge, 2008.

Weindling, Paul Julian. *Nazi Medicine and the Nuremberg Trials: From Medical War Crimes to Informed Consent*. Houndsmills and New York, 2004.

Weinke, Annette. *Die Nürnberger Prozesse*. 2nd rev. ed. Munich, 2015.

Wells, Wyatt. *Antitrust and the Formation of the Postwar World*. New York, 2002.

West, Rebecca. *A Train of Powder: Six Reports on the Problem of Guilt and Punishment in Our Time*. Chicago, New York, 1955 [Reprint].

Wickel, Helmut. *I.-G. Deutschland: Ein Staat im Staate*. Berlin, 1932.

Wiesen, S. Jonathan. "Overcoming Nazism: Big Business, Public Relations, and the Politics of Memory, 1945–1950." *Central European History* 29, no. 2 (1996): 201–26.

——. *West German Industry and the Challenge of the Nazi Past, 1945–1955*. Chapel Hill, 2001.

——. "Die Verteidigung der deutschen Wirtschaft: Nürnberg, das Industriebüro und die Herausbildung des Neuen Industriellen." In *NMT: Die Nürnberger Militärtribunale zwischen Geschichte, Gerechtigkeit und Rechtschöpfung*, ed. Kim C. Priemel and Alexa Stiller, 630–52. Hamburg, 2013.

Wilkins, Robert P., and Wynona Huchette Wilkins. *North Dakota: A Bicentennial History*. New York, 1977.

Williams, T. Harry. *Huey Long*. New York, 1969.

Willis, James F. *Prologue to Nuremberg: The Politics and Diplomacy of Punishing War Criminals of World War I*. Westport, Connecticut, 1982.

Wilmowsky, Tilo Freiherr von. *Warum wurde Krupp verurteilt? Legende und Justizirrtum*. 2nd ed. Stuttgart, 1950.

Winter, Jay, and Antoine Prost. *René Cassin and Human Rights: From the Great War to the Universal Declaration*. Cambridge, 2013.

Zeck, William. "Nuremberg: Proceedings Subsequent to Goering et al." *The North Carolina Law Review* 26, no. 4 (June 1948): 350–89.

Zummersch, Maren. *Heinrich Hörlein (1882–1954): Wissenschaftler, Manager und Netzwerker in der pharmazeutischen Industrie. Eine Schlüsselfigur der pharmazeutischen Forschung und Entwicklung bei Bayer*. Stuttgart, 2019.

Zuppi, Alberto L. "Slave Labor in Nuremberg's I. G. Farben Case: The Lonely Voice of Paul M. Hebert." *Louisiana Law Review* 66 (2005–2006): 495–526.

Index

Terms that are pervasive throughout the book have been omitted from the index to avoid redundancy (e.g., I. G. Farben trial, I. G. Farbenindustrie AG, National Socialism, Nuremberg Trials).

www.ingramcontent.com/pod-product-compliance
Ingram Content Group UK Ltd.
Pitfield, Milton Keynes, MK11 3LW, UK
UKHW021837150926
8656IPUK00004B/30

9 781836 952664